ALCOHOL,
TOBACCO, AND
ILLICIT DRUGS

ISSN 1938-8896

ALCOHOL, TOBACCO, AND ILLICIT DRUGS

Sandra M. Alters

INFORMATION PLUS® REFERENCE SERIES
Formerly Published by Information Plus, Wylie, Texas

THOMSON
GALE

Detroit • New York • San Francisco • New Haven, Conn. • Waterville, Maine • London

Alcohol, Tobacco, and Illicit Drugs
Sandra M. Alters
Paula Kepos, Series Editor

Project Editors
Kathleen J. Edgar, John McCoy

Permissions
Jackie Jones, Jhanay Williams

Composition and Electronic Prepress
Evi Seoud

Manufacturing
Cynde Bishop

ISBN-13: 978-0-7876-5103-9 (set)
ISBN-10: 0-7876-5103-6 (set)
ISBN-13: 978-1-4144-0744-9
ISBN-10: 1-4144-0744-0
ISSN 1938-8896

This title is also available as an e-book.
ISBN-13: 978-1-4144-2948-9 (set), ISBN-10: 1-4144-2948-7 (set)
Contact your Gale Group sales representative for ordering information.

Printed in the United States of America
10 9 8 7 6 5 4 3 2 1

TABLE OF CONTENTS

PREFACE

Alcohol, Tobacco, and Illicit Drugs is part of the *Information Plus Reference Series.* The purpose of each volume of the series is to present the latest facts on a topic of pressing concern in modern American life. These topics include today's most controversial and most studied social issues: abortion, capital punishment, care of senior citizens, crime, the environment, health care, immigration, minorities, national security, social welfare, women, youth, and many more. Although written especially for the high school and undergraduate student, this series is an excellent resource for anyone in need of factual information on current affairs.

By presenting the facts, it is the Gale Group's intention to provide its readers with everything they need to reach an informed opinion on current issues. To that end, there is a particular emphasis in this series on the presentation of scientific studies, surveys, and statistics. These data are generally presented in the form of tables, charts, and other graphics placed within the text of each book. Every graphic is directly referred to and carefully explained in the text. The source of each graphic is presented within the graphic itself. The data used in these graphics are drawn from the most reputable and reliable sources, in particular from the various branches of the U.S. government and from major independent polling organizations. Every effort has been made to secure the most recent information available. The reader should bear in mind that many major studies take years to conduct and that additional years often pass before the data from these studies are made available to the public. Therefore, in many cases the most recent information available in 2007 dated from 2004 or 2005. Older statistics are sometimes presented as well if they are of particular interest and no more-recent information exists.

Although statistics are a major focus of the *Information Plus Reference Series*, they are by no means its only content. Each book also presents the widely held posi-

tions and important ideas that shape how the book's subject is discussed in the United States. These positions are explained in detail and, where possible, in the words of their proponents. Some of the other material to be found in these books includes: historical background; descriptions of major events related to the subject; relevant laws and court cases; and examples of how these issues play out in American life. Some books also feature primary documents or have pro and con debate sections giving the words and opinions of prominent Americans on both sides of a controversial topic. All material is presented in an even-handed and unbiased manner; the reader will never be encouraged to accept one view of an issue over another.

HOW TO USE THIS BOOK

Both legal and illicit drugs—substances that can affect a person's mood or physiology—are used by people from all segments of American society. Legal drugs include prescription medications but also popular and widely available substances such as alcohol, tobacco, and caffeine. Illegal drugs are those with no currently accepted medical use in the United States, such as heroin, lysergic acid diethylamide (LSD), ecstasy, and inhalants. This book provides an overview of legal and illicit drugs, including their health impact, addictive nature, and potential for abuse. Also discussed are the political and economic ramifications of such substances; their use among youth; possible treatments; drug trafficking; antidrug efforts and campaigns; and criticisms of the "war on drugs."

Alcohol, Tobacco, and Illicit Drugs consists of nine chapters and three appendixes. Each of the chapters is devoted to a particular aspect of alcohol, tobacco, and illicit drugs in the United States. For a summary of the information covered in each chapter, please see the synopses provided in the Table of Contents at the front of the book. Chapters generally begin with an overview of the basic facts and background information on the chapter's topic, then proceed to examine subtopics of particular interest. For example, Chapter 6: Drug Treatment begins with a discussion of drug abuse and addiction. It details the number of people being treated as well as the characteristics of those admitted for treatment. The chapter outlines the types of treatment available as well as their effectiveness. Readers can find their way through a chapter by looking for the section and subsection headings, which are clearly set off from the text. They can also refer to the book's extensive Index if they already know what they are looking for.

Statistical Information

The tables and figures featured throughout *Alcohol, Tobacco, and Illicit Drugs* will be of particular use to the reader in learning about this issue. These tables and figures represent an extensive collection of the most recent and important statistics on alcohol, tobacco, illicit drugs, and related issues—for example, graphics in the book cover the amount of alcoholic beverages consumed per capita by American citizens over the past several decades; alcohol's involvement in fatal automobile crashes; diseases associated with tobacco use; number of youth who use illicit drugs; and prevalence rates of hallucinogen use among students. The Gale Group believes that making this information available to the reader is the most important way in which we fulfill the goal of this book: to help readers to understand the issues and controversies surrounding alcohol, tobacco, and illicit drugs in the United States and to reach their own conclusions.

Each table or figure has a unique identifier appearing above it for ease of identification and reference. Titles for the tables and figures explain their purpose. At the end of each table or figure, the original source of the data is provided.

In order to help readers understand these often complicated statistics, all tables and figures are explained in the text. References in the text direct the reader to the relevant statistics. Furthermore, the contents of all tables and figures are fully indexed. Please see the opening section of the Index at the back of this volume for a description of how to find tables and figures within it.

Appendixes

In addition to the main body text and images, *Alcohol, Tobacco, and Illicit Drugs* has three appendixes. The first is the Important Names and Addresses directory. Here the reader will find contact information for a number of government and private organizations that can provide further information on alcohol, tobacco, and/or illicit drugs. The second appendix is the Resources section, which can also assist the reader in conducting his or her own research. In this section the author and editors of *Alcohol, Tobacco, and Illicit Drugs* describe some of the sources that were most useful during the compilation of this book. The final appendix is the Index.

ADVISORY BOARD CONTRIBUTIONS

The staff of Information Plus would like to extend its heartfelt appreciation to the Information Plus Advisory Board. This dedicated group of media professionals provides feedback on the series on an ongoing basis. Their comments allow the editorial staff who work on the project to make the series better and more user-friendly. Our top priorities are to produce the highest-quality and most useful books possible, and the Advisory Board's contributions to this process are invaluable.

The members of the Information Plus Advisory Board are:

- Kathleen R. Bonn, Librarian, Newbury Park High School, Newbury Park, California

- Madelyn Garner, Librarian, San Jacinto College— North Campus, Houston, Texas

- Anne Oxenrider, Media Specialist, Dundee High School, Dundee, Michigan

- Charles R. Rodgers, Director of Libraries, Pasco-Hernando Community College, Dade City, Florida

- James N. Zitzelsberger, Library Media Department Chairman, Oshkosh West High School, Oshkosh, Wisconsin

COMMENTS AND SUGGESTIONS

The editors of the *Information Plus Reference Series* welcome your feedback on *Alcohol, Tobacco, and Illicit Drugs*. Please direct all correspondence to:

Editors
Information Plus Reference Series
27500 Drake Rd.
Farmington Hills, MI 48331-3535

CHAPTER 1

DRUGS: A DEFINITION

Drugs are nonfood chemicals that alter the way a person thinks, feels, functions, or behaves. This includes everything from prescription medications, to illegal chemicals such as heroin, to popular and widely available substances such as alcohol, tobacco, and caffeine. A wide variety of laws, regulations, and government agencies exists to control the possession, sale, and use of drugs. Different drugs are held to different standards based on their perceived dangers and usefulness, a fact that sometimes leads to disagreement and controversy.

Illegal drugs are those with no currently accepted medical use in the United States, such as heroin, lysergic acid diethylamide (LSD), and marijuana. It is illegal to buy, sell, possess, and use these drugs except for research purposes. They are supplied only to registered, qualified researchers. Legal drugs, by contrast, are drugs whose sale, possession, and use as intended are not forbidden by law. Their use may be restricted, however. For example, the U.S. Drug Enforcement Administration (DEA) controls the use of legal psychoactive (mood- or mind-altering) drugs that have potential for abuse. These drugs, which include narcotics, depressants, and stimulants, are available only with a prescription and are called controlled substances. The term "illicit drugs" is used by the Substance Abuse and Mental Health Services Administration to describe both controlled substances that are used in violation of the law and drugs that are completely illegal.

The goal of the DEA is to ensure that controlled substances are readily available for medical use or research purposes while preventing their illegal sale and abuse. The agency works toward accomplishing its goal by requiring people and businesses that manufacture, distribute, prescribe, and dispense controlled substances to register with the DEA. Registrants must abide by a series of requirements relating to drug security, records accountability, and adherence to standards. The DEA also enforces the controlled substances laws and regula-

tions of the United States by investigating and prosecuting those who violate these laws.

The U.S. Food and Drug Administration (FDA) also plays a role in drug control. This agency regulates the manufacture and marketing of prescription and nonprescription drugs, requiring the active ingredients in a product to be safe and effective before allowing the drug to be sold.

Alcohol and tobacco are monitored and specially taxed by the Alcohol and Tobacco Tax and Trade Bureau (TTB). The TTB was formed in January 2003 as a provision of the Homeland Security Act of 2002, which split the Bureau of Alcohol, Tobacco, and Firearms (ATF) into two new agencies. One of these agencies, the TTB, took over the taxation duties for alcohol, tobacco, and firearms and remained a part of the Bureau of the Treasury. The TTB also ensures that alcohol and tobacco products are legally labeled, advertised, and marketed; regulates the qualification and operations of distilleries, wineries, and breweries; tests alcoholic beverages to ensure that their regulated ingredients are within legal limits; and screens applicants who wish to manufacture, import, or export tobacco products.

The other agency split from the "old" ATF is the "new" ATF: the Bureau of Alcohol, Tobacco, Firearms, and Explosives. The ATF is now a principal law enforcement agency within the Department of Justice, enforcing federal criminal laws and regulating the firearms and explosives industries. It also investigates illegal trafficking of alcohol and tobacco products.

FIVE CATEGORIES OF SUBSTANCES

Drugs may be classified into five categories:

- Depressants, including alcohol and tranquilizers: These substances slow down the activity of the nervous system. They produce sedative (calming) and hypnotic (trancelike) effects as well as drowsiness. If taken in large doses, depressants can cause intoxication (drunkenness).

- Hallucinogens, including marijuana, phencyclidine (PCP), and LSD: Hallucinogens produce abnormal and unreal sensations such as seeing distorted and vividly colored images. Hallucinogens can also produce frightening psychological responses such as anxiety, depression, and the feeling of losing control of one's mind.

- Narcotics, including heroin and opium, from which morphine and codeine are derived: Narcotics are drugs that alter the perception of pain and induce sleep and euphoria (an intense feeling of well-being; a "high").

- Stimulants, including caffeine, nicotine, cocaine, amphetamine, and methamphetamine: These substances speed up the processing rate of the central nervous system. They can reduce fatigue, elevate mood, increase energy, and help people stay awake. In large doses stimulants can cause irritability, anxiety, sleeplessness, and even psychotic behavior. Caffeine is the most commonly used stimulant in the world.

- Other compounds, including anabolic steroids and inhalants: Anabolic steroids are a group of synthetic substances that are chemically related to testosterone and are promoted for their muscle-building properties. Inhalants are solvents and aerosol products that produce vapors having psychoactive effects. These substances dull pain and can produce euphoria.

Table 1.1 provides an overview of alcohol, nicotine, and other selected psychoactive substances. It includes the DEA schedule for each drug listed. Developed as part of the Controlled Substances Act of 1970 (PL 91-513), the DEA drug schedules are categories into which controlled substances are placed depending on characteristics such as medical use, potential for abuse, safety, and danger of dependence. The types of drugs categorized in each of the five schedules, with examples, are shown in Table 1.2.

DRUGS DISCUSSED IN THIS BOOK

This book focuses on substances widely used throughout the world: alcohol, tobacco, and illicit drugs. Not only are alcohol and tobacco legal, relatively affordable, and more or less socially acceptable (depending on time, place, and circumstance) but they are also important economic commodities. Industries exist to produce, distribute, and sell these products, creating jobs and income and contributing to economic well-being. Thus, whenever discussions of possible government regulation of alcohol and tobacco arise, the topic brings with it significant economic and political issues.

Illicit drugs are those that are unlawful to possess or distribute under the Controlled Substances Act. Some controlled substances can be taken under the supervision of health care professionals licensed by the DEA. The Controlled Substances Act provides penalties for the unlawful manufacture, distribution, and dispensing of controlled substances, based on the schedule of the drug or substance and enforced by the DEA. Nonetheless, illicit drugs have fostered huge illicit drug marketing and drug trafficking (buying and selling) networks (see Chapter 8). Tobacco, beer, wine, and spirits are exempt from the Controlled Substances Act and the DEA drug schedules.

Figure 1.1 shows trends in cigarette, illicit drug, and alcohol use in the twentieth century and beyond. It gives an overview of the ebb and flow of the use and abuse of these substances in the United States. This chapter will take a historical look at the use and abuse of each, and the chapters that follow will present more up-to-date information.

WHAT ARE ABUSE AND ADDICTION?

Many drugs, both legal and illicit, have potential for abuse and addiction. Research and treatment experts identify three general levels of interaction with drugs: use, abuse, and dependence (or addiction). In general, abuse involves a compulsive use of a substance and impaired social or occupational functioning. Dependence (addiction) includes these traits, plus evidence of physical tolerance (a need to take increasingly higher doses to achieve the same effect) or withdrawal symptoms when use of the drug is stopped.

The progression from use to dependence is complex, as are the abused substances themselves. Researchers find no standard boundaries between using a substance, abusing a substance, and being addicted to a substance. They believe these lines vary widely from substance to substance and from individual to individual.

Scientists do not know why some people who use addictive substances become addicted and why others do not. Results of many studies of identical and fraternal (nonidentical) twins and families with histories of substance abuse and addiction indicate that there is a genetic component to addiction. In the article "The Genetics of Alcohol Dependence" (*Current Psychiatry Reports*, April 2006), Danielle M. Dick and Laura J. Bierut review several of the specific genes that would distinguish people who are predisposed to becoming addicted. Furthermore, results of Andrew R. Tapper et al.'s study, "Nicotine Activation of alpha4 Receptors: Sufficient for Reward, Tolerance, and Sensitization" (*Science*, November 5, 2004), show that a mutation in certain brain receptors lowers the threshold for nicotine dependence in mice with the mutation.

TABLE 1.1

Commonly abused drugs

Substance: category and name	Examples of *commercial* and street names	DEA Schedule[a]/how administered[b]	*Intoxication effects*/potential health consequences
Depressants			
Alcohol	Beer, wine, hard liquor	Not scheduled/swallowed	*Reduced anxiety; feeling of well-being; lowered inhibitions; slowed pulse and breathing; lowered blood pressure; poor concentration*/fatigue; confusion; impaired coordination, memory, judgment; addiction; respiratory depression and arrest, death
Barbiturates	*Amytal, Nembutal, Seconal, Phenobarbital;* barbs, reds, red birds, phennies, tooies, yellows, yellow jackets	II, III, V/injected, swallowed	*Also, for barbiturates—sedation, drowsiness*/depression, unusual excitement, fever, irritability, poor judgment, slurred speech, dizziness, life-threatening withdrawal.
Benzodiazepines (other than flunitrazepam)	*Ativan, Halcion, Librium, Valium, Xanax;* candy, downers, sleeping pills, tranks	IV/swallowed, injected	*For benzodiazepines—sedation, drowsiness*/dizziness
Flunitrazepam[c]	*Rohypnol;* forget-me pill, Mexican Valium, R2, Roche, roofies, roofinol, rope, rophies	IV/swallowed, snorted	*For flunitrazepam—visual and gastrointestinal disturbances, urinary retention, memory loss for the time under the drug's effects*
GHB[c]	*gamma-hydroxybutyrate;* G, Georgia home boy, grievous bodily harm, liquid ecstasy	I/swallowed	*For GHB—drowsiness, nausea*/vomiting, headache, loss of consciousness, loss of reflexes, seizures, coma, death
Methaqualone	*Quaalude, Sopor, Parest;* ludes, mandex, quad, quay	I/injected, swallowed	*For methaqualone—euphoria*/depression, poor reflexes, slurred speech, coma
Cannabinoids (hallucinogens)			
Hashish	Boom, chronic, gangster, hash, hash oil, hemp	I/swallowed, smoked	*Euphoria, slowed thinking and reaction time, confusion, impaired balance and coordination*/cough, frequent respiratory infections; impaired memory and learning; increased heart rate, anxiety; panic attacks; tolerance, addiction
Marijuana	Blunt, dope, ganja, grass, herb, joints, Mary Jane, pot, reefer sinsemilla, skunk, weed	I/swallowed, smoked	
Dissociative anesthetics (hallucinogens)			
Ketamine	*Ketalar SV;* cat Valiums, K, Special K, vitamin K	III/injected, snorted, smoked	*Increased heart rate and blood pressure, impaired motor function/memory loss;* numbness; nausea/vomiting *Also, for ketamine—at high doses, delirium, depression, respiratory depression and arrest*
PCP and analogs	*phencyclidine;* angel dust, boat, hog, love boat, peace pill	I, II/injected, swallowed, smoked	*For PCP and analogs—possible decrease in blood pressure and heart rate, panic, aggression, violence*/loss of appetite, depression
Hallucinogens			*Altered states of perception and feeling; nausea;* persisting perception disorder (flashbacks)
LSD	*Lysergic acid diethylamide;* acid, blotter, boomers, cubes, microdot, yellow	I/swallowed, absorbed through mouth tissues	*Also, for LSD and mescaline—increased body temperature, heart rate, blood pressure; loss of appetite, sleeplessness, numbness, weakness, tremors*
Mescaline	Buttons, cactus, mesc, peyote	I/swallowed, smoked	*For LSD—persistent mental disorders*
Psilocybin	Magic mushroom, purple passion, shrooms	I/swallowed	*For psilocybin—nervousness, paranoia*
Opioids and morphine derivatives (narcotics)			
Codeine	*Empirin with Codeine, Fiorinal with Codeine, Robitussin A-C, Tylenol with Codeine;* Captain Cody, Cody, schoolboy; (with glutethimide) doors & fours, loads, pancakes and syrup	II, III, IV/injected, swallowed	*Pain relief, euphoria, drowsiness*/nausea, constipation, confusion, sedation, respiratory depression and arrest, tolerance, addiction, unconsciousness, coma, death
Fentanyl and fentanyl analogs	*Actiq, Duragesic, Sublimaze;* Apache, China girl, China white, dance fever, friend, goodfella, jackpot, murder 8, TNT, Tango and Cash	I, II/injected smoked, snorted	*Also, for codeine—less analgesia, sedation, and respiratory depression than morphine*
Heroin	*Diacetylmorphine;* brown sugar, dope, H, horse, junk, skag, skunk, smack, white horse	I/injected smoked, snorted	*For heroin—staggering gait*
Morphine	*Roxanol, Duramorph;* M, Miss Emma, monkey, white stuff	II, III/injected, swallowed, smoked	
Opium	*Laudanum, paregoric;* big O, black stuff, block, gum, hop	II, III, V/swallowed, smoked	
Oxycodone HCL	*Oxycontin;* Oxy, O.C., killer	II/swallowed, snorted, injected	
Hydrocodone bitartrate, acetaminophen	*Vicodin;* vike, Watson-387	II/swallowed	

Physiological, Psychological, and Sociocultural Factors

Some researchers maintain that the principal causes of substance use are external social influences, such as peer pressure, whereas substance abuse and/or dependence result primarily from internal psychological and physiological needs and pressures, including inherited tendencies. Additionally, psychoactive drug use at an early age may be a risk factor (a characteristic that increases likelihood) for subsequent dependence.

TABLE 1.1

Commonly abused drugs [CONTINUED]

Substance: category and name	Examples of *commercial* and *street* names	DEA Schedule[a]/how administered[b]	*Intoxication effects*/potential health consequences
Stimulants			*Increased heart rate, blood pressure, metabolism; feelings of exhilaration, energy, increased mental alertness*/rapid or irregular heart beat; reduce appetite, weight loss, heart failure, nervousness, insomnia
Amphetamine	*Biphetamine, Dexedrine;* bennies, black beauties, crosses, hearts, LA turnaround, speed, truck drivers, uppers	II/injected, swallowed, smoked, snorted	*Also, for amphetamine—rapid breathing*/tremor, loss of coordination; irritability, anxiousness, restlessness, delirium, panic, paranoia, impulsive behavior, aggressiveness, tolerance, addiction, psychosis
Cocaine	*Cocaine hydrochloride;* blow, bump, C, candy Charlie, coke, crack, flake, rock, snow, toot	II/injected, smoked, snorted	*For cocaine—increased temperature*/chest pain, respiratory failure, nausea, abdominal pain, strokes, seizures, headaches, malnutrition, panic attacks
MDMA (methylenedioxy-methamphetamine)	Adam, clarity, ecstasy, Eve, lover's speed, peace, STP, X, XTC	I/swallowed	*For MDMA—mild hallucinogenic effects, increased tactile sensitivity, empathic feelings*/impaired memory and learning, hyperthermia, cardiac toxicity, renal failure, liver toxicity
Methamphetamine	*Desoxyn;* chalk, crank, crystal, fire, glass, go fast, ice, meth, speed	II/injected, swallowed, smoked, snorted	*For methamphetamine—aggression, violence, psychotic behavior*/memory loss, cardiac and neurological damage; impaired memory and learning, tolerance, addiction
Methylphenidate (safe and effective for treatment of ADHD)	*Ritalin;* JIF, MPH, R-ball, Skippy, the smart drug, vitamin R	II/injected, swallowed, snorted	
Nicotine	Cigarettes, cigars, smokeless tobacco, snuff, spit tobacco, bidis, chew	Not scheduled/smoked, snorted, taken in snuff and spit	*For nicotine—additional effects attributable to tobacco exposure, adverse pregnancy outcomes, chronic lung disease, cardiovascular, chronic lung disease, cardiovascular disease, stroke, cancer, tolerance, addiction
Other compounds			
Anabolic steroids	*Anadrol, Oxandrin, Durabolin, Depo-Testosterone, Equipoise;* roids, juice	III/injected, swallowed, applied to skin	*No intoxication effects*/hypertension, blood clotting and cholesterol changes, liver cysts and cancer, kidney cancer, hostility and aggression, acne; in adolescents, premature stoppage of growth; in males, prostate cancer, reduced sperm production, shrunken testicles, breast enlargement; in females, menstrual irregularities, development of beard and other masculine characteristics
Inhalants	*Solvents (paint thinners, gasoline, glues), gases (butane, propane, aerosol propellants, nitrous oxide), nitrites (isoamyl, isobutyl, cyclohexyl);* laughing gas, poppers, snappers, whippets	Not scheduled/inhaled through nose or mouth	*Stimulation, loss of inhibition; headache; nausea or vomiting; slurred speech, loss of motor coordination; wheezing*/unconsciousness, cramps, weight loss, muscle weakness, depression, memory impairment, damage to cardiovascular and nervous systems, sudden death

[a]Schedule I and II drugs have a high potential for abuse. They require greater storage security and have a quota on manufacturing, among other restrictions. Schedule I drugs are available for research only and have no approved medical use; schedule II drugs are available only by prescription (unrefillable) and require a form for ordering. Schedule III and IV drugs are available by prescription, may have five refills in 6 months, and may be ordered orally. Most schedule V drugs are available over the counter.
[b]Taking drugs by injection can increase the risk of infection through needle contamination with staphylococci, HIV, hepatitis, and other organisms.
[c]Associated with sexual assaults.

SOURCE: Adapted from "Commonly Abused Drugs," National Institutes of Health, National Institute on Drug Abuse, http://www.nida.nih.gov/DrugPages/DrugsofAbuse.html (accessed October 2, 2006)

Physically, mood-altering substances affect brain processes. Most drugs that are abused stimulate the reward or pleasure centers of the brain by causing the release of dopamine, which is a neurotransmitter—a chemical in the brain that relays messages from one nerve cell to another.

Psychologically, a person may become dependent on a substance because it relieves pain, offers escape from real or perceived problems, or makes the user feel more relaxed or confident in certain social settings. A successful first use of a substance may reduce the user's fear of the drug and thus lead to continued use and even dependence.

Socially, substance use may be widespread in some groups or environments. The desire to belong to a special group is a strong human characteristic, and those who use one or more substances may become part of a subculture that encourages and promotes use. An individual may be influenced by one of these groups to start using a substance, or he or she may be drawn to such a group after starting use somewhere else. In addition, a person—especially a young person—may not have access to alternative rewarding or pleasurable groups or activities that do not include substance use.

Figure 1.2 illustrates some relationships between physiological, psychological, and cultural factors that influence drinking and drinking patterns. Constraints (inhibitory factors) and motivations influence drinking patterns. In turn, drinking patterns influence the relationship between routine activities related to drinking and acute (immediate) consequences of drinking.

TABLE 1.2

FIGURE 1.1

Drug schedules established by the Controlled Substances Act (CSA), 1970

Schedule I

- The drug or other substance has a high potential for abuse.
- The drug or other substance has no currently accepted medical use in treatment in the United States.
- There is a lack of accepted safety for use of the drug or other substance under medical supervision.
- Examples of Schedule I substances include heroin, lysergic acid diethylamide (LSD), marijuana, and methaqualone.

Schedule II

- The drug or other substance has a high potential for abuse.
- The drug or other substance has a currently accepted medical use in treatment in the United States or a currently accepted medical use with severe restrictions.
- Abuse of the drug or other substance may lead to severe psychological or physical dependence.
- Examples of Schedule II substances include morphine, phencyclidine (PCP), cocaine, methadone, and methamphetamine.

Schedule III

- The drug or other substance has less potential for abuse than the drugs or other substances in Schedules I and II.
- The drug or other substance has a currently accepted medical use in treatment in the United States.
- Abuse of the drug or other substance may lead to moderate or low physical dependence or high psychological dependence.
- Anabolic steroids, codeine and hydrocodone with aspirin or Tylenol, and some barbiturates are examples of Schedule III substances.

Schedule IV

- The drug or other substance has a low potential for abuse relative to the drugs or other substances in Schedule III.
- The drug or other substance has a currently accepted medical use in treatment in the United States.
- Abuse of the drug or other substance may lead to limited physical dependence or psychological dependence relative to the drugs or other substances in Schedule III.
- Examples of drugs included in Schedule IV are Darvon, Talwin, Equanil, Valium and Xanax.

Schedule V

- The drug or other substance has a low potential for abuse relative to the drugs or other substances in Schedule IV.
- The drug or other substance has a currently accepted medical use in treatment in the United States.
- Abuse of the drug or other substances may lead to limited physical dependence or psychological dependence relative to the drugs or other substances in Schedule IV.
- Cough medicines with codeine are examples of Schedule V drugs.

SOURCE: Adapted from *Drugs of Abuse, 2005 Edition*, U.S. Department of Justice, U.S. Drug Enforcement Administration, 2005, http://www.usdoj.gov/dea/pubs/abuse/doap.pdf (accessed October 2, 2006)

Definitions of Abuse and Dependence

Two texts provide the most commonly used medical definitions of substance abuse and dependence. The *Diagnostic and Statistical Manual of Mental Disorders* (*DSM*) is published by the American Psychiatric Association. The *International Classification of Diseases* (*ICD*) is published by the World Health Organization (WHO). Even though the definitions of dependence in these two manuals are almost identical, the definitions of abuse are not.

DSM **DEFINITION OF ABUSE.** The text revision of the fourth edition of the *DSM*, *Diagnostic and Statistical Manual of Mental Disorders-IV Text Revision* (*DSM-IV-TR*), was published in 2000 and was the most recent revision available in 2007. The *DSM-IV-TR* defines abuse as an abnormal pattern of recurring use that leads to

Trends in cigarette, illicit drug, and alcohol use, selected years 1850–2004

Annual per capita consumption of cigarettes for those 18 years and over

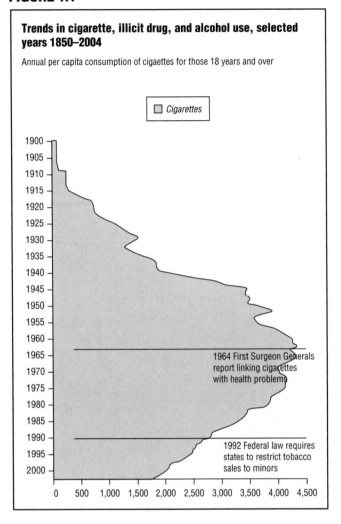

"significant impairment or distress," marked by one or more of the following in a twelve-month period:

- Failure to fulfill major obligations at home, school, or work (e.g., repeated absences, poor performance, or neglect)

- Use in hazardous or potentially hazardous situations, such as driving a car or operating a machine while impaired

- Legal problems, such as arrest for disorderly conduct while under the influence of the substance

- Continued use in spite of social or interpersonal problems caused by the use of the substance, such as fights or family arguments

ICD **DEFINITION OF HARMFUL USE.** The tenth and most recent revision (as of 2007) of the *ICD* (*ICD-10*), which was endorsed by the Forty-third World Health Assembly in May 1990 and has been used in WHO Member States since 1994, uses the term *harmful use* rather than *abuse*. It defines harmful use as "a pattern of psychoactive substance use that is causing damage to health," either physical or mental.

FIGURE 1.1

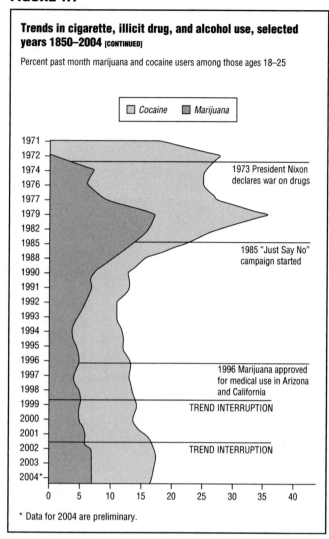

Trends in cigarette, illicit drug, and alcohol use, selected years 1850–2004 [CONTINUED]

Percent past month marijuana and cocaine users among those ages 18–25

* Data for 2004 are preliminary.

FIGURE 1.1

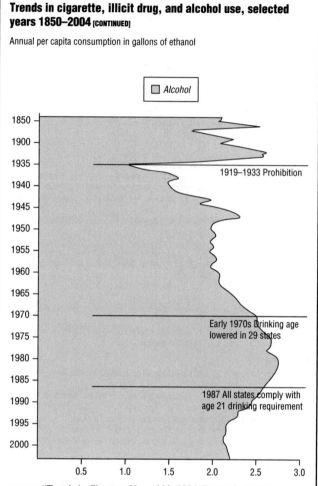

Trends in cigarette, illicit drug, and alcohol use, selected years 1850–2004 [CONTINUED]

Annual per capita consumption in gallons of ethanol

SOURCE: "Trends in Cigarette Use, 1900–2004, Trends in Illicit Drug Use, 1974–2004, Trends in Alcohol Use, 1850–2002," in *National Drug Control Strategy*, Executive Office of the President of the United States, Office of National Drug Control Policy, February 2006, http://www.whitehousedrugpolicy.gov/publications/policy/ndcs06/ndcs06.pdf (accessed November 9, 2006). Copyright © 2006 Robert Wood Johnson Foundation. Used with permission from the Robert Wood Johnson Foundation in Princeton, New Jersey.

Because the *ICD* manual is targeted toward international use, its definition must be broader than the *DSM* definition, which is intended for use by Americans. Cultural customs of substance use vary widely, sometimes even within the same country.

DEFINITIONS OF DEPENDENCE. In general, the *DSM-IV-TR* and the *ICD-10* manuals agree that dependence is present if three or more of the following occur in a twelve-month period:

- Increasing need for more of the substance to achieve the same effect (occurs as the user builds up a tolerance to the substance), or a reduction in effect when using the same amount as used previously

- Withdrawal symptoms if use of the substance is stopped or reduced

- Progressive neglect of other pleasures and duties

- A strong desire to take the substance or a persistent but unsuccessful desire to control or reduce the use of the substance

- Continued use in spite of physical or mental health problems caused by the substance

- Use of the substance in larger amounts or over longer periods of time than originally intended, or difficulties in controlling the amount of the substance used or when to stop taking it

- Considerable time spent in obtaining the substance, using it, or recovering from its effects

Progression from Use to Dependence

The rate at which individuals progress from drug use to drug abuse to drug dependence (or addiction) depends on many of the aforementioned factors. In general, each level is more dangerous, more invasive in the user's life, and more likely to cause social

FIGURE 1.2

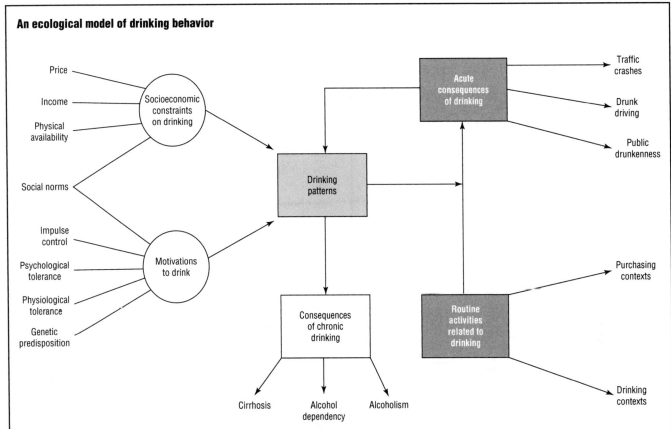

An ecological model of drinking behavior

SOURCE: Paul J. Gruenewald and Alex B. Millar, "An Ecological Model of Drinking Behavior," in "Alcohol Availability and the Ecology of Drinking Behavior," *Alcohol Health & Research World*, vol. 17, no. 1, 1993 (updated October 2000), http://www.niaaa.nih.gov/Resources/GraphicsGallery/TreatmentPrevention/gruen.htm (accessed October 2, 2006)

interventions, such as family pressure to enter treatment programs or prison sentences for drug offenses, than the previous level.

Figure 1.3 is a diagram of the progression to addiction. Notice that the intensification of use leads to abuse and that abuse leads to dependence. The right side of the diagram shows social interventions appropriate at various stages of drug use, abuse, and dependence. The dotted lines to the left show that relapse after recovery may lead to renewed drug use, abuse, or dependence.

HISTORY OF ALCOHOL USE

Ethyl alcohol (ethanol), the active ingredient in beer, wine, and other liquors, is the oldest known psychoactive drug. It is also the only type of alcohol used as a beverage. Other alcohols, such as methanol and isopropyl alcohol, when ingested even in small amounts, can produce severe negative health effects and often death.

The basic characteristics of alcoholic beverages have remained unchanged from early times. Beer and wine is created through the natural chemical process called fermentation. Fermentation can only produce beverages with an alcohol content of up to 14%. More potent drinks

such as rum or vodka—known as spirits or liquors—can be produced through distillation. This is a process that involves using heat to separate and concentrate the alcohol found in fermented beverages, and can result in drinks that are 50% or more alcohol.

Early Uses and Abuses of Alcohol

Beer and wine have been used since ancient times in religious rituals, celebrations of councils, coronations, war, peacemaking, festivals, hospitality, and the rites of birth, initiation, marriage, and death. In ancient times, just as today, the use of beer and wine sometimes led to drunkenness. One of the earliest written works on temperance (controlling one's drinking or not drinking at all) was written in Egypt nearly three thousand years ago. These writings can be thought of as similar to present-day pamphlets espousing moderation in alcohol consumption. Similar recommendations have been found in early Greek, Roman, Indian, Japanese, and Chinese writings, as well as in the Bible.

Drinking in Colonial America

In colonial America people drank much more alcohol than they do today, with estimates ranging from three to seven times more alcohol per person per year. Liquor was

FIGURE 1.3

Drug use, abuse, and dependence

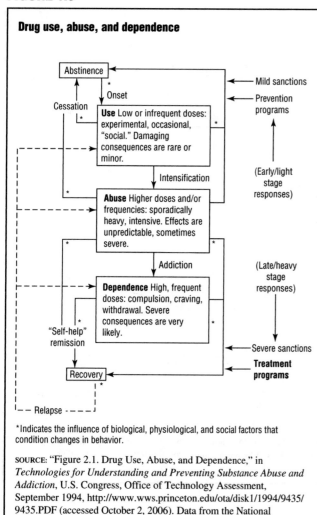

*Indicates the influence of biological, physiological, and social factors that condition changes in behavior.

SOURCE: "Figure 2.1. Drug Use, Abuse, and Dependence," in *Technologies for Understanding and Preventing Substance Abuse and Addiction*, U.S. Congress, Office of Technology Assessment, September 1994, http://www.wws.princeton.edu/ota/disk1/1994/9435/9435.PDF (accessed October 2, 2006). Data from the National Academy of Sciences, Institute of Medicine.

An Inquiry into the Effects of Ardent Spirits on the Mind and Body. The pamphlet became popular among the growing number of people concerned about the excessive drinking of many Americans. Such concern gave rise to the temperance movement.

The temperance movement in the United States began in the early 1800s and lasted until roughly 1890. Initially, the goal of the temperance movement was to promote moderation in the consumption of alcohol. By the 1850s large numbers of people were completely giving up alcohol, and by the 1870s the goal of the temperance movement had become to promote abstinence from alcohol. Reformers were concerned about the effects of alcohol on the family, the labor force, and the nation, all of which needed sober participants if they were to remain healthy and productive. Temperance supporters also saw alcoholism as a problem of personal immorality.

Prohibition

In 1919 reform efforts led to the passage of the Eighteenth Amendment of the U.S. Constitution, which prohibited the "manufacture, sale, or transportation of intoxicating liquors" and their importation and exportation. The Volstead Act of 1919, which passed over President Woodrow Wilson's veto, was the Prohibition law that enforced the Eighteenth Amendment.

Outlawing alcohol did not stop most people from drinking; instead, alcohol was manufactured and sold illegally by gangsters, who organized themselves efficiently and gained considerable political influence from the money they earned. In addition, many individuals illegally brewed alcoholic beverages at home or smuggled alcohol from Canada and Mexico. Ultimately, the Eighteenth Amendment was repealed in 1933 with the passage of the Twenty-first Amendment.

Understanding the Dangers of Alcohol

As the decades passed, recognition of the dangers of alcohol increased. In 1956 the American Medical Association endorsed classifying and treating alcoholism as a disease. In 1970 Congress created the National Institute on Alcohol Abuse and Alcoholism, establishing a public commitment to alcohol-related research. During the 1970s, however, many states lowered their drinking age to eighteen when the legal voting age was lowered to this age.

Traffic fatalities rose after these laws took effect, and many such accidents involved people between the ages of eighteen and twenty-one who had been drinking and driving. Organizations such as Mothers against Drunk Driving and Students against Drunk Driving sought to educate the public about the great harm drunk drivers had done to others. As a result, and because of pressure from the federal government, by 1988 all states raised their

used to ease the pain and discomfort of many illnesses and injuries such as the common cold, fever, broken limbs, toothaches, frostbite, and the like. Parents often gave liquor to children to relieve their minor aches and pains or to help them sleep. Until 1842, when modern surgical anesthesia began with the use of ether, only heavy doses of alcohol were consistently effective to ease pain during operations.

As early as 1619 drunkenness was illegal in the American colony of Virginia. It was punished in various ways: whipping, placement in the stocks, fines, and even wearing a red *D* (for *drunkard*). By the eighteenth century all classes of people were getting drunk with greater frequency, even though it was well known that alcohol affected the senses and motor skills and that drunkenness led to increased crime, violence, accidents, and death.

Temperance

In 1784 Dr. Benjamin Rush, a physician and signer of the Declaration of Independence, published the booklet

minimum drinking age to twenty-one. In the report *Traffic Safety Facts, 2005 Data—Young Drivers* (2006, http://www-nrd.nhtsa.dot.gov/Pubs/youngdriverstsf05.PDF), the National Highway Traffic Safety Administration estimates that laws making twenty-one the minimum drinking age have saved an estimated 24,560 lives since 1975. By 1989 warning labels noting the deleterious effects of alcohol on health were required on all retail containers of alcoholic beverages. Nonetheless, the misuse and abuse of alcohol remain major health and social problems today.

HISTORY OF TOBACCO USE

Tobacco is a commercially grown plant that contains nicotine, an addictive drug. Tobacco is native to North America, where since ancient times it has played an important part in Native American social and religious customs. Additionally, Native Americans believed that tobacco had medicinal properties, so it was used to treat pain, epilepsy, colds, and headaches.

From Pipes to Cigarettes

As European explorers and settlers came to North America in the fifteenth and sixteenth centuries, Native Americans introduced them to tobacco. Its use soon spread among the settlers, and throughout Europe and Asia, although some rulers and nations opposed it and sought to outlaw it. At this time tobacco was smoked in pipes, chewed, or taken as snuff. Snuff is finely powdered tobacco that can be chewed, rubbed on the gums, or inhaled through the nose.

Cigar smoking was introduced to the United States in about 1762. Cigars are tobacco leaves rolled and prepared for smoking. U.S. consumption of cigars exceeded four billion in 1898, according to various tobacco-related Web sites. Cigarettes—cut tobacco rolled in a paper tube—would soon become the choice of most smokers, however, thanks to the 1881 invention of a cigarette-making machine that allowed them to be mass-produced and sold cheaply.

Early Antismoking Efforts in the United States

The first antismoking movement in the United States was organized in the 1830s (just as the temperance movement was growing in the country). Reformers characterized tobacco as an unhealthy and even fatal habit. Tobacco use was linked to increased alcohol use and lack of cleanliness. Antismoking reformers also suggested that tobacco exhausted the soil, wasted money, and promoted laziness, promiscuity, and profanity. Their efforts to limit or outlaw smoking met with only small, temporary, successes until well into the twentieth century.

A Boom in Smoking in the United States

The National Center for Chronic Disease Prevention and Health Promotion reports in "Consumption Data" (2006, http://www.cdc.gov/tobacco/research_data/economics/consump1.htm) that cigarette usage increased dramatically in the early 1900s, with total consumption increasing from 2.5 billion cigarettes in 1901 to 13.2 billion cigarettes in 1912. By 1919 cigarette consumption reached forty-eight billion. In 1913 the R. J. Reynolds Company introduced Camel cigarettes, an event that is often called the birth of the modern cigarette. During World War I (1914–18) cigarettes were shipped to U.S. troops fighting overseas (this also occurred during World War II, 1939–45). They were included in soldiers' rations and were dispensed by groups such as the American Red Cross and the Young Men's Christian Association. Women began openly smoking in larger numbers as well, something tobacco companies noticed; in 1919 the first advertisement featuring a woman smoking cigarettes appeared.

Cigarette smoking was very common and an accepted part of society, but doubts about its safety were growing. In July 1957, following a joint report by the National Cancer Institute, the National Heart Institute, the American Cancer Society, and the American Heart Association, U.S. Surgeon General Leroy E. Burney (a smoker himself) delivered an official statement that "the weight of the evidence is increasingly pointing in one direction; that excessive smoking is one of the causative factors in lung cancer." Nevertheless, cigarette ads of the 1950s touted cigarette smoking as pleasurable, sexy, relaxing, flavorful, and fun. (See Figure 1.4.)

Health Risks Lead to Diminished Smoking

In 1964 U.S. Surgeon General Luther L. Terry released *Smoking and Health: Report of the Advisory Committee to the Surgeon General of the Public Health Service* (January 1964, http://www.cdc.gov/Tobacco/sgr/sgr_1964/sgr64.htm). This landmark document was the United States' first widely publicized official recognition that cigarette smoking is a cause of lung cancer and laryngeal cancer in men, a probable cause of lung cancer in women, and the most important cause of chronic bronchitis.

Increased attention was paid to the potential health risks of smoking throughout the rest of the 1960s and the 1970s. The first health warnings appeared on cigarette packages in 1966. In 1970 the WHO took a public stand against smoking. On January 1, 1971, the Public Health Cigarette Smoking Act of 1969 (PL 91-222) went into effect, removing cigarette advertising from radio and television in the United States. A growing number of individuals, cities, and states filed lawsuits against U.S. tobacco companies. Some individuals claimed they had been deceived about the potential harm of smoking. Some states filed lawsuits to recoup money spent on smokers' Medicaid bills. In 1998 forty-six states, five territories, and the District of

FIGURE 1.4

A cigarette advertisement from the 1950s. © *Robert Landau/Corbis.*

Columbia signed the Master Settlement Agreement with the major tobacco companies to settle all state lawsuits for $206 billion. Excluded from the settlement were Florida, Minnesota, Mississippi, and Texas, which had already concluded previous settlements with the tobacco industry. Chapter 8 includes more recent information on the Master Settlement Agreement and its long-term effects.

EARLY HISTORY OF NARCOTIC, STIMULANT, AND HALLUCINOGEN USE

Humans have experimented with narcotic and hallucinogenic plants since before recorded history, discovering their properties as they tested plants for edibility or were attracted by the odors of some leaves when the leaves were burned. Ancient cultures used narcotic plants to relieve pain or to heighten pleasure and hallucinogenic plants to induce trancelike states during religious ceremonies. Natural substances, used directly or in refined extracts, have also served simply to increase or dull alertness, to invigorate the body, or to change the mood.

Narcotic Use through the Nineteenth Century

As mentioned earlier, narcotics, including heroin and opium, are drugs that alter the perception of pain and induce sleep and euphoria. Opium is a dried powdered extract derived from the opium poppy plant *Papaver somniferum.* Morphine and heroin are made from opium, and all three of these addicting narcotics are called opiates.

Opium itself has been used as a pain reliever in Europe and Asia for thousands of years. In 1803 Friedrich Wilhelm Sertürner, a German pharmacist, discovered how to isolate the highly potent morphine from opium. In 1832 Pierre-Jean Robiquet, a French chemist, isolated codeine from opium, which is milder than morphine. It came to be used in cough remedies. The development of the hypodermic needle in the early 1850s made it easier to use morphine. It became a common medicine for treating severe pain, such as battlefield injuries. During the U.S. Civil War, so many soldiers became addicted to morphine that the addiction was later called soldier's disease.

The most potent narcotic derived from opium is heroin, which was first synthesized in 1874 by C. R. Alder

Wright at St. Mary's Hospital in London. In "History of Heroin" (January 1953, http://www.unodc.org/unodc/bulletin/bulletin_1953-01-01_2_page004.html), the United Nations Office on Drugs and Crime notes that the Bayer Company in Eberfeld, Germany, began to market the drug as a cough remedy and painkiller under the brand name Heroin, the word derived from the German word for "heroic," which was intended to convey the drug's power and potency. The drug was an instant success and was soon exported to twenty-three countries.

Stimulant Use through the Nineteenth Century

The use of stimulants dates back to about 3000 B.C.E. with native South American societies. Even then, the people of this region knew that cocaine, which was extracted from the leaves of the coca tree *Erythroxylon coca*, was capable of producing euphoria, hyperactivity, and hallucinations. This small coca tree is native to tropical mountain regions in Peru and Bolivia.

After the Spanish conquest of the Incas in the early 1500s and ensuing Spanish immigration into South America, coca was grown on plantations and used as wages to pay workers. The drug seemed to negate the effects of exhaustion and malnutrition, especially at high altitudes. Many South Americans still chew coca leaves to alleviate the effects of high altitudes.

The spread of the use of coca is attributed to Paolo Mantegazza, an Italian doctor who came to value the restorative powers of coca while living in Lima, Peru, in the 1850s. His book praised the drug and led to interest in coca in the United States and Europe. In 1863 the French chemist Angelo Mariani extracted cocaine from coca leaves and used it as the main ingredient in his coca wine, called Vin Mariani. Shortly thereafter, cough syrups and tonics holding drops of cocaine in solution became popular. Eventually, extracts from coca leaves not only appeared in wine but also in chewing gum, tea, and throat lozenges.

The temperance movement in the United States from 1800 to 1890 helped fuel the public's fondness for non-alcoholic products containing coca. In the mid-1880s Atlanta, Georgia, became one of the first major U.S. cities to forbid the sale of alcohol. It was there that the pharmacist John Pemberton first marketed Coca-Cola, a syrup that then contained extracts of both coca and the kola nut, as a "temperance drink."

Hallucinogen Use through the Nineteenth Century

Naturally occurring hallucinogens, which are derived from plants, have been used by various cultures for magical, religious, recreational, and health-related purposes for thousands of years. For more than two thousand years Native American societies often used hallucinogens, such as the psilocybin mushroom (*Psilocybe mexicana*) of Mexico and the peyote cactus (*Lophophora williamsii*) of the U.S. Southwest, in religious ceremonies. Although scientists were slow to discover the medicinal possibilities of hallucinogens, by 1919 they had isolated mescaline from the peyote cactus and recognized its resemblance to the adrenal hormone epinephrine (or adrenaline).

Arthur C. Gibson notes in "The Weed of Controversy" (February 1999, http://www.botgard.ucla.edu/html/botanytextbooks/economicbotany/Cannabis/index.html) that cannabis, also a hallucinogen, is the term generally applied to the Himalayan hemp plant *Cannabis sativa* from which marijuana, bhang, and ganja (hashish) are derived. Bhang is equivalent to the U.S.-style marijuana, consisting of the leaves, fruits, and stems of the plant. Ganja, which is prepared by crushing the flowering tips of cannabis and collecting a resinous paste, is more potent than marijuana and bhang.

Cannabis dates back more than five thousand years to Central Asia and China; from there it spread to India and the Near East. Cannabis was highly regarded as a medicinal plant used in folk medicines. It was long valued as an analgesic, topical anesthetic, antispasmodic, antidepressant, appetite stimulant, antiasthmatic, and antibiotic.

NARCOTIC, STIMULANT, AND HALLUCINOGEN USE AT THE TURN OF THE NINETEENTH CENTURY AND BEYOND

In late nineteenth-century America it was possible to buy, in a store or by mail order, many medicines (or alleged medicines) containing morphine, cocaine, and even heroin. Until 1903 the soft drink Coca-Cola contained cocaine. The cocaine was later removed and more caffeine (already present in the drink from the kola nut) was added. Pharmacies sold cocaine in pure form, as well as many drugs made from opium, such as morphine and heroin.

Beginning in 1898 heroin became widely available when the Bayer Company marketed it as a powerful cough suppressant. According to the U.S. Government Office of Technology Assessment, in "Technologies for Understanding and Preventing Substance Abuse and Addiction: Appendix A, Drug Control Policy in the United States—Historical Perspectives" (December 2005, http://www.drugtext.org/library/reports/ota/appa.htm), physician prescriptions of these drugs increased from 1% of all prescriptions in 1874 to 20–25% in 1902. These drugs were not only available but also widely used, with little concern for negative health consequences.

Soon, however, cocaine, heroin, and other drugs were taken off the market for a number of reasons. A growing awareness of the dangers of drug use and food contamination led to the passage of laws such as the Pure Food and Drug Act of 1906 (PL 59-384). Among other things, the act required the removal of false claims from patent medicines. Medical labels also had to state the amount of any narcotic ingredient the medicine contained and whether that medicine was habit-forming. A growing temperance movement, the development of safe, alternative painkillers (such as aspirin), and more alternative medical treatments contributed to the passage of laws limiting drug use, although these laws did not completely outlaw the drugs.

Besides health-related worries, by the mid- to late 1800s drug use had come to be associated with "undesirables." When drug users were thought to live only in the slums, drug use was considered solely a criminal problem; but when it was finally recognized in middle-class neighborhoods, it came to be seen as a mental health problem. By the turn of the nineteenth century the use of narcotics was considered an international problem. In 1909 the International Opium Commission met to discuss drugs. This meeting led to the signing of a treaty two years later in the Netherlands requiring all signatories to pass laws limiting the use of narcotics for medicinal purposes. After nearly three years of debate Congress passed in 1914 the Harrison Narcotic Act (PL 63-223), which called for the strict control of opium and coca (although coca is a stimulant and not a narcotic).

Regulating Narcotics, Stimulants, and Hallucinogens

During the 1920s the federal government regulated drugs through the U.S. Treasury Department. In 1930 President Herbert Hoover created the Federal Bureau of Narcotics, headed by Harry J. Anslinger, the commissioner of narcotics. Believing that all drug users were deviant criminals, Anslinger vigorously enforced the law for the next thirty-two years. Marijuana, for example, was presented as a "killer weed" that threatened the very fabric of American society. It is thought that the drug was introduced to the United States by Mexican immigrants.

According to the U.S. Government Office of Technology Assessment, it is widely believed that anti-Mexican attitudes, as well as Anslinger's considerable influence, prompted the passage of the Marijuana Tax Act of 1937 (PL 75-238). The act made the use or sale of marijuana without a tax stamp a federal offense. Because by this time the sale of marijuana was illegal in most states, buying a federal tax stamp would alert the police in a particular state to who was selling drugs. Naturally, no marijuana dealer wanted to buy a stamp and expose his or her identity to the police.

From the 1940s through the 1960s the FDA, based on the authority granted by the Food, Drug, and Cosmetic Act of 1938 (52 Stat. 1040), began to police the sale of certain drugs. The act had required the FDA to stipulate if specific drugs, such as amphetamines, barbiturates, and sulfa drugs, were safe for self-medication.

After studying most amphetamines (stimulants) and barbiturates (depressants), the agency concluded that it simply could not declare them safe for self-medication. (See Table 1.1 for listings of stimulants and depressants.) Therefore, it ruled that these drugs could only be used under medical supervision—that is, with a physician's prescription. For all pharmaceutical products other than narcotics, this marked the beginning of the distinction between prescription and over-the-counter (without a prescription) drugs.

For twenty-five years undercover FDA inspectors tracked down pharmacists who sold amphetamines and barbiturates without a prescription and doctors who wrote illegal prescriptions. In the 1950s, with the growing sale of amphetamines, barbiturates, and, eventually, LSD and other hallucinogens at cafés, truck stops, flophouses, and weight-reduction salons and by street-corner pushers, FDA authorities went after these other illegal dealers. In 1968 the drug-enforcement responsibilities of the FDA were transferred to the U.S. Department of Justice.

War on Drugs

From the mid-1960s to the late 1970s the demographic profile of drug users changed. Previously, drug use had generally been associated with minorities, lower classes, or young "hippies" and "beatniks." During this period drug use among middle-class whites became widespread and more generally accepted. Cocaine, an expensive drug, began to be used by middle- and upper-class whites, many of whom looked on it as a nonaddictive recreational drug and status symbol. In addition, drugs had become much more prevalent in the military because they were cheap and plentiful in Vietnam.

Whereas some circles viewed drug use with wider acceptance, other public sectors came to see drugs as a threat to their communities—much as, forty years earlier, alcohol had acquired a negative image, leading to Prohibition. Drugs not only symbolized poverty but also were associated with protest movements against the Vietnam War and the "Establishment." Many parents began to perceive the widespread availability of drugs as a threat to their children. By the end of the 1960s such views began to acquire a political expression.

When he ran for president in 1968, Richard Nixon included a strong antidrug plank in his law-and-order platform, calling for a war on drugs. After he was elected president, Nixon created the President's National Commission on Marihuana and Drug Abuse, which published its findings in the report *Marihuana: A Signal of Misunderstanding* (March 1972, http://www.druglibrary.org/ schaffer/library/studies/nc/ncmenu.htm). Nixon ignored the commission's findings, which called for the legalization of marijuana. Since that time the U.S. government has been waging a war on drugs in some form or another.

In 1973 Congress authorized the formation of the Drug Enforcement Administration to reduce the supply of drugs. A year later the National Institute on Drug Abuse (NIDA) was created to lead the effort to reduce the demand for drugs and to direct research and federal prevention and treatment services.

Under the Nixon, Ford, and Carter administrations federal spending tended to emphasize the treatment of drug abusers. Meanwhile, a growing number of parents, fearing that their children were being exposed to drugs, began to pressure elected officials and government agencies to do more about the growing use of drugs. In response, the NIDA began widely publicizing the dangers of marijuana and other drugs once thought not to be particularly harmful.

The Reagan administration favored a strict approach to drug use, popularized the phrase "war on drugs," and increased enforcement efforts. According to the Government Office of Technology Assessment, the budget to fight drugs rose from $1.5 billion in 1981 to $4.2 billion in 1989. By the end of the Reagan administration two-thirds of all drug control funding went for law enforcement and one-third went for treatment and prevention. First Lady Nancy Reagan vigorously campaigned against drug use, urging children to "just say no!" The Crime Control Act of 1984 (PL 98-473) dramatically increased the penalties for drug use and drug trafficking.

INTRODUCTION OF CRACK COCAINE. Cocaine use increased dramatically in the 1960s and 1970s, but the drug's high cost restricted its use to the more affluent. In the early 1980s cocaine dealers discovered a way to prepare the cocaine so that it could be smoked in small and inexpensive but powerful and highly addictive amounts. The creation of this so-called crack cocaine meant that poor people could now afford to use the drug, and a whole new market was opened up. In addition, the acquired immune deficiency syndrome (AIDS) epidemic caused some intravenous drug users to switch to smoking crack to avoid exposure to the human immunodeficiency virus (HIV), which can be contracted by sharing needles with an infected user.

Battles for control of the distribution and sale of the drug led to a violent black market. The easy availability of sophisticated firearms and the huge amounts of money to be made selling crack and other drugs transformed many areas of the nation—but particularly the inner cities—into dangerous places.

The widespread fear of crack cocaine led to increasingly harsh laws and penalties. Authorities warned that crack was instantly addictive and spreading rapidly, and they predicted a subsequent generation of "crack babies"—that is, babies born addicted to crack because their mothers were using it during pregnancy.

HEROIN GETS CHEAPER AND PURER. The dangers associated with crack cocaine caused changes in the use of heroin in the 1990s. Many reported deaths from heroin overdosing had lessened the drug's attraction in the 1980s. In addition, heroin had to be injected by syringe, and concerns regarding HIV infection contributed to the dangers of using the drug. In the 1990s an oversupply of heroin, innovations that produced a smokable variety of the drug, and the appearance of purer forms of the drug restored its attractiveness to the relatively small number of people addicted to "hard" drugs. It was no longer necessary to take the drug intravenously—it could be sniffed like cocaine—although many users continued to use needles.

The War Continues: The Office of National Drug Control Policy

The Anti-Drug Abuse Act of 1988 (PL 100-690) created the Office of National Drug Control Policy (ONDCP), to be headed by a director—popularly referred to as the "drug czar"—who would coordinate the nation's drug policy. The Government Office of Technology Assessment reports that spending for drug control rose from $4.2 billion under President Ronald Reagan to $12.7 billion in the last year of President George H. W. Bush's term. As was the case during the Reagan administration, the monetary split was roughly two-thirds for law enforcement and one-third for treatment and prevention. By 1990 every state that had once decriminalized the use of marijuana had repealed those laws.

The Government Office of Technology Assessment indicates that when President Bill Clinton took office in 1993, he cut the ONDCP staff from 146 to 25, while at the same time raising the director of the ONDCP to cabinet status. Clinton called for one hundred thousand more police officers on the streets and advocated drug treatment on demand. According to *The National Drug Control Strategy, 1998: Budget Summary* (February 1998, http://www.ncjrs.gov/ondcppubs/publications/pdf/budget98.pdf), in 1998 drug control funding totaled $16 billion, with the split remaining at about two-thirds for law enforcement and one-third for treatment and prevention. (It is important to note that in the mid-1990s changes were made in the list of expenditures included in this tally, making it difficult to analyze historical drug control spending trends.)

Taking office in 2001, President George W. Bush promised to continue national efforts to eradicate illicit drugs in the United States and abroad. On May 10, 2001, he appointed John Walters as the new drug czar. Together, they pledged to continue "an all out effort to reduce illicit drug use in America," according to the White House news release announcing the appointment. Their proposed goals included increased spending on treatment, intensified work with foreign nations, and an adamant opposition to the legalization of any currently illicit drugs. The Bush administration also wove its anti-drug message into its arguments for invading Afghanistan. Even though Bush's case was built primarily on the notion that Afghanistan's Taliban leaders had harbored the terrorist Osama bin Laden, he regularly referred to Afghanistan's role as the world's biggest producer of opium poppies.

Over the course of Bush's presidency, White House budget documents indicate that federal spending on drug control started at $9.5 billion in 2001 and grew to $12.6 billion in 2006, with treatment accounting for 23.8% of the total in the requested 2007 budget, according to the *National Drug Control Strategy: FY 2007 Budget Summary* (February 2006, http://www.whitehousedrugpolicy.gov/publications/policy/07budget/partii_funding_tables.pdf).

Questioning the War on Drugs

By 2007 there was considerable controversy surrounding the necessity and effectiveness of the war on drugs. Decades of effort have led to large numbers of people serving prison sentences for manufacturing, selling, or using drugs. Yet the illicit drug trade continued to thrive. Many critics argue that a different approach is necessary and question whether illicit drugs are an enemy worth waging war against, especially such a costly war during a time of rapidly rising federal budget deficits. In the October 2006 "Most Important Problem" Gallup Poll, adult Americans rated drugs as a low priority—the fifteenth most important noneconomic problem. The noneconomic problems they perceived as more important included the war in Iraq, terrorism, dissatisfaction with the government, illegal immigration, poverty, crime, the situation in North Korea, poor education, and Social Security.

CHAPTER 2
ALCOHOL

Contrary to popular belief, ethanol (the alcohol in alcoholic beverages) is not a stimulant, but a depressant. Although many of those who drink alcoholic beverages feel relaxation, pleasure, and stimulation, these feelings are in fact caused by the depressant effects of alcohol on the brain.

WHAT CONSTITUTES A DRINK?

In the United States a standard drink contains about twelve grams (about 0.5 fluid ounces) of pure alcohol. The following beverages contain nearly equal amounts of alcohol and are approximately standard drink equivalents:

- One shot (1.5 ounces) of spirits (eighty-proof whiskey, vodka, gin, etc.)
- One 2.5-ounce glass of a cordial, liqueur, or aperitif
- One five-ounce glass of table wine
- One three- to four-ounce glass of fortified wine, such as sherry or port
- One twelve-ounce bottle or can of beer
- One eight- to nine-ounce bottle or can of malt liquor

ALCOHOL CONSUMPTION IN THE UNITED STATES

After caffeine, alcohol is the most commonly used drug in the United States. Although researchers frequently count how many people are drinking and how often, the statistics do not necessarily reflect the true picture of alcohol consumption in the United States. People tend to underreport their drinking. Furthermore, survey interviewees are typically people living in households; therefore, the results of survey research may not include the homeless, a portion of the U.S. population traditionally at risk for alcoholism (alcohol dependence).

Per Capita Consumption of Alcohol

According to Table 2.1, the yearly per capita consumption of alcoholic beverages peaked at 28.8 gallons in 1981. (The per capita consumption includes the total resident population and all age groups.) Per capita consumption declined to 24.7 gallons in 1995 and has climbed only slightly since then. In 2004 the per capita consumption of alcoholic beverages was 25.2 gallons.

Beer remained the most popular alcoholic beverage in 2004, being consumed at a rate of 21.6 gallons per person. Nonetheless, this level of consumption (also seen in 2003 and 1997) is the lowest level since 1976, when 21.5 gallons were consumed. Beer consumption peaked in 1981 at 24.6 gallons per person, but its consumption declined steadily to its present relatively stable level by 1995. The per capita consumption of wine and spirits in the United States is much lower than that of beer; the 2004 per capita consumption of wine was 2.3 gallons, while per capita consumption of distilled spirits (liquor) was 1.4 gallons.

A complex set of factors contributes to variations in alcohol use over people's life spans. Part of the decline in alcohol consumption is a result of population trends. In the 1980s and 1990s the number of people in their early twenties—the leading consumers of alcohol—declined fairly steadily. The United States is also seeing a growing number of residents in their fifties and sixties. This is a group that is, in general, unlikely to consume as much alcohol as younger people.

Individual Consumption of Alcohol

The data for alcohol consumption noted in the previous section are per capita figures, which are determined by taking the total consumption of alcohol per year and dividing by the total resident population, including children. This figure is useful to see how consumption changes from year to year because it takes into account changes in the size of the resident population. Nonetheless,

TABLE 2.1

Per capita consumption of beer, wine, and distilled spirits, 1966–2004

Year	Total resident population			
	Beer	Wine[a]	Distilled spirits	Total[b]
		Gallons		
1966	16.5	1.0	1.6	19.0
1967	16.8	1.0	1.6	19.4
1968	17.3	1.1	1.7	20.1
1969	17.8	1.2	1.8	20.8
1970	18.5	1.3	1.8	21.6
1971	18.9	1.5	1.8	22.3
1972	19.3	1.6	1.9	22.8
1973	20.1	1.6	1.9	23.6
1974	20.9	1.6	2.0	24.5
1975	21.3	1.7	2.0	25.0
1976	21.5	1.7	2.0	25.2
1977	22.4	1.8	2.0	26.1
1978	23.0	2.0	2.0	26.9
1979	23.8	2.0	2.0	27.8
1980	24.3	2.1	2.0	28.3
1981	24.6	2.2	2.0	28.8
1982	24.4	2.2	1.9	28.5
1983	24.2	2.3	1.8	28.3
1984	24.0	2.4	1.8	28.1
1985	23.8	2.4	1.8	28.0
1986	24.1	2.4	1.6	28.2
1987	24.0	2.4	1.6	28.0
1988	23.8	2.3	1.5	27.6
1989	23.6	2.1	1.5	27.2
1990	23.9	2.0	1.5	27.5
1991	23.1	1.8	1.4	26.3
1992	22.7	1.9	1.4	25.9
1993	22.4	1.7	1.3	25.5
1994	22.3	1.7	1.3	25.3
1995	21.8	1.7	1.2	24.7
1996	21.7	1.9	1.2	24.8
1997	21.6	1.9	1.2	24.7
1998	21.7	1.9	1.2	24.8
1999	21.8	2.0	1.2	25.0
2000	21.7	2.0	1.3	24.9
2001	21.8	2.0	1.3	25.0
2002	21.8	2.1	1.3	25.2
2003	21.6	2.2	1.3	25.1
2004	21.6	2.3	1.4	25.2

Notes: Alcoholic beverage per capita figures are calculated by Economic Research Service using industry data. Uses U.S. resident population, July.
[a]Beginning in 1983, includes winecoolers.
[b]Computed from unrounded data.

SOURCE: "Alcoholic Beverages: Per Capita Consumption," U.S. Department of Agriculture, Economic Research Service, December 21, 2005, http://www.ers.usda.gov/data/foodconsumption/spreadsheets/beverage.xls#PccLiq!a1 (accessed October 2, 2006)

babies and small children generally do not consume alcohol, so it is also useful to look at consumption figures based on U.S. residents aged twelve and over.

Table 2.2 shows the percentage of respondents aged twelve and over who reported consuming alcohol in the past month in 2004 and 2005 when questioned for the annual National Survey on Drug Use and Health, which is conducted by the Substance Abuse and Mental Health Services Administration. In 2005, 51.8% of this total population had consumed alcohol in the month prior to the survey, as opposed to 50.3% of the total population in 2004. A higher percentage of males consumed alcoholic beverages in the past month than did females in both

years. Table 2.2 also shows that alcohol consumption varies by race. A higher percentage of whites had used alcohol within the month prior to the survey than had African-Americans or Hispanics.

Prevalence of Problem Drinking

Table 2.2 also shows the percentages of Americans aged twelve and older who engaged in binge drinking or heavy alcohol use in the month prior to the survey. Binge drinking means that a person had five or more drinks on the same occasion, that is, within a few hours of each other. Heavy alcohol use means that a person had five or more drinks on the same occasion on each of five or more days in the past thirty days. All heavy alcohol users are binge drinkers, but not all binge drinkers are heavy alcohol users.

People aged eighteen to twenty-five were more likely than people in other age groups to have binged on alcohol and been heavy alcohol users in both 2004 and 2005. Much higher percentages of males binge drank and used alcohol heavily than females in the month prior to each of these surveys. In addition, American Indians and Alaskan Natives were the most likely to have engaged in binge and heavy alcohol use.

DEFINING ALCOHOLISM

Most people consider an alcoholic to be someone who drinks too much and cannot control his or her drinking. Alcoholism, however, does not merely refer to heavy drinking or getting drunk a certain number of times. The diagnosis of alcoholism applies only to those who show specific symptoms of addiction, which the Institute of Medicine (1996, http://www.iom.edu/) defines as a brain disease "manifested by a complex set of behaviors that are the result of genetic, biological, psychological, and environmental interactions."

Robert M. Morse and Daniel K. Flavin, in "The Definition of Alcoholism" (*Journal of the American Medical Association*, August 1992), define alcoholism as:

> A primary, chronic disease with genetic, psychosocial, and environmental factors influencing its development and manifestations. The disease is often progressive and fatal. It is characterized by impaired control over drinking, preoccupation with the drug alcohol, use of alcohol despite adverse consequences, and distortions in thinking, most notably denial. Each of these symptoms may be continuous or periodic.

"Primary" refers to alcoholism as a disease independent from any other psychological disease (for example, schizophrenia), rather than as a symptom of some other underlying disease. "Adverse consequences" for an alcoholic can include physical illness (liver disease, withdrawal symptoms, etc.), psychological problems, interpersonal difficulties (such as marital problems or domestic violence),

TABLE 2.2

Percentage of past-month alcohol use, binge alcohol use, and heavy alcohol use among drinkers aged 12 and older, by demographic characteristics, 2004 and 2005

	Type of alcohol use					
	Alcohol use		Binge alcohol use		Heavy alcohol use	
Demographic characteristic	2004	2005	2004	2005	2004	2005
Total	50.3	51.8	22.8	22.7	6.9	6.6
Age						
12–17	17.6	16.5	11.1	9.9	2.7	2.4
18–25	60.5	60.9	41.2	41.9	15.1	15.3
26 or older	53.0	55.1	21.1	21.0	6.1	5.6
Gender						
Male	56.9	58.1	31.1	30.5	10.6	10.3
Female	44.0	45.9	14.9	15.2	3.5	3.1
Hispanic origin and race						
Not Hispanic or Latino	51.8	53.2	22.6	22.5	7.2	6.7
White	55.2	56.5	23.8	23.4	7.9	7.4
Black or African American	37.1	40.8	18.3	20.3	4.4	4.2
American Indian or Alaska Native	36.2	42.4	25.8	32.8	7.7	11.5
Native Hawaiian or other Pacific Islander	*	37.3	*	25.7	4.9	5.3
Asian	37.4	38.1	12.4	12.7	2.7	2.0
Two or more races	52.4	47.3	23.5	20.8	6.9	5.6
Hispanic or Latino	40.2	42.6	24.0	23.7	5.3	5.6

*Low precision; no estimate reported.
Note: Binge alcohol use is defined as drinking five or more drinks on the same occasion (i.e., at the same time or within a couple of hours of each other) on at least 1 day in the past 30 days. Heavy alcohol use is defined as drinking five or more drinks on the same occasion on each of 5 or more days in the past 30 days; all heavy alcohol users are also binge alcohol users.

SOURCE: "Table 2.52B. Alcohol Use, Binge Alcohol Use, and Heavy Alcohol Use in the Past Month among Persons Aged 12 or Older, by Demographic Characteristics: Percentages, 2004 and 2005," in *Results from the 2005 National Survey on Drug Use and Health: Detailed Tables*, U.S. Department of Health and Human Services, Substance Abuse and Mental Health Services Administration, Office of Applied Studies, 2006, http://www.oas.samhsa.gov/nsduh/2k5nsduh/tabs/Sect2peTabs47to56.pdf (accessed October 3, 2006)

and problems at work. "Denial" includes a number of psychological maneuvers by the drinker to avoid the fact that alcohol is the cause of his or her problems. Family and friends may reinforce an alcoholic's denial by covering up his or her drinking (for example, calling an employer to say the alcoholic has the flu rather than a hangover). Such behavior is also known as enabling. In other words, the friends and family make excuses for the drinker and enable him or her to continue drinking as opposed to having to face the repercussions of his or her alcohol abuse. Denial is a major obstacle in recovery from alcoholism.

ALCOHOLISM AND ALCOHOL ABUSE

The American Psychiatric Association (APA), which publishes the *Diagnostic and Statistical Manual of Mental Disorders* (*DSM*), first defined alcoholism in 1952. *DSM-III*, the third edition of the APA's publication, renamed alcoholism as alcohol dependence and introduced the phrase *alcohol abuse*. According to *DSM-III*'s definitions of alcohol abuse, the condition involves a compulsive use of alcohol and impaired social or occupational functioning, whereas alcohol dependence includes physical tolerance and withdrawal symptoms when the drug is stopped. *DSM-IV-TR*, the most recent edition, refines these definitions further, but the basic definitions remain the same.

TABLE 2.3

Four symptoms of alcoholism

Alcoholism, also known as "alcohol dependence," is a disease that includes four symptoms:

- Craving: A strong need, or compulsion, to drink.
- Loss of control: The inability to limit one's drinking on any given occasion.
- Physical dependence: Withdrawal symptoms, such as nausea, sweating, shakiness, and anxiety, occur when alcohol use is stopped after a period of heavy drinking.
- Tolerance: The need to drink greater amounts of alcohol in order to "get high."

SOURCE: Adapted from *Alcoholism: Getting the Facts*, U.S. Department of Health and Human Services, National Institutes of Health, National Institute on Alcohol Abuse and Alcoholism, revised 2004, http://pubs.niaaa.nih.gov/publications/GettheFacts_HTML/Facts.pdf (accessed October 6, 2006)

The World Health Organization publishes the *International Classification of Diseases* (*ICD*), which is designed to standardize health data collection throughout the world. The tenth edition (*ICD-10*) generally defines abuse and tolerance similarly to the *DSM-IV-TR*.

The National Institute on Alcohol Abuse and Alcoholism (NIAAA), in its September 2004 update of *Alcoholism: Getting the Facts*, states that alcoholism (alcohol dependence) is a disease that includes the four symptoms listed and described in Table 2.3.

Four symptoms of alcohol abuse

Alcohol abuse is defined as a pattern of drinking that results in one or more of the following situations within a 12-month period:

- Failure to fulfill major work, school, or home responsibilities;
- Drinking in situations that are physically dangerous, such as while driving a car or operating machinery;
- Having recurring alcohol-related legal problems, such as being arrested for driving under the influence of alcohol or for physically hurting someone while drunk; and
- Continued drinking despite having ongoing relationship problems that are caused or worsened by the drinking.

SOURCE: Adapted from *Alcoholism: Getting the Facts*, U.S. Department of Health and Human Services, National Institutes of Health, National Institute on Alcohol Abuse and Alcoholism, revised 2004 http://pubs.niaaa.nih.gov/publications/GettheFacts_HTML/Facts.pdf (accessed October 6, 2006)

According to the NIAAA, "alcohol abuse differs from alcoholism in that it does not include an extremely strong craving for alcohol, loss of control over drinking, or physical dependence." The symptoms of alcohol abuse are listed in Table 2.4. The NIAAA notes that "although alcohol abuse is basically different from alcoholism, many effects of alcohol abuse are also experienced by alcoholics."

Other characteristics of alcohol abuse include the need to drink before facing certain situations, frequent drinking sprees, a steady increase in intake, solitary drinking, early morning drinking, and the occurrence of blackouts. Blackouts for heavy drinkers are not episodes of passing out, but are periods drinkers cannot remember later, even though they appeared to be functioning at the time.

Prevalence of Alcohol Dependence, Alcohol Abuse, Binge Drinking, and Heavy Drinking

The *Strategic Plan 2001–2005* of the NIAAA notes that nearly fourteen million Americans—one in every thirteen adults—have alcohol-abuse or alcohol-dependence problems.

Figure 2.1 shows the percentages of people who engaged in alcohol use, binge drinking, and heavy alcohol use in 2005 by age group. The graph shows that people aged eighteen to twenty-nine are more likely to engage in binge drinking and heavy alcohol use than those aged twelve to seventeen or those aged thirty and older. The graph also shows that as people grow older, alcohol use (not binge or heavy) becomes prevalent, and binge and heavy alcohol use decline.

Table 2.2 compares the rates of binge drinking for males and females across all age groups. In 2004 and 2005 the rate of binge drinking in males was substantially higher than that of females. The percentage of males who binge drank in 2004 and 2005 was 31.1% and 30.5%, respectively, whereas the percentage of females who binge drank was about half that, at approximately 15%.

In addition, heavy alcohol use was much more prevalent in males than in females. Approximately 10% of males were heavy alcohol users in 2004 and 2005, whereas only about 3% of females were in this group.

ALCOHOL ABUSE AND ALCOHOLISM IN VARIOUS RACIAL AND ETHNIC GROUPS

As shown in Table 2.2, patterns of alcohol consumption vary across racial and ethnic groups. The NIAAA suggests that low alcoholism rates occur in certain groups because the drinking customs and sanctions (permissions) are well established and consistent with the rest of the culture. Conversely, multicultural populations have mixed feelings about alcohol and no common rules; they tend to have higher alcoholism rates. Frank H. Galvan and Raul Caetano note in "Alcohol Use and Related Problems among Ethnic Minorities in the United States" (*Alcohol Research and Health*, Winter 2003) that a population's alcohol norms (how one should behave in relation to alcohol) and attitudes (general beliefs about drinking) have been found to be strong predictors of drinking.

In addition, certain populations may be at a higher or lower risk because of the way their bodies metabolize (chemically process) alcohol. For example, many Asians have an inherited deficiency of aldehyde dehydrogenase, a chemical that breaks down ethyl alcohol in the body. Without it, toxic substances build up after drinking alcohol and rapidly lead to flushing, dizziness, and nausea. Therefore, many Asians experience warning signals very early on and are less likely to continue drinking. Conversely, research results suggest that Native Americans may lack these warning signals. They are less sensitive to the intoxicating effects of alcohol and are more likely to develop alcoholism. Table 2.2 shows that the prevalence of binge alcohol use and heavy alcohol use is the lowest for Asians and the highest in for Native Americans.

RISK FACTORS OF ALCOHOL ABUSE AND ALCOHOLISM

The development of alcoholism is the result of a complex mix of biological, psychological, and social factors. Table 2.5 summarizes risk factors for alcohol use, abuse, and dependence. Genetics and alcohol reactivity (sensitivity) are biological factors. The rest are psychosocial factors.

Biological Factors

GENETICS. A variety of studies investigating family history, adopted versus biological children living in the same families, and twins separated and living in different families all indicate that genetics plays a substantial role in some forms of alcohol dependence and heavy drinking. For example, in "Genetics of Alcohol and Tobacco Use in Humans" (*Annals of Medicine*, 2003), Rachel F. Tyndale

FIGURE 2.1

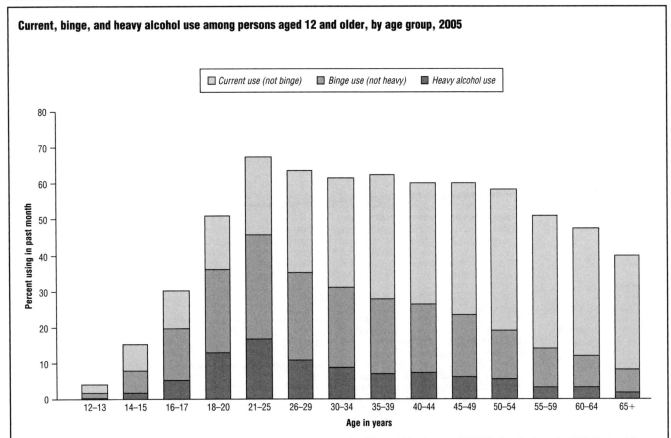

Current, binge, and heavy alcohol use among persons aged 12 and older, by age group, 2005

SOURCE: "Figure 3.1. Current, Binge, and Heavy Alcohol Use among Persons Aged 12 or Older, by Age: 2005," in *Results from the 2005 National Survey on Drug Use and Health: National Findings*, U.S. Department of Health and Human Services, Substance Abuse and Mental Health Services Administration, Office of Applied Studies, 2006, http://www.oas.samhsa.gov/nsduh/2k5nsduh/2k5Results.pdf (accessed October 12, 2006)

indicates that many genes are likely to be involved, each contributing a small part of the overall risk.

ALCOHOL REACTIVITY (SENSITIVITY). Alcohol reactivity or sensitivity refers to the sense of intoxication one has when drinking alcohol. The research on this topic has been conducted primarily on sons of alcoholics and reveals that, in general, they have a lower reactivity to alcohol. That is, when given moderate amounts of alcohol, sons of alcoholics report a lower subjective sense of intoxication compared with sons of nonalcoholics. Sons of alcoholics also show fewer signs of intoxication on certain physiological indicators than do sons of nonalcoholics. Without early signals of intoxication, men with a low reactivity to alcohol may tend to drink more before they begin to feel drunk and thus may develop a high physiological tolerance for alcohol, which magnifies the problem. Susan Nolen-Hoeksema notes in "Gender Differences in Risk Factors and Consequences for Alcohol Use and Problems" (*Clinical Psychology Review*, December 2004) that "long-term studies of men with low reactivity to moderate doses of alcohol suggest they are significantly more likely to become alcoholics over time than are men with greater reactivity to moderate doses of alcohol." (See Table 2.5.)

Psychosocial Factors

SOCIAL SANCTIONS, GENDER ROLES, AND COPING STYLES. Social sanctions are a mechanism of social control for enforcing a society's standards. Social sanctions may be one factor explaining why men drink more alcohol than women. A "double standard" appears to exist for men and women in American society with regard to consuming alcohol. Research findings support this idea. For example, Nancy D. Vogeltanz and Sharon C. Wilsnack find in "Alcohol Problems in Women: Risk Factors, Consequences, and Treatment Strategies" (Sheryle J. Gallant, Gwendolyn Puryear Keita, Reneé Royak-Schaler, eds., *Health Care for Women: Psychological, Social, and Behavioral Influences*, 1997) that in 1996 women thought that 50% of people at a party would disapprove of a woman getting drunk but that only 30% would disapprove of a man doing the same.

Besides social sanctions against women drinking as heavily as men, American culture appears to identify alcohol consumption as more of a part of the male gender role than of the female gender role. While discussing and reviewing the results of several studies, Nolen-Hoeksema "find[s] that people, particularly women, who endorse

TABLE 2.5

Risk factors for alcohol use, abuse, and dependence

Risk factor	Evidence
Genetics	Most studies find genetics contribute to alcoholism and alcohol use in both women and men; some studies suggest genetics play a stronger role in alcoholism for men than for women.
Alcohol reactivity	Studies of men find low alcohol reactivity is associated with a history of familial risk for alcohol use disorders and the development of alcohol use disorders in men. There are only a few small studies of women, but these studies also tend to find an association between familial risk for alcoholism and low alcohol reactivity. It is unknown whether there are gender differences in alcohol reactivity, but other studies find women may be more cognitively and motorically impaired at lower doses of alcohol, suggesting they have greater alcohol reactivity.
Social sanctions	Social sanctions are perceived to be greater for women drinking than for men drinking. It is unclear whether or not women actually suffer more negative social consequences as a result of heavy drinking than men.
Gender roles	Feminine traits (e.g., nurture and warmth) are associated with less use and fewer alcohol problems. Undesirable masculine traits (aggressiveness and overcontrol) are associated with heavy and problematic alcohol use. Socially desirable masculine traits (instrumentality) are associated with fewer drinking problems. Patterns are generally the same for males and females. One study found that gender differences in gender role traits mediated gender differences in alcohol use and problems.
Coping styles	Avoidant coping is more consistently associated with alcohol consumption and drinking problems in men than in women. It is not clear whether there are gender differences in avoidant coping.
Motives and expectancies	Drinking to cope with distress and positive expectancies for the outcomes of alcohol consumption (e.g., that it will reduce distress) are associated with alcohol consumption and problem drinking; this relationship tends to be stronger for men than for women. Men tend to be more likely than women to report drinking to cope and positive expectancies for alcohol use.
Depression/distress	Among social drinkers, some studies show a stronger relationship between distress and drinking for men than women, whereas others show the opposite gender pattern; among alcoholics, the relationship between distress and alcohol use or problems is stronger for women than men.
Self-esteem	Some evidence suggests that low self-esteem is associated with alcohol-related problems in women more than men, but this result is inconsistent.
Behavioral undercontrol/ sensation-seeking/impulsivity	Men score higher than women on measures of behavioral undercontrol, sensation-seeking, and impulsivity. These variables are consistently associated with alcohol use and problems in men, less consistently so in women.
Antisociality	Males are more likely to show symptoms of antisociality and delinquency than females. Antisociality is associated with alcohol use and disorders in both males and females.
Interpersonal relationships	There are strong similarities between partners in heterosexual couples in drinking patterns. It is not clear whether the effects of a partner on the individual's drinking are stronger for women or men.
Sexual assault	A history of sexual assault is associated with problem drinking and alcohol use disorders in both women and men. Women are more likely to have a history of sexual assault.

SOURCE: Reprinted from Susan Nolen-Hoeksema, "Gender Differences in Risk Factors and Consequences for Alcohol Use and Problems," in *Clinical Psychology Review*, vol. 24, no. 8, 2004, 981=1010, http://www.sciencedirect.com/science?_ob=ArticleURL&_udi=B6VB8-4DG3DCH-1&_user=10&_handle=V-WA-A-W-E-MsSAYVW-UUA-U-AAZZEZBYWZ-AAZVCVVZWZ-EYBCEWVZ-E-U&_fmt=summary&_coverDate=12%2F01%2F2004&_rdoc=4&_orig=browse&_srch=%23toc%235920%232004%23999759991%23527116!&_cdi=5920&_acct=C000050221&_version=1&_urlVersion=0&_userid=10&md5=40d785e3d01008ef15122c95de7802f7 (accessed October 6, 2006). Copyright © 2004 with permission from Elsevier.

traditionally feminine traits (nurturance, emotional expressivity) report less quantity and frequency of alcohol use." (See Table 2.5.) In contrast, traits often associated with the male gender role, such as aggressiveness and overcontrol of emotions, have been associated with heavy and problem alcohol use in both men and women. In fact, heavy drinking may be a way that some people cope with stress and avoid emotions, a behavior referred to as "avoidant coping."

DRINKING MOTIVES, EXPECTATIONS, AND DEPRESSION/ DISTRESS. People consume alcohol for various reasons: as part of a meal, to celebrate certain occasions, and to reduce anxiety in social situations. Nolen-Hoeksema comments that people also consume alcohol to cope with distress or depression or to escape from negative feelings. Consequently, people expect that drinking alcohol will reduce tension, increase social or physical pleasure, and facilitate social interaction. Those who have positive expectations for their drinking, such as the belief that alcohol will reduce distress, tend to drink more than those who have negative expectancies, such as the belief that alcohol will interfere with the ability to cope with distress. In general, men have more positive expectations concerning alcohol consumption than women. These stronger motives to drink are more strongly associated with alcohol-related problems in men than in women, although Nolen-Hoeksema reports that the relationships among depression, general distress, alcohol consumption, and problems are quite complex. (See Table 2.5.)

SELF-ESTEEM, IMPULSIVITY, SENSATION-SEEKING, BEHAVIORAL UNDERCONTROL, AND ANTISOCIALITY. As Table 2.5 shows, research results are inconclusive regarding the relationship between self-esteem and alcohol use. However, impulsivity, sensation-seeking, and behavioral undercontrol (not controlling one's behavior well) are consistently associated with alcohol use and problems in men. This association is less clear in women and may be another factor determining why a higher percentage of men than women are alcohol dependent.

Antisociality is a personality disorder that includes a chronic disregard for the rights of others and an absence of remorse for the harmful effects of these behaviors on others. People with this disorder are usually involved in aggressive and illegal activities. They are often impulsive and reckless and are more likely to become alcohol dependent. Males are more likely than females to demonstrate antisociality. (See Table 2.5.)

INTERPERSONAL RELATIONSHIPS AND SEXUAL ASSAULT. Married couples often have strongly similar levels of drinking. It is unclear whether men and women with problem drinking patterns seek out partners with similar drinking patterns or whether either is influenced by the other to drink during the marriage. However, marital discord is often present when spouses' drinking patterns differ significantly.

Being a victim of sexual assault is a risk factor for problem drinking. The results of many studies show that women who have experienced a history of sexual assault, whether during childhood or as an adult, are at increased risk for problem drinking and alcohol abuse. According to Nolen-Hoeksema, the correlation is not as clear in men.

Effects of Alcoholism on Family Members

Living with someone who has an alcohol problem affects every member of the family. Children seem to suffer the most. The National Association for Children of Alcoholics, in the fact sheet "Children of Addicted Parents: Important Facts" (2000, http://www.nacoa.net/pdfs/addicted.pdf), estimates that there are more than twenty-eight million children of alcoholics in the United States, including more than eleven million under the age of eighteen. Researchers suspect that children of alcoholics have a risk for alcoholism and other drug abuse two to nine times greater than that of children of non-alcoholics. They are also thought to be more likely to suffer from attention-deficit hyperactivity disorder, behavioral problems, and anxiety disorders. They tend to score lower on tests that measure cognitive and verbal skills. Children of alcoholics are also more likely to be truant, repeat grades, drop out of school, or be referred to a school counselor or psychologist.

SHORT-TERM EFFECTS OF ALCOHOL ON THE BODY

When most people think about how alcohol affects them, they think of a temporary light-headedness or a hangover the next morning. Many are also aware of the serious damage that continuous, excessive alcohol use can do to the liver. Alcohol, however, affects many organs of the body and has been linked to cancer, mental and/or physical retardation in newborns, heart disease, and other health problems.

Low to moderate doses of alcohol produce a slight, brief increase in heartbeat and blood pressure. Large doses can reduce the pumping power of the heart and produce irregular heartbeats. In addition, blood vessels within muscles constrict, but those at the surface expand, causing rapid heat loss from the skin and a flushing or reddening. Thus, large doses of alcohol decrease body temperature and, additionally, may cause numbness of the skin, legs, and arms, creating a false feeling of warmth. Figure 2.2 illustrates and describes in more detail the path alcohol takes through the body after it is consumed.

Alcohol affects the endocrine system (a group of glands that produce hormones) in several ways. One effect is increased urination. Urination increases not only because of fluid intake but also because alcohol stops the release of an antidiuretic hormone—ADH, or vasopressin—from the pituitary gland. This hormone controls how much water the kidneys reabsorb from the urine as it is being produced and how much water the kidneys excrete. Therefore, heavy alcohol intake can result in both dehydration and an imbalance in electrolytes, which are chemicals dissolved in body fluids that conduct electrical currents. Both of these conditions are serious health hazards.

Alcohol is sometimes believed to be an aphrodisiac (sexual stimulant). Whereas low to moderate amounts of alcohol can reduce fear and decrease sexual inhibitions, larger doses tend to impair sexual performance. Alcoholics sometimes report difficulties in their sex lives.

Intoxication

The speed of alcohol absorption affects the rate at which one becomes intoxicated. Intoxication occurs when alcohol is absorbed into the blood faster than the liver can oxidize it (or break it down into water, carbon dioxide, and energy). In a 160-pound man, alcohol is metabolized (absorbed and processed by the body) at a rate of about one drink every two hours. The absorption of alcohol is influenced by several factors:

- Body weight—Heavier people are less affected than lighter people by the same amount of alcohol because there is more blood and water in their system to dilute the alcohol intake. In addition, the greater the body muscle weight, the lower the blood alcohol concentration (BAC) for a given amount of alcohol.

- Speed of drinking—The faster alcohol is drunk, the faster the BAC level rises.

- Presence of food in the stomach—Eating while drinking slows down the absorption of alcohol by increasing the amount of time it takes the alcohol to get from the stomach to the small intestine.

- Drinking history and body chemistry—The longer a person has been drinking, the greater his or her tolerance (in other words, the more alcohol it takes him or her to get drunk). An individual's physiological functioning or "body chemistry" may also affect his or her reactions to alcohol. Women are more easily affected by alcohol regardless of weight because women metabolize alcohol differently than men. Women are known to have less body water than

FIGURE 2.2

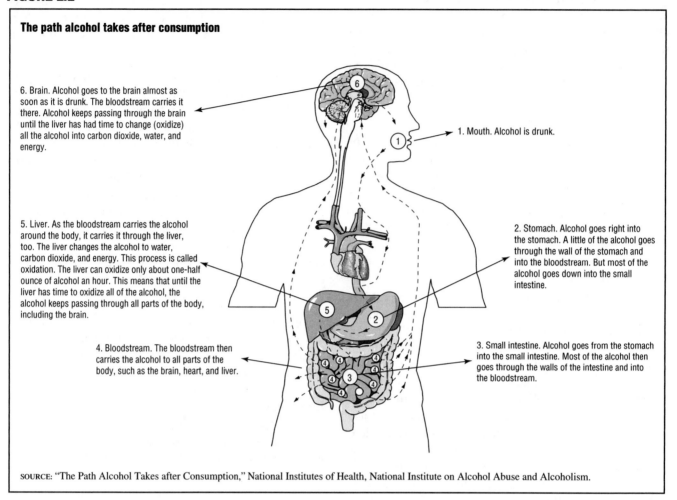

The path alcohol takes after consumption

6. Brain. Alcohol goes to the brain almost as soon as it is drunk. The bloodstream carries it there. Alcohol keeps passing through the brain until the liver has had time to change (oxidize) all the alcohol into carbon dioxide, water, and energy.

5. Liver. As the bloodstream carries the alcohol around the body, it carries it through the liver, too. The liver changes the alcohol to water, carbon dioxide, and energy. This process is called oxidation. The liver can oxidize only about one-half ounce of alcohol an hour. This means that until the liver has time to oxidize all of the alcohol, the alcohol keeps passing through all parts of the body, including the brain.

4. Bloodstream. The bloodstream then carries the alcohol to all parts of the body, such as the brain, heart, and liver.

1. Mouth. Alcohol is drunk.

2. Stomach. Alcohol goes right into the stomach. A little of the alcohol goes through the wall of the stomach and into the bloodstream. But most of the alcohol goes down into the small intestine.

3. Small intestine. Alcohol goes from the stomach into the small intestine. Most of the alcohol then goes through the walls of the intestine and into the bloodstream.

SOURCE: "The Path Alcohol Takes after Consumption," National Institutes of Health, National Institute on Alcohol Abuse and Alcoholism.

men of the same body weight, so equivalent amounts of alcohol result in higher concentrations of alcohol in the blood of women than men.

As a person's BAC rises, there are somewhat predictable responses in behavior.

- At a BAC of about 0.05 g/dL (0.05 grams of alcohol per 1 deciliter of blood), thought processes, judgment, and restraint are more lax. The person may feel more at ease socially. Also, reaction time to visual or auditory stimuli slows down as the BAC rises. (Note: A measurement of g/dL—a mass/volume measure—is approximately equal to a volume/volume—or a percentage—measurment when calculating BAC, and the two are often used interchangeably; so, a BAC of 0.05 g/dL can also mean a BAC of 0.05%.)

- At 0.10 g/dL, voluntary motor actions become noticeably clumsy. (It is illegal to drive with a BAC of 0.08 g/dL or higher.)

- At 0.20 g/dL, the entire motor area of the brain becomes significantly depressed. The person staggers, may want to lie down, may be easily angered, or may shout or weep.

- At 0.30 g/dL, the person generally acts confused or may be in a stupor.

- At 0.40 g/dL, the person usually falls into a coma.

- At 0.50 g/dL or more, the medulla is severely depressed, and death generally occurs within several hours, usually from respiratory failure. The medulla is the portion of the brainstem that regulates many involuntary processes, such as breathing.

There have been some cases of delayed death from circulatory failure as long as sixteen hours after the last known ingestion of alcohol. Without immediate medical attention, a person whose BAC reaches 0.50 g/dL will almost certainly die. Death may even occur at a BAC of 0.40 g/dL if the alcohol is "chugged," or consumed quickly and in a large amount, causing the BAC to rise rapidly.

Sobering Up

Time is the only way to rid the body of alcohol. The more slowly a person drinks, the more time the body has to process the alcohol, so less alcohol accumulates in the bloodstream. According to the National Clearinghouse

TABLE 2.6

Symptoms of a hangover

Alertness (lack of)	Laziness, fatigue
Clumsiness, uncoordination	Lightheadedness, dizziness
Dazed state	Loose bowels
Difficulty concentrating	Muscle aches
Drowsiness, mental slowness	Nausea
Dry mouth	Sleepiness
Exhaustion	Stomach pains
Headache	Thirst
Hunger	Trembling hands
Irritability	Tremor

SOURCE: Max H. Pittler, Adrian R. White, Clare Stevinson, and Edzard Ernst, "Box 1. Symptoms Assessed in Hangover Questionnaire," in "Effectiveness of Artichoke Extract in Preventing Alcohol-Induced Hangovers: A Randomized Controlled Trial," in *Canadian Medical Association Journal*, vol. 169, no. 12, December 9, 2003, http://www.cmaj.ca/cgi/reprint/169/12/1269?maxtoshow=&HITS=10&hits=10&RESULTFORMAT=&fulltext=hangover&searchid=1&FIRSTINDEX=0&volume=169&issue=12&resourcetype=HWCIT (accessed November 24, 2006). Copyright © 2003 Canadian Medical Association or its licensors. Reprinted by permission of the publisher.

for Alcohol and Drug Information, five drinks consumed in quick succession by a 180-pound man will produce a BAC of 0.11 g/dL. In a 140-pound man this intake will produce a BAC of 0.13 g/dL. In a 120-pound woman it will produce a BAC of 0.19 g/dL. The body takes nearly seven hours to metabolize this blood concentration of alcohol. Under normal conditions five drinks consumed with an hour or so between each drink will produce a BAC of only 0.02 g/dL, depending on the gender and weight of the person. It will likely produce a BAC higher than 0.02 g/dL in women and people weighing less than 180 pounds.

Hangovers

Hangovers cause a great deal of misery as well as absenteeism and loss of productivity at work or school. A person with a hangover experiences two or more physical symptoms after drinking and fully metabolizing alcohol. The major symptoms of a hangover are listed in Table 2.6, but the causes of these symptoms are not well known. Results from Jeff Wiese et al.'s study "Effect of *Opuntia ficus indica* on Symptoms of the Alcohol Hangover" (*Archives of Internal Medicine*, June 28, 2004) support the idea that the symptoms of a hangover are largely because of an inflammatory response of the body to impurities in alcohol and by-products of alcohol metabolism. Fluctuations in body hormones and dehydration intensify hangover symptoms.

There is no scientific evidence to support popular hangover cures, such as black coffee, raw egg, chili pepper, steak sauce, "alkalizers," and vitamins. To treat a hangover, health care practitioners usually prescribe bed rest as well as eating food and drinking nonalcoholic fluids.

LONG-TERM EFFECTS OF ALCOHOL ON THE BODY

The results of scientific research help health care practitioners and the general public understand both the positive and negative health consequences of drinking alcohol. Table 2.7 summarizes major diseases and injury conditions related to alcohol use and the proportions attributable to alcohol worldwide. As Table 2.7 notes, about one-fifth of mouth and throat cancers are related to drinking alcohol. Nearly one-third of cancers of the esophagus (food tube) and one-fourth of cancers of the liver are linked to alcohol consumption as well. Alcohol consumption is also related to heart disease and stroke and is associated with cirrhosis of the liver, a condition in which the liver becomes scarred and dysfunctional. In addition, one-fifth of motor vehicle accidents are related to alcohol consumption.

Scientists have developed research-based hypotheses (explanations) about the interaction between alcoholism and various characteristics, such as aging, gender, family history, and vitamin deficiency. They have also developed explanations about how alcohol affects the brain. These explanations are based on evidence from scientific studies, brain scans, and analyses of brain tissue after death. For example, results from Marlene Oscar-Berman and Ksenija Marinkovic's study "Hypotheses Proposed to Explain the Consequences of Alcoholism for the Brain" (*Alcohol Research and Health*, Spring 2003) support the idea that alcoholism accelerates aging, affects women more than men, and runs in families.

Not all the effects of alcohol consumption are harmful to health. Table 2.8 presents five tables (A to E) that list levels of alcohol consumption and the relative risk for total mortality and a variety of other diseases and conditions. Table A in Table 2.8 shows alcohol consumption versus relative risk of total mortality in men aged forty to eighty-five. To obtain these data, researchers compared total mortality (death rate; similar to life expectancy) among those who rarely or never drank alcohol with those who did drink alcohol. Those who rarely or never drank were assigned a value of 1.00 for their risk of total mortality. Numbers above 1.00 mean a higher risk of total mortality (lower life expectancy). Numbers below 1.00 mean a lower risk of total mortality (higher life expectancy). Table A shows that men aged forty to eighty-five who drank up to (and possibly slightly over) two drinks per day had a lower total mortality risk than those who did not drink. That is, this level of drinking was good for the men's overall health and life expectancy.

Table B in Table 2.8 shows alcohol consumption versus relative risk of hypertension (chronic high blood pressure) in women aged twenty-five to forty-two. This table shows that women in this age group who had up to

TABLE 2.7

Major diseases and injuries linked to alcohol and the extent of effects worldwide, 2005

	Men	Women	Both
Malignant neoplasms			
Mouth and oropharynx cancers	22%	9%	19%
Oesophageal cancer	37%	15%	29%
Liver cancer	30%	13%	25%
Breast cancer	n/a	7%	7%
Neuropsychiatric disorders			
Unipolar depressive disorders	3%	1%	2%
Epilepsy	23%	12%	18%
Alcohol use disorders: alcohol dependence and harmful use	100%	100%	100%
Diabetes mellitus	−1%	−1%	−1%
Cardiovascular disorders			
Ischaemic heart disease	4%	−1%	2%
Haemorrhagic stroke	18%	1%	10%
Ischaemic stroke	3%	−6%	−1%
Gastrointestinal diseases			
Cirrhosis of the liver	39%	18%	32%
Unintentional injury			
Motor vehicle accidents	25%	8%	20%
Drownings	12%	6%	10%
Falls	9%	3%	7%
Poisonings	23%	9%	18%
Intentional injury			
Self-inflicted injuries	15%	5%	11%
Homicide	26%	16%	24%

SOURCE: Reprinted from Robin Room, Thomas Babor, and Jürgen Rehm, "Table 1. Major Diseases and Injury Conditions Related to Alcohol and Proportions Attributable to Alcohol Worldwide," in "Alcohol and Public Health," in *The Lancet*, vol. 365, February 5, 2005, 519=530, http://www .thelancet.com (accessed October 3, 2006). Copyright © 2005, with permission from Elsevier.

TABLE 2.8

Alcohol consumption and risk of death or serious health problems, by age and gender

(A) Alcohol consumption and total mortality in men aged 40–85

Alcohol consumption	Relative risk[a]
Rarely/never	1.0
1–3 drinks/month	0.86
1 drink/week	0.74
2–4 drinks/week	0.77
5–6 drinks/week	0.78
1 drink/day	0.82
≥2 drinks/day	0.95

(B) Alcohol consumption and risk of hypertension in women aged 25–42

Alcohol consumption	Relative risk
≤02.5 drinks/day	0.95
0.26–0.50 drinks/day	0.86
0.51–1.00 drinks/day	0.92
1.01–1.50 drinks/day	1.0
1.51–2.00 drinks/day	1.2
>2.00 drinks/day	1.31

(C) Alcohol consumption and risk of dementia in adults aged 65 and older

Alcohol consumption	Relative risk
<1 drink/week	0.65
1–6 drinks/week	0.46
7–13 drinks/week	0.69
≥14 drinks/week	1.22

(D) Alcohol consumption and risk of macular degeneration in men aged 40–84

Alcohol consumption	Relative risk
1 drink/week[b]	1.0
2–4 drinks/week	0.68
5–6 drinks/week	1.32
1 or more drinks/day	1.27

(E) Alcohol consumption and risk of breast cancer in women aged 40–59

Alcohol consumption	Relative risk
1–10 g/day	1.01
11–20 g/day	1.16
21–30 g/day	1.27
31–40 g/day	0.77
41–50 g/day	1.0
>50 g/day	1.7

Note: One drink is approximately 14g of alcohol
[a]Adjusted for age and other cardiovascular risk factors.
[b]Less than 1 drink/week was the referent group.

SOURCE: Adapted from Ronald C. Hamdy and Melissa McManama Aukerman, "Alcohol on Trial: The Evidence," in *Southern Medical Journal*, vol. 98, no. 1, 2005, 35–56, http://www.sma.org/smj/ (accessed October 9, 2006)

one drink per day had a lower risk of hypertension than women in the same age group who did not drink alcohol. Drinking slightly more than one drink per day to 1.5 drinks per day put these drinkers at equal relative risk for hypertension as those who did not drink alcohol. Drinking more than 1.5 drinks per day was detrimental and put these heavier drinkers at a higher relative risk for hypertension than their nondrinking counterparts.

Table C in Table 2.8 shows a similar pattern of alcohol consumption versus relative risk. Drinking small amounts of alcohol had positive health effects, whereas drinking above a certain threshold limit had negative health effects. With respect to dementia in adults aged sixty-five and over, those consuming one to six drinks weekly had a lower risk of dementia than those who abstained from drinking. Those consuming fourteen or more drinks per week had a higher risk of dementia than those who abstained.

Tables D and E in Table 2.8 show somewhat different patterns than tables A to C. Although drinking two to four drinks per week reduced the risk of age-related macular degeneration (a disease of the retina of the eye), one drink per week had no protective effect and five to six drinks per week appeared to raise the relative risk of this disease in men aged forty to eighty-five.

Table E shows that women who drank even small amounts of alcohol raised their relative risk of breast cancer. Although Table E shows that drinking 31 to 40 grams per day of alcohol (about 2.5 to 3.5 drinks per day) may have a protective effect, the results of most studies on this topic do not show this effect. They conversely show that a moderately high consumption of alcohol is linked to a greater risk of breast cancer.

With so many studies and so many health-related factors to take into account, how does a person know how much alcohol is beneficial and how much is too much? The American Cancer Society (2006, http:// www.cancer.org/) recommends that people should "drink alcohol only occasionally, and sparingly." The National Cancer Institute (2005, http://progressreport.cancer.gov/) states that "in general, these [cancer] risks increase after about one daily drink for women and two daily drinks for men. . . . Also, using alcohol with tobacco is riskier than using either one alone, because it further increases the chances of getting cancers of the mouth, throat, and esophagus." The American Heart Association (December 7, 2006, http://www.americanheart.org/presenter.jhtml?identifier=4422) weighs in with the following: "If you drink alcohol, do so in moderation. This means an average of one to two drinks per day for men and one drink per day for women. . . . Drinking more alcohol increases such dangers as alcoholism, high blood pressure, obesity, stroke, breast cancer, suicide and accidents. Also, it's not possible to predict in which people alcoholism will become a problem. Given these and other risks, the American Heart Association cautions people NOT to start drinking . . . if they do not already drink alcohol. Consult your doctor on the benefits and risks of consuming alcohol in moderation."

EFFECTS OF ALCOHOL ON SEX AND REPRODUCTION

Alcohol consumption can affect sexual response and reproduction in profound ways. Many alcoholics suffer from impotence and/or reduced sexual drive. Some studies, such as Jane Y. Polsky et al.'s "Smoking and Other Lifestyle Factors in Relation to Erectile Dysfunction" (*BJU International*, 2005), suggest that alcohol consumption, even at low levels, is associated with a greater risk of erectile dysfunction (impotence). Many alcoholics suffer from depression, which may further impair their sexual function. In addition, Jerrold S. Greenberg, Clint E. Bruess, and Debra Haffner report in *Exploring the Dimensions of Human Sexuality* (2004) that alcohol use is associated with poor sperm quality in men.

In premenopausal women chronic heavy drinking can contribute to a variety of reproductive disorders. According to Greenberg, Bruess, and Haffner, these disorders include the cessation of menstruation, irregular menstrual cycles, failure to ovulate, early menopause, increased risk of spontaneous miscarriages, and lower rates of conception. Some of these disorders can be caused directly by the interference of alcohol with the hormonal regulation of the reproductive system. They may also be caused indirectly through other disorders associated with alcohol abuse, such as liver disease, pancreatic disease, malnutrition, or fetal abnormalities.

Fetal Alcohol Spectrum Disorders

Research shows that alcohol consumption during pregnancy can result in severe harm to the fetus (unborn child). The development of such defects can begin early

FIGURE 2.3

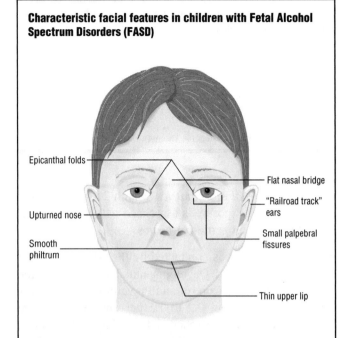

Characteristic facial features in children with Fetal Alcohol Spectrum Disorders (FASD)

Epicanthal folds

Flat nasal bridge

"Railroad track" ears

Upturned nose

Smooth philtrum

Small palpebral fissures

Thin upper lip

Notes: An epicanthal fold is skin of the upper eyelid that partially covers the inner corner of the eye. A palpebral fissure is the opening between the upper and lower eyelids. "Railroad track" ears refers to the parallel-lined appearance of the upper part of the ears in which the underdeveloped upper part is flattened and parallel to the crease below it. The philtrum is the vertical groove between the upper lip and the nose. Structural abnormalities of the brain along with reduced brain size are also characteristic of fetal alcohol spectrum disorders. Structural abnormalities of the brain along with reduced brain size are also characteristic of fetal alcohol spectrum disorder.

SOURCE: Adapted from Darryl Leja, National Human Genome Research Institute, National Institutes of Health, in Daniel J. Wattendorf and Maximilian Muenke, "Fetal Alcohol Spectrum Disorders," in *American Family Physician*, vol. 72, no. 2, 2005, http://www.aafp.org/afp/20050715/279.html (accessed October 4, 2006)

in pregnancy when the mother-to-be may not even know she is pregnant.

Drinking during pregnancy can cause fetal alcohol spectrum disorders (FASD). As Edward P. Riley and Christie L. McGee note in "Fetal Alcohol Spectrum Disorders: An Overview with Emphasis on Changes in Brain and Behavior" (*Experimental Biology and Medicine*, 2005), "The term FASD . . . is an umbrella term that describes the range of effects that can occur in an individual whose mother drank alcohol during pregnancy. These effects can be physical, mental, or behavioral, with possible lifelong implications."

The key facial characteristics of a child born with FASD are shown in Figure 2.3. These characteristics are the most pronounced in fetal alcohol syndrome (FAS), the most recognizable form of FASD. Children with FASD also exhibit a complex pattern of behavioral and cognitive dysfunctions, which are listed in Table 2.9. Besides these characteristics and dysfunctions, results of studies, such as Maria de Los Angeles Avaria et al.'s "Peripheral Nerve Conduction Abnormalities in Children Exposed to Alcohol

TABLE 2.9

Cognitive and behavioral characteristics typical of Fetal Alcohol Spectrum Disorders (FASD)

Low IQ
Attention deficit
Slow reaction time
Delayed motor development
Disruptive and impulsive behavior
Difficulties in learning and in abstract thinking

SOURCE: Created by Sandra Alters for Thomson Gale, 2006

TABLE 2.10

Key points in the U.S. Surgeon General's advisory on alcohol use during pregnancy, 2005

Based on the current, best science available we now know the following:

- Alcohol consumed during pregnancy increases the risk of alcohol related birth defects, including growth deficiencies, facial abnormalities, central nervous system impairment, behavioral disorders, and impaired intellectual development.
- No amount of alcohol consumption can be considered safe during pregnancy.
- Alcohol can damage a fetus at any stage of pregnancy. Damage can occur in the earliest weeks of pregnancy, even before a woman knows that she is pregnant.
- The cognitive deficits and behavioral problems resulting from prenatal alcohol exposure are lifelong.
- Alcohol-related birth defects are completely preventable.

For these reasons:

1. A pregnant woman should not drink alcohol during pregnancy.
2. A pregnant woman who has already consumed alcohol during her pregnancy should stop in order to minimize further risk.
3. A woman who is considering becoming pregnant should abstain from alcohol.
4. Recognizing that nearly half of all births in the United States are unplanned, women of childbearing age should consult their physician and take steps to reduce the possibility of prenatal alcohol exposure.
5. Health professionals should inquire routinely about alcohol consumption by women of childbearing age, inform them of the risks of alcohol consumption during pregnancy, and advise them not to drink alcoholic beverages during pregnancy.

SOURCE: Adapted from "Surgeon General's Advisory on Alcohol Use in Pregnancy," in *News Release: U.S. Surgeon General Releases Advisory on Alcohol Use in Pregnancy*, U.S. Department of Health and Human Services Press Office, February 21, 2005, http://www.hhs.gov/surgeongeneral/pressreleases/sg02222005.html (accessed October 30, 2006)

in Utero" (*Journal of Pediatrics*, March 2004), show that prenatal alcohol exposure is associated with abnormalities in the electrical properties of nerves.

Results of studies conducted by the National Center on Birth Defects and Developmental Disabilities of the Centers for Disease Control and Prevention (CDC) show FAS rates range from 0.2 to 1.5 per one thousand live births. In addition, researchers believe that other prenatal alcohol-related conditions less severe than FAS, such as alcohol-related neurodevelopmental disorder (ARND) and alcohol-related birth defects (ARBD), occur approximately three times as often as FAS. ARND and ARBD were formerly and collectively known as fetal alcohol effects. Now all prenatal alcohol-related conditions are collectively known as FASD.

In February 2005 U.S. Surgeon General Richard H. Carmona issued an advisory on alcohol use in pregnancy. Key points of the advisory are listed in Table 2.10. As noted in the advisory, there is no known safe level of alcohol consumption during pregnancy. The CDC emphasizes, along with the surgeon general, that FAS and other prenatal alcohol-related disorders are 100% preventable if a woman does not drink alcohol while she is pregnant or if she is of reproductive age and is not using birth control. Yet, data show that some women who might become pregnant, or who are pregnant, consume alcohol and put themselves at risk for having a child with FASD.

Table 2.11 shows that 12.1% of pregnant women consumed alcohol in the past month in 2004–05 when questioned for the annual National Survey on Drug Use and Health. This figure was up from 9.8% in the 2002–03 period. In 2002–03 and 2004–05 approximately one-fifth (19.6% and 20.6%, respectively) drank during their first trimester of pregnancy, a time when all the organ systems of the fetus are developing. Fewer women drank in their second and third trimesters. More than half of women who might become pregnant (51.3% and 51.4%, respectively) used alcohol.

In the report "Alcohol Consumption among Women Who Are Pregnant or Who Might Become Pregnant—United States, 2002" (December 24, 2004, http://www

.cdc.gov/MMWR/preview/mmwrhtml/mm5350a4.htm), the CDC reports that in 2002, 2% of pregnant women engaged in binge drinking and 2% in frequent use of alcohol when they were pregnant. In addition, greater binge drinking prevalence was reported among younger women, non-Hispanic whites, current smokers, unmarried women, and impaired drivers.

ALCOHOL'S INTERACTION WITH OTHER DRUGS

Because alcohol is easily available and such an accepted part of American social life, people often forget that it is a drug. When someone takes a medication while drinking alcohol, he or she is taking two drugs. Alcohol consumed with other drugs—for example, an illegal drug such as cocaine, an over-the-counter (without a prescription) drug such as cough medicine, or a prescription drug such as an antibiotic—may make the combination harmful or even deadly or may counteract the effectiveness of a prescribed medication.

To promote the desired chemical or physical effects, a medication must be absorbed into the body and must reach its site of action. Alcohol may prevent an appropriate amount of the medication from reaching its site of action. In other cases alcohol can alter the drug's effects once it reaches the site. Alcohol interacts negatively with more than 150 medications. Table 2.12 shows some possible effects of combining alcohol and other types of drugs.

TABLE 2.11

Percentage of past-month alcohol use among females aged 15–44, by pregnancy status, 2002–03 and 2004–05

	Total[a]		Pregnancy status			
			Pregnant		Not pregnant	
Demographic characteristic	2002–2003	2004–2005	2002–2003	2004–2005	2002–2003	2004–2005
Total	51.3	51.4	9.8	12.1	53.0	53.1
Age						
15–17	28.5	27.6	14.5	13.9	28.7	27.7
18–25	55.7	55.7	10.5	9.7	58.7	58.5
26–44	53.0	53.4	8.9	13.5	54.6	55.0
Hispanic origin and race						
Not Hispanic or Latino	53.7	54.1	10.1	13.4	55.3	55.7
White	57.8	58.9	10.8	13.8	59.6	60.7
Black or African American	41.0	40.5	6.4	13.4	42.2	41.6
American Indian or Alaska Native	49.8	44.3	*	*	51.7	45.0
Native Hawaiian or other Pacific Islander	40.9	*	*	*	42.1	*
Asian	34.9	31.2	*	*	36.0	32.4
Two or more races	53.3	60.5	*	*	55.6	61.8
Hispanic or Latino	37.9	37.4	8.6	6.8	39.6	39.1
Trimester[b]						
First	N/A	N/A	19.6	20.6	N/A	N/A
Second	N/A	N/A	6.1	10.2	N/A	N/A
Third	N/A	N/A	4.7	6.7	N/A	N/A

*Low precision; no estimate reported.
N/A: Not applicable.
[a]Estimates in the total column are for all females aged 15 to 44, including those with unknown pregnancy status.
[b]Pregnant females aged 15 to 44 not reporting trimester were excluded.

SOURCE: "Table 7.73B. Alcohol Use in the Past Month among Females Aged 15 to 44, by Pregnancy Status and Demographic Characteristics: Percentages, Annual Averages Based on 2002–2003 and 2004–2005," in *Results from the 2005 National Survey on Drug Use and Health: Detailed Tables*, U.S. Department of Health and Human Services, Substance Abuse and Mental Health Services Administration, Office of Applied Studies, 2006, http://www.oas.samhsa.gov/nsduh/2k5nsduh/tabs/Sect7peTabs68to75.pdf (accessed October 17, 2006)

TABLE 2.12

Interactions between alcohol and medications

Substances	Interactions
Antidepressants	Alcohol slows the breakdown of these drugs and increases their toxicity.
Acetaminophen (aspirin substitute)	Alcohol can increase this pain killer's toxic effects on the liver.
Aspirin	Aspirin may increase stomach irritation caused by alcohol.
Antihistamines	Alcohol increases the sedative effects of these drugs.
Sedatives	Alcohol increases the effects of many of these drugs and can be dangerously toxic.
Antacid histamine blockers	These drugs can interfere with the metabolism of alcohol, making it more intoxicating.

SOURCE: Created by Staff of Information Plus for Thomson Gale

The U.S. Food and Drug Administration recommends that anyone who regularly has three alcoholic drinks per day should check with a physician before taking aspirin, acetaminophen (such as Tylenol or Excedrin), or any other over-the-counter painkiller. Combining alcohol with aspirin, ibuprofen (such as Advil or Motrin), or related pain relievers may promote stomach bleeding. Combining alcohol with acetaminophen may promote liver damage.

ALCOHOL-RELATED DEATHS

In *Deaths: Final Data for 2003* (April 19, 2006, http://www.cdc.gov/nchs/data/nvsr/nvsr54/nvsr54_13.pdf), Donna L. Hoyert et al. report that 20,687 people in the United States died of alcohol-induced causes in 2003. This category included deaths from dependent use of alcohol, nondependent use of alcohol, and accidental alcohol poisoning. It excluded accidents, homicides, and other causes indirectly related to alcohol use, as well as deaths because of fetal alcohol syndrome. The age-adjusted death rate for males was 3.3 times the rate for females. In 2003, 12,360 people died from alcoholic liver disease.

MOTOR VEHICLE AND PEDESTRIAN ACCIDENTS

The National Highway Traffic Safety Administration (NHTSA) of the U.S. Department of Transportation defines a traffic crash as alcohol-related if either the driver or an involved pedestrian had a BAC of 0.01 g/dL or greater. People with a BAC of 0.08 g/dL or higher are considered intoxicated.

The NHTSA reports that 42,636 people were killed in traffic accidents in 2004, with 16,694 of them caused by alcohol-related crashes. (See Table 2.13.) These

TABLE 2.13

Fatalities in motor vehicle accidents, by blood alcohol concentration (BAC) at time of crash, 1982–2004

Year	BAC=.00 (no impairment)		BAC=.01–.07 (slight to significant impairment)		BAC=.08 + (impaired)		Total number	Total fatalities in alcohol-related crashes	
	Number	Percent	Number	Percent	Number	Percent		Number	Percent
1982	17,773	40	2,927	7	23,246	53	43,945	26,173	60
1983	17,955	42	2,594	6	22,041	52	42,589	24,635	58
1984	19,496	44	3,046	7	21,715	49	44,257	24,762	56
1985	20,659	47	3,081	7	20,086	46	43,825	23,167	53
1986	21,070	46	3,546	8	21,471	47	46,087	25,017	54
1987	22,297	48	3,398	7	20,696	45	46,390	24,094	52
1988	23,254	49	3,234	7	20,599	44	47,087	23,833	51
1989	23,159	51	2,893	6	19,531	43	45,582	22,424	49
1990	22,012	49	2,980	7	19,607	44	44,599	22,587	51
1991	21,349	51	2,560	6	17,599	42	41,508	20,159	49
1992	20,960	53	2,443	6	15,847	40	39,250	18,290	47
1993	22,242	55	2,361	6	15,547	39	40,150	17,908	45
1994	23,409	57	2,322	6	14,985	37	40,716	17,308	43
1995	24,085	58	2,490	6	15,242	36	41,817	17,732	42
1996	24,316	58	2,486	6	15,263	36	42,065	17,749	42
1997	25,302	60	2,290	5	14,421	34	42,013	16,711	40
1998	24,828	60	2,465	6	14,207	34	41,501	16,673	40
1999	25,145	60	2,321	6	14,250	34	41,717	16,572	40
2000	24,565	59	2,511	6	14,870	35	41,945	17,380	41
2001	24,796	59	2,542	6	14,858	35	42,196	17,400	41
2002	25,481	59	2,432	6	15,093	35	43,005	17,524	41
2003	25,779	60	2,427	6	14,678	34	42,884	17,105	40
2004	25,942	61	2,285	5	14,409	34	42,636	16,694	39

Note: The National Highway Traffic Safety Administration estimates alcohol involvement when alcohol test results are unknown.

SOURCE: "Table 13. Persons Killed, by Highest Blood Alcohol Concentration (BAC) in the Crash, 1982–2004," in *Traffic Safety Facts 2004*, U.S. Department of Transportation, National Center for Statistics and Analysis, National Highway Traffic Safety Administration, January 2006, http://www-nrd.nhtsa.dot.gov/pdf/nrd-30/NCSA/TSFAnn/TSF2004.pdf (accessed October 6, 2006)

alcohol-related traffic deaths represented 39% of all car crash fatalities in 2004. The percentage of alcohol-related traffic fatalities has declined somewhat steadily from a high of 60% in 1982. The peak number of fatalities occurred in 1988, when 47,087 traffic accident deaths (including both alcohol related and nonalcohol related) were recorded.

A number of important factors contribute to the decline of drunk driving fatalities. Mothers against Drunk Driving was founded in 1980. This organization's most significant achievement was lobbying to get the legal drinking age raised to twenty-one in all states, which occurred in 1988. There were also successful campaigns such as "Friends Don't Let Friends Drive Drunk." The use of seat belts has also helped reduce deaths in motor vehicle accidents.

As of July 2004 all states, the District of Columbia, and Puerto Rico had lowered the BAC limit for drunk driving from 0.1 g/dL to 0.08 g/dL, with all states implementing this limit by August 2005. According to the Insurance Institute for Highway Safety (http://www.iihs.org/laws/state_laws/dui.html), by June 2006 forty-one states and the District of Columbia also had administrative license revocation laws, which require prompt, mandatory suspension of drivers' licenses for failing or refusing to take the BAC test. This immediate suspen-sion, before conviction and independent of criminal procedures, is invoked right after arrest.

As Table 2.14 shows, in both 1995 and 2005 drivers aged twenty-one to forty-four were the ones most likely to be involved in fatal crashes in which the driver had a BAC of 0.08 g/dL or higher. Whereas the percentage of drivers within the twenty-one- to twenty-four-year-old age group stayed steady over the decade shown, the percentages in the twenty-five to forty-four group declined.

In 2005 the percentage of male drivers involved in fatal crashes who had a BAC of 0.08 g/dL or greater was nearly twice that of female drivers involved in fatal crashes (23% versus 13%, respectively). When compared with 1995, the percentage of drunk male drivers in fatal accidents in 2005 dropped. (See Table 2.14.)

Alcohol was related to a higher percentage of fatal crashes by motorcycles (27%) in 2005 than for crashes involving automobiles (22%) and light trucks (21%). Fatal crashes involving large trucks were very unlikely to be alcohol related (1%). (See Table 2.14.)

As Table 2.15 shows, in both 1995 and 2005 about half of all pedestrians aged twenty-one to forty-four who were killed in a traffic accident had a BAC of 0.08 g/dL or higher. This percentage was considerably higher than that for other age groups.

TABLE 2.14

Drivers with a blood alcohol count (BAC) of 0.08 or higher killed in motor vehicle crashes, by age, gender, and vehicle type, 1995 and 2005

	Total drivers					
	1995			2005		
		BAC .08 g/dL or higher			BAC .08 g/dL or higher	
	Total number of drivers	Number	Percent of total	Total number of drivers	Number	Percent of total
Total	56,164	12,366	22	59,104	11,921	20
Drivers by age group (years)						
16–20	7,725	1,203	16	7,293	1,198	16
21–24	6,263	1,994	32	6,548	2,086	32
25–34	13,048	3,953	30	11,378	3,162	28
35–44	10,677	2,784	26	10,733	2,490	23
45–54	6,815	1,206	18	9,403	1,752	19
55–64	4,079	555	14	6,041	714	12
65–74	3,251	246	8	3,212	210	7
75+	2,989	118	4	3,003	116	4
Drivers by sex						
Male	41,235	10,302	25	43,060	9,906	23
Female	14,184	1,835	13	14,974	1,878	13
Drivers by vehicle type						
Passenger cars	30,773	6,957	23	24,908	5,486	22
Light trucks	17,483	4,300	25	22,757	4,842	21
Large trucks	4,410	100	2	4,881	61	1
Motorcycles	2,262	747	33	4,652	1,246	27

Note: Numbers shown for groups of drivers do not add to the total number of drivers due to unknown or other data not included.

SOURCE: Adapted from "Table 6. Drivers in Fatal Crashes with BAC 0.08 gm/dl or Higher by Age, Gender, and Vehicle Type, 1995 and 2005," in *Traffic Safety Facts 2005 Data Alcohol*, National Highway Traffic Safety Administration, National Center for Statistics and Analysis, October 2006, http://www-nrd.nhtsa.dot.gov/pdf/nrd-30/NCSA/TSF2005/AlcoholTSF05.pdf (accessed October 29, 2006)

TABLE 2.15

Pedestrians and pedalcyclists with a blood alcohol count (BAC) of 0.08 or higher killed in motor vehicle crashes, by age group, 1995 and 2005

| | 1995 | | | 2005 | | |
| | | BAC .08 g/dL or higher | | | BAC .08 g/dL or higher | |
Nonoccupant fatalities	Total number of fatalities	Number	Percent of total	Total number of fatalities	Number	Percent of total
Pedestrian fatalities by age group (years)						
<16	753	11	1	387	12	3
16–20	296	70	26	281	76	27
21–24	292	137	48	296	137	46
25–34	836	459	54	613	295	48
35–44	954	487	54	804	404	50
45–64	1,142	441	41	1,456	527	36
65+	1,263	125	10	981	85	9
Unknown	48	16	35	63	24	39
Total	5,584	1,822	33	4,881	1,560	32
Pedalcyclist fatalities						
<16	281	4	2	144	4	3
16–20	59	7	12	47	8	17
21–24	44	12	26	41	13	31
25–34	129	53	41	76	26	34
35–44	142	54	38	150	47	31
45–64	115	33	29	237	74	31
65+	55	3	6	81	4	5
Unknown	8	2	30	8	4	48
Total	833	169	20	784	181	23

Note: Includes pedestrians age 15 and younger and pedestrians of unknown age.

SOURCE: "Table 4. Nonoccupants with BAC 0.08 gm/dl or Higher Killed in Motor Vehicle Crashes by Age Group, 1995 and 2005," in *Traffic Safety Facts: 2005 Data—Alcohol*, U.S. Department of Transportation, National Center for Statistics and Analysis, National Highway Traffic Safety Administration, October 2006, http://www-nrd.nhtsa.dot.gov/pdf/nrd-30/NCSA/TSF2005/AlcoholTSF05.pdf (accessed October 29, 2006)

ALCOHOL-RELATED OFFENSES

Table 2.16 shows arrest trends for alcohol-related offenses and driving under the influence from 1970 to 2004. Arrests were the highest for alcohol-related offenses from 1975 to 1992, with 1981 being the peak year. Arrests for driving under the influence were highest from 1977 to 1996, with 1983 being the peak year.

In 2004 there were nearly 2.4 million alcohol-related arrests; slightly more than one million of those arrests were for driving under the influence. (See Table 2.16.) According to the Federal Bureau of Investigation report *Crime in the United States, 2004* (February 17, 2006, http://www.fbi.gov/ucr/cius_04/documents/CIUS2004.pdf), there were nearly fourteen million arrests in 2004. Of those, more than 2.6 million were alcohol-related arrests.

Doris J. James mentions in *Profile of Jail Inmates* (July 2004, http://www.ojp.usdoj.gov/bjs/pub/pdf/pji02.pdf) that in 2002, 33.4% of convicted jail inmates reported that they had been under the influence of alcohol alone (not in combination with any other drug) when they committed their offenses. This figure decreased since 1996. A higher percentage of jail inmates used alcohol when committing a violent offense than did those committing other types of crimes, such as property or drug offenses.

In the report *ADAM Preliminary Finds on Drug Use and Drug Markets* (December 2001, http://www.ncjrs.gov/pdffiles1/nij/189101.pdf), a 2001 study of adult male arrestees in thirty-two U.S. cities, the U.S. Department of Justice finds that many had used alcohol before committing their crimes. More than 50% of the adult arrestees reported binge drinking in the thirty days before they were interviewed. Rates ran as low as 39.3% of arrestees in New York City to 70.1% in Albuquerque, New Mexico. In Phoenix, Arizona, 54.1% of arrestees reported binge drinking; 57.6% reported it in Spokane, Washington, 62.1% in Oklahoma City, and 64.8% in Denver, Colorado. A significant percentage of male arrestees also reported heavy drinking in the thirty days before their interview as well.

TABLE 2.16

Arrests for alcohol-related offenses and driving under the influence, 1970–2004

[In thousands]

	Alcohol-related offenses	Driving under the influence
1970	2,849	424
1971	2,914	490
1972	2,835	604
1973	2,539	654
1974	2,297	617
1975	3,044	909
1976	2,790	838
1977	3,303	1,104
1978	3,406	1,205
1979	3,455	1,232
1980	3,535	1,304
1981	3,745	1,422
1982	3,640	1,405
1983	3,729	1,613
1984	3,153	1,347
1985	3,418	1,503
1986	3,325	1,459
1987	3,248	1,410
1988	2,995	1,294
1989	3,180	1,333
1990	3,270	1,391
1991	3,000	1,289
1992	3,061	1,320
1993	2,886	1,229
1994	2,698	1,080
1995	2,578	1,033
1996	2,677	1,014
1997	2,510	986
1998	2,451	969
1999	2,238	931
2000	2,218	916
2001	2,224	947
2002	2,401	1,020
2003	2,301	1,006
2004	2,373	1,014

Note: This table presents data from all law enforcement agencies submitting complete reports for 12 months. Alcohol-related offenses include driving under the influence, liquor law violations, drunkenness, disorderly conduct, and vagrancy.

SOURCE: Ann L. Pastore and Kathleen Maguire, eds. "Table 4.27.2004. Arrests for Alcohol-Related Offenses and Driving under the Influence, United States, 1970–2004," in *Sourcebook of Criminal Justice Statistics Online, 31st Edition*, U.S. Department of Justice, Bureau of Justice Statistics, University at Albany School of Criminal Justice, Hindelang Criminal Justice Research Center, http://www.albany.edu/sourcebook/pdf/t4272004.pdf (accessed October 29, 2006)

CHAPTER 3
TOBACCO

In the mid-twentieth century smoking in the United States was often associated with romance, relaxation, and adventure; movie stars oozed glamour on screen while smoking, and movie tough guys were never more masculine than when lighting up. Songs such as "Smoke Gets in Your Eyes" topped the hit parade. Smoking became a rite of passage for many young males and a sign of increasing independence for women.

Since the 1990s, however, there has been an increase of opposition to tobacco use. Health authorities warn of the dangers of smoking and chewing tobacco, and nonsmokers object to secondhand smoke—because of both the smell and the health dangers of breathing smoke from other people's cigarettes. Today, a smoker is more likely to ask for permission before lighting up, and the answer is often "no." Because of health concerns, smoking has been banned on airplanes, in hospitals, and in many workplaces, restaurants, and bars.

PHYSICAL PROPERTIES OF NICOTINE

Tobacco is a plant native to the Western Hemisphere. It contains nicotine, a drug classified as a stimulant, although it has some depressive effects as well. Nicotine is a poisonous alkaloid that is the major psychoactive (mood-altering) ingredient in tobacco. (Alkaloids are carbon- and nitrogen-containing compounds that are found in some families of plants. They have both poisonous and medicinal properties.)

Nicotine's effects on the body are complex. The drug affects the brain and central nervous system as well as the hypothalamus and pituitary glands of the endocrine (hormone) system. Nicotine easily crosses the blood-brain barrier (a series of capillaries and cells that controls the flow of substances from the blood to the brain), and it accumulates in the brain—faster than caffeine or heroin, but slower than diazepam (a sedative medicine used to treat anxiety). In the brain nicotine imitates the actions of the hormone epinephrine (adrenaline) and the neurotransmitter acetylcholine, both of which heighten awareness. Nicotine also triggers the release of dopamine, which enhances feelings of pleasure, and endorphins, "the brain's natural opiates," which have a calming effect.

As noted earlier, nicotine acts as both a stimulant and a depressant. By stimulating certain nerve cells in the spinal cord, nicotine relaxes the nerves and slows some reactions, such as the knee-jerk reflex. Small amounts of nicotine stimulate some nerve cells, but these cells are depressed by large amounts. In addition, nicotine stimulates the brain cortex (the outer layer of the brain) and affects the functions of the heart and lungs.

TRENDS IN TOBACCO USE
Cigarettes

CONSUMPTION DATA. According to the Centers for Disease Control and Prevention (CDC), the consumption of cigarettes, the most widely used tobacco product, has decreased over the past generation among adults. After increasing rather consistently for sixty years, the per capita (per person) consumption of cigarettes peaked in the 1960s at well over four thousand cigarettes per year ("Chronic Disease Notes and Reports," Fall 2001, http://www.cdc.gov/nccdphp/publications/cdnr/pdf/CDNRfall 2001.pdf). The steady decline in smoking came shortly after 1964, when the *Smoking and Health: Report of the Advisory Committee to the Surgeon General of the Public Health Service* (January 1964, http://www.cdc.gov/Tobacco/sgr/sgr_1964/sgr64.htm) concluded that cigarette smoking is a cause of lung and laryngeal cancer in men, a probable cause of lung cancer in women, and the most important cause of chronic bronchitis in both genders. By 2006 the annual per capita consumption of cigarettes for those aged eighteen and over was 1,691. (See Table 3.1.)

TABLE 3.1

Per capita consumption of tobacco products, 1996–2006

Year	Per capita 16 years and over	Per capita 18 years and over				Per male 18 years and over		
		Cigarettes[a]	Snuff[b]		All tobacco products	Large cigars & cigarillos	Smoking tobacco[b]	Chewing tobacco[b]
	Number	**Number**	**Pounds**			**Number**	**Pounds**	
1996	2,355	2,445	4.1	0.31	4.83	31.9	0.52	0.12	0.63
1997	2,290	2,422	4.1	0.31	4.85	37.3	0.61	0.11	0.60
1998	2,190	2,275	3.6	0.31	4.32	37.1	0.61	0.12	0.53
1999	2,022	2,101	3.5	0.32	4.23	38.5	0.63	0.13	0.51
2000	1,974	2,049	3.4	0.33	4.10	38.0	0.62	0.13	0.48
2001	1,976	2,051	3.5	0.34	4.30	41.2	0.68	0.15	0.47
2002	1,909	1,982	3.4	0.34	4.16	41.8	0.68	0.16	0.43
2003	1,820	1,890	3.2	0.35	3.97	44.5	0.73	0.16	0.40
2004	1,747	1,814	3.1	0.36	3.87	47.9	0.79	0.15	0.37
2005	1,675	1,716	2.9	0.36	3.69	46.9	0.77	0.16	0.36
2006[c]	1,650	1,691	2.9	0.38	3.69	47.8	0.78	0.15	0.37

[a]Unstemmed processing weight.
[b]Finished product weight.
[c]Preliminary.

SOURCE: Tom Capehart, "Table 2. Per Capita Consumption of Tobacco Products in the United States (including Overseas Forces), 1996–2006," in *Tobacco Outlook*, U.S. Department of Agriculture, Economic Research Service, September 26, 2006, http://usda.mannlib.cornell.edu/usda/ers/TBS//2000s/2006/TBS-09-26-2006.pdf (accessed October 10, 2006)

TABLE 3.2

Percentage of lifetime, past-year, and past-month cigarette users, by age group, gender, and ethnicity, 2004 and 2005

Demographic characteristic	Time period					
	Lifetime		Past year		Past month	
	2004	2005	2004	2005	2004	2005
Total	67.3	66.6	29.1	29.1	24.9	24.9
Age						
12–17	29.2	26.7	18.4	17.3	11.9	10.8
18–25	68.7	67.3	47.5	47.2	39.5	39.0
or 26 older	72.3	71.9	27.3	27.6	24.1	24.3
Gender						
Male	72.4	71.3	32.5	31.9	27.7	27.4
Female	62.4	62.1	25.9	26.5	22.3	22.5
Hispanic origin and race						
Not Hispanic or Latino	69.4	68.3	29.4	29.3	25.4	25.3
White	73.0	72.2	30.4	30.1	26.4	26.0
Black or African American	56.6	55.7	27.4	27.4	23.5	24.5
American Indian or Alaska Native	77.2	69.2	37.1	42.0	31.0	36.0
Native Hawaiian or other Pacific Islander	*	64.4	*	35.0	*	28.8
Asian	43.5	41.1	13.4	17.4	10.3	13.4
Two or more races	74.1	61.7	43.0	35.2	38.3	30.9
Hispanic or Latino	52.9	55.3	26.8	27.9	21.3	22.1

*Low precision; no estimate reported.

SOURCE: "Table 2.31B. Cigarette Use in Lifetime, Past Year, and Past Month among Persons Aged 12 or Older, by Demographic Characteristics: Percentages, 2004 and 2005," in *Results from the 2005 National Survey on Drug Use and Health: Detailed Tables*, U.S. Department of Health and Human Services, Substance Abuse and Mental Health Services Administration, Office of Applied Studies, 2006, http://www.drugabusestatistics.samhsa.gov/NSDUH/2k5NSDUH/Tabs/Sect2peTabs31to36.pdf (accessed October 10, 2006)

Each year the Substance Abuse and Mental Health Services Administration surveys U.S. households on drug use for the National Survey on Drug Use and Health (NSDUH). The 2005 NSDUH reports that 66.6% of the U.S. population had smoked cigarettes at some time in their lives and that 24.9% were current smokers (meaning that they had smoked within the month prior to the survey). (See Table 3.2.)

In 2005 men (27.4%) were more likely than women (22.5%) to be current smokers. Additionally, whites (26%) were more likely to be current smokers than African-Americans

FIGURE 3.1

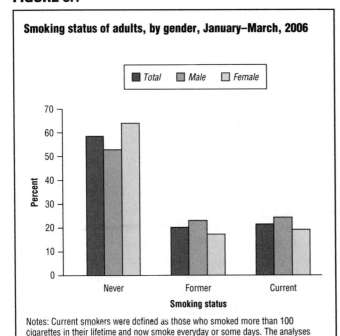

Smoking status of adults, by gender, January–March, 2006

Notes: Current smokers were defined as those who smoked more than 100 cigarettes in their lifetime and now smoke everyday or some days. The analyses excluded 71 persons (1.2%) with unknown smoking status.

SOURCE: J. S. Schiller and P. Barnes, "Figure 8.2. Percent Distribution of Smoking Status among Adults Aged 18 Years and Over, by Sex: United States, January–March 2006," in *Early Release of Selected Estimates Based on Data from the January–March 2006 National Health Interview Survey,* U.S. Department of Health and Human Services, Centers for Disease Control and Prevention, National Center for Health Statistics, September 28, 2006, http://www.cdc.gov/nchs/data/nhis/earlyrelease/200609_08.pdf (accessed October 10, 2006)

FIGURE 3.2

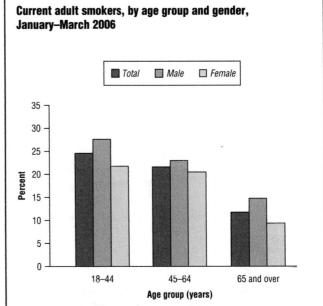

Current adult smokers, by age group and gender, January–March 2006

Notes: Current smokers were defined as those who smoked more than 100 cigarettes in their lifetime and now smoke everyday or some days. The analyses excluded 71 persons (1.2%) with unknown smoking status.

SOURCE: J. S. Schiller and P. Barnes, "Figure 8.3. Prevalence of Current Smoking among Adults Aged 18 Years and Over, by Age Group and Sex: United States, January–March 2006," in *Early Release of Selected Estimates Based on Data from the January–March 2006 National Health Interview Survey,* U.S. Department of Health and Human Services, Centers for Disease Control and Prevention, National Center for Health Statistics, September 28, 2006, http://www.cdc.gov/nchs/data/nhis/earlyrelease/200609_08.pdf (accessed October 10, 2006)

(24.5%), Hispanics (22.1%), or Asian-Americans (13.4%). Those aged eighteen to twenty-five had the highest rates of current smoking at 39%, compared with 10.8% for twelve- to seventeen-year-olds and 24.3% for those aged twenty-six and older. (See Table 3.2.) In general, rates of cigarette smoking remained the same or declined from 2004 to 2005 for most groups. A notable increase in smoking occurred, however, in the American Indian and Alaskan Native group.

The National Health Interview Survey (NHIS), which is conducted annually by the National Center for Health Statistics, reports findings similar to those of the NSDUH. Preliminary findings from the January–March 2006 NHIS show that 21.5% of adults in the United States were current smokers in early 2006, down from 24.7% in 1997. Like the NSDUH, the NHIS finds that men are more likely than women to smoke. Just over 24% of adult men and 19.1% of adult women were current smokers. Women were more likely than men to have never smoked. (See Figure 3.1.)

Although the NHIS uses different age groups than the NHSDA, results of both surveys show that younger people smoke at a higher rate than older people. Figure 3.2 shows that those aged eighteen to forty-four are slightly more likely than those aged forty-five to sixty-four to smoke. The rate of smoking in the sixty-five and over age group was dramatically lower than in either of the two younger groups. Men in all age categories were more likely than women in the same age group to smoke.

Also, like the NHSDA, the NHIS finds that the prevalence of current smoking among various races and ethnicities is highest for non-Hispanic whites (23.5%). Non-Hispanic African-Americans (23.1%) were slightly less likely to smoke, whereas Hispanics (13.8%) were the least likely to smoke. (See Figure 3.3.)

Cigars, Pipes, and Other Forms of Tobacco

According to the NSDUH, 3.2% of those aged twelve and older were current users of smokeless tobacco (chewing tobacco and/or snuff), and 5.6% were current users of cigars. Only 0.9% smoked pipes. These percentages remained relatively constant from 2002 to 2005. (See Figure 3.4.)

According to the U.S. Department of Agriculture, in 2006 the per capita consumption by males aged eighteen and over was 47.8 large cigars and small, narrow cigars called cigarillos. (See Table 3.1.) This figure is much higher than in 1996 when the per capita consumption

FIGURE 3.3

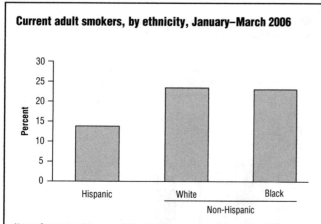

Current adult smokers, by ethnicity, January–March 2006

Notes: Current smokers were defined as those who smoked more than 100 cigarettes in their lifetime and now smoke everyday or somedays. The analyses excluded 71 persons (1.2%) with unknown smoking status. Estimates are age-sex adjusted using the projected 2000 U.S. population as the standard population using five age groups: 18–24 years, 25–34 years, 35–44 years, 45–64 years, and 65 years and over.

SOURCE: J. S. Schiller and P. Barnes, "Figure 8.4. Age-Sex-Adjusted Prevalence of Current Smoking Adults Aged 18 Years and Over, by Race/Ethnicity: United States, January–March 2006," in *Early Release of Selected Estimates Based on Data from the January–March 2006 National Health Interview Survey*, U.S. Department of Health and Human Services, Centers for Disease Control and Prevention, National Center for Health Statistics, September 28, 2006, http://www.cdc.gov/nchs/data/nhis/earlyrelease/200609_08.pdf (accessed October 10, 2006)

among this group was 31.9 cigars and cigarillos. The use of snuff has increased as well, although not as much as cigars. In 2006 the per capita consumption of snuff was 0.38 of a pound. In 1996 the per capita consumption of this tobacco product was 0.31 of a pound. Snuff is powdered tobacco that is inhaled through the nose.

ADDICTIVE NATURE OF NICOTINE

Is tobacco addictive? In *The Health Consequences of Smoking—Nicotine Addiction: A Report of the Surgeon General* (1988, http://www.cdc.gov/tobacco/sgr/sgr_1988/index.htm), researchers examined this question. They determined that the pharmacological (chemical and physical) effects and behavioral processes that contribute to tobacco addiction are similar to those that contribute in the addiction to drugs such as heroin and cocaine. Many researchers consider nicotine to be as potentially addictive as cocaine and heroin and note that it can create dependence quickly in some users.

Researchers have also discovered that some cigarettes have a "kick," in that they contain thirty-five times more freebase nicotine than other cigarettes. According to the article "'Crack' Nicotine in Cigarettes" (*Journal of Chemical Research in Toxicology*, July 28, 2003), the danger of this freebase nicotine is that it is in a volatile,

FIGURE 3.4

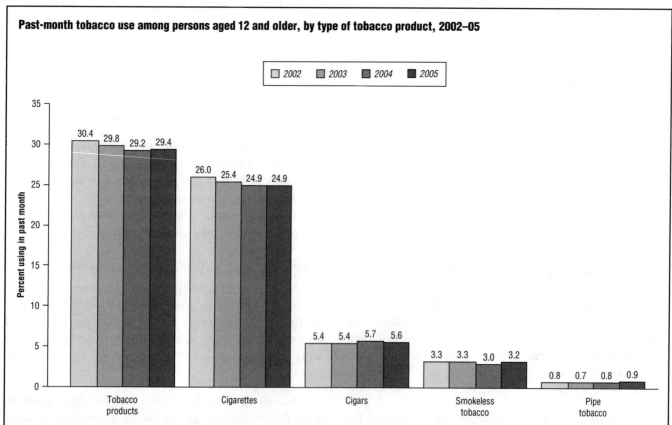

Past-month tobacco use among persons aged 12 and older, by type of tobacco product, 2002–05

SOURCE: "Figure 4.1. Past Month Tobacco Use among Persons Aged 12 or Older: 2002–2005," in *Results from the 2005 National Survey on Drug Use and Health: National Findings*, U.S. Department of Health and Human Services, Substance Abuse and Mental Health Services Administration, Office of Applied Studies, 2006, http://www.oas.samhsa.gov/nsduh/2k5nsduh/2k5Results.pdf (accessed October 12, 2006)

uncombined form that is absorbed by the lungs and brain at a faster rate than standard forms of nicotine. Researchers sometimes refer to this raw form of nicotine as "crack nicotine," because it potentially has the same addictive quality as crack cocaine. (A drug's addictiveness is measured by the speed at which it reaches the brain.)

Cigarette smoking results in rapid distribution of nicotine throughout the body, reaching the brain within ten seconds of inhalation. However, the intense effects of nicotine disappear in a few minutes, causing smokers to continue smoking frequently throughout the day to maintain its pleasurable effects and to prevent withdrawal. Tolerance develops after repeated exposure to nicotine, and higher doses are required to produce the same initial stimulation. Because nicotine is metabolized fairly quickly, disappearing from the body in a few hours, some tolerance is lost overnight. Smokers often report that the first cigarette of the day is the most satisfying. The more cigarettes smoked during the day, the more tolerance develops, and the less effect subsequent cigarettes have.

Is There a Genetic Basis for Nicotine Addiction?

Smoking is influenced by both environment and genetics. The results of many scientific studies, such as Viba Malaiyandi, Edward M. Sellers, and Rachel F. Tyndale's "Implications of *CYP2A6* Genetic Variation for Smoking Behaviors and Nicotine Dependence" (*Perspectives in Clinical Pharmacology*, March 2005), show that about 60% of the initiation of nicotine dependence and about 70% of the maintenance of dependent smoking behavior is genetically influenced.

The Collaborative Study on the Genetics of Alcoholism, in "Co-occurring Risk Factors for Alcohol Dependence and Habitual Smoking" (*Alcohol Research and Health*, Winter 2000), reports the results that support the hypothesis that some common genetic factors are involved in the susceptibility for developing both alcohol and nicotine addiction. Moreover, studies of twins support the role of common genetic factors in the development of both disorders.

Nicotine May Not Be the Only Addictive Substance in Cigarettes

Research results suggest that nicotine may not be the only psychoactive ingredient in tobacco. Some as-yet-unknown compound in cigarette smoke decreases the levels of monoamine oxidase (MAO), an enzyme responsible for breaking down the brain chemical dopamine. The decrease in MAO results in higher dopamine levels and may be another reason that smokers continue to smoke—to sustain the high dopamine levels that result in pleasurable effects and the desire for repeated cigarette use.

One issue that complicates any efforts by a longtime smoker to quit is nicotine withdrawal, which is often referred to as craving. This urge for nicotine is not well understood by researchers. Withdrawal may begin within a few hours after the last cigarette. According to the National Institute on Drug Abuse, high levels of craving may persist six months or longer. Besides craving, withdrawal can include irritability, attention deficits, interruption of thought processes, sleep disturbances, and increased appetite.

Some researchers also point out the behavioral aspects involved in smoking. The purchasing, handling, and lighting of cigarettes may be just as pleasing psychologically to the user as the chemical properties of tobacco itself.

HEALTH CONSEQUENCES OF TOBACCO USE
Respiratory System Effects

Cigarette smoke contains almost four thousand different chemical compounds, many of which are toxic, mutagenic (capable of increasing the frequency of mutation), and carcinogenic (cancer-causing). At least forty-three carcinogens have been identified in tobacco smoke. Besides nicotine, the most damaging substances are tar and carbon monoxide (CO). Smoke also contains hydrogen cyanide and other chemicals that can damage the respiratory system. These substances and nicotine are absorbed into the body through the linings of the mouth, nose, throat, and lungs. About ten seconds later they are delivered by the bloodstream to the brain.

Tar, which adds to the flavor of cigarettes, is released by the burning of tobacco. As it is inhaled, it enters the alveoli (air cells) of the lungs. There, the tar hampers the action of cilia—small, hairlike extensions of cells that clean foreign substances from the lungs—allowing the substances in cigarette smoke to accumulate.

CO affects the blood's ability to distribute oxygen throughout the body. CO is chemically similar to carbon dioxide (CO_2), which bonds with the hemoglobin in blood so that the CO_2 can be carried to the lungs for elimination. Hemoglobin has two primary functions: to carry oxygen to all parts of the body and to remove excess CO_2 from the body's tissues. CO bonds to hemoglobin more tightly than CO_2 and leaves the body more slowly, which allows CO to build up in the hemoglobin, in turn reducing the amount of oxygen the blood can carry. Lack of adequate oxygen is damaging to most of the body's organs, including the heart and brain.

Diseases and Conditions Linked to Tobacco Use

Results of medical research show an association between smoking and cancer, as well as heart and circulatory disease, fetal growth retardation, and low birth weight babies. The 1983 *Health Consequences of Smoking—Cardiovascular Disease: Report of the Surgeon General* (http://profiles.nlm.nih.gov/NN/B/B/T/D/_/nnbbtd.pdf) linked cigarette smoking to cerebrovascular disease (stroke) and associated it with cancer of the uterine cervix. Two 1992 studies showed that people who smoke double their risk of forming cataracts, the leading cause of blindness. Recent research links smoking to unsuccessful pregnancies, increased infant mortality, and peptic ulcer disease. In 2004 U.S. Surgeon General Richard H. Carmona released a comprehensive report on smoking and health, *The Health Consequences of Smoking: A Report of the Surgeon General* (http://www.cdc.gov/Tobacco/sgr/ sgr_2004/index.htm), revealing for the first time that cigarette smoking causes diseases in nearly every organ of the body. Table 3.3 lists diseases—including cancers—and other adverse health effects for which cigarette smoking is identified as a cause.

The National Cancer Institute, in "Questions and Answers about Cigar Smoking and Cancer" (2000, http:// www.cancer.gov/cancertopics/factsheet/Tobacco/cigars), notes that cigar smoking is associated with cancers of the lip, tongue, mouth, throat, larynx (voice box), lungs, and esophagus (food tube). Those who smoke cigars daily and inhale the smoke are at increased risk for developing heart and lung disease.

Smokeless tobacco, which includes chewing tobacco and snuff, also creates health hazards for its users. The 1979 *Smoking and Health: A Report of the Surgeon General* (http://profiles.nlm.nih.gov/NN/B/C/ M/D/_/nnbcmd.pdf) noted that smokeless tobacco was associated with oral cancers; and the 1986 *Health Consequences of Involuntary Smoking: A Report of the Surgeon General* concluded that it was a cause of these diseases. The nicotine in smokeless tobacco is absorbed into the bloodstream through the lining of the mouth and has been linked to periodontal (gum) disease and, more important, to cancers of the lip, gum, and mouth. The CDC, in "Smokeless Tobacco: Fact Sheet" (November 2005, http://www.cdc.gov/Tobacco/factsheets/smoke lesstobacco.htm), reminds the public that smokeless tobacco can lead to nicotine addiction. Thus, people who use smokeless tobacco are more likely than nontobacco users to become smokers.

Premature Aging

Smoking cigarettes contributes to premature aging in a variety of ways. Results of research over two decades, such as Marysia Placzek et al.'s "Tobacco Smoke Is Phototoxic" (*British Journal of Dermatology*, May 2004), show that smoking enhances facial aging and skin wrinkling. Additionally, smoking has been associated with a decline in overall fitness in women.

Interactions with Other Drugs

Smoking can have adverse effects when combined with over-the-counter (without a prescription) and prescription medications that a smoker may be taking. In many cases tobacco smoking reduces the effectiveness of medications, such as pain relievers (acetaminophen), antidepressants, tranquilizers, sedatives, ulcer medications, and insulin. With estrogen and oral contraceptives, tobacco smoking may increase the risk of heart and blood vessel disease and can cause strokes and blood clots.

SMOKING AND PUBLIC HEALTH

A study in the 1920s found that men who smoked two or more packs of cigarettes per day were twenty-two times more likely than nonsmokers to die of lung cancer. At the time, these results surprised researchers and medical authorities alike. Some forty years ago, the U.S. government first officially recognized the negative health consequences of smoking. In 1964 the Advisory Committee to the Surgeon General released a groundbreaking survey of studies on tobacco use. In *Smoking and Health: Report of the Advisory Committee to the Surgeon General of the Public Health Service*, U.S. Surgeon General Luther L. Terry reported that cigarette smoking increased overall mortality in men and caused lung and laryngeal cancer, as well as chronic bronchitis. The report concluded, "Cigarette smoking is a health hazard of sufficient importance in the United States to warrant appropriate remedial action," but what action should be taken was left unspecified at that time.

Later surgeons general issued additional reports on the health effects of smoking and the dangers to nonsmokers of passive or secondhand smoke. Besides general health concerns, the reports have addressed specific health consequences and populations. Table 3.4 shows a listing of reports of the surgeon general and the years in which they were published. The later reports concluded that smoking increased the morbidity (proportion of diseased people in a particular population) and mortality (proportion of deaths in a particular population) of both men and women.

In 1965 Congress passed the Federal Cigarette Labeling and Advertising Act (PL 89-92), which required the following health warning on all cigarette packages: "Caution: Cigarette smoking may be hazardous to your health." The Public Health Cigarette Smoking Act of 1969 (PL 91-222) strengthened the warning to read: "Warning: The Surgeon General has determined that cigarette smoking is dangerous to your health." Still later acts resulted in four different health warnings to be used in rotation.

The April 2, 1999, *Morbidity and Mortality Weekly Report* (http://www.cdc.gov/mmwr/PDF/wk/mm4812.pdf) included "recognition of tobacco use as a health hazard" as one of the country's ten greatest public health achievements of the twentieth century, along with vaccination, control of infectious diseases, safer and healthier food, healthier mothers and babies, family planning, safer workplaces, motor-vehicle

TABLE 3.3

Diseases and other adverse health effects caused by cigarette smoking, according to the U.S. Surgeon General, 2004

Disease	Highest level conclusion from previous Surgeon General's reports (year)	Conclusion from the 2004 Surgeon General's report
Cancer		
Bladder cancer	"Smoking is a cause of bladder cancer; cessation reduces risk by about 50 percent after only a few years, in comparison with continued smoking." (1990)	"The evidence is sufficient to infer a causal relationship between smoking and . . . bladder cancer."
Cervical cancer	"Smoking has been consistently associated with an increased risk for cervical cancer." (2001)	"The evidence is sufficient to infer a causal relationship between smoking and cervical cancer."
Esophageal cancer	"Cigarette smoking is a major cause of esophageal cancer in the United States." (1982)	"The evidence is sufficient to infer a causal relationship between smoking and cancers of the esophagus."
Kidney cancer	"Cigarette smoking is a contributory factor in the development of kidney cancer in the United States. The term 'contributory factor' by no means excludes the possibility of a causal role for smoking in cancers of this site." (1982)	"The evidence is sufficient to infer a causal relationship between smoking and renal cell, [and] renal pelvis . . . cancers."
Laryngeal cancer	"Cigarette smoking is causally associated with cancer of the lung, larynx, oral cavity, and esophagus in women as well as in men. . . ." (1980)	"The evidence is sufficient to infer a causal relationship between smoking and cancer of the larynx."
Leukemia	"Leukemia has recently been implicated as a smoking-related disease . . . but this observation has not been consistent." (1990)	"The evidence is sufficient to infer a causal relationship between smoking and acute myeloid leukemia."
Lung cancer	"Additional epidemiological, pathological, and experimental data not only confirm the conclusion of the Surgeon General's 1964 report regarding lung cancer in men but strengthen the causal relationship of smoking to lung cancer in women." (1967)	"The evidence is sufficient to infer a causal relationship between smoking and lung cancer."
Oral cancer	"Cigarette smoking is a major cause of cancers of the oral cavity in the United States." (1982)	"The evidence is sufficient to infer a causal relationship between smoking and cancers of the oral cavity and pharynx."
Pancreatic cancer	"Smoking cessation reduces the risk of pancreatic cancer, compared with continued smoking, although this reduction in risk may only be measurable after 10 years of abstinence." (1990)	"The evidence is sufficient to infer a causal relationship between smoking and pancreatic cancer."
Stomach cancer	"Data on smoking and cancer of the stomach . . . are unclear." (2001)	"The evidence is sufficient to infer a causal relationship between smoking and gastric cancers."
Cardiovascular diseases		
Abdominal aortic aneurysm	"Death from rupture of an atherosclerotic abdominal aneurysm is more common in cigarette smokers than in nonsmokers." (1983)	"The evidence is sufficient to infer a causal relationship between smoking and abdominal aortic aneurysm."
Atherosclerosis	"Cigarette smoking is the most powerful risk factor predisposing to atherosclerotic peripheral vascular disease." (1983)	"The evidence is sufficient to infer a causal relationship between smoking and subclinical atherosclerosis."
Cerebrovascular disease	"Cigarette smoking is a major cause of cerebrovascular disease (stroke), the third leading cause of death in the United States." (1989)	"The evidence is sufficient to infer a causal relationship between smoking and stroke."
Coronary heart disease	"In summary, for the purposes of preventive medicine, it can be concluded that smoking is causally related to coronary heart disease for both men and women in the United States." (1979)	"The evidence is sufficient to infer a causal relationship between smoking and coronary heart disease."
Respiratory diseases		
Chronic obstructive pulmonary disease	"Cigarette smoking is the most important of the causes of chronic bronchitis in the United states, and increases the risk of dying from chronic bronchitis." (1964)	"The evidence is sufficient to infer a causal relationship between active smoking and chronic obstructive pulmonary disease morbidity and mortality."
Pneumonia	"Smoking cessation reduces rates of respiratory symptoms such as cough, sputum production, and wheezing, and respiratory infections such as bronchitis and pneumonia, compared with continued smoking." (1990)	"The evidence is sufficient to infer a causal relationship between smoking and acute respiratory illnesses, including pneumonia, in persons without underlying smoking-related chronic obstructive lung disease."
Respiratory effects in utero	"In utero exposure to maternal smoking is associated with reduced lung function among infants. . . ." (2001)	"The evidence is sufficient to infer a causal relationship between maternal smoking during pregnancy and a reduction of lung function in infants."
Respiratory effects in childhood and adolescence	"Cigarette smoking during childhood and adolescence produces significant health problems among young people, including cough and phlegm production, an increased number and severity of respiratory illnesses, decreased physical fitness, an unfavorable lipid profile, and potential retardation in the rate of lung growth and the level of maximum lung function." (1994)	"The evidence is sufficient to infer a causal relationship between active smoking and impaired lung growth during childhood and adolescence." "The evidence is sufficient to infer a causal relationship between active smoking and the early onset of lung function decline during late adolescence and early adulthood." "The evidence is sufficient to infer a causal relationship between active smoking and respiratory symptoms in children and adolescents, including coughing, phlegm, wheezing, and dyspnea." "The evidence is sufficient to infer a causal relationship between active smoking and asthma-related symptoms (i.e., wheezing) in childhood and adolescence."
Respiratory effects in adulthood	"Cigarette smoking accelerates the age-related decline in lung function that occurs among never smokers. With sustained abstinence from smoking, the rate of decline in pulmonary function among former smokers returns to that of never smokers." (1990)	"The evidence is sufficient to infer a causal relationship between active smoking in adulthood and a premature onset of and an accelerated age-related decline in lung function." "The evidence is sufficient to infer a causal relationship between active sustained cessation from smoking and a return of the rate of decline in pulmonary function to that of persons who had never smoked."
Other respiratory effects	"Smoking cessation reduces rates of respiratory symptoms such as cough, sputum production, and wheezing, and respiratory infections such as bronchitis and pneumonia, compared with continued smoking." (1990)	"The evidence is sufficient to infer a causal relationship between active smoking and all major respiratory symptoms among adults, including coughing, phlegm, wheezing, and dyspnea." "The evidence is sufficient to infer a causal relationship between active smoking and poor asthma control."

TABLE 3.3

Diseases and other adverse health effects caused by cigarette smoking, according to the U.S. Surgeon General, 2004 [CONTIUNED]

Disease	Highest level conclusion from previous Surgeon General's reports (year)	Conclusion from the 2004 Surgeon General's report
Reproductive effects		
Fetal death and stillbirths	"The risk for perinatal mortality—both stillbirth and neonatal deaths—and the risk for sudden infant death syndrome (SIDS) are increased among the offspring of women who smoke during pregnancy." (2001)	"The evidence is sufficient to infer a causal relationship between sudden infant death syndrome and maternal smoking during and after pregnancy."
Fertility	"Women who smoke have increased risks for conception delay and for both primary and secondary infertility." (2001)	"The evidence is sufficient to infer a causal relationship between smoking and reduced fertility in women."
Low birth weight	"Infants born to women who smoke during pregnancy have a lower average birth weight . . . than . . . infants born to women who do not smoke." (2001)	"The evidence is sufficient to infer a causal relationship between maternal active smoking and fetal growth restriction and low birth weight."
Pregnancy complications	"Smoking during pregnancy is associated with increased risks for preterm premature rupture of membranes, abruptio placentae, and placenta previa, and with a modest increase in risk for preterm delivery." (2001)	"The evidence is sufficient to infer a casual relationship between maternal active smoking and premature rupture of the membranes, placenta previa, and placental abruption." "The evidence is sufficient to infer a causal relationship between maternal active smoking and preterm delivery and shortened gestation."
Other effects		
Cataract	"Women who smoke have an increased risk for cataract." (2001)	"The evidence is sufficient to infer a causal relationship between smoking and nuclear cataract."
Diminished health status/morbidity	"Relationships between smoking and cough or phlegm are strong and consistent; they have been amply documented and are judged to be causal. . . ." (1984)	"The evidence is sufficient to infer a causal relationship between smoking and diminished health status that may be manifest as increased absenteeism from work and increased use of medical care services."
	"Consideration of evidence from many different studies has led to the conclusion that cigarette smoking is the overwhelmingly most important cause of cough, sputum, chronic bronchitis, and mucus hypersecretion." (1984)	"The evidence is sufficient to infer a causal relationship between smoking and increased risks for adverse surgical outcomes related to wound healing and respiratory complications."
Hip fractures	"Women who currently smoke have an increased risk for hip fracture compared with women who do not smoke." (2001)	"The evidence is sufficient to infer a causal relationship between smoking and hip fractures."
Low bone density	"Postmenopausal women who currently smoke have lower bone density than do women who do not smoke." (2001)	"In postmenopausal women, the evidence is sufficient to infer a causal relationship between smoking and low bone density."
Peptic ulcer disease	"The relationship between cigarette smoking and death rates from peptic ulcer, especially gastric ulcer, is confirmed. In addition, morbidity data suggest a similar relationship exists with the prevalence of reported disease from this cause." (1967)	"The evidence is sufficient to infer a causal relationship between smoking and peptic ulcer disease in persons who are helicobacter pylori positive."

SOURCE: "Table 1.1. Diseases and Other Adverse Health Effects for Which Smoking Is Identified as a Cause in the Current Surgeon General's Report," in *The Health Consequences of Smoking: A Report of the Surgeon General*, U.S. Department of Health and Human Services, Centers for Disease Control and Prevention, National Center for Chronic Disease Prevention and Health Promotion, Office on Smoking and Health, http://www.cdc.gov/tobacco/sgr/sgr_2004/pdf/chapter1.pdf (accessed October 10, 2006)

safety, decline in deaths from coronary heart disease and stroke, and fluoridation of drinking water. These ten accomplishments were chosen based on their contributions to prevention and their impact on illness, disability, and death in the United States.

DEATHS ATTRIBUTED TO TOBACCO USE

According to the *Health Consequences of Smoking: A Report of the Surgeon General*, cigarette smoking is the leading cause of preventable death in the United States and produces substantial health-related economic costs to society. The report notes that smoking caused an estimated 440,100 deaths in the United States each year from 1995 to 1999. Nationwide, smoking kills more people each year than alcohol, drug abuse, car crashes, murders, suicides, fires, and acquired immune deficiency syndrome combined.

In 2004 diseases linked to smoking accounted for four of the top five leading causes of death in the United States. (See Table 3.5.) According to the CDC, about 655,000 people died of various heart diseases in 2004

(down from about 761,000 in 1980). Approximately 550,000 died of cancer, and cerebrovascular disease (stroke) claimed about 150,000 lives. Chronic lower respiratory diseases, including chronic bronchitis, asthma, and emphysema, claimed nearly 124,000 lives.

In *Cancer Facts and Figures, 2006* (2006, http://www.cancer.org/downloads/STT/CAFF2006PWSecured.pdf), the American Cancer Society estimated that 162,460 Americans died of lung and bronchus cancer in 2006. While not all lung and bronchus cancer deaths are directly attributable to smoking, a large proportion of them are. Lung cancer is the leading cause of cancer mortality in both men and women in the United States. It has been the leading cause of cancer deaths among men since the early 1950s and, in 1987, surpassed breast cancer to become the leading cause of cancer deaths in women.

SECONDHAND SMOKE

Secondhand smoke, also known as environmental tobacco smoke (ETS) or passive smoke, is a health hazard for nonsmokers who live or work with smokers. The

TABLE 3.4

Twenty-nine Surgeon General's reports on smoking and health, selected years 1964–2006

1964	Smoking and Health: Report of the Advisory Committee to the Surgeon General of the Public Health Service
1967	The Health Consequences of Smoking: A Public Health Service Review
1968	The Health Consequences of Smoking: 1968 Supplement to the 1967 Public Health Service Review
1969	The Health Consequences of Smoking: 1969 Supplement to the 1967 Public Health Service Review
1971	The Health Consequences of Smoking
1972	The Health Consequences of Smoking
1973	The Health Consequences of Smoking
1974	The Health Consequences of Smoking
1975	The Health Consequences of Smoking
1976	The Health Consequences of Smoking
1978	The Health Consequences of Smoking, 1977–1978
1979	Smoking and Health
1980	The Health Consequences of Smoking for Women
1981	The Health Consequences of Smoking—The Changing Cigarette
1982	The Health Consequences of Smoking—Cancer
1983	The Health Consequences of Smoking—Cardiovascular Disease
1984	The Health Consequences of Smoking—Chronic Obstructive Lung Disease
1985	The Health Consequences of Smoking—Cancer and Chronic Lung Disease in the Workplace
1986	The Health Consequences of Involuntary Smoking
1988	The Health Consequences of Smoking—Nicotine Addiction
1989	Reducing the Health Consequences of Smoking—25 Years of Progress
1990	The Health Benefits of Smoking Cessation
1992	Smoking and Health in the Americas
1994	Preventing Tobacco Use among Young People
1998	Tobacco Use among U.S. Racial/Ethnic Minority Groups
2000	Reducing Tobacco Use
2001	Women and Smoking
2004	The Health Consequences of Smoking
2006	The Health Consequences of Involuntary Exposure to Tobacco Smoke

Note: Smoking remains the leading cause of preventable death and has negative health impacts on people at all stages of life. It harms unborn babies, infants, children, adolescents, adults, and seniors.

SOURCE: Adapted from "28 Surgeon General's Reports on Smoking and Health, 1964–2004," U.S. Department of Health and Human Services, Centers for Disease Control and Prevention, National Center for Chronic Disease Prevention and Health Promotion, Tobacco Information and Prevention Source (TIPS), http://www.cdc.gov/tobacco/sgr/sgr_2004/Factsheets/11.htm (accessed October 30, 2006), and "The Health Consequences of Involuntary Exposure to Tobacco Smoke: A Report of the Surgeon General," U.S. Department of Health and Human Services, Centers for Disease Control and Prevention, National Center for Chronic Disease Prevention and Health Promotion, Office on Smoking and Health, http://www.surgeongeneral.gov/library/secondhandsmoke/report/executive summary.pdf (accessed November 24, 2006).

National Cancer Institute (2006, http://www.cancer.gov/Templates/db_alpha.aspx?CdrID=46431) defines second-hand smoke as "smoke that comes from the burning of a tobacco product and smoke that is exhaled by smokers. . . . Inhaling ETS is called involuntary or passive smoking."

The first scientific paper on the harmful effects of sec-ondhand smoke was Takeshi Hirayama's "Non-smoking Wives of Heavy Smokers Have a Higher Risk of Lung Cancer: A Study from Japan" (*British Medical Journal*, 1981). Hirayama studied 92,000 nonsmoking wives of smoking husbands and a similarly sized group of women married to nonsmokers. He discovered that nonsmoking wives of husbands who smoked faced a 40% to 90% elevated risk of lung cancer (depending on how fre-quently their husbands smoked) compared with the wives of nonsmoking husbands.

Other studies have followed. The U.S. Environmen-tal Protection Agency (EPA), in *Respiratory Health Effects of Passive Smoking: Lung Cancer and Other Disorders* (December 1992, http://cfpub2.epa.gov/ncea/cfm/recordisplay.cfm?deid=2835), concluded that the "widespread exposure to environmental tobacco smoke (ETS) in the United States presents a serious and sub-stantial public health impact." In Elizabeth T. H. Fon-tham et al.'s "Environmental Tobacco Smoke and Lung Cancer in Nonsmoking Women: A Multicenter Study" (*Journal of the American Medical Association*, June 1994), a large case-control study on secondhand smoke, compelling links were found between passive smoke and lung cancer. In 2000 the Environmental Health Informa-tion Service's *Ninth Report on Carcinogens* classified secondhand smoke as a Group A (Human) Carcino-gen—a substance known to cause cancer in humans. According to the EPA, there is no safe level of exposure to such Group A toxins.

In 2005 more evidence accumulated on the risks of passive smoking. In "Environmental Tobacco Smoke and Risk of Respiratory Cancer and Chronic Obstructive Pul-monary Disease in Former Smokers and Never Smokers in the EPIC Prospective Study" (*British Medical Journal*, 2005), the European Prospective Investigation into Can-cer and Nutrition reveals that those who had been exposed to secondhand smoke during childhood for many hours each day had more than triple the risk of develop-ing lung cancer compared with people who were not exposed. In addition, Sarah M. McGhee et al., in "Mor-tality Associated with Passive Smoking in Hong Kong" (*British Medical Journal*, January 2005), show that there is a correlation between an increased risk of dying from various causes (including lung cancer and other lung diseases, heart disease, and stroke) and the number of smokers in the home. Risk increased by 24% when one smoker lived in the home and by 74% with two smokers in the household.

In June 2006 the twenty-ninth report of the surgeon general on smoking—*The Health Consequences of Invol-untary Exposure to Tobacco Smoke* (http://www.surgeon general.gov/library/secondhandsmoke/report/)—was pub-lished. The report notes that:

> With regard to the involuntary exposure of nonsmokers to tobacco smoke, the scientific evidence now supports the following major conclusions:
>
> 1. Secondhand smoke causes premature death and disease in children and in adults who do not smoke.

TABLE 3.5

Leading causes of death, 1980 and 2004

Rank order	1980 Cause of death		2004 Cause of death
	All causes		All causes
1	Diseases of heart	1	Diseases of heart
2	Malignant neoplasms	2	Malignant neoplasms
3	Cerebrovascular diseases	3	Cerebrovascular diseases
4	Unintentional injuries	4	Chronic lower respiratory diseases
5	Chronic obstructive pulmonary diseases	5	Accidents (unintentional injuries)
6	Pneumonia and influenza	6	Diabetes mellitus
7	Diabetes mellitus	7	Alzheimer's disease
8	Chronic liver disease and cirrhosis	8	Influenza and pneumonia
9	Atherosclerosis	9	Nephritis, nephrotic syndrome and nephrosis
10	Suicide	10	Septicemia

SOURCE: Adapted from "Table 32. Leading Causes of Death and Numbers of Deaths, according to Sex, Race, and Hispanic Origin: United States, 1980 and 2000," in *Health, United States, 2002,* U.S. Department of Health and Human Services, Centers for Disease Control and Prevention, National Center for Health Statistics, September 2002, and Arialdi M. Minino, Melonie P. Heron, and Betty L. Smith, "Table 7. Deaths and Death Rates for the 10 Leading Causes of Death in Specified Age Groups: United States, Preliminary 2004," in "Deaths: Preliminary Data for 2004," in *National Vital Statistics Reports*, vol. 54, no. 19, U.S. Department of Health and Human Services, Centers for Disease Control and Prevention, National Center for Health Statistics, June 28, 2006, http://www.cdc.gov/nchs/data/nvsr/nvsr54/nvsr54_19.pdf (accessed October 10, 2006)

2. Children exposed to secondhand smoke are at an increased risk for sudden infant death syndrome (SIDS), acute respiratory infections, ear problems, and more severe asthma. Smoking by parents causes respiratory symptoms and slows lung growth in their children.

3. Exposure of adults to secondhand smoke has immediate adverse effects on the cardiovascular system and causes coronary heart disease and lung cancer.

4. The scientific evidence indicates that there is no risk-free level of exposure to secondhand smoke.

5. Many millions of Americans, both children and adults, are still exposed to secondhand smoke in their homes and workplaces despite substantial progress in tobacco control.

6. Eliminating smoking in indoor spaces fully protects nonsmokers from exposure to secondhand smoke. Separating smokers from nonsmokers, cleaning the air, and ventilating buildings cannot eliminate exposures of nonsmokers to secondhand smoke.

A MOVEMENT TO BAN SMOKING

Many efforts have been initiated over the years to control public smoking or to separate smokers and nonsmokers. In 1975 the Clean Indoor Air Act in Minnesota became the nation's first statewide law to require the separation of smokers and nonsmokers. The purpose of the law was to protect public health, public comfort, and the environment by banning smoking in public places and at public meetings, except in designated smoking areas.

Other states soon followed Minnesota. In 1977 Berkeley became the first community in California to limit smoking in restaurants and other public places. In 1990 San Luis Obispo, California, became the first city to ban smoking in all public buildings, bars, and restaurants. In 1994 smoking was restricted in many government buildings in California. In that same year the fast-food giant McDonald's banned smoking in all of its establishments. In 1995 New York City banned smoking in the dining areas of all restaurants with more than thirty-five seats. As of July 2003, all public and workplaces in New York City became smoke-free, including bars and restaurants. Laws vary from state to state and from city to city, but by 2005 smoking was banned in most workplaces, hospitals, government buildings, museums, schools, theaters, and many restaurants throughout the United States.

Gallup conducted a poll regarding secondhand smoke after the 2006 surgeon general's report on the subject was published. Gallup notes that the document had "little immediate impact on public attitudes about the risks" of passive smoking. The 2006 poll revealed that 56% of those surveyed perceived the risk of secondhand smoke to be very harmful. Twenty-nine percent believed that secondhand smoke was somewhat harmful, and 12% thought it was not too harmful or not at all harmful in the 2006 survey. (See Figure 3.5.)

STOPPING SMOKING

The CDC, in "Cigarette Smoking among Adults—United States, 2005" (October 27, 2006, http://www.cdc.gov/mmwr/PDF/wk/mm5542.pdf), estimates that in 2005 there were 45.1 million current smokers. Furthermore, the CDC reports in "Smoking Prevalence among U.S. Adults" (October 2006, http://www.cdc.gov/tobacco/research_data/adults_prev/prevali.htm) that there continues to be a decline in adult smokers. In 1965, 42.4% of adults smoked; by 2005, 20.9% of adults smoked.

Many cigarette smokers are trying to stop smoking—or would at least like to. In the 2006 Gallup poll "Tobacco and Smoking," smokers were asked if they would like to give up smoking. Seventy-five percent answered yes. This figure is down from 82% in 2004 and 76% in 1999 but up from 66% in 1977.

According to the article "U.S. Has New Plan against Smoking" (*New York Times*, October 5, 1991), the federal government began a massive antismoking campaign in 1991 that was intended to prevent 1.2 million smoking-related deaths. The goal of the multiyear program was to help 4.5 million adults stop smoking, prevent two million

FIGURE 3.5

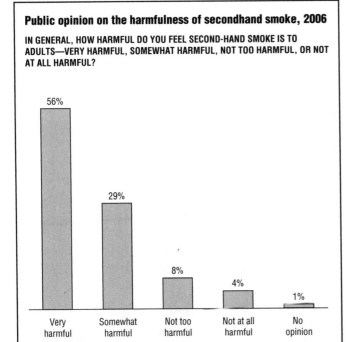

Public opinion on the harmfulness of secondhand smoke, 2006

IN GENERAL, HOW HARMFUL DO YOU FEEL SECOND-HAND SMOKE IS TO ADULTS—VERY HARMFUL, SOMEWHAT HARMFUL, NOT TOO HARMFUL, OR NOT AT ALL HARMFUL?

SOURCE: Lydia Saad, "In general, how harmful do you feel second-hand smoke is to adults—very harmful, somewhat harmful, not too harmful, or not at all harmful?" in *Many Americans Still Downplay Risk of Passive Smoking: No Perceived Change as a Result of Recent Government Report*, Gallup Poll News Service, July 6–9, 2006, http://www.galluppoll.com (accessed November 1, 2006). Copyright © 2006 by The Gallup Organization. Reproduced by permission of The Gallup Organization.

youths from starting, and reduce the number of smokers to 15% of the population.

The government reports *Reducing Tobacco Use* (2000, http://www.cdc.gov/Tobacco/sgr/sgr_2000/Full Report.pdf) and *Investment in Tobacco Control State Highlights* (2002, http://www.cdc.gov/tobacco/statehi/statehi_2002.htm) say that drug treatment for nicotine addiction, combined with other treatment methods, will enable 20–25% of users to refrain from smoking one year after treatment. Even physicians who simply advise their patients to quit smoking can produce a cessation increase of 5–10%.

Global Efforts to Reduce Tobacco Use

According to the World Health Organization (WHO), in *Tobacco: Deadly in Any Form or Disguise* (2006, http://www.who.int/tobacco/communications/events/wntd/2006/Tfi_Rapport.pdf), an estimated 1.3 billion adults around the world use tobacco. In addition, the WHO notes that tobacco causes five million deaths per year.

In May 2003 member states of the WHO adopted the world's first international public health treaty for global cooperation in reducing the negative health consequences of tobacco use. The WHO Framework Convention on Tobacco Control is designed to reduce tobacco-related deaths and disease worldwide. In February 2005 the treaty came into force after being ratified by member countries. Each of the 168 countries that signed the treaty must now pass it into law. Although the United States signed the treaty in May 2004, indicating its general acceptance, by the end of 2006 it had not yet ratified (become bound by) the treaty. The treaty has many measures, which include requiring countries to impose restrictions on tobacco advertising, sponsorship, and promotion; establishing new packaging and labeling of tobacco products; establishing clean indoor air controls; and promoting taxation as a way to cut consumption and fight smuggling.

Benefits of Stopping

The Health Benefits of Smoking Cessation: A Report of the Surgeon General (1990, http://profiles.nlm.nih.gov/NN/B/B/C/T/_/nnbbct.pdf) notes that quitting offers major and immediate health benefits for both sexes and for all ages. This first comprehensive report on the benefits of quitting showed that many of the ill effects of smoking can be reversed. The surgeon general's report *Health Consequences of Smoking* reveals that deaths attributable to smoking can be reduced dramatically if the prevalence of smoking is cut.

According to Arialdi M. Miniño et al. in *Deaths: Preliminary Data for 2004* (June 28, 2006, http://www.cdc.gov/nchs/data/nvsr/nvsr54/nvsr54_19.pdf), heart disease was the number-one killer of Americans in 2004 and cancer was the number-two killer. Of all cancers, lung cancer is the number-one killer of both men and women. People who quit smoking in middle age or before middle age avoid more than 90% of the lung cancer risk attributable to tobacco. Results of Richard Peto et al.'s "Smoking, Smoking Cessation, and Lung Cancer in the UK since 1950: Combination of National Statistics with Two Case-Control Studies" (*British Medical Journal*, August 5, 2000) reveal the extent to which smoking cessation lowers lung cancer risk. For men who stopped smoking at aged sixty, fifty, forty, and thirty, the cumulative risks of lung cancer by the age of seventy-five were 10%, 6%, 3%, and 2%, respectively. These results were supported by the findings of Anna Crispo et al., in "The Cumulative Risk of Lung Cancer among Current, Ex- and Never-Smokers in European Men" (*British Journal of Cancer*, October 2004), that led to the conclusion that, for long-term smokers, giving up smoking in middle age allows people to avoid most of the subsequent risk of lung cancer.

For smokers who quit, the risk of heart disease drops rapidly after smoking cessation. After one year's abstinence from smoking, the risk of heart disease is reduced by about 50% and continues to decline gradually. After five to ten years of smoking cessation, the risk has declined to that of a person who has never smoked. In addition, Gay Sutherland reports in "Smoking: Can We Really Make a Difference?" (*Heart*, May 2003) that stopping smoking reduces the risk of stroke to that of a nonsmoker after five years of smoking cessation.

The study "Effects of Multiple Attempts to Quit Smoking and Relapses to Smoking on Pulmonary Function" (*Journal of Clinical Epidemiology*, December 1998) by Robert P. Murray et al. investigated whether short periods of quitting were beneficial to smokers' health. Results revealed that those who made several attempts to quit smoking had less loss of lung function than those who continued to smoke. Therefore, even intermittent lapses in smoking are beneficial.

Quitting and Pregnancy

The 2005 NSDUH finds that from 10.4% to 26.4% of pregnant women smoked cigarettes in the month prior to the survey. Those aged eighteen to twenty-five had the highest percentage of smokers. Nonetheless, in the fifteen- to seventeen-year-old group a higher percentage of pregnant girls smoked than nonpregnant girls, 22.3% versus 18.5%, respectively. (See Figure 3.6.)

Smoking during pregnancy can compromise the health of the developing fetus. The 2004 surgeon general's report *Health Consequences of Smoking* notes that evidence suggests the possibility of a causal relationship between maternal smoking and ectopic pregnancy, a situation in which the fertilized egg implants in the fallopian tube rather than in the uterus. This situation is quite serious and is life-threatening to the mother. Smoking by pregnant women is also linked to an increased risk of miscarriage, stillbirth, premature delivery, and sudden infant death syndrome, and is a cause of low birth weight in infants. A woman who stops smoking before pregnancy or during her first trimester (three months) of pregnancy significantly reduces her chances of having a low birth weight baby. Research finds that it takes smokers longer to get pregnant than nonsmokers, but that women who quit are as likely to get pregnant as those who have never smoked.

Complaints about Quitting

A major side effect of smoking cessation is nicotine withdrawal. The short-term consequences of nicotine withdrawal may include anxiety, irritability, frustration, anger, difficulty concentrating, and restlessness. Possible long-term consequences are urges to smoke and increased appetite. Nicotine withdrawal symptoms peak in the first few days after quitting and subside during the following weeks. Improved self-esteem and an increased sense of control often accompany long-term abstinence.

FIGURE 3.6

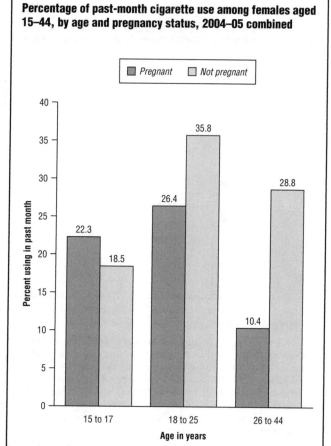

Percentage of past-month cigarette use among females aged 15–44, by age and pregnancy status, 2004–05 combined

SOURCE: "Figure 4.5. Past Month Cigarette Use among Women Aged 15 to 44, by Age and Pregnancy Status, 2004–2005 Combined," in *2005 National Survey on Drug Use and Health*, U.S. Department of Health and Human Services, Substance Abuse and Mental Health Services Administration, Office of Applied Studies, 2006, http://www.oas.samhsa.gov/NSDUH/2k5NSDUH/2k5results.htm#Ch4 (accessed October 10, 2006)

One of the most common complaints among former smokers is that they gain weight when they stop smoking. Many reasons explain this weight gain, but two primary reasons are the metabolism changes when nicotine is withdrawn from the body and many former smokers use food in an attempt to manage their withdrawal cravings. To combat weight gain, some former smokers start exercise programs.

Ways to Stop Smoking

Nicotine replacement treatments can be effective for many smokers. Nicotine patches and gum are two types of nicotine replacement therapy (NRT). The nicotine in a patch is absorbed through the skin, and the nicotine in gum is absorbed through the mouth and throat. NRT helps a smoker cope with nicotine withdrawal symptoms that discourage many smokers trying to stop. Nicotine patches and gum are available over the counter. Other NRT products are the nicotine nasal spray and the nicotine inhaler, which are available by prescription.

The nonnicotine therapy bupropion (an antidepressant drug such as Zyban and Wellbutrin) is also available by prescription for the relief of nicotine withdrawal symptoms. In addition, behavioral treatments, such as smoking-cessation programs, are useful for some smokers who want to quit. Behavioral methods are designed to create an aversion to smoking, develop self-monitoring of smoking behavior, and establish alternative coping responses.

Quitting smoking is not easy. Sutherland notes that the expected one-year success rates of quitting smoking vary among stop-smoking interventions. Only 1–2% of smokers trying to quit will remain smoke-free for a year with no advice or support from a doctor or other health care professional and no treatment (NRT or bupropion). Five percent of those who receive three minutes' advice from a health care professional to help them quit will remain smoke-free for a year. Advice plus treatment raises the percentage of those who remain smoke free to 10%. Intensive behavioral support from a specialist plus treatment can lead to a 25% success rate.

CHAPTER 4
ILLICIT DRUGS

Illegal drugs are those with no currently accepted medical use in the United States, such as heroin, lysergic acid diethylamide (LSD), and marijuana. Controlled substances are legal drugs whose sale, possession, and use are restricted because they are psychoactive (mood- or mind-altering) drugs that have potential for abuse. These drugs are medications, such as certain narcotics, depressants, and stimulants, which physicians prescribe for various conditions. The term *illicit drugs* is used by the Substance Abuse and Mental Health Services Administration (SAMHSA) to mean both illegal drugs and controlled substances that are used illegally.

WHO USES ILLICIT DRUGS?

The 2005 National Survey on Drug Use and Health (NSDUH) is an annual survey conducted by the SAMHSA, and its results are published in *Results from the 2005 National Survey on Drug Use and Health: National Findings* (September 2006, http://www.oas. samhsa.gov/nsduh/2k5nsduh/2k5Results.pdf). The NSDUH reveals that an estimated 19.7 million Americans aged twelve or older were current illicit drug users in 2005. By "current" the SAMHSA means that the people who were surveyed about their drug use had taken an illicit drug during the month prior to taking the SAMHSA survey. (Current users are "past month" users.) This figure represented 8.1% of the U.S. population in 2005.

Table 4.1 presents a demographic profile of this population of drug users. Most drug users are twenty-five years old or younger. In 2005, 20.1% of those aged eighteen to twenty-five were current illicit drug users, and 9.9% of those aged twelve to seventeen were. In contrast, only 5.8% of those aged twenty-five and over were current illicit drug users.

Figure 4.1 shows a more detailed look at current illicit drug use by age. In 2005 the age group having the highest percentage of illicit drug users was the eighteen- to twenty-year-olds. At 22.3% of their population, over one out of every five young people aged eighteen to twenty were current illicit drug users in that year. The age group with the next-highest percentage of current illicit drug users was the twenty-one- to twenty-five-year-olds (18.7%), followed by the sixteen- and seventeen-year-olds (17%).

Regarding other demographics of illicit drug use, Table 4.1 shows that more males than females were current, past-year, or lifetime illicit drug users from 2004 to 2005. (Past-year users took a specific drug in the twelve months prior to taking the SAMHSA survey. Lifetime users took a specific drug at least once in their lifetime.) Those of American Indian or Alaskan Native heritage had the highest percentage of current illicit drug users in their population (12.8% in 2005). Those of two or more races were next (12.2%), followed by African-Americans (9.7%). Asian-Americans had the lowest percentage of current illicit drug users in their population (3.1%).

WHICH ILLICIT DRUGS ARE USED MOST FREQUENTLY?

Figure 4.2 shows the types of illicit drugs used in 2005. Those who used only marijuana made up more than half (54.5%) the population of current illicit drug users in 2005. Nearly one out of five (19.6%) used marijuana and another illicit drug. Only one-quarter (25.8%) used illicit drugs but did not use marijuana. Clearly, marijuana was the drug used by the greatest percentage of illicit drug users in the United States in 2005.

In the years 2002 through 2005 marijuana was used by the largest percentage of the population, roughly 6%. (See Figure 4.3.) Psychotherapeutics were the next most used group of illicit drugs, ranging from 2.5% to 2.7% of the population from 2002 to 2005. Psychotherapeutics are a group of drugs that include pain relievers, tranquilizers,

TABLE 4.1

Use of illicit drugs among persons aged 12 and older, by time of use and demographic characteristics, 2004–05

Demographic characteristic	Lifetime		Past year		Past month	
	2004	2005	2004	2005	2004	2005
Total	45.8	46.1	14.5	14.4	7.9	8.1
Age						
12–17	30.0	27.7	21.0	19.9	10.6	9.9
18–25	59.2	59.2	33.9	34.2	19.4	20.1
or 26 older	45.6	46.3	10.2	10.2	5.5	5.8
Gender						
Male	50.7	50.8	16.9	16.8	9.9	10.2
Female	41.1	41.6	12.2	12.1	6.1	6.1
Hispanic origin and race						
Not Hispanic or Latino	47.3	47.4	14.7	14.5	8.0	8.2
White	49.1	48.9	15.0	14.5	8.1	8.1
Black or African American	43.3	44.7	14.6	16.0	8.7	9.7
American Indian or Alaska Native	58.4	60.9	26.2	21.3	12.3	12.8
Native Hawaiian or other Pacific Islander	*	54.3	*	15.5	*	8.7
Asian	24.3	28.1	6.9	7.1	3.1	3.1
Two or more races	54.9	45.8	21.0	19.1	13.3	12.2
Hispanic or Latino	35.4	37.3	12.9	13.9	7.2	7.6

*Low precision; no estimate reported.
Note: Illicit drugs include marijuana/hashish, cocaine (including crack), heroin, hallucinogens, inhalants, or prescription-type psychotherapeutics used nonmedically.

SOURCE: "Table 1.28B. Illicit Drug Use in Lifetime, Past Year, and Past Month among Persons Aged 12 or Older, by Demographic Characteristics: Percentages, 2004 and 2005," in *Results from the 2005 National Survey on Drug Use and Health: Detailed Tables*, U.S. Department of Health and Human Services, Substance Abuse and Mental Health Services Administration, Office of Applied Studies, 2006, http://www.oas.samhsa.gov/nsduh/2k5nsduh/tabs/Sect1peTabs28to32.pdf (accessed October 13, 2006)

stimulants (including methamphetamine), and sedatives. This group does not include over-the-counter (without a prescription) drugs. The next most used illicit drugs were cocaine, hallucinogens, and inhalants, from most used to least used.

CANNABIS AND MARIJUANA

Cannabis sativa, the hemp plant from which marijuana is made, grows wild throughout most of the world's tropic and temperate regions, including Mexico, the Middle East, Africa, and India. For centuries its therapeutic potential has been explored, including uses as an analgesic (painkiller) and anticonvulsant. However, with the advent of new, synthetic drugs and the passage of the Marijuana Tax Act of 1937 (PL 75-238), interest in marijuana—even for medicinal purposes—faded. In 1970 the Controlled Substances Act (PL 91-513) classified marijuana as a Schedule I drug, having "no currently accepted medical use in the United States," though this classification is debated by those in favor of using it for medical and recreational purposes. (See Chapter 9.)

Besides regular marijuana, there are two alternate forms: ditchweed and sinsemilla. All three are tobacco-like substances produced by drying the leaves and flow-

ery tops of cannabis plants. Potency varies considerably among the three, depending on how much of the chemical THC (delta-9-tetrahydrocannabinol) is present. Ditchweed, or wild U.S. marijuana, is the least potent form of marijuana and generally has a THC content of less than 0.5%. Sinsemilla is the most potent form of marijuana. The name is Spanish for "without seed" and refers to the unpollinated, and therefore seedless, female cannabis plant. Sinsemilla can contain up to nearly 15% THC. (See Table 8.7 in Chapter 8.) The marijuana generally cultivated in the United States has a THC content of about 3%, but marijuana from other countries has a higher potency of up to 7%.

Effects of Marijuana

Marijuana is usually smoked in the form of loosely rolled cigarettes called joints, in hollowed-out commercial cigars called blunts, or in water pipes called bongs. Sometimes it is ingested. The effects are felt within minutes, usually peaking in ten to thirty minutes and lingering for two to three hours. Low doses induce restlessness and an increasing sense of well-being, followed by a dreamy state of relaxation and, frequently, hunger. Changes in sensory perception—a more vivid sense of sight, smell, touch, taste, and hearing—may occur, with

FIGURE 4.1

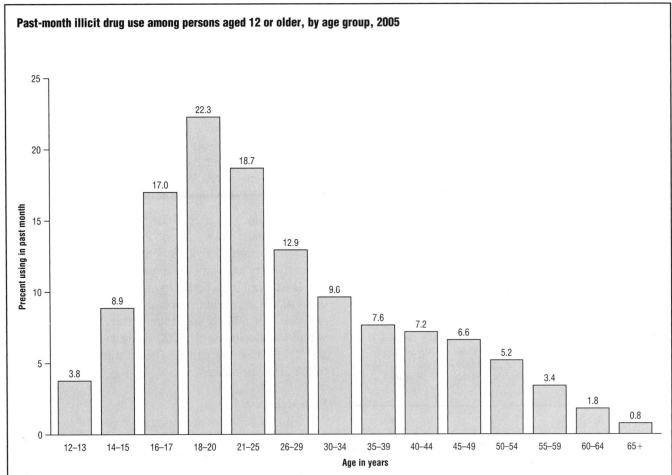

Past-month illicit drug use among persons aged 12 or older, by age group, 2005

SOURCE: "Figure 2.4. Past Month Illicit Drug Use among Persons Aged 12 or Older, by Age: 2005," in *Results from the 2005 National Survey on Drug Use and Health: National Findings*, U.S. Department of Health and Human Services, Substance Abuse and Mental Health Services Administration, Office of Applied Studies, 2006, http://www.oas.samhsa.gov/nsduh/2k5nsduh/2k5Results.pdf (accessed October 12, 2006)

subtle alterations in thought formation and expression. However, the Drug Enforcement Administration (DEA) reports in *Drugs of Abuse* (2005, http://www.usdoj.gov/dea/pubs/abuse/doa-p.pdf) that along with the pleasant side effects of smoking marijuana come some not-so-pleasant effects with extended use: short-term memory loss, lung damage, adverse effects on reproductive function, suppression of the immune system, apathy, impairment of judgment, and loss of interest in personal appearance and pursuit of goals.

The immediate physical effects of marijuana include a faster heartbeat (by as much as 50%), bloodshot eyes, and a dry mouth and throat. It can alter one's sense of time and reduce concentration and coordination. Some users experience lightheadedness and giddiness, whereas others feel depressed and sad. Many users have also reported experiencing severe anxiety attacks.

Although the immediate effects of marijuana usually disappear in about four to six hours, it takes about three days for 50% of the drug to be broken down and eliminated from the body. It takes three weeks to completely

excrete the THC from one marijuana cigarette. If a user smokes two joints per week, it takes months for all traces of the THC to disappear from the body.

Hashish and Hash Oil

Two other drugs besides marijuana come from the cannabis plant: hashish and hash oil. Hashish is made from the THC-rich, tar-like material that can be collected from the cannabis plant. This resin is dried and compressed into a variety of forms, including balls and cakes. Larger pieces are broken into smaller pieces and smoked. Most hashish comes from the Middle East, North Africa, Pakistan, and Afghanistan. According to *Drugs of Abuse*, the THC content of hashish in the United States hovered around 5% during the 1990s. Demand in the United States is limited.

Despite the name, hash oil is not directly related to hashish. It is produced by extracting the cannabinoids from the cannabis plant with a solvent. The color and odor of hash oil depend on the solvent used. According to *Drugs of Abuse*, seized hash oil has ranged from amber to

FIGURE 4.2

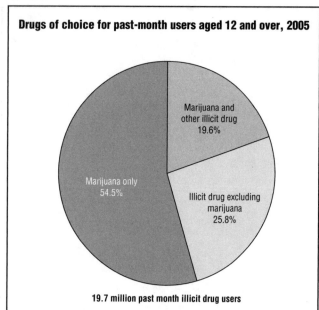

Drugs of choice for past-month users aged 12 and over, 2005

Marijuana and other illicit drug
19.6%

Marijuana only
54.5%

Illicit drug excluding marijuana
25.8%

19.7 million past month illicit drug users

SOURCE: "Figure 2.1. Types of Drugs Used by Past Month Illicit Drug Users Aged 12 or Older: 2005," in *Results from the 2005 National Survey on Drug Use and Health: National Findings*, U.S. Department of Health and Human Services, Substance Abuse and Mental Health Services Administration, Office of Applied Studies, 2006, http://www.oas.samhsa.gov/nsduh/2k5nsduh/2k5Results.pdf (accessed October 12, 2006)

dark brown with about 15% THC. In terms of effect, a drop or two of hash oil on a cigarette is equal to a single joint of marijuana.

Prevalence of Use of Marijuana

Figure 4.4 shows the lifetime, annual, and thirty-day (current) use of marijuana among people eighteen to forty-five years old. Current and annual use generally drops with age: Younger people are more likely to have used marijuana during the past year or past month than older people. However, by the age of forty-five, 79% of the U.S. population in 2005 had tried marijuana sometime in their life.

In 2005, 20% of eighteen-year-olds were current users of marijuana. Use rates dropped to 19% for nineteen- to twenty-year-olds, and to 18% for twenty-one- to twenty-two-year olds. By the age of thirty, 12% of the population were current users of marijuana, and by the age of forty-five, this figure had dropped to 7%. (See Figure 4.4.)

For each year from 2002 to 2005 just over two million people over the age of twelve tried marijuana for the first time. (See Figure 4.5.) The average age of those "first-timers" ranged from 16.8 years in 2003 to 17.4 years in 2005, indicating in general that the average age at which people tried marijuana for the first time is at about seventeen.

PSYCHOTHERAPEUTICS

Psychotherapeutics, a group of drugs that includes pain relievers, tranquilizers, stimulants (including methamphetamine), and sedatives, were the second most used group of illicit drugs from 2002 to 2005. (See Figure 4.3.) SAMHSA data show that use of prescription-type pain relievers as recreational drugs rather than for medical purposes has slowly risen from 1965 to 1995, after which it dramatically rose. Similar trends are seen for other prescription drugs, such as tranquilizers, stimulants, and sedatives. The use of these drugs reached early peaks in the mid- to late 1970s. All but the sedatives reached new highs since 2000, with pain relievers leading the way.

According to the NSDUH, 6.4 million people aged twelve or older were current users of prescription-type psychotherapeutic drugs for nonmedical reasons in 2005. Pain relievers were still the most used and sedatives were the least used psychotherapeutics. Of the 6.4 million users of illicit psychotherapeutics, 4.7 million used pain relievers, 1.8 million used tranquilizers, 1.1 million used stimulants (including 512,000 using methamphetamine), and 272,000 used sedatives. These estimates were similar to the 2004 estimates.

Pain Relievers

Table 4.2 shows percentages of people aged twelve or older who used prescription pain relievers for nonmedical reasons in their lifetime, during the past year, and during the past month in 2004 and 2005. Current users were slightly less than 2% of the population for both 2004 (1.8%) and 2005 (1.9%). Nearly 5% of people used painkillers for nonmedical reasons within the past year in both 2004 (4.7%) and 2005 (4.9%), and more than 13% had tried them at least once in their lifetime.

Most current users of illicit pain relievers in 2004 and 2005 were young adults aged eighteen to twenty-five (4.7% in both 2004 and 2005). Those aged twelve to seventeen were the next most likely to take these drugs (3% in 2004 and 2.7% in 2005). Only 1.2% of those aged twenty-six and older were current illicit users of prescription pain relievers in 2004, and 1.3% in 2005. (See Table 4.2.)

The percentage of current users of illicit pain relievers among most racial groups ranges between 1.4% and 2% of their populations. In 2005, however, the Native Hawaiian and Other Pacific Islander group had a current rate of use of 2.9%, and the American Indian and Alaskan Native group had the highest percentage of current users at 4.6%, a figure that is considerably above the national average. (See Table 4.2.)

NARCOTICS: OXYCONTIN, VICODIN, AND MORPHINE. Two prescription pain relievers that have been popular with users of illicit prescription drugs are OxyContin and Vicodin. Both contain strong narcotic pain relievers.

FIGURE 4.3

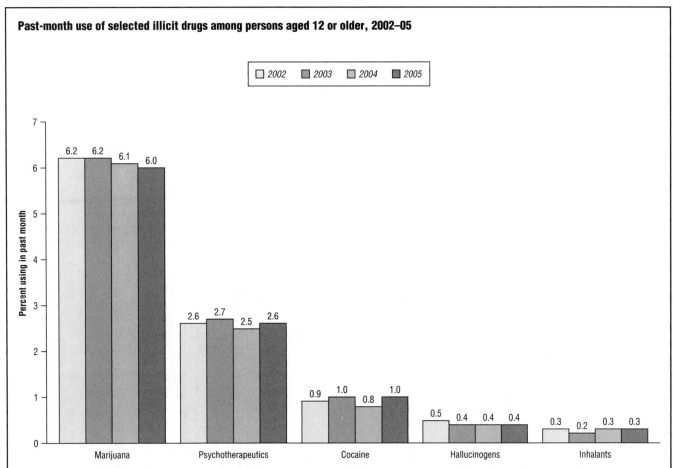

Past-month use of selected illicit drugs among persons aged 12 or older, 2002–05

☐ *2002* ◼ *2003* ☐ *2004* ◼ *2005*

SOURCE: "Figure 2.2. Past Month Use of Selected Illicit Drugs among Persons Aged 12 or Older: 2002–2005," in *Results from the 2005 National Survey on Drug Use and Health: National Findings*, U.S. Department of Health and Human Services, Substance Abuse and Mental Health Services Administration, Office of Applied Studies, 2006, http://www.oas.samhsa.gov/nsduh/2k5nsduh/2k5Results.pdf (accessed October 12, 2006)

OxyContin contains the narcotic oxycodone, and Vicodin contains the narcotic hydrocodone. Narcotics are addictive drugs, such as morphine, codeine, and opium, which reduce pain, alter mood and behavior, and usually induce sleep. Whereas morphine, codeine, and opium are natural narcotics extracted from the juice of the opium poppy, oxycodone and hydrocodone are semisynthetic narcotics; that is, they are made in the laboratory from codeine.

Hydrocodone and oxycodone are two of the most commonly prescribed narcotic painkillers in the United States. Although they are designed to have a less euphoric effect than morphine, they are still highly sought after by recreational users and addicts. Like morphine, these drugs have enough potential for abuse that they are classified as Schedule II substances. (See Table 1.2 in Chapter 1.)

In 2001 OxyContin received an enormous amount of media attention. Although oxycodone, the active ingredient, has been around for a long time in drugs such as Percocet and Percodan, OxyContin contains large amounts of opioids in a time-release caplet. Physicians often prescribe this drug to terminally ill cancer patients who have tremendous pain. When used properly it allows patients to swallow fewer pills yet have pain relief for three times as long as previous preparations of oxycodone. Illicit users of OxyContin crush, chew, or dissolve and inject the drug so that they receive all of the oxycodone at once, giving them a heroin-like high. Emergency rooms have reported serious injuries and deaths from the abuse of OxyContin, often by teenagers and young adults.

The National Drug Intelligence Center reports that as of 2003 abuse of OxyContin was still on the rise, and according to the NSDUH in 2005 there were 526,000 new nonmedical users of OxyContin aged twelve or older. *Monitoring the Future National Survey Results on Drug Use, 1975–2005, Volume 1: Secondary School Students* (2006, http://www.monitoringthefuture.org/pubs/monographs/vol1_2005.pdf) by the National Institute on Drug Abuse (NIDA) and the University of Michigan Institute for Social Research reports that 3.2% of high school seniors had tried OxyContin at least once in their lifetime. The less dangerous drug, Vicodin, showed a lifetime rate of use of 4.5% for high school seniors in 2005.

FIGURE 4.4

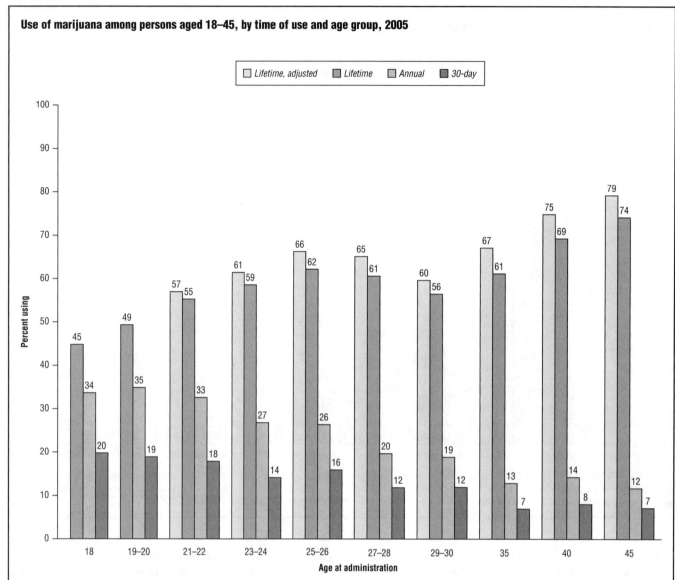

Use of marijuana among persons aged 18–45, by time of use and age group, 2005

Note: Lifetime prevalence estimates were adjusted for inconsistency in self-reports of drug use over time.

SOURCE: L. D. Johnston, P. M. O'Malley, J. G. Bachman, and J. E. Schulenberg, "Figure 4.3. Marijuana: Lifetime, Annual, and Thirty-Day Prevalence among High School Seniors and Adults through Age 45, 2005, by Age Group," in *Monitoring the Future National Survey Results on Drug Use,1975–2005, Volume 2: College Students and Adults Ages 19–45*, National Institute on Drug Abuse and the University of Michigan Institute for Social Research, 2006, http://www.monitoringthefuture.org/pubs/monographs/vol2_2005.pdf (accessed October 6, 2006)

Morphine is extracted from opium and is one of the most effective drugs known for pain relief. It is marketed in the form of oral solutions, sustained-release tablets, and injectable preparations. Morphine is used legally only in hospitals or hospice care, usually to control the severe pain resulting from illnesses such as cancer. Tolerance and dependence develop rapidly in the morphine abuser. According to *Monitoring the Future*, the lifetime rate of use of morphine for high school seniors in 2005 was 2.1%.

Tranquilizers

A tranquilizer is a calming medication that relieves tension and anxiety. Tranquilizers are central nervous system depressants and include a group of drugs called benzodiazepines. They are also known as sleeping pills, "downers," or "tranks." Benzodiazepines have a relatively slow onset but long duration of action. They also have a greater margin of safety than other depressants. According to the DEA, benzodiazepines are among the most widely prescribed medications in the United States. Xanax (alprazolam), Librium (zepoxide), and Valium (diazepam) are in this group.

According to *Monitoring the Future*, most illicit tranquilizer use reported in recent years involved the drugs Valium and Xanax. In 2005 over 3.1% of high school seniors had taken Valium at least once, and 2.3% had taken Xanax at least once.

FIGURE 4.5

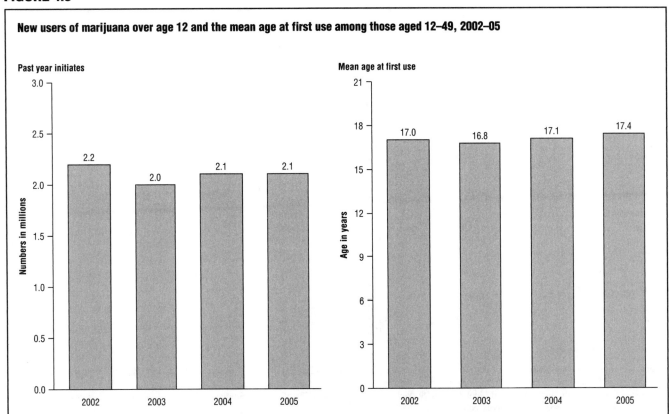

New users of marijuana over age 12 and the mean age at first use among those aged 12–49, 2002–05

SOURCE: "Figure 5.3. Past Year Marijuana Initiates among Persons Aged 12 or Older and Mean Age at First Use of Marijuana among Past Year Marijuana Initiates Aged 12 to 49: 2002–2005," in *Results from the 2005 National Survey on Drug Use and Health: National Findings*, U.S. Department of Health and Human Services, Substance Abuse and Mental Health Services Administration, Office of Applied Studies, 2006, http://www.oas.samhsa.gov/nsduh/2k5nsduh/2k5Results.pdf (accessed October 12, 2006)

Prolonged use of excessive doses of tranquilizers may result in physical and psychological dependence. Because benzodiazepines are eliminated from the body slowly, withdrawal symptoms generally develop slowly, usually seven to ten days after continued high doses are stopped. When these drugs are used illicitly, they are often taken with alcohol or marijuana to achieve a euphoric "high."

ROHYPNOL—THE "DATE RAPE" DRUG. Rohypnol (flunitrazepam), another benzodiazepine, has become increasingly popular among young people. Manufactured as a short-term treatment for severe sleeping disorders, the drug is not marketed legally in the United States and must be smuggled in. It is widely known as a "date rape drug" because would-be rapists have been known to drop it secretly into a woman's drink to facilitate sexual assault. In a sufficiently large dose it can leave a victim physically incapacitated and cause amnesia that may prevent them from recalling an assault. Several states— including Florida, Idaho, Minnesota, New Mexico, North Dakota, Oklahoma, and Pennsylvania—placed the drug under Schedule I control, and the United States has banned its importation and imposed stiff federal penalties for its sale. Responding to pressure from the U.S. government, Roche, the Mexican producer of Rohypnol, began

putting a blue dye in the pill so that it can be seen when dissolved in a drink.

Synthetic Stimulants

Stimulants (uppers) are drugs that produce a sense of euphoria or wakefulness. They are used to increase alertness, boost endurance and productivity, and suppress the appetite. Examples of stimulants are caffeine, nicotine, amphetamine, methamphetamine, and cocaine.

Potent stimulants, such as amphetamine and methamphetamine, make users feel stronger, more decisive, and self-possessed. Chronic users often develop a pattern of using uppers in the morning and depressants (downers), such as alcohol or sleeping pills, at night. Such manipulation interferes with normal body processes and can lead to mental and physical illness.

Large doses of stimulants can produce paranoia and auditory and visual hallucinations. Overdoses can also produce dizziness, tremors, agitation, hostility, panic, headaches, flushed skin, chest pain with palpitations, excessive sweating, vomiting, and abdominal cramps. When withdrawing from stimulants, chronic high-dose users exhibit depression, apathy, fatigue, and disturbed sleep.

TABLE 4.2

Nonmedical use of pain relievers among persons aged 12 and older, by time of use and demographic characteristics, 2004 and 2005

Demographic characteristic	Time period					
	Lifetime		Past year		Past month	
	2004	2005	2004	2005	2004	2005
Total	13.2	13.4	4.7	4.9	1.8	1.9
Age						
12–17	11.4	9.9	7.4	6.9	3.0	2.7
18–25	24.3	25.5	11.9	12.4	4.7	4.7
26 or older	11.5	11.8	3.0	3.3	1.2	1.3
Gender						
Male	14.8	15.4	5.1	5.3	1.9	2.1
Female	11.7	11.6	4.3	4.4	1.8	1.8
Hispanic origin or race						
Not Hispanic or Latino	13.6	13.7	4.8	4.8	1.8	1.9
White	14.6	14.6	5.2	5.1	2.0	2.0
Black or African American	9.0	9.7	3.0	3.8	1.4	1.6
American Indian or Alaska Native	18.1	21.4	5.2	9.0	2.1	4.6
Native Hawaiian or other Pacific Islander	*	12.9	7.8	3.7	*	2.9
Asian	6.2	8.4	1.6	2.7	0.7	1.3
Two or more races	18.9	15.6	7.5	4.3	2.9	1.6
Hispanic or Latino	10.9	11.9	4.1	4.9	1.7	1.9

*Low precision; no estimate reported.

SOURCE: "Table 1.63 B. Nonmedical Use of Pain Relievers in Lifetime, Past Year, and Past Month among Persons Aged 12 or Older, by Demographic Characteristics: Percentages, 2004 and 2005," in *Results from the 2005 National Survey on Drug Use and Health: Detailed Tables*, U.S. Department of Health and Human Services, Substance Abuse and Mental Health Services Administration, Office of Applied Studies, 2006, http://www.oas.samhsa.gov/NSDUH/2k5nsduh/tabs/Sect1peTabs63to67.pdf (accessed October 13, 2006)

AMPHETAMINE AND METHAMPHETAMINE. *Drugs of Abuse* notes that amphetamine has been used to treat sleeping disorders and during World War II to keep soldiers awake. Abuse of amphetamine was noticed in the 1960s: Amphetamine was used by truckers to help them stay alert during long hauls. Athletes used amphetamine to help them train longer. Many people used amphetamine to lose weight. An intravenous form of amphetamine, methamphetamine, was abused by a sub-culture of people dubbed "speed freaks."

In 1965 the federal government realized that amphetamine products had tremendous potential for abuse, so it amended food and drug laws to place stricter controls on their distribution and use. All amphetamines are now Schedule II drugs, in the same category as morphine and cocaine.

Methamphetamine is a powerful stimulant that is relatively easy for drug traffickers to synthesize in home-made labs, so its illegal synthesis, distribution, and sale developed after new laws made amphetamine more difficult to get. Two products that come out of these clandestine labs are the injectable form of methamphetamine ("meth") and the crystallized form ("crystal meth" or "ice") that is smoked. As the DEA (October 27, 2006, http://www.dea.gov/concern/meth.html) notes, both forms are highly addictive and toxic. Chronic abuse results in a schizophrenic-like mental illness characterized by paranoia, picking at the skin, and hallucinations.

Figure 4.6 shows data on past-year meth initiates and meth use during the past year from 2002 to 2005. In 2005, 192,000 people aged twelve and older began using methamphetamine. This figure was down from 318,000 initiates the previous year. In addition, Figure 4.6 shows that the average age at which meth users first used the drug ranged from 18.6 to 20.6 from 2002 to 2005.

Monitoring the Future notes that in 2005 annual methamphetamine use was highest among twenty-one-to twenty-two-year-olds and then declined with age. It determined that annual prevalence in the twenty-one- to twenty-two-year-old group was 3.7% (shown as 4% in Figure 4.7) in 2005 and declined to 1.4% (shown as 1% in Figure 4.7) by the age of twenty-nine to thirty. The use of crystal meth is much lower. Thus, the combined data from both studies show that those who use meth typically take the drug for the first time at about the age of nineteen to twenty. The population of users quickly peaks at the age of twenty-one to twenty-two and then gradually declines by the age of thirty.

Sedatives

Like tranquilizers, sedatives are calming, soothing drugs. They relieve tension and anxiety. Also, like tranquilizers, sedatives are central nervous system depressants, but they include a group of drugs called barbiturates, which are generally stronger than tranquilizers.

FIGURE 4.6

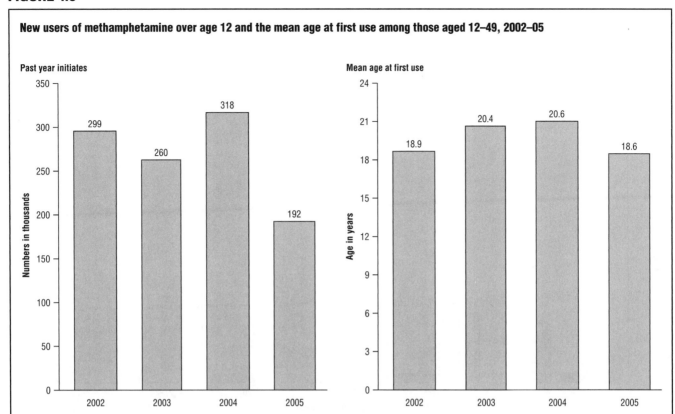

New users of methamphetamine over age 12 and the mean age at first use among those aged 12–49, 2002–05

Past year initiates

Mean age at first use

SOURCE: "Figure 5.4. Past Year Methamphetamine Initiates among Persons Aged 12 or Older and Mean Age at First Use of Methamphetamine among Past Year Methamphetamine Initiates Aged 12 to 49: 2002–2005," in *Results from the 2005 National Survey on Drug Use and Health: National Findings*, U.S. Department of Health and Human Services, Substance Abuse and Mental Health Services Administration, Office of Applied Studies, 2006, http://www.oas.samhsa.gov/nsduh/2k5nsduh/2k5Results.pdf (accessed October 12, 2006)

Barbiturates have many street names, including "barbs," "yellows," and "reds."

Small therapeutic doses of sedatives calm nervous conditions; larger doses cause sleep within a short period. A feeling of excitement precedes the sedation. Because of the usual rapid onset and brief duration of effect, drug abusers find these drugs unattractive. They were the least used illicit psychotherapeutics in 2005. The primary danger of sedatives is that too large a dose can bring a person through stages of sedation, sleep, and coma and ultimately cause death via respiratory failure and cardiovascular complications.

COCAINE

After marijuana and psychotherapeutics, cocaine was the next most used illicit drug in 2005. (See Figure 4.3.) Cocaine is a powerful stimulant of natural origin: It is extracted from the leaves of the coca plant (*Erythroxylon coca*). These plants have been cultivated in the Andean highlands of South America since prehistoric times. In these regions of South America coca leaves are frequently chewed for refreshment and relief from fatigue—in much the same way some North Americans chew tobacco.

According to the Office of National Drug Control Policy (October 30, 2006, http://www.whitehousedrugpolicy.gov/drugfact/cocaine/index.html), pure cocaine was first isolated in the 1880s and used as a local anesthetic in eye surgery. In the late nineteenth and early twentieth centuries it became popular in this country as an anesthetic for nose and throat surgery and dental procedures. Since then, other drugs, such as lidocaine and novocaine, have replaced it as an anesthetic.

Illicit cocaine is distributed as a white crystalline powder, often contaminated, or "cut," with sugars or local anesthetics. The drug is commonly sniffed, or "snorted," through the nasal passages. Less commonly, it is mixed with water and injected, which brings a more intense high because the drug reaches the brain more rapidly.

Cocaine produces a short but extremely powerful rush of energy and confidence. Because the pleasurable effects are so intense, cocaine can lead to severe mental dependency, destroying a person's life as the need for the drug supersedes any other considerations. Physically, cocaine users risk permanent damage to their noses by exposing the cartilage and dissolving the nasal septum (membrane), resulting in a collapsed nose. Cocaine

FIGURE 4.7

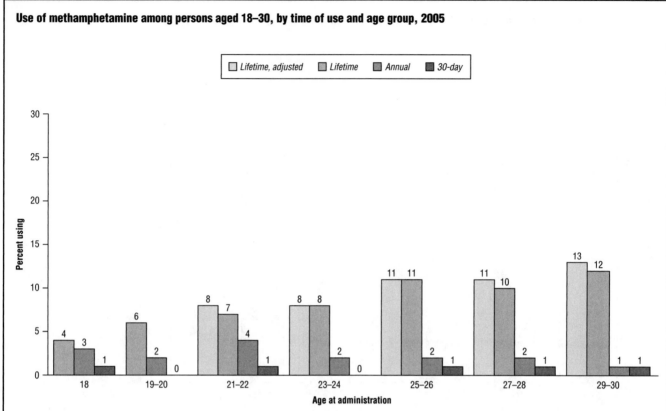

Use of methamphetamine among persons aged 18–30, by time of use and age group, 2005

Legend: ☐ *Lifetime, adjusted* ☐ *Lifetime* ■ *Annual* ■ *30-day*

Note: Lifetime prevalence estimates were adjusted for inconsistency in self-reports of drug use over time.

SOURCE: L. D. Johnston, P. M. O'Malley, J. G. Bachman, and J. E. Schulenberg, "Figure 4.5. Methamphetamine: Lifetime, Annual, and Thirty-Day Prevalence among High School Seniors and Adults through Age 45, 2005, by Age Group," in *Monitoring the Future National Survey Results on Drug Use, 1975–2005, Volume 2: College Students and Adults Ages 19–45*, National Institute on Drug Abuse and the University of Michigan Institute for Social Research, 2006, http://www.monitoringthefuture.org/pubs/monographs/vol2_2005.pdf (accessed October 6, 2006)

significantly increases the risk of heart attack in the first hour after use. Heavy use (two grams or more per week) impairs memory, decision making, and manual dexterity.

Freebasing is a process in which dissolved cocaine is mixed with ether or rum and sodium hydroxide or baking powder. The salt base dissolves, leaving granules of pure cocaine. These are next heated in a pipe until they vaporize. The vapor is inhaled directly into the lungs, causing an immediate high that lasts about ten minutes.

There is a danger of being badly burned if the open flame gets too close to the ether or the rum, causing them to flare up as they burn. When the actor-comedian Richard Pryor set himself on fire while freebasing in 1980, many users started to search for a safer way to achieve the same high. The dangers inherent in freebasing may have been the catalyst for the development of crack cocaine.

Crack Cocaine

Cocaine hydrochloride, the powdered form of cocaine, is soluble in water, can be injected, and is fairly insensitive to heat. When cocaine hydrochloride is converted to cocaine base, it yields a substance that becomes

volatile when heated. According to the NIDA (April 2006, http://www.nida.nih.gov/Infofacts/cocaine.html), "crack" is processed by mixing cocaine with baking soda and heating it to remove the hydrochloride rather than by the more volatile method of using ether. The resultant chips, or "rocks," of pure cocaine are usually smoked in a pipe or added to a cigarette or marijuana joint. The name comes from the crackling sound made when the mixture is smoked.

Inhaling the cocaine fumes produces a rapid, intense, and short-lived effect. This incredible intensity is followed within minutes by an abnormally disconcerting and anxious "crash," which leads almost inevitably to the need for more of the drug—and a great likelihood of addiction.

Prevalence of Cocaine Use

Figure 4.3 shows that about 1% of the population aged twelve and over were current users of cocaine from 2002 to 2005. Narrowing the survey population from eighteen to forty-five gives a clearer picture of actual use, because most users are within this age range. Figure 4.8 shows that in 2005 about 2% of eighteen-through twenty-eight-year-olds were current users of

FIGURE 4.8

Use of cocaine among persons aged 18–45, by time of use and age group, 2005

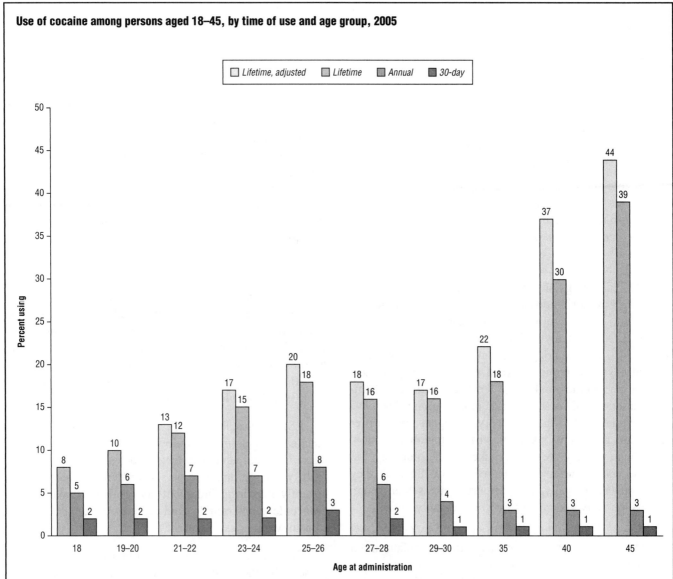

Note: Lifetime prevalence estimates were adjusted for inconsistency in self-reports of drug use over time.

SOURCE: L. D. Johnston, P. M. O'Malley, J. G. Bachman, and J. E. Schulenberg, "Figure 4.7. Cocaine: Lifetime, Annual, and Thirty-Day Prevalence among High School Seniors and Adults through Age 45, 2005, by Age Group," in *Monitoring the Future National Survey Results on Drug Use, 1975–2005, Volume 2: College Students and Adults Ages 19–45*, National Institute on Drug Abuse and the University of Michigan Institute for Social Research, 2006, http://www.monitoringthefuture.org/pubs/monographs/vol2_2005.pdf (accessed October 6, 2006)

about 5% to 8% were annual users. About 1% of twenty-nine- to forty-five-year-olds were current users and 3% to 4% were annual users.

HALLUCINOGENS

After marijuana, psychotherapeutics, and cocaine, hallucinogenic drugs were the next most used illicit drugs in 2005. (See Figure 4.3.) Hallucinogens, also known as psychedelics, are natural or synthetic substances that distort the perceptions of reality. They cause excitation, which can vary from a sense of well-being to severe depression. Time may appear to stand still, and forms and colors seem to change and take on new meaning.

Typically, the heart rate increases, blood pressure rises, and the pupils dilate. The experience may be pleasurable or extremely frightening. The effects of hallucinogens vary from use to use and cannot be predicted.

The most common danger of using hallucinogens is impaired judgment, which can lead to rash decisions and accidents. Long after hallucinogens have been eliminated from the body, users may experience "flashbacks," in the form of perceived intensity of color, the apparent motion of fixed objects, or illusions that present one object when another one is present. Some hallucinogens are present in plants (for example, mescaline in the peyote cactus); others, such as LSD, are synthetic.

Peyote and Mescaline

Mescaline is a psychoactive chemical found naturally in the peyote cactus (*Lophophora williamsii*), which is a small, spineless plant native to Mexico and the U.S. Southwest. The top of the cactus, often called the crown, consists of disk-shaped buttons that can be cut off and dried. These buttons are generally chewed or soaked in water to produce an intoxicating liquid. A dose of 350 to 500 milligrams produces hallucinations lasting from five to twelve hours. Mescaline can be extracted from peyote or produced synthetically.

Peyote and mescaline have long been used by Native Americans in religious ceremonies. A series of court cases resulted in the ruling that the legality of the use of peyote in these ceremonies is decided by individual states.

MDMA and Other Designer Drugs

Designer drugs are those produced in the laboratory by making minor modifications in the chemical structure of existing drugs, resulting in new substances with similar effects. DOM (4-methyl-2,5-dimethoxyamphetamine), DOB (4-bromo-2,5-dimethoxyamphetamine), MDA (3,4-methylenedioxyamphetamine), MDMA (3,4-methylenedioxymethamphetamine), and other "designer drugs" are chemical variations of mescaline and amphetamine that have been synthesized in the laboratory. Designer drugs differ from one another in speed of onset, duration of action, and potency. They are usually taken orally, but they can also be snorted or injected intravenously. Because they are produced illegally, designer drugs are seldom pure. Dosage quantity and quality vary considerably.

The most noted designer drug is MDMA (also called ADAM, ecstasy, or X). It acts as both a stimulant and a psychedelic and is noted for enhancing a user's sense of touch. It was first banned by the DEA in 1985. The Anti-Drug Abuse Act of 1986 (PL 99-570) made all designer drugs illegal. Widespread abuse placed MDMA in Schedule I of the Controlled Substances Act.

Designer drugs such as MDMA are often used at "raves"—large, all-night dance parties once held in unusual places such as warehouses or railroad yards. Although many raves became mainstream events that are professionally organized and held at public venues, the underground style and culture of raves remains an alluring draw to many teenagers. Part of the allure is drug use. For this reason, such drugs are also called "club drugs." (Club drugs include MDMA, Rohypnol, LSD, and methamphetamine, among others.)

Users of MDMA have been known to suffer serious psychological effects—including confusion, depression, sleep problems, drug craving, severe anxiety, and paranoia—both during and sometimes weeks after taking the drug. Physical symptoms include muscle tension, involuntary teeth clenching, nausea, blurred vision, rapid eye movement, faintness, and chills or sweating. MDMA can also interfere with the body's ability to regulate temperature, and severe dehydration, particularly among users who dance for hours while under the drug's influence, is a serious hazard.

According to *Monitoring the Future*, past-year MDMA/ecstasy use by high school seniors rose from 3.6% in 1998 to 9.2% in 2001. Since then a dramatic decline in ecstasy use in this group occurred. By 2005 only about 3% of high school seniors used ecstasy in the past year. Similar declines have occurred among college students and young adults. Survey researchers suggest that the decline is due in large part to educational campaigns on the adverse effects of ecstasy and the wearing off of the novelty effect of all-night raves.

LSD

LSD is one of the most potent mood-changing chemicals in existence. It is often called "acid." Odorless, colorless, and tasteless, it is produced from a substance derived from ergot fungus or from a chemical found in morning glory seeds. Both chemicals are found in Schedule III of the Controlled Substances Act, whereas LSD itself is a Schedule I substance.

LSD is usually sold in tablets ("microdots"), thin squares of gelatin ("window panes"), or impregnated paper ("blotter acid"). Effects of doses higher than thirty to fifty micrograms can persist for ten to twelve hours, severely impairing judgment and decision making. Tolerance develops rapidly, and more of the drug is needed to achieve the desired effect.

Because of its structural similarity to a chemical present in the brain, LSD was originally used as a research tool to study the mechanism of mental illness. It was later adopted by the drug culture of the 1960s. LSD use dropped in the 1980s but showed a resurgence in the 1990s. It is inexpensive, nonaddictive, and one hit can last for eight to twelve hours. Many young people have rediscovered the drug, taking it in a liquid form dropped on the tongue or in the eyes with an eye dropper or by placing impregnated blotter paper on their tongue.

Phencyclidine and Related Drugs

Many drug-treatment professionals believe that phencyclidine (PCP) poses greater risks to the user than any other drug. In the United States most PCP is manufactured in clandestine laboratories and sold on the black market. This drug is sold under at least fifty different names, many of which reflect its bizarre and volatile effects: "Angel Dust," "Crystal," "Supergrass," "Killer Weed," "Embalming Fluid," "Rocket Fuel," and others. It is often sold to users who think they are buying mescaline or LSD.

Because PCP is an anesthetic, it produces an inability to feel pain, which can lead to serious bodily injury. Unlike other hallucinogens, PCP produces depression in some individuals. Regular use often impairs memory, perception, concentration, motor movement, and judgment. PCP can also produce a psychotic state in many ways indistinguishable from schizophrenia, or it can lead to hallucinations, mood swings, paranoia, and amnesia.

Because of the extreme psychic disorders associated with repeated use, or even one dose, of PCP and related drugs, Congress passed the Psychotropic Substances Act of 1978 (PL 95-633). The penalties imposed for the manufacture or possession of these chemicals are the stiffest of any nonnarcotic violation under the Controlled Substances Act.

In its pure form PCP is a white crystalline powder that readily dissolves in water. It can also be taken in tablet or capsule form. It can be swallowed, sniffed, smoked, or injected. It is commonly applied to a leafy material, such as parsley, mint, oregano, or marijuana, and smoked.

Prevalence of Hallucinogen Use

According to the NSDUH, about 1.1 million people aged twelve and over (0.4%) used hallucinogens in the past month in 2005, which was similar to the rate of current use in 2004. As shown in Figure 4.9, current users were concentrated among eighteen- to twenty-four-year-olds, while annual use persisted up into the twenty-nine- to thirty-year-old group. Although ages younger than eighteen years are not shown on Figure 4.9, the NSDUH reports that most of the MDMA/ecstasy initiates in 2005 were aged eighteen and older the first time they used the drug. *Monitoring the Future* shows a lifetime prevalence for hallucinogen use was 3.8% for eighth graders, 5.8% for tenth graders, and 8.8% for twelfth graders in 2005.

INHALANTS

As shown in Figure 4.3, inhalants were the least used group of illicit drugs in 2005. Inhalants are volatile liquids, such as cleaning fluids, glue, gasoline, paint, and turpentine, the vapors of which are inhaled. Sometimes the sprays of aerosols are inhaled, such as those of spray paints, spray deodorants, hair spray, or fabric protector spray. According to the NSDUH, an estimated 877,000 people tried inhalants for the first time in 2005. As in past years, this group was dominated by those aged eighteen and under, representing 72.3% of new users. A small proportion of adults aged twenty-six and older (0.1%) were current inhalant users in 2005.

OTHER ILLICIT DRUGS
Heroin

Heroin is a narcotic, as are OxyContin, Vicodin, and morphine. Heroin, however, is not used as a medicine, so it is not included with the psychotherapeutics.

Heroin is extracted from morphine, which is extracted from opium. This drug was not used extensively until the Bayer Company of Germany began commercial production in 1898. It was widely accepted as a painkiller for years, with the medical profession largely unaware of its potential for addiction. The Harrison Narcotic Act of 1914 (PL 63-223) established control of heroin in the United States.

Pure heroin, a bitter white powder, is usually dissolved and injected. Heroin found "on the street" may vary in color from white to dark brown, depending on the amount of impurities left from the extraction process or the presence of additives, such as food coloring, cocoa, or brown sugar.

"Black tar" heroin is popular in the western United States. A crudely processed form of heroin, black tar is manufactured illegally in Mexico and derives its name from its sticky, dark brown or black appearance. According to USNoDrugs.com, black tar is often sold on the street in its tarlike state and can have purities ranging from 20% to 80%. It can be diluted with substances such as burned cornstarch or converted into a powder. It is most commonly injected.

In the past heroin was usually injected—intravenously (the preferred method), subcutaneously ("skin popping"), or intramuscularly. The increased availability of high-purity heroin, however, meant that users could snort or smoke the drug, which contributed to an increase in heroin use. Snorting or smoking is more appealing to users who fear contracting the human immunodeficiency virus and hepatitis through needles shared with potentially infected users; users who smoke or snort heroin also avoid the historical stigma attached to heroin use: the marks of the needle left on one's skin. Once hooked, however, many abusers who start by snorting or smoking the drug shift to intravenous use.

Symptoms and signs of heroin use include euphoria, drowsiness, respiratory depression, constricted pupils, and nausea. Withdrawal symptoms include watery eyes, runny nose, yawning, loss of appetite, tremors, panic, chills, sweating, nausea, diarrhea, muscle cramps, and insomnia. Elevations in blood pressure, pulse, respiratory rate, and temperature occur as withdrawal progresses. Because heroin abusers are often unaware of the actual strength of the drug and its true contents, they are at risk of overdose. Symptoms of overdose, which may result in death, include shallow breathing, clammy skin, convulsions, and coma. In *Mortality Data from the Drug Abuse Warning Network, 2002* (January 2004, http://oas .samhsa.gov/DAWN2k2/2k2mortality.pdf), the SAMHSA reports that heroin is a frequently reported drug in drug-abuse deaths, either singly or in combination with cocaine and/or alcohol.

FIGURE 4.9

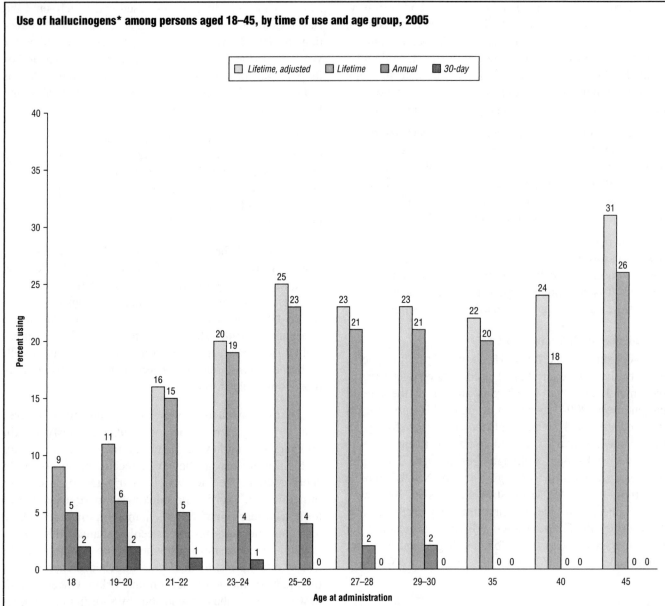

Use of hallucinogens* among persons aged 18–45, by time of use and age group, 2005

Note: Lifetime prevalence estimates were adjusted for inconsistency in self-reports of drug use over time.
*Unadjusted for the possible underreporting of PCP.

SOURCE: L. D. Johnston, P. M. O'Malley, J. G. Bachman, and J. E. Schulenberg, "Figure 4.10. Hallucinogens: Lifetime, Annual, and Thirty-Day Prevalence Among High School Seniors and Adults Through Age 45, 2005 by Age Group," in *Monitoring the Future National Survey Results on Drug Use, 1975–2005, Volume 2: College Students and Adults Ages 19–45*, National Institute on Drug Abuse and the University of Michigan Institute for Social Research, 2006, http://www.monitoringthefuture.org/pubs/monographs/vol2_2005.pdf (accessed October 6, 2006)

The NSDUH reports that 136,000 Americans aged twelve and older were current heroin users in 2005. This is similar to the 2004 estimate.

Anabolic Steroids

Anabolic steroids are drugs derived from the male sex hormone testosterone. They are used illegally by some athletes, including weight lifters, bodybuilders, long-distance runners, cyclists, and others who believe that these drugs can give them a competitive advantage or improve their physical appearance. When used in combination with exercise training and a high-protein diet, anabolic steroids can lead to increased size and strength of muscles, improved endurance, and shorter recovery time between workouts.

Steroids are taken orally or by intramuscular injection. Most are smuggled into the United States and sold at gyms and competitions or by mail-order companies. Concerns about the drug led Congress in 1991 to place anabolic steroids into Schedule III of the Controlled Substances Act.

There is growing evidence of serious health problems from taking anabolic steroids, including cardiovascular and liver damage and harm to reproductive organs. The Department of Justice and the DEA's Diversion Control Program lists the effects of steroids in "Anabolic Steroids—Hidden Dangers" (March 2004, http://www.deadiversion.usdoj.gov/pubs/brochures/steroids/hidden/). Physical side effects include elevated blood pressure and cholesterol levels, severe acne, premature balding, reduced sexual desire, and atrophying of the testicles. Males may develop breasts, whereas females may experience a deepening of the voice, increased body-hair growth, fewer menstrual cycles, and diminished breast size. Some of these effects can be irreversible. In adolescents, bone development may stop, causing stunted growth. Some users become violently aggressive.

By the turn of the twenty-first century some professional sports agencies had begun to acknowledge that widespread steroid use was taking place in their ranks. In 2005 Major League Baseball initiated regular testing of players for steroid use.

Steroid use is not limited to professional athletes, however. The Centers for Disease Control and Prevention (CDC), in "Youth Risk Behavior Surveillance—United States, 2005" (June 9, 2006, http://www.cdc.gov/mmwr/PDF/SS/SS5505.pdf), reports that in 2006, 4.2% of male high school students and 2.3% of female students had used illegal steroids by the time they were seniors. *Monitoring the Future* determined annual prevalence rates for androstenedione, a precursor to anabolic steroids, which was available over the counter until early 2005. Among males, annual prevalence rates of this drug in 2005 were 1%, 1.4%, and 2.7% in eighth, tenth, and twelfth grades, respectively. The rates among females in 2005 were much lower than among males: 0.3%, 0.4%, and 0.5% in eighth, tenth, and twelfth grades, respectively.

ILLICIT DRUG USE DURING PREGNANCY

Illicit drug use during pregnancy places both mother and the embryo/fetus at risk for serious health problems. For example, a fetus may become addicted to heroin in its mother's womb—provided the fetus reaches full term and is born (fetal death is a possibility). Cocaine use by the pregnant mother carries similar risks to the fetus and may kill the mother as well. LSD use may lead to birth defects. PCP users may have smaller-than-normal babies who later turn out to have poor muscle control. Learning disabilities are associated with children born to pregnant women using cocaine and MDMA/ecstasy. Smoking marijuana may prevent an embryo from attaching to the uterine wall and halt pregnancies.

The NSDUH surveyed pregnant women as to their illicit drug use. Results from this 2005 survey, as well as

from those conducted in 2002, 2003, and 2004, are shown in Table 4.3. A smaller percentage of pregnant women took illicit drugs than did women who were not pregnant. However, illicit drug use did occur: In 2004–05, 3.9% of pregnant women took drugs. The most prevalent illicit drug use during pregnancy was smoking marijuana and hashish: 2.8% in 2004–05, down from 3.5% in 2002–03. Although smoking marijuana may seem safe to some pregnant women, it is not. The NIDA, in *NIDA Info-Facts: Marijuana* (April 2006, http://www.nida.nih.gov/infofacts/marijuana.html), lists many of the effects of marijuana abuse during pregnancy, all of which relate to detrimental effects on the developing brain and other parts of the nervous system of the fetus.

The next most used illicit drugs during pregnancy are psychotherapeutics taken for nonmedical reasons. Over 1% of pregnant women in 2002–03 and 2004–05 took these prescription drugs, such as pain relievers, tranquilizers, stimulants, and sedatives. Of the psychotherapeutics, pain relievers were taken the most often. The percentage of pregnant women who took heroin, hallucinogens, or inhalants during their pregnancies was low. (See Table 4.3.)

DRUGS PLAY A MAJOR ROLE IN ARRESTS

The Bureau of Justice Statistics (BJS) estimates in *Drugs and Crime Facts* (September 21, 2006, http://www.ojp.usdoj.gov/bjs/pub/pdf/dcf.pdf) that there were more than 1.8 million arrests for drug abuse violations in 2005. As Figure 4.10 shows, the estimated number of arrests for drug abuse violations has been increasing steadily since the early 1990s. Drug arrests also increased as a percentage of all arrests, from 7.4% in 1987 to 13.1% in 2005. Drug abuse violations topped the list of the seven leading arrest offenses in the United States in 2005. That year more people were arrested for drug abuse violations than were arrested for driving under the influence (1.4 million), simple assault (1.3 million), larceny/theft (1.1 million), disorderly conduct (678,000), liquor laws (568,000), or drunkenness (556,000).

Possession versus Sale

Most people arrested for drug offenses are charged with possession—carrying some kind of drug—rather than with trafficking—the sale or manufacture of drugs. In *Drugs and Crime Facts*, the BJS states that more than four-fifths of those arrested for drug law violations were for possession.

ARRESTEE DRUG USE

The National Institute of Justice published the annual *Arrestee Drug Abuse Monitoring* (*ADAM*) report from 1987 to 2003. The most recent report, *2000 Arrestee Drug Abuse Monitoring: Annual Report* (April 2003,

TABLE 4.3

Percentage of past-month illicit drug use among females aged 15–44, by pregnancy status, 2002–03 and 2004–05

	Total[a]		Pregnancy status			
			Pregnant		Not pregnant	
Drug	2002–2003	2004–2005	2002–2003	2004–2005	2002–2003	2004–2005
Illicit drugs[b]	10.2	9.6	4.3	3.9	10.4	9.9
Marijuana and hashish	7.4	6.9	3.5	2.8	7.6	7.1
Cocaine	1.0	1.1	0.3	0.3	1.0	1.1
Crack	0.2	0.3	0.0	0.1	0.2	0.3
Heroin	0.1	0.1	0.0	0.1	0.1	0.1
Hallucinogens	0.6	0.4	0.3	0.2	0.6	0.4
LSD	0.1	0.0	0.0	0.1	0.1	0.0
PCP	0.0	0.0	0.1	*	0.0	0.0
Ecstasy	0.4	0.3	0.1	0.1	0.4	0.3
Inhalants	0.2	0.2	0.0	0.1	0.2	0.2
Nonmedical use of psychotherapeutics[c]	3.8	3.8	1.2	1.3	3.9	3.9
Pain relievers	2.6	2.7	0.9	1.2	2.7	2.8
OxyContin®	—	0.2	—	0.1	—	0.2
Tranquilizers	1.1	1.1	0.2	0.3	1.2	1.1
Stimulants	0.8	0.8	0.3	0.1	0.8	0.9
Methamphetamine	0.3	0.4	0.0	0.1	0.3	0.4
Sedatives	0.2	0.2	0.1	0.0	0.2	0.2
Illicit drugs other than marijuana[b]	**4.8**	**4.7**	**1.4**	**1.6**	**4.9**	**4.9**

*Low precision; no estimate reported.
— Not available.
[a]Estimates in the total column are for all females aged 15 to 44, including those with unknown pregnancy status.
[b]Illicit drugs include marijuana/hashish, cocaine (including crack), heroin, hallucinogens, inhalants, or prescription-type psychotherapeutics used nonmedically. Illicit drugs other than marijuana include cocaine (including crack), heroin, hallucinogens, inhalants, or prescription-type psychotherapeutics used nonmedically.
[c]Nonmedical use of prescription-type psychotherapeutics includes the nonmedical use of pain relievers, tranquilizers, stimulants, or sedatives and does not include over-the-counter drugs.

SOURCE: "Table 7.68B. Types of Illicit Drug Use in the Past Month among Females Aged 15 to 44, by Pregnancy Status: Percentages, Annual Average Based on 2002–2003 and 2004–2005," in *Results from the 2005 National Survey on Drug Use and Health: Detailed Tables*, U.S. Department of Health and Human Services, Substance Abuse and Mental Health Services Administration, Office of Applied Studies, 2006, http://www.oas.samhsa.gov/nsduh/2k5nsduh/tabs/Sect7peTabs68to75.pdf (accessed October 17, 2006)

FIGURE 4.10

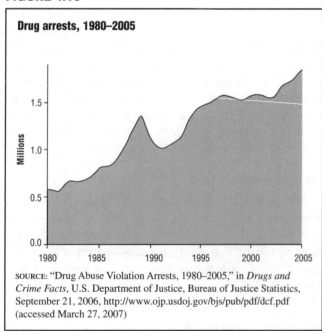

Drug arrests, 1980–2005

SOURCE: "Drug Abuse Violation Arrests, 1980–2005," in *Drugs and Crime Facts*, U.S. Department of Justice, Bureau of Justice Statistics, September 21, 2006, http://www.ojp.usdoj.gov/bjs/pub/pdf/dcf.pdf (accessed March 27, 2007)

http://www.ncjrs.gov/pdffiles1/nij/193013.pdf), analyzes data gathered through 2000. The report surveyed arrestees in thirty-five urban sites about drug use in the past year and conducted urinalyses to determine if ten different drugs had been used recently. The *2000 ADAM* reports on drugs in six categories: cocaine (crack or powder), marijuana, opiates, methamphetamine, phencyclidine (PCP), and "any drug," which could include the remainder of the other five drugs. The report asserts that "people who come to the attention of the criminal justice system by being arrested are more often than not users of drugs and/or alcohol." This claim is supported by the finding that in half of the sites surveyed by the report, urinalysis revealed that more than 64% of adult male arrestees had used at least one of five drugs: marijuana, cocaine, opiates, methamphetamine, or PCP. Use ranged from a low of 52% of arrestees in Anchorage, Alaska, to a high of 80% in New York, but was consistently a majority of those arrested. In half the sites at least 21% tested positive for more than one drug, with a low of 10% in Anchorage and Albany, New York, and a high of 34% in Chicago.

The *ADAM* program ended in 2004 in response to budgetary considerations, with plans of being resumed when funding became available. As of early 2007, the program had not been reinstituted.

FIGURE 4.11

Impact of drugs on state prison populations, 1980–2003

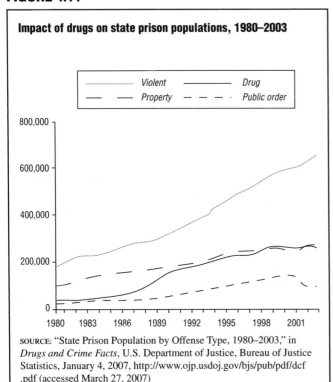

SOURCE: "State Prison Population by Offense Type, 1980–2003," in *Drugs and Crime Facts*, U.S. Department of Justice, Bureau of Justice Statistics, January 4, 2007, http://www.ojp.usdoj.gov/bjs/pub/pdf/dcf.pdf (accessed March 27, 2007)

Arrests and Race

Enforcing the official public policy on drugs has a significant impact on the nation's justice system: local policing, the courts, and the state and federal corrections systems. A relatively small percentage of total users are arrested, but at increasing rates. Sentencing policies have changed to require mandatory incarceration of those who possess, not just those who sell, drugs. Prison populations have swollen as a consequence, putting pressure on prison capacities. According to Paige M. Harrison and Allen J. Beck, in *Prisoners in 2005* (January 19, 2007, http://www.ojp.usdoj.gov/bjs/pub/pdf/p05.pdf), from 1995 to 2004 drug offenders accounted for nearly half of the growth in the federal inmate population.

However, arrest, sentencing, and incarceration rates are different for whites, African-Americans, and Hispanics. The BJS reports in the *Compendium of Federal Justice Statistics, 2004* (December 2006, http://www.ojp.usdoj.gov/bjs/pub/pdf/cfjs04.pdf) that in 2004 two-thirds (66%) of federal drug offense arrestees were white, and most of the remaining third (31%) were African-American. The majority of suspects arrested for amphetamines, marijuana, heroin, and other drugs were white, whereas more African-Americans (57%) were arrested for cocaine-related drug use than were whites (41%).

In *Drugs and Crime Facts*, the BJS reports that of the 158,426 sentenced inmates under federal jurisdiction at the close of 2003, more than half (86,972 inmates or 55%)

TABLE 4.4

Percent of sentenced offenders in state prisons, by race and offense, 2003

	White	Black	Hispanic
Total	**100%**	**100%**	**100%**
Violent	50	52	53
Property	27	18	17
Drug	14	24	23
Public order	9	6	6

SOURCE: "Estimated Percent of Sentenced Prisoners under State Jurisdiction, by Race and Offense, 2003," in *Drugs and Crime Facts*, U.S. Department of Justice, Bureau of Justice Statistics, January 4, 2007, http://www.ojp.usdoj.gov/bjs/pub/pdf/dcf.pdf (accessed March 27, 2007)

were drug offenders. As Figure 4.11 shows, the number of people in state correctional facilities for drug offenses more than doubled from 120,100 in 1989 to 250,900 in 2003. By 2003 drug offenses accounted for 20% of prisoners under state jurisdiction. That year, nearly one-quarter of African-Americans (24%) and Hispanics (23%), compared with 14% of whites in state prison populations, were sentenced for drug offenses. (See Table 4.4.)

When drug abuse violation arrest rates by race are compared with the general U.S. population, African-Americans are arrested disproportionately. For example, according to the BJS, in the *Sourcebook of Criminal Justice Statistics Online* (2005, http://www.albany.edu/sourcebook/), the U.S. Census Bureau estimated in 2004 that the U.S. population was 80.4% and 12.9% African-American, with other races making up the remainder. An analysis of drug arrests in 2004 reveals that 65.8% of those arrested were white—underrepresented in comparison to the population statistic of 80.4%—and 32.9% of those arrested were African-American—more than twice as many as would be expected if arrest rates reflected population statistics. (See Table 4.5.)

CONVICTION AND SENTENCING TRENDS

According to the BJS, in *Drugs and Crime Facts*, drug prosecutions account for an increasing proportion of the criminal caseload, growing from 21% of defendants in 1982 to 27% in 2004. Similarly, the number of convictions of drug defendants increased from 76% to 92% during the same period. Along with higher conviction rates came more and longer prison sentences for drug offenses. The proportion of drug offenders sentenced to prison rose from 79% in 1988 to 91% in 2002. Table 4.6 shows that the duration of sentences increased from 78 months in 1988 to 85.7 months in 2005.

Convictions and Race

The BJS notes in *Drugs and Crime Facts* that of the 266,465 adults arrested for drug trafficking in 2002, 212,810 were convicted. Of those convicted, 85% were

TABLE 4.5

Drug arrests by race, 2004

Offense charged	Total arrests					Percent*				
	Total	White	Black	American Indian or Alaskan Native	Asian or Pacific Islander	Total	White	Black	American Indian or Alaskan Native	Asian or Pacific Islander
Drug abuse violations	1,249,088	822,307	410,552	7,868	8,361	100.0	65.8	32.9	0.6	0.7

*Because of rounding, percents may not add to total.

SOURCE: Adapted from Ann L. Pastore and Kathleen Maguire, eds.,"Table 4.10.2004. Arrests by Offense Charged, Age Group, and Race, United States, 2004," in *Sourcebook of Criminal Justice Statistics Online*, U.S. Department of Justice, Bureau of Justice Statistics, University at Albany School of Criminal Justice, Hindelang Criminal Justice Resource Center, 2005, http://www.albany.edu/sourcebook/pdf/t4102004.pdf (accessed March 27, 2007)

male, 51% were white, and 47% were African-American. In absolute numbers, more whites are arrested and convicted for drug violations than African-Americans, but African-Americans are much more likely not only to be arrested but also to be convicted in proportion to their representation in the population.

Once convicted for drug offenses, more African-Americans, on average, are incarcerated than whites, and more whites, on average, receive milder jail sentences (less than a year) than African-Americans or get probation or split sentences. According to the BJS, in the *Sourcebook of Criminal Justice Statistics, 1996–2001* (2001), of all whites convicted of drug offenses in 2000, 63% were incarcerated, versus 73% of all African-Americans convicted of drug offenses. Among convicted whites, 30% went to prison (sentences of a year or longer), and among African-Americans this figure was 48%. About one-third (32%) of whites were given a milder jail sentence, versus 25% of African-Americans. A higher proportion of whites received nonincarceration sentences (37%) than African-Americans (28%). The same was true for probation, which was received by 32% of whites versus 24% of African-Americans.

The Human Rights Watch (HRW), an independent, nongovernmental organization dedicated to protecting the human rights of people around the world, documents racial disparities in the incarceration of state drug offenders. The HRW considers crime rates, law enforcement priorities, and sentencing legislation as factors that contribute to creating racial disparities in incarceration. It contends that African-Americans have been disproportionately affected by the war on drugs, which largely aims to arrest, prosecute, and imprison street-level drug offenders from inner-city areas.

The HRW briefing "Race and Incarceration in the United States" (February 27, 2002, http://www.hrw.org/backgrounder/usa/race/) reports that in at least fifteen states African-American men are sent to prison on drug charges at rates ranging from twenty to fifty-seven times those of white men. The HRW asserts that racial profiling

of minorities by the criminal justice system contributes to the overrepresentation of minorities in the incarcerated population and observes that in the federal courts African-Americans are prosecuted more frequently than whites for crack cocaine offenses. As a result, African-Americans disproportionately experience the consequences of the longer sentences for crack versus powder cocaine mandated by federal law.

Truth-in-Sentencing

Sentence lengths do not, however, fully convey the picture. The time actually served for an offense is a better indicator of the actual "price" society extracts for an offense. Thus, for instance, a person sentenced to five years who serves 60% of the sentence and is then paroled serves as long as a person sentenced to four years who serves 75% of the sentence. In both cases time served will be three years. Public perceptions in the late 1970s that felons were sentenced only to walk free after doing a brief stint in prison culminated in the truth-in-sentencing movement, an attempt at the state and federal levels to reform sentencing practices. Washington State passed the first truth-in-sentencing statute in 1984. Congress established the U.S. Sentencing Commission in the same year with the purpose of setting mandatory sentence lengths. The consequence of these actions (forty-two states and the District of Columbia have passed truth-in-sentencing laws since 1984) was an increase in time served even as, in some areas, the average length of the formal sentences grew shorter.

Under federal sentencing guidelines, people who are sentenced are required to serve 85% of the imposed sentence; however, there is no comparable requirement at the state level. In *Felony Sentences in State Courts, 2002* (December 2004, http://www.ojp.usdoj.gov/bjs/pub/pdf/fssc02.pdf), Matthew R. Durose and Patrick A. Langan report that in 2002 people convicted of drug trafficking convictions in the state courts were sentenced to an average of fifty-five months in prison, but generally served less than half of the sentence—about

TABLE 4.6

Drug charges, by type and sentence lengths, in U.S. District Courts, 1945–2005

		Type of sentence									Average sentence to imprisonment (in months)[d]	Average sentence to probation (in months)[e]
		Imprisonment										
		Regular sentences[a]										
	Total	Total regular	1 through 12 months	13 through 35 months	36 through 60 months	Over 60 months	Life sentences	Other[b]	Probation	Fine and other[c]		
1945	861	X	308	360	140	53	NA	X	287	37	22.2	NA
1946	949	X	430	377	108	34	NA	X	369	20	18.7	NA
1947	1,128	X	471	452	161	44	NA	X	504	38	19.7	NA
1948	1,048	X	488	408	122	30	NA	X	411	23	18.6	NA
1949	1,187	X	541	451	152	43	NA	X	398	13	18.9	NA
1950	1,654	X	595	736	218	105	NA	X	471	11	21.9	NA
1951	1,659	X	473	671	328	187	NA	X	345	24	27.1	NA
1952	1,551	X	221	652	402	276	NA	X	312	6	35.2	NA
1953	1,586	X	108	789	358	331	NA	X	403	14	38.4	NA
1954	1,483	X	72	681	360	370	NA	X	411	16	41.3	NA
1955	1,457	X	47	648	360	402	NA	X	329	17	43.5	NA
1956	1,258	X	30	511	341	376	NA	X	250	13	45.8	NA
1957	1,432	X	16	326	248	842	NA	X	220	2	66.0	NA
1958	1,351	X	25	167	141	1,018	NA	X	282	8	69.4	NA
1959	1,151	X	43	126	95	887	NA	X	224	3	74.2	NA
1960	1,232	X	33	145	148	906	NA	X	271	3	72.8	NA
1961	1,258	X	42	126	105	985	NA	X	252	5	74.0	NA
1962	1,173	X	38	129	106	900	NA	X	217	13	70.5	NA
1963	1,085	X	39	144	113	789	NA	X	304	17	70.1	NA
1964	1,076	X	28	142	157	749	NA	X	309	23	63.7	NA
1965	1,257	X	53	186	197	821	NA	X	480	18	60.3	NA
1966	1,272	X	85	154	276	757	NA	X	589	13	61.3	NA
1967	1,180	X	83	139	245	713	NA	X	620	22	62.0	NA
1968	1,368	X	93	141	293	841	NA	X	728	33	64.4	NA
1969	1,581	X	110	179	500	892	NA	X	1,110	18	63.7	NA
1970	1,283	X	101	166	276	740	NA	X	1,156	22	64.8	NA
1971	1,834	X	249	300	428	857	NA	X	1,258	70	58.5	NA
1972	3,050	X	882	396	789	983	NA	X	2,068	130	46.4	NA
1973	5,097	X	1,445	744	1,343	1,565	NA	X	2,591	126	45.5	NA
1974	5,125	X	1,547	792	1,390	1,396	NA	X	3,039	81	43.7	NA
1975	4,887	X	1,366	706	1,441	1,374	NA	X	3,209	55	45.3	NA
1976	5,039	X	1,221	790	1,544	1,484	NA	X	2,927	75	47.6	NA
1977	5,223	X	1,505	886	1,366	1,466	NA	X	2,324	88	47.3	NA
1978	4,119	3,605	885	623	956	1,141	NA	514	1,630	68	51.3	38.6
1979	3,641	2,820	369	614	868	969	NA	821	1,379	47	50.8	37.8
1980	3,479	2,547	281	565	792	909	NA	932	1,232	38	54.5	38.7
1981	3,856	2,865	403	578	748	1,136	NA	991	1,371	119	55.5	36.6
1982	4,586	3,516	383	729	966	1,438	NA	1,070	1,617	133	61.4	34.1
1983	5,449	4,150	447	890	1,011	1,802	NA	1,299	1,893	148	63.8	33.7
1984	5,756	4,306	354	845	1,173	1,934	NA	1,450	1,584	119	65.7	43.2
1985	6,786	5,207	411	1,103	1,459	2,234	NA	1,579	2,039	238	64.8	36.2
1986	8,152	6,601	506	1,271	1,808	3,016	NA	1,551	2,353	259	70.0	38.7
1987	9,907	8,188	613	1,491	2,049	4,035	NA	1,719	2,680	112	73.0	39.9
1988	9,983	8,560	708	1,466	1,577	4,809	NA	1,423	3,042	137	78.0	33.4
1989	11,626	10,838	1,270	2,343	1,844	5,381	NA	788	2,358	155	73.8	32.8
1990	13,838	13,462	1,490	3,047	1,801	7,124	NA	376	2,135	215	79.3	32.3
1991	14,382[f]	14,286	1,687	2,828	3,063	6,708	34	61	1,896	68	95.7	53.4
1992	16,040	15,775	1,810	3,423	3,397	7,145	80	185	2,011	194	87.8	38.7
1993	16,995[f]	16,639	2,097	3,383	4,128	7,031	186	169	1,943	310	83.2	35.8
1994	15,623	15,130	1,836	3,074	3,798	6,422	238	255	1,908	73	84.3	34.4
1995	14,157	13,734	1,606	2,716	3,311	6,101	150	273	1,597	107	88.7	33.6
1996	18,333	16,684	1,643	3,334	4,025	7,113	197	372	1,534	112	82.5	35.0
1997	18,231[f]	17,456	1,687	4,166	4,445	7,158	228	546	1,523	79	79.3	34.9
1998	19,809	19,062	2,100	4,443	4,517	8,002	180	567	1,629	91	78.0	34.9
1999	22,443[f]	21,513	2,670	5,074	5,240	8,529	205	724	1,719	85	74.6	34.2
2000	23,120	22,207	2,523	5,095	5,452	9,137	148	765	1,591	75	75.7	35.1
2001	24,011	23,127	2,780	5,350	5,670	9,327	122	762	1,671	133	73.8	34.5
2002	25,031	23,838	2,825	5,250	5,727	10,036	168	1,025	1,947	148	75.9	33.4
2003	25,060	23,937	2,632	4,781	5,967	10,557	157	966	1,781	145	80.2	32.2
2004	23,920	22,984	2,581	4,181	5,553	10,669	146	790	1,598	184	82.5	28.4
2005	24,786	23,831	2,389	4,296	5,719	11,427	151	804	1,508	294	85.7	32.7

two years. Similarly, the average prison sentence for drug possession was thirty-five months, of which the average time served was estimated to be fourteen months. As these data show, there remains a rather wide gap between the average sentence imposed and the actual time served.

DRUGS' IMPACT ON PRISONS

According to the BJS, in "Probation and Parole Statistics" (November 30, 2006, http://www.ojp.usdoj.gov/bjs/pandp.htm), on December 31, 2005, there were 4.9 million prisoners held in federal or state prisons or in local jails. The BJS reports in the *Compendium of*

TABLE 4.6

Drug charges, by type and sentence lengths, in U.S. District Courts, 1945–2005 [CONTINUED]

Note: Two reporting changes were made during fiscal year 1976. Beginning Oct. 1, 1975, all minor offenses (offenses involving penalties that do not exceed 1 year imprisonment or a fine of more than $1,000), with the exception of most petty offenses (offenses involving penalties that do not exceed 6 months incarceration and/or a fine of not more than $500), are included. Minor offenses are generally disposed of by magistrate judges and, in past years, most of these minor offenses would not have been counted in the workload of the district courts. Second, when the federal government's motion to dismiss an original indictment or information is granted, the superseding indictment or information does not become a new case as in the years prior to 1976, but remains the same case. (An indictment is the charging document of the grand jury, and an information is the charging document of the U.S. attorney.) Data for 1945–91 are reported for the 12-month period ending June 30. Beginning in 1992, data are reported for the federal fiscal year, which is the 12-month period ending September 30. These data were taken from the first year they were reported and do not reflect revisions made in subsequent years.

The District of Columbia is excluded from these data through 1973. The territorial courts of the Virgin Islands, Canal Zone, and Guam are excluded through 1976. Between 1991 and 2004, defendants charged in two or more cases that were terminated during the year are counted only once. Beginning in 2005, defendants charged in two or more cases that were terminated during the year are counted separately for each case.

[a]Includes sentences of more than 6 months that are to be followed by a term of probation (mixed sentences). Beginning in 1991, includes sentences of at least 1 month that may be followed by a term of probation.
[b]From 1978–88, "other" includes split sentences, indeterminate sentences, and Youth Corrections Act and youthful offender sentences. In 1989 and 1990, the category includes split sentences and indeterminate sentences. Beginning in 1991, "other" includes deportation, suspended and sealed sentences, imprisonment of 4 days or less, and no sentence.
[c]Includes supervised release, probation of 4 days or less, suspended sentences, sealed sentences, and no sentence.
[d]From 1978–90, split sentences, Youth Corrections Act and youthful offender sentences, and life sentences were not included in computing average sentence. Beginning in 1991, life sentences, death sentences, deportation, suspended and sealed sentences, imprisonment of 4 days or less, and no sentence also are not included in computing average sentence.
[e]From 1986–90, split sentences, indeterminate sentences, and Youth Corrections Act and youthful offender sentences were not included in computing average sentence. Beginning in 1991, supervised release, probation of 4 days or less, suspended sentences, sealed sentences, and no sentence also are not included in computing average sentence.
[f]Includes one death sentence.

SOURCE: Ann L. Pastore and Kathleen Maguire, eds., "Table 5.38.2005. Defendants Sentenced for Violation of Drug Laws in U.S. District Courts," in *Sourcebook of Criminal Justice Statistics Online*, U.S. Department of Justice, Bureau of Justice Statistics, University at Albany School of Criminal Justice, Hindelang Criminal Justice Resource Center, 2005, http://www.albany.edu/sourcebook/pdf/t5382005.pdf (accessed March 27, 2007)

Federal Justice Statistics, 2004 that of those held in state prisons in 2003, the most recent year for which data are available, about one in five were in prison for drug offenses. Drug offenders outnumbered those held for burglary, larceny, auto theft, fraud, and all other property crimes.

According to *Drugs and Crime Facts*, the BJS indicates that over a period of twenty years prisoners incarcerated for drug violations have become the second most populous category at the state level and the largest group in the federal prison system. People incarcerated in state prison systems for drug offenses increased by 1,220% between 1980 and 2003. In 2004 drug offenders made up 55% of the federal prison system population.

The BJS indicates in *Drugs and Crime Facts* that people in prison for drug offenses were 6% of the state prison population in 1980. By 1990 they peaked at 21.8% of the prison population and then dropped slightly to 20.2% in 2003.

Harrison and Beck note that in 2003 the state prison population of drug offenders (250,900 people in 2003) were overwhelmingly male (90%). The majority (53%) of these prisoners were African-American, about a quarter (26%) were white, and one-fifth (20%) were Hispanic.

Crowded Prisons and Growing Costs

Overcrowding has been an issue in America's prison system for many years. In 2005 state prisons operated on average at 101% of capacity and federal prisons operated at 134% of capacity. Pressures on correctional facilities are the result of growing rates of drug arrests that result in felony convictions combined with truth-in-sentencing policies that cause actual time served to increase.

According to the BJS (March 2007, http://www.albany.edu/sourcebook/pdf/t192003.pdf), state expenditures on corrections were $4.2 billion in 1980, at a time when people serving time for drug offenses were just 6% of all state prisoners. Therefore, in 1980 about $252 million was used to house, hold, guard, feed, clothe, and provide medical care for drug offenders. By 2003 costs of state corrections had risen to $36.9 billion. Drug offenders were about one-fifth of state prison populations at this time, meaning that nearly $7.4 billion was spent to imprison them.

THE BROADER RELATIONSHIP BETWEEN ILLICIT DRUGS AND CRIME

The relationship between illicit drugs and crime goes beyond the fact that illicit drug use is inherently illegal. There are strong correlations between drug use and a variety of nondrug crimes. There are usually three reasons given for this correlation:

1. Drugs may reduce inhibitions or stimulate aggression and interfere with the ability to earn legitimate income.

2. People who develop a dependence on an illegal drug need a substantial income to pay for them and may commit crimes to fund their habit.

3. Drug trafficking may lead to crimes such as extortion, aggravated assault, and homicide. For example, the Department of Justice (September 2006, http://www.ojp.usdoj.gov/bjs/dcf/duc.htm) reports that about 4% to 7% of homicides committed each year between 1987 and 2005 were drug related.

In *Adult Patterns of Criminal Behavior* (June 1996, http://www.ncjrs.gov/pdffiles/adultpat.pdf), Julie Horney,

TABLE 4.7

TABLE 4.8

Drug use among state and federal prisoners, by type of offense, 2004

| | Percent of prisoners who reported— | | | |
| | use in the month before the offense | | use at the time of the offense | |
Type of offense	State	Federal	State	Federal
Total[a]	**56.0%**	**50.2%**	**32.1%**	**26.4%**
Violent offenses	49.6%	49.1%	27.7%	24.0%
Homicide	48.9	44.9	27.3	16.8
Sexual assault[b]	32.3	17.0	17.4	13.8
Robbery	66.6	56.9	40.7	29.4
Assault	48.9	42.3	24.1	20.1
Property offenses	64.0%	27.7%	38.5%	13.6%
Burglary	67.7	—	41.1	—
Larceny/theft	66.6	—	40.1	—
Motor vehicle theft	65.4	—	38.7	—
Fraud	56.3	22.8	34.1	9.3
Drug offenses	71.9%	57.3%	43.6%	32.3%
Possession	76.4	46.4	46.0	20.9
Trafficking	70.0	58.8	42.3	33.8
Public-order offenses[c]	49.9%	41.2%	25.4%	18.7%
Weapons	53.3	53.8	27.6	27.8
Other public-order	48.7	26.5	24.6	8.0

— Not calculated; too few cases to permit calculation.
[a]Includes offenses not shown.
[b]Includes rape and other sexual assault.
[c]Excluding driving while intoxicated (DWI) and driving under the influence (DUI).

SOURCE: Christopher J. Mumola and Jennifer C. Karberg, "Table 4. Drug Use of State and Federal Prisoners, by Type of Offense, 2004," in *Drug Use and Dependence, State and Federal Prisoners, 2004*, U.S. Department of Justice, Office of Justice Programs, Bureau of Justice Statistics, October 2006, http://www.ojp.usdoj.gov/bjs/pub/pdf/dudsfp04.pdf (accessed October 13, 2006)

Drug use among state and federal prisoners in the month before their offense, by demographic characteristics, 1997 and 2004

| | State | | Federal | |
Characteristic	2004	1997	2004	1997
All prisoners	56.0%	56.5%	50.2%	44.8%
Gender				
Male	55.7%	56.1%	50.4%	45.4%
Female	59.3	62.4	47.6	36.7
Race/Hispanic origin				
White[a]	57.7%	55.2%	58.2%	49.4%
Black[a]	56.0	58.3	52.7	47.2
Hispanic	53.5	55.0	38.4	37.5
Other[a, b]	52.9	52.7	48.4	38.5
Age				
24 or younger	66.2%	63.2%	62.0%	57.2%
25–34	60.9	60.0	56.7	48.5
35–44	54.9	56.5	47.9	46.8
45–54	47.4	40.4	44.9	35.2
55 or older	19.2	18.4	20.9	24.3

[a]Excludes persons of Hispanic origin.
[b]Includes Asians, American Indians, Alaska Natives, Native Hawaiians, other Pacific Islanders, and inmates who specified more than one race.

SOURCE: Christopher J. Mumola and Jennifer C. Karberg, "Table 3. Drug Use in the Month before the Offense, by Selected Characteristics of State and Federal Prisoners, 1997 and 2004," in *Drug Use and Dependence, State and Federal Prisoners, 2004*, U.S. Department of Justice, Office of Justice Programs, Bureau of Justice Statistics, October 2006, http://www.ojp.usdoj.gov/bjs/pub/pdf/dudsfp04.pdf (accessed October 13, 2006)

D. Wayne Osgood, and Ineke Haen Marshall studied 658 newly convicted male prisoners sentenced to the Nebraska Department of Correctional Services between 1989 and 1990. Horney, Osgood, and Marshall wanted to determine if changes in life circumstances, such as being unemployed or living with a wife or girlfriend, influenced their criminal behavior. They find that "use of illegal drugs was related to all four measures of offending [any crime, property crime, assault, and drug crime]. For example, during months of drug use, the odds of committing a property crime increased by 54 percent; the odds of committing an assault increased by over 100 percent. Overall, illegal drug use increased the odds of committing any crime sixfold."

Table 4.7 shows the drug use of state and federal prisoners by the type of offense they committed in 2004. Overall, more than half of state and federal prisoners (56% and 50.2%, respectively) reported using illicit drugs in the month before their offense. Unsurprisingly, a high percentage of those in state prison for drug offenses (71.9%) had used drugs in the month prior to their offense. The correlation between drug use and nondrug crimes can be seen, however, in the fact that 64% of state prisoners who committed property offenses and nearly 50% of those who committed violent offenses had used drugs in the month before their offense. The percentages for federal prisoners were lower but still substantial, with 57.3% of drug offenders, 49.1% of violent offenders, and 27.7% of property offenders reporting drug use in the month before their offense. Furthermore, more than one-quarter of state and federal prisoners (32.1% and 26.4%, respectively) reported they were using illicit drugs at the time of their offense.

Table 4.8 shows drug use in the month before the offense by selected characteristics of state and federal prisoners, comparing results from 1997 and 2004. For state prisoners the likelihood that they used drugs in the month before the offense stayed the same from 1997 to 2004, at approximately 56%. The likelihood that federal prisoners used drugs in the month before their offense rose from 44.8% in 1997 to 50.2% in 2004. For state prisoners women were more likely than men to have used drugs in the month before their offense in both years. Federal prisoners showed the opposite trend: Men were more likely than women to have used drugs in the month before their offense in both years.

For both state and federal prisoners people aged twenty-four or younger were the ones most likely to have used drugs in the month before the offense in both years. The likelihood of drug use fell with age in both years and for both sets of prisoners. In general whites were slightly more likely than African-Americans to have used drugs in the month before their offenses. Hispanics were the least likely of the three racial groups to have used drugs in the month before their offenses. However, the incidence of drug use was nearly 50% or above for all groups except Hispanics in federal prison. Only slightly more than one-third of Hispanic federal prisoners used drugs in the month before their offenses. (See Table 4.8.)

TRENDS IN DRUG-RELATED DEATHS

The SAMHSA's Drug Abuse Warning Network (DAWN) program collects data on drug-related mortality. The data are collected and published for metropolitan areas and counties. According to DAWN, its locally collected data cannot be used for national estimates of drug-abuse-related mortality because, among other reasons, the samples are skewed toward urban areas and are also incomplete. National data, however, are available from the National Center for Health Statistics (NCHS), which is part of the CDC.

Sherry L. Murphy of the NCHS reports in *Deaths: Final Data for 1998* (July 24, 2000, http://www.cdc.gov/ nchs/data/nvsr/nvsr48/nvs48_11.pdf) that there were 7,101 drug-related deaths in 1979. By 2003 Donna L. Hoyert et al. note in *Deaths: Final Data for 2003* (April 19, 2006 http://www.cdc.gov/nchs/data/nvsr/nvsr54/nvsr54_13 .pdf) that these deaths increased to 28,723.

NCHS death rate measurements are not exclusively restricted to the use of illicit drugs. NCHS data also include accidental poisonings and assaults by drugs. For instance, the anthrax poisoning deaths of late 2001 would be included, but documented murders by poisoning would not. The inclusion of accidents and chemical assaults where intent is unknown somewhat weaken the data for tracking drug-abuse trends, but most cases are related to the use of drugs.

According to the SAMHSA report *Drug Abuse Warning Network, 2003: Area Profiles of Drug-Related Mortality* (March 2005, https://dawninfo.samhsa.gov/ pubs/mepubs/default.asp), cocaine and opioids such as heroin, oxycodone, and hydrocodone were the drugs most frequently associated with drug deaths in 2003. Club drugs and hallucinogens were reported infrequently in that year as causes of death.

CHAPTER 5

ALCOHOL, TOBACCO, ILLICIT DRUGS, AND YOUTH

"What do you think is the most important problem facing people your age today?" This question was asked of 480 teenagers aged thirteen to seventeen in the Gallup Youth Survey conducted December 5, 2005, to January 16, 2006. The results show that nearly one-third (31%) of this teenaged population placed the consumption of alcohol, tobacco, and drugs at the top of their list of concerns. The next most important problem cited by only 17% of the teens was peer pressure/fitting in/looks/popularity. Sexual issues, such as teen pregnancy, abortion, and sexually transmitted diseases, shared the number-three spot with education; 14% of the teens thought that those were the top problems faced by people their age.

Gallup pollsters then separated the teens into two response groups: thirteen- to fifteen-year-olds and sixteen- to seventeen-year-olds. In both groups the top problem was the same: the consumption of alcohol, tobacco, and drugs, although the younger teens mentioned this problem more frequently (35%) than did the older teens (26%). When separated by sex, male and female teens responded in near-equal percentages (32% and 31%, respectively) that the consumption of alcohol, tobacco, and drugs was the top problem facing people their age.

PROBLEM BEHAVIORS BEGIN EARLY IN LIFE

The Centers for Disease Control and Prevention (CDC), in its Youth Risk Behavior Survey (YRBS), 2005, asked high school students if they had smoked a whole cigarette, had drunk alcohol, or had tried marijuana before the age of thirteen. The results are shown in Table 5.1.

A higher percentage of younger students than older students reported having initiated cigarette, alcohol, or marijuana use before age thirteen. The most frequently reported behavior was drinking alcohol before the age of thirteen. One-third (33.9%) of ninth graders reported they had done so, as had one-quarter (26.2%) of tenth graders

and one-fifth of both eleventh graders (20.5%) and twelfth graders (19.3%). Males throughout all grades (29.2%) were more likely to report having had a drink before age thirteen than females (22%). Hispanics (29.8%) were the most likely ethnic group to report having an alcoholic drink before the age of thirteen, followed by African-Americans (27.9%) and then whites (23.7%).

Table 5.1 shows that the next most frequently reported behavior was smoking an entire cigarette before the age of thirteen. Once again, males throughout all grades (18.3%) were more likely than females (13.6%) to report having smoked a cigarette before age thirteen. Whites (16.4%) were slightly more likely than Hispanics (16%) to report having smoked before their teens. African-Americans (13.8%) reported this behavior less frequently.

The same pattern between males and females emerged with the least frequently reported behavior of trying marijuana before the age of thirteen. However, the ethnic group most likely to report this early behavior were Hispanics (12.5%), followed by African-Americans (9.1%) and then whites (7.7%).

ALCOHOL AND YOUTH
Age of First Use

The data in the previous section clearly show that the use of alcohol, tobacco, and marijuana often begins early in life, especially alcohol use. Elizabeth J. D'Amico and Denis M. McCarthy, in "Escalation and Initiation of Younger Adolescents' Substance Use: The Impact of Perceived Peer Use" (*Journal of Adolescent Health*, October 2006), note that the middle school years are peak years for the first-time use of alcohol, tobacco, and marijuana.

TABLE 5.1

Percentage of high school students who drank alcohol, smoked cigarettes, or tried marijuana before age 13, by gender, ethnicity, and grade, 2005

	Smoked a whole cigarette before age 13 years			Drank alcohol before age 13 years[a]			Tried marijuana before age 13 years		
	Female	Male	Total	Female	Male	Total	Female	Male	Total
Category	%	%	%	%	%	%	%	%	%
Race/ethnicity									
White[b]	14.8	18.0	16.4	20.5	26.9	23.7	6.0	9.5	7.7
Black[b]	10.6	17.2	13.8	24.2	31.9	27.9	5.5	12.9	9.1
Hispanic	12.0	20.0	16.0	24.7	34.8	29.8	8.3	16.5	12.5
Grade									
9	15.8	21.3	18.6	31.3	36.4	33.9	9.0	13.3	11.2
10	14.0	17.9	16.0	22.2	30.0	26.2	7.3	10.9	9.1
11	12.7	16.2	14.4	17.0	24.2	20.5	4.7	9.7	7.1
12	11.4	16.3	13.9	15.4	23.2	19.3	3.3	9.0	6.2
Total	**13.6**	**18.3**	**16.0**	**22.0**	**29.2**	**25.6**	**6.3**	**11.0**	**8.7**

[a]Other than a few sips.
[b]Non-Hispanic.

SOURCE: Adapted from "Table 38. Percentage of High School Students Who Used Drugs for the First Time before Age 13 Years, by Sex, Race/Ethnicity, and Grade—United States, Youth Risk Behavior Survey, 2005," in "Youth Risk Behavior Surveillance—United States, 2005," *Morbidity & Mortality Weekly Report*, vol. 55, no. SS-5, U.S. Department of Health and Human Services, Centers for Disease Control and Prevention, 2006, http://www.cdc.gov/mmwr/PDF/SS/SS5505.pdf (accessed October 10, 2006)

Although the precise reasons for increasing rates of alcohol and drug use at younger ages have not yet been pinpointed, Drew W. Edwards and Mark S. Gold, in "Facts about Marijuana Use" (February 6, 2001, http://psychcentral.com/library/sa_factsm.htm), speculate that a variety of factors contribute to lower ages of first use. These include media and other cultural influences that minimize the dangers and glamorize the use of illegal drugs; increasing parental expectations and acceptance of a certain amount of experimentation with illegal drugs; and easier access to alcohol, tobacco, and marijuana. Furthermore, in "Middle Childhood and Early Adolescence: Growth and Change" (2004, http://www.childrenssummit.umn.edu/docs/growthandchange.pdf), the 2004 Minnesota Children's Summit: Staying Strong through Challenge and Change cites less face-to-face contact with working parents and limited parental monitoring of behavior; reduced access to after-school programs and safety concerns that limit children's ability for outdoor, unstructured play, which has increased time spent home alone and unsupervised; and greater access to undesirable content via television, music, and the Internet.

The 2004 National Survey on Drug Use and Health (NSDUH; September 2005, http://oas.samhsa.gov/nsduh/2k4nsduh/2k4overview/2k4overview.htm) by the Substance Abuse and Mental Health Services Administration (SAMHSA) reports that in 2004, 4.4 million people used alcohol for the first time. The number of initiates ("first-timers") increased from 3.9 million in 2002 and from 4.1 million in 2003. Most (86.9 percent) of the 4.4 million 2004 alcohol initiates were younger than the age of twenty-one when they took their first drink.

Reasons for Drinking

Findings from a 2003 nationwide survey of thirteen- to seventeen-year-olds by the *Roper Youth Report, 2003* (2003, http://www.gfkamerica.com) revealed that 69% of respondents cited parents as the most influential factor in their decision whether to smoke and drink. Best friends were the second-most important factor influencing a young person's decision to smoke or drink, according to the Roper report. The attitudes of one's peer group can hold tremendous sway over a young person's alcohol and tobacco choices. Results of research conducted by Bruce Simons-Morton et al., in "Peer and Parent Influences on Smoking and Drinking among Early Adolescents" (*Health Education and Behavior*, February 2001), agree with this conclusion, reporting that teens with friends who smoked and drank were nine times more likely to participate in these behaviors than those with friends who did not smoke and drink.

However, D'Amico and McCarthy note that perception of peer use of alcohol is an important factor in the onset of use of this drug. They state, "Specifically, for alcohol, if youth thought that many of their friends used alcohol, they initiated alcohol use during the academic year." D'Amico and McCarthy indicate that students make assumptions about their peers' behaviors and that these assumptions may not be accurate, so risky behaviors often begin based on false assumptions. They also suggest that peer influence may outweigh parental influence in the initiation and escalation of substance use in early adolescence.

TABLE 5.2

Percentage of high school students who drank alcohol, by time and type of use and demographic characteristics, 2005

Category	Lifetime alcohol use[a]			Current alcohol use[b]			Episodic heavy drinking[c]		
	Female	Male	Total	Female	Male	Total	Female	Male	Total
	%	%	%	%	%	%	%	%	%
Race/ethnicity									
White[d]	75.7	75.0	75.3	45.9	47.0	46.4	28.1	31.8	29.9
Black[d]	71.4	66.5	69.0	32.5	29.6	31.2	10.4	11.9	11.1
Hispanic	79.0	79.9	79.4	44.8	48.9	46.8	21.9	28.7	25.3
Grade									
9	66.5	66.6	66.5	36.2	36.3	36.2	17.3	20.7	19.0
10	75.6	73.2	74.4	42.7	41.4	42.0	24.1	25.1	24.6
11	77.1	75.5	76.3	44.2	47.8	46.0	25.0	30.4	27.6
12	81.8	81.5	81.7	49.6	52.0	50.8	29.2	36.2	32.8
Total	**74.8**	**73.8**	**74.3**	**42.8**	**43.8**	**43.3**	**23.5**	**27.5**	**25.5**

[a]Had at least one drink of alcohol on ≥1 day during their life.
[b]Had at least one drink of alcohol on ≥1 of the 30 days preceding the survey.
[c]Had ≥ 5 drinks of alcohol in a row (i.e., within a couple of hours) on ≥ 1 of the 30 days preceding the survey.
[d]Non-Hispanic.

SOURCE: Adapted from "Table 28. Percentage of High School Students Who Drank Alcohol, by Sex, Race/Ethnicity, and Grade—United States, Youth Risk Behavior Survey, 2005," in "Youth Risk Behavior Surveillance—United States, 2005," *Morbidity & Mortality Weekly Report*, vol. 55, no. SS-5, U.S. Department of Health and Human Services, Centers for Disease Control and Prevention, 2006, http://www.cdc.gov/mmwr/PDF/SS/SS5505.pdf (accessed October 10, 2006)

Current Use of Alcohol in High School Students

It is illegal for high school students to purchase alcoholic beverages, yet in 2005 slightly more than 43.3% of high school students had consumed alcohol at least once in the thirty days prior to taking the CDC's YRBS. (See Table 5.2.) These students are considered current users. *Monitoring the Future National Survey Results on Drug Use, 1975–2005, Volume 1: Secondary School Students* (2006, http://www.monitoringthefuture .org/pubs/monographs/vol1_2005.pdf) by the National Institute on Drug Abuse and the University of Michigan Institute for Social Research also provides data on current alcohol use among eighth, tenth, and twelfth graders. Data from the *Monitoring the Future* survey shown in Table 5.3 and the YRBS overlap in current drinking data for tenth and twelfth graders. Comparing the "total" figures in Table 5.2 and Table 5.3 for those grades, the YRBS study shows a slightly higher prevalence of current drinking for twelfth graders (50.8% in YRBS and 47% in *Monitoring the Future*) and for tenth graders (42% for YRBS and 33.2% for *Monitoring the Future*). The *Monitoring the Future* data also show that the prevalence of current drinking in eighth graders was 17.1% in 2005.

The 2004 NSDUH also collected data on alcohol use. It reported that an estimated 10.8 million people aged twelve to twenty (28.2% of this age group) used alcohol in the month prior to the survey. The 2005 NSDUH, the results of which are published in *Results from the 2005 National Survey on Drug Use and Health: National Findings* (September 2006, http://www.oas.samhsa.gov/nsduh/ 2k5nsduh/2k5Results.pdf), presents rates of current alcohol use in 2005 among various age groups: 4.2% among twelve- to thirteen-year-olds (grades seventh and eighth), 15.1% of fourteen- to fifteen-year-olds (grades ninth and tenth), 30.1% of sixteen- to seventeen-year-olds (grades eleventh and twelfth), and 51.1% of eighteen- to twenty-year-olds. The peak age of current alcohol use was twenty-one to twenty-five years at 67.4% of this population. (See Figure 2.1 in Chapter 2; note that the top of the bar shows the percentage for current use.)

What can be gleaned from all these studies? Looking at all the data presented here, each study shows 2005 current rates of alcohol use in high school students rising with grade level. As students grew older, they drank more. Looking at the studies together, the percentage of tenth graders who were current alcohol users in 2005 ranged from about 15% to 42%. The percentage of twelfth graders who were current alcohol users in 2005 ranged from about 30% to 51%. Taken separately or together, data from these surveys present a picture of a high percentage of teens who use alcohol, which can cause bodily harm, serious diseases, and possibly death. (See Chapter 2.) The teens who responded to the Gallup Youth Survey that alcohol was one of the most important problems facing young people today appeared to understand the state of current alcohol use of high school students.

Alcohol Use among College Students and Other Young Adults

In the previous section, data from the 2005 NSDUH indicate that 51.1% of eighteen- to twenty-year-olds and 67.4% of twenty-one to twenty-five-year-olds (the peak

TABLE 5.3

Past-month use of alcohol by eighth, tenth, and twelfth graders, 2005

[Entries are percentages]

Grade:	Alcohol			Been drunk			Flavored alcoholic beverages		
	8th	10th	12th	8th	10th	12th	8th	10th	12th
Total	17.1	33.2	47.0	6.0	17.6	30.2	12.9	23.1	30.5
Gender:									
Male	16.2	32.8	50.7	5.9	18.2	33.6	11.4	20.3	28.3
Female	17.9	33.6	43.3	6.2	16.8	26.4	14.4	25.8	33.2
College plans:									
None or under 4 years	32.6	44.9	52.8	15.7	27.8	34.3	24.9	33.8	34.2
Complete 4 years	15.5	31.6	45.5	5.1	16.3	28.5	11.8	21.7	29.6
Region:									
Northeast	14.5	37.0	54.5	4.2	20.5	38.7	11.0	22.4	38.1
North central	16.9	31.9	48.0	6.2	17.4	31.3	12.6	23.4	33.4
South	19.0	33.4	43.9	7.1	17.2	26.9	14.6	23.7	25.9
West	16.4	30.7	43.6	5.8	15.2	26.5	11.9	22.5	27.9
Population density:									
Large MSA	17.2	31.1	46.6	5.4	16.2	28.2	11.5	22.0	29.9
Other MSA	17.9	34.4	47.6	6.1	18.3	31.5	14.0	23.1	29.9
Non-MSA	15.6	33.5	46.1	6.9	17.8	29.9	12.8	24.4	32.2
Parental education:*									
1.0–2.0 (Low)	23.8	36.5	38.2	9.3	15.8	22.0	19.5	24.9	22.2
2.5–3.0	20.4	36.0	47.8	8.4	19.4	29.9	18.0	28.1	33.3
3.5–4.0	18.8	33.5	47.8	6.7	17.5	31.3	16.2	23.6	31.7
4.5–5.0	14.6	31.8	50.2	4.6	17.5	31.3	10.3	22.6	30.2
5.5–6.0 (High)	13.1	31.8	46.0	3.5	17.0	32.2	7.3	17.3	30.2

Note: MSA stands for metropolitan statistical areas.

*Parental education is an average score of mother's education and father's education reported on the following scale: (1) completed grade school or less, (2) some high school, (3) completed high school, (4) some college, (5) completed college, (6) graduate or professional school after college. Missing data were allowed on one of the two variables.

SOURCE: Adapted from L. D. Johnston, P. M. O'Malley, J. G. Bachman, and J. E. Schulenberg, "Table 4.7. Thirty-Day Prevalence of Use of Various Drugs by Subgroups: Eighth, Tenth, and Twelfth Graders, 2005," in *Monitoring the Future National Survey Results on Drug Use, 1975–2005, Volume 1: Secondary School Students*, National Institute on Drug Abuse and the University of Michigan Institute for Social Research, 2006. http://www.monitoringthefuture.org/pubs/monographs/vol1_2005.pdf (accessed October 6, 2006).

age group) used alcohol in 2005. These college-aged students and recent graduates are a part of the youth of this nation; many of them are using a potentially dangerous drug, and those under twenty-one are using it illegally.

Monitoring the Future National Survey Results on Drug Use, 1975–2005, Volume 2: College Students and Adults Ages 19–45 (2006, http://www.monitoringthefuture.org/pubs/monographs/vol2_2005.pdf) reports drug use results for college students and adults. Table 5.4 shows the annual prevalence of the use of alcohol and flavored alcoholic beverages for college students and noncollege students who are one to four years beyond high school. The results show that both groups have a high annual prevalence of alcohol use (83% for full-time college students and 76.9% for noncollege students of the same age), but college students have the higher rate of use. Female college students are slightly more likely to have consumed alcohol in the past year (83.4%) than male college students (82.4%). The reverse is true for noncollege students one to four years beyond high school: Males (77.4%) are more likely than females (76.6%) to have consumed alcohol in the past year.

TABLE 5.4

Annual prevalence of alcohol use by full-time college students vs. other young adults 1–4 years beyond high school, 2005

[Entries are percentages]

	Total		Males		Females	
	Full-time college	Others	Full-time college	Others	Full-time college	Others
Alcohol	83.0	76.9	82.4	77.4	83.4	76.6
Flavored alcoholic beverage	67.0	50.6	55.5	46.3	74.0	54.0

SOURCE: Adapted from L. D. Johnston, P. M. O'Malley, J. G. Bachman, and J. E. Schulenberg, "Table 8.2. Annual Prevalence of Use for Various Types of Drugs, 2005: Full-Time College Students vs. Others among Respondents 1–4 Years beyond High School," in *Monitoring the Future National Survey Results on Drug Use, 1975–2005, Volume 2: College Students and Adults Ages 19–45*, National Institute on Drug Abuse and the University of Michigan Institute for Social Research, 2006, http://www.monitoringthefuture.org/pubs/monographs/vol2_2005.pdf (accessed October 6, 2006).

Table 5.5 shows the trend of lifetime prevalence of alcohol use from 1980 to 2005 among those aged nineteen to twenty-eight years. Throughout the 1980s the annual prevalence of alcohol use for this group remained relatively steady at around 94% to 95%. In the 1990s

TABLE 5.5

Trends in lifetime prevalence of alcohol use among young adults, 1980–2005

[By percentage]

Respondents aged 19–28	1980	1981	1982	1983	1984	1985	1986	1987	1988	1989	1990	1991	1992	1993	1994	1995	1996	1997	1998	1999	2000	2001	2002	2003	2004	2005	'04–'05 change
Alcohol	94.3	95.2	95.2	95.0	94.2	95.3	94.9	94.1	94.9	93.7	93.1	93.6	91.8	89.3	88.2	88.5	88.4	87.3	88.5	88.0	86.6	86.1	86.0	86.2	84.6	86.6	+2.1
Flvd. alcoholic bvg.	NA	NA	NA	NA	NA	NA	NA	NA	NA	NA	NA	NA	NA	NA	NA	NA	NA	NA	NA	NA	NA	NA	NA	NA	79.0	84.5	+5.5
College students 1–4 years beyond high school																											
Alcohol	NA	NA	NA	NA	NA	NA	94.8	94.9	94.8	94.5	94.3	94.1	93.4	92.1	91.2	91.6	91.2	90.7	90.6	90.2	90.7	89.9	90.2	89.3	89.4	89.1	−0.2
Flvd. alcoholic bvg.	NA	NA	NA	NA	NA	NA	NA	NA	NA	NA	NA	NA	NA	NA	NA	NA	NA	NA	NA	NA	NA	NA	NA	NA	83.2	84.6	+1.4

NA indicates data not available

SOURCE: Adapted from L. D. Johnston, P. M. O'Malley, J. G. Bachman, and J. E. Schulenberg, "Table 5.1. Trends in Lifetime Prevalence of Various Types of Drugs among Respondents of Modal Ages 19–28," and "Table 9-1. Trends in Lifetime Prevalence of Various Types of Drugs among College Students 1–4 Years beyond High School," in *Monitoring the Future National Survey Results on Drug Use, 1975–2005, Volume 2: College Students and Adults Ages 19–45*, National Institute on Drug Abuse and the University of Michigan Institute for Social Research, 2006, http://www.monitoringthefuture.org/pubs/monographs/vol2_2005.pdf (accessed October 6, 2006)

annual prevalence fell; by 1999 the annual prevalence of alcohol use for this group was 88%. In 2004 the lifetime prevalence reached a low of 84.6% but then jumped to 86.6% in 2005. The lifetime prevalence of drinking flavored alcoholic beverages (the data for which has only recently been gathered) for nineteen- to twenty-eight-year-olds was 79% in 2004 and rose to 84.5% in 2005.

Table 5.5 also shows the trend of lifetime prevalence of alcohol use among college students one to four years beyond high school. The lifetime prevalence of alcohol use in this group is slightly higher (89.1% in 2005) than that for the nineteen- to twenty-eight-year-old group (86.6% in 2005).

Heavy Drinking, Binge Drinking, and Drunkenness

Merriam-Webster's Collegiate Dictionary defines the term *drunk* as "having the faculties impaired by alcohol." According to the *Monitoring the Future* survey, rates of occurrences of drunkenness among high school students generally declined between 2000 and 2005 from the increases of the 1990s. The highest rate for eighth graders occurred in 1996, when 9.6% reported having been drunk in the past thirty days. The highest rate for tenth graders came in 2000, when the rate hit 23.5%, although it fell to 18.2% three years later. The highest rate for twelfth graders was 34.2% in 1997. In 2005 the *Monitoring the Future* survey's having "been drunk" rates were 6% of eighth graders, 17.6% of tenth graders, and 30.2% of twelfth graders reported being drunk during the previous month in 2005. (See Table 5.3.)

The National Institute on Alcohol Abuse and Alcoholism defines binge drinking as the consumption of five or more drinks of alcoholic beverages on at least one occasion during the past month. Heavy drinking is an average of more than one drink per day for women and more than two drinks per day for men. (There is a male-female difference because the same amount of alcohol affects women more than it does men. Women's bodies have less water than men's bodies, so a given amount of alcohol becomes more highly concentrated in a woman's body than in a man's.)

The YRBS used the term *episodic heavy drinking* and defined it using the same definition as binge drinking, rather than asking students if they had "been drunk" (with no definition) as did the *Monitoring the Future* survey. According to the YRBS, in 2005 nearly 26% of high school students were current binge drinkers. The incidence of binge drinking increased with grade level: 19% in ninth grade, 24.6% in tenth grade, 27.6% in eleventh grade, and 32.8% in twelfth grade. (See Table 5.2.)

Demographic Factors in Youth Alcohol Use

GENDER, RACIAL, AND ETHNIC DIFFERENCES. In 2005 high school males were only slightly more likely (43.8%) to be current alcohol users than females (42.8%). (See Table 5.2.) Males (27.5%) were more likely than females (23.5%) to engage in episodic heavy drinking.

Similarly, results from the *Monitoring the Future* survey (Table 5.3) show close percentages of current alcohol use for males and females in grades eight and ten in 2005, but in this survey with the female rates slightly higher. However, the data show that twelfth-grade males (50.7%) were more likely to have been current drinkers in 2005 than females (43.3%). The 2005 results in the *Monitoring the Future* survey for being drunk were similar to those in the YRBS for binge drinking: males in grades ten (18.2%) and twelve (33.6%) were more likely than females in those grades (16.8% and 26.4%, respectively) to have been drunk. The data for eighth-grade males (5.9%) and females (6.2%) show a similar likelihood of having been drunk.

The *Monitoring the Future* survey also shows data for males and females among full-time college students versus others one to four years beyond high school. (See Table 5.4.) The 2005 annual prevalence rates for alcohol use were similar for males and females of both groups. However, the survey shows gender differences in the consumption of flavored alcoholic beverages. Full-time college females were more likely (74%) than full-time college males (55.5%) to drink these beverages. The same was true for noncollege students in the same age group: females were more likely (54%) than males (46.3%) to drink flavored alcoholic beverages. A female preference for these drinks was also seen among eighth, tenth, and twelfth graders in Table 5.3.

Table 5.2 also shows that in 2005 Hispanic high school students (79.4%) were more likely than white high school students (75.3%) or African-American high school students (69%) to have consumed alcohol in their lifetime, but whites were more likely to have engaged in episodic heavy drinking (29.9% versus 11.1% of African-Americans and 25.3% of Hispanics). White and Hispanic high school students were equally likely to be current drinkers in 2005 (46.4% and 46.8%, respectively), and African-Americans were less likely to be current drinkers (31.2%).

WHERE STUDENTS LIVE. The *Monitoring the Future* survey looked at population density as a factor in student drinking patterns. (See Table 5.3.) In that category MSA stands for "metropolitan statistical area," which means that the area contains at least one town that has more than fifty thousand inhabitants. Large MSAs are the biggest cities in the United States, such as New York, Los Angeles, Chicago, Philadelphia, and Boston. Little difference was found in the percentage of students who were current drinkers based on whether they lived in a large MSA, smaller-sized MSA, or non-MSA. However, students who lived in the Northeast were more likely to be current alcohol users than students who lived in other parts of the country. (See Table 5.3.)

FIGURE 5.1

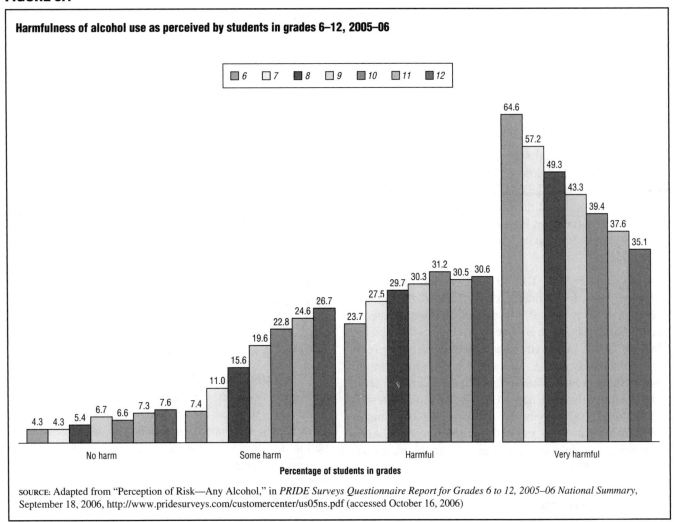

Harmfulness of alcohol use as perceived by students in grades 6–12, 2005–06

☐ 6 ☐ 7 ■ 8 ☐ 9 ■ 10 ☐ 11 ■ 12

Percentage of students in grades

No harm: 4.3, 4.3, 5.4, 6.7, 6.6, 7.3, 7.6

Some harm: 7.4, 11.0, 15.6, 19.6, 22.8, 24.6, 26.7

Harmful: 23.7, 27.5, 29.7, 30.3, 31.2, 30.5, 30.6

Very harmful: 64.6, 57.2, 49.3, 43.3, 39.4, 37.6, 35.1

SOURCE: Adapted from "Perception of Risk—Any Alcohol," in *PRIDE Surveys Questionnaire Report for Grades 6 to 12, 2005–06 National Summary*, September 18, 2006, http://www.pridesurveys.com/customercenter/us05ns.pdf (accessed October 16, 2006)

PARENTAL EDUCATION. Table 5.3 shows an inverse relationship between current alcohol use in eighth graders and parental education: the less parental education, the more likely eighth graders were to drink. This relationship is not as strong in tenth graders and is not apparent in twelfth graders. In addition, students in all three grades who had no college plans were more likely to be current drinkers, to have been drunk in the past thirty days, and to drink flavored alcoholic beverages than those with plans to complete four years of college.

Perception of Harmfulness of Alcohol Use

The PRIDE Survey (formerly the Parents Resource Institute for Drug Education) also asks adolescents and teenagers questions about drug and alcohol use. Figure 5.1 shows results from the *PRIDE Surveys Questionnaire Report for Grades 6 to 12, 2005–06 National Survey*. The report reveals that most sixth graders perceived alcohol as very harmful (64.6%). Perception of alcohol being very harmful decreased with increasing grade level. Only 35.1% of twelfth graders perceived alcohol as being very harmful. Thus, when perception of risk decreased, use of

alcohol increased (as shown in Table 5.2 and Table 5.3). The report also notes that easy access to alcohol increases the probability that adolescents and teenagers will drink. The survey results show that access to alcohol increased as grade level increased.

Drinking and Young Drivers

The National Highway Traffic Safety Administration (NHTSA), in *Traffic Safety Facts, 2005 Data—Young Drivers* (2006, http://www-nrd.nhtsa.dot.gov/Pubs/young driverstsf05.PDF), reports that in 2005 a total of 7,460 drivers aged fifteen to twenty were involved in fatal crashes—a 7% decrease from the 7,979 involved in 1995. Twenty-three percent of the drivers fifteen to twenty years of age who were killed in crashes were intoxicated (had a blood alcohol level of 0.08 grams per deciliter [g/dL] or higher). For young male drivers aged fifteen to twenty, fatalities rose 5% between 1995 and 2005, compared with a 1% decrease for females.

When alcohol is involved, the severity of a traffic accident generally increases. The NHTSA defines a traffic accident as alcohol related if either the driver or an involved nonoccupant, such as a pedestrian, has a BAC of 0.01 g/dL of blood or greater. According to *Traffic Safety Facts, 2005*, of those who survived the 7,460 crashes in 2005, 4% had blood alcohol concentration (BAC) levels between 0.01 and 0.07 g/dL and 10% had levels of 0.08 g/dL or higher. For those fatally injured, 5% had BAC levels between 0.01 and 0.07 g/dL and 23% had levels of 0.08 g/dL or higher.

As of July 2004 all states, the District of Columbia, and Puerto Rico had lowered the legal BAC limit for driving to 0.08 g/dL. The NHTSA estimates that between 1975 and 2005 the minimum drinking age laws have reduced traffic fatalities involving drivers aged eighteen to twenty by 13%, saving approximately 24,560 lives since 1975.

All states and the District of Columbia have zero-tolerance laws for drinking drivers under the age of twenty-one. It is illegal for drivers under the age of twenty-one to drive with BAC levels of 0.02 g/dl or greater. Matthew Gever, in "Environmental Strategies for Preventing Underage Drinking" (September 30, 2006, http://www.ncsl.org/programs/health/forum/uderagedrinking.htm), reports that early evidence on the results of the law is encouraging. Heavy episodic drinking for both males and females has been reduced by 13% to 18%. Also, the number of drinks consumed in a month by males has decreased by 20%.

TOBACCO AND YOUTH
Health Consequences of Early Tobacco Use
John K. Wiencke et al., in "Early Age at Smoking Initiation and Tobacco Carcinogen DNA Damage in the Lung" (*Journal of the National Cancer Institute*, April 1999), indicate that the age at which smoking is initiated is a significant factor in the risk of developing lung cancer. Smoking in the teen years appears to cause permanent genetic changes in the lungs, increasing the risk of lung cancer—even if the smoker quits. The younger a person starts smoking, the more lasting damage is done to his or her lungs. Such damage is less likely among smokers who start in their twenties.

An earlier study, *Preventing Tobacco Use among Young People: A Report of the Surgeon General* (March 1994, http://www.cdc.gov/Tobacco/sgr/sgr_1994/index.htm), indicated that cigarette smoking during adolescence seems to retard lung growth and reduce maximum lung function. As a result, young smokers are less likely than their nonsmoking peers to be physically fit and more likely to experience shortness of breath, coughing spells, wheezing, and overall poorer health. These health problems pose a clear risk for developing other chronic conditions in adulthood, such as chronic obstructive pulmonary disease, including emphysema and chronic

bronchitis. Early smoking has also been linked to an increased risk of cardiovascular diseases, such as high cholesterol and triglyceride levels, atherosclerosis (arterial plaque), and early onset of heart disease.

Smokeless tobacco also has undesirable health effects on young users. Adolescent use is linked to the development of periodontal disease, soft-tissue damage, and oral cancers. In addition, young people who use smokeless tobacco are more likely than their nonusing peers to become cigarette smokers.

Age of First Use
Even though these health effects of early tobacco use are known, most cigarette smokers begin their habit early in life. The results of the *Monitoring the Future* survey show that in 2005, 12.5% of the eighth graders surveyed reported that they had their first cigarette in the sixth and seventh grades, and 10% reported having their first cigarette even earlier—in fifth grade. The twelfth graders who were surveyed responded that their daily smoking habit began primarily in grades seven through eleven.

The *Monitoring the Future* survey reveals that smokeless tobacco use begins early in life as well. Smokeless tobacco is chewing tobacco or finer-cut tobacco that is inhaled (snuff). The highest rates of initiation in smokeless tobacco use are in grades seven through ten. In 2005, 5.1% of the eighth graders surveyed reported that they began to use smokeless tobacco by the sixth grade, and another 5% started by the eighth grade.

Current Use of Tobacco by High School Students
The 2005 NSDUH determines that 13.1% of students aged twelve to seventeen used various tobacco products in the month prior to the survey; that is, they were current users. The use of tobacco products among this age group declined from 15.2% in 2002. This decline was due primarily to the decline in the use of cigarettes. In 2002, 13% of students aged twelve to seventeen were current cigarette smokers, and in 2005, 10.8% were. Use of other tobacco products—cigars, smokeless tobacco, and pipe tobacco—remained relatively steady. In 2005, 4.2% of students aged twelve to seventeen were current cigar smokers, 2.1% were smokeless tobacco users, and 0.6% were pipe tobacco users.

Table 5.6 shows the results for current tobacco use, current smokeless tobacco use, and current cigar use from the YRBS. The YRBS focuses on students in grades nine through twelve, not students aged twelve to seventeen as does the NSDUH. The YRBS finds that 28.4% of high school students in 2005 reported current tobacco use. The *Monitoring the Future* results are lower (13.1% of twelve- to seventeen-year-olds), but it includes younger students, who are less likely to use

TABLE 5.6

Current high school users of smokeless tobacco, smoked cigars, and any tobacco product, by gender, ethnicity, and grade, 2005

Category	Current smokeless tobacco use[a]			Current cigar use[b]			Current tobacco use[c]		
	Female	Male	Total	Female	Male	Total	Female	Male	Total
	%	%	%	%	%	%	%	%	%
Race/ethnicity									
White[d]	2.7	17.6	10.2	8.6	21.0	14.9	29.3	35.7	32.5
Black[d]	0.4	3.0	1.7	8.3	12.3	10.3	14.9	18.1	16.5
Hispanic	1.5	8.6	5.1	9.1	20.0	14.6	19.2	30.6	24.9
Grade									
9	3.4	11.8	7.6	8.7	15.5	12.2	22.0	26.8	24.4
10	1.9	12.8	7.5	9.4	15.7	12.6	24.6	28.2	26.4
11	2.1	14.8	8.4	7.3	21.3	14.3	25.4	34.6	29.9
12	1.3	15.5	8.4	9.4	25.8	17.5	29.3	39.1	34.2
Total	**2.2**	**13.6**	**8.0**	**8.7**	**19.2**	**14.0**	**25.1**	**31.7**	**28.4**

[a]Used chewing tobacco, snuff, or dip on ≥1 of the 30 days preceding the survey.
[b]Smoked cigars, cigarillos, or little cigars on ≥1 of the 30 days preceding the survey
[c]Current cigarette use, current smokeless tobacco use, or current cigar use.
[d]Non-Hispanic

SOURCE: Adapted from "Table 26, Percentage of High School Students Who Currently Used Smokeless Tobacco, Currently Smoked Cigars, and Currently Used Tobacco, by Sex, Race/Ethnicity, and Grade—United States, Youth Risk Behavior Survey, 2005," in "Youth Risk Behavior Surveillance—United States, 2005," in *Morbidity & Mortality Weekly Report*, vol. 55, no. SS-5, U.S. Department of Health and Human Services, Centers for Disease Control and Prevention, 2006, http://www.cdc.gov/mmwr/PDF/SS/SS5505.pdf (accessed October 10, 2006)

TABLE 5.7

Prevalence of cigarette use by students in grades 9–12, selected years 1991–2005

1991	1993	1995	1997	1999	2001	2003	2005	Changes from 1991–2003	Change from 2003–2005
Lifetime cigarette use									
(Ever tried cigarette smoking, even one or two puffs.)									
70.1	69.5	71.3	70.2	70.4	63.9	58.4	54.3	No change, 1991–1999 Decreased, 1999–2005	No change
Current cigarette use									
(Smoked cigarettes on ≥1 of the 30 days preceding the survey.)									
27.5	30.5	34.8	36.4	34.8	28.5	21.9	23.0	Increased, 1991–1997 Decreased, 1997–2005	No change
Current frequent cigarette use									
(Smoked cigarettes on ≥20 of the 30 days preceding the survey.)									
12.7	13.8	16.1	16.7	16.8	13.8	9.7	9.4	Increased, 1991–1999 Decreased, 1999–2005	No change
Smoked cigarettes on school property									
(On ≥1 of the 30 days preceding the survey.)									
NA	13.2	16.0	14.6	14.0	9.9	8.0	6.8	No change, 1993–1995 Decreased, 1995–2005	No change

NA=Not available.

SOURCE: Adapted from "Trends in the Prevalence of Cigarette Use," in *National Youth Risk Behavior Survey: 1991–2005*," U.S. Department of Health and Human Services, Centers for Disease Control and Prevention, 2006, http://www.cdc.gov/HealthyYouth/yrbs/pdf/trends/2005_YRBS_Cigarette_Use.pdf (accessed October 10, 2006)

---

tobacco, and does not include eighteen-year-olds, who are more likely to use tobacco and who are likely present in the cohort of high school seniors surveyed for the YRBS. The YRBS finds that 14% of high school students in 2005 were current cigar smokers (*Monitoring the Future* reports 4.2%) and 8% were current smokeless tobacco users (*Monitoring the Future* reports 2.1%). The YRBS results also show that, in general, tobacco use increases with grade level.

Trends in Prevalence of Cigarette Use in High School Students

The YRBS also determined trends in the prevalence of cigarette smoking in high school students from 1991 to 2005. The YRBS results reveal that in 2005, 23% of high school students were current cigarette smokers. (See Table 5.7.) This rate is down from the 1991 rate of 27.5%. Current cigarette smoking rates rose from 1991 to 1993, however, and continued to rise through 1997. The rates then fell to 21.9% in 2003 before rising again slightly by 2005.

What are the causes of the general decrease in current smoking rates among high school students after 1997? *Monitoring the Future* provides a possible answer to this question:

> We think that the extensive adverse publicity generated by the state attorneys general, the President, and Congress in the debate over a possible legal settlement with the tobacco companies likely contributed importantly to this turnaround by influencing youth attitudes toward cigarette companies and their products. Substantial price increases, the removal of some forms of advertising (such as billboard advertising and the Joe Camel campaign), the implementation of vigorous antismoking advertising (particularly that launched by the American Legacy Foundation and some of the states), and strong prevention programs in some states all may have contributed.

According to the YRBS, lifetime cigarette use among high school students was also lower in 2005 than in 1991. In 1991 nearly three-quarters (70.1%) of all high school students had tried smoking. In 2005 slightly more than half (54.3% had tried.) The lifetime rates did not begin to fall, however, until the turn of the twenty-first century. The percentage of high school students who are current, frequent users of cigarettes is also down from 1991 (12.7% versus 9.4%), as is the percentage of students who smoked cigarettes on school property (13.2% in 1993 versus 6.8% in 2005).

Tobacco Use among College Students and Other Young Adults

The *Monitoring the Future* survey reports drug use results for college students and adults. In 2005 the rates of current cigarette smoking for young adults increased steadily by age, from 23% for eighteen-year-olds to 31% for twenty-five- to twenty-six-year-olds. It then decreased to 24% for twenty-nine- to thirty-year-olds. These current smoking rates are down considerably from the past. Current cigarette use rates for eighteen-year-olds were 38.8% in 1976 and dropped to 23.2% by 2005. Decreases are apparent in all age groups, but they are not as dramatic as with the eighteen-year-olds. For example, current smoking rates for twenty-five- to twenty-six-year-olds were 33.7% in 1984 and dropped only to 30.7% in 2005.

The *Monitoring the Future* survey looked at trends in current cigarette smoking among college students and noncollege students who are one to four years beyond high school. In 2005 noncollege students had a higher rate of current cigarette use (35%) than college students (23%), opposite to the results of alcohol use described earlier in this chapter. This difference in current cigarette use between college and noncollege students of the same

age has been documented since 1980, when *Monitoring the Future* first assessed these rates in these populations.

"Part-Time" Current Smokers

According to the *Monitoring the Future* study and the CDC, in the late 1990s there was a noticeable increase in people who currently smoked, but only occasionally. These individuals have been described as "part-time" or "social" smokers. These smokers do not see the harm in having the occasional cigarette—for example, after a meal or with their morning coffee. As reported by Tom Majeski in "Young Smokers Playing with Fire" (Knight Ridder/Tribune News Service, July 25, 2003), Marc Manley, the executive director for the Center for Tobacco Reduction and Health Improvement at Blue Cross/Blue Shield of Minnesota, warns of the dangers of such thinking: "Everyone who becomes addicted does so because it sneaks up on them. There are many people who don't consider themselves smokers because they only smoke on weekends. However, many of them will wake up some day and realize they want a cigarette. People are playing with fire when they take on risks with nicotine."

Demographic Factors in Youth Tobacco Use

GENDER, RACIAL, AND ETHNIC DIFFERENCES. According to the YRBS, in 2005 high school males were much more likely to currently use various tobacco products (31.7%) than females (25.1%). (See Table 5.6.) They were also much more likely to be current cigar smokers (19.2% for males versus 8.7% for females) and current smokeless tobacco users (13.6% for males versus 2.2% for females). The *Monitoring the Future* survey shows similar differences in current smokeless tobacco use between males and females in grades eight (5.3% for males and 1.5% for females), ten (9.7% versus 1.6%), and twelve (12.7% versus 1.9%).

Looking at current cigarette use alone, the *Monitoring the Future* survey shows female rates of cigarette smoking to be slightly higher than that of males in the eighth grade (9.7% for females versus 8.7% for males) and the tenth grade (15.1% for females versus 14.5% for males). However, there was a dramatic shift in twelfth grade: 24.8% of males were current smokers, whereas 20.7% of females were.

In 2005 female and male college students had equal rates (nearly 25%) of current cigarette smoking, but it has not always been that way. According to the *Monitoring the Future* study, female college students were more likely to be current smokers than male college students from 1980 to 1994. In 1994 their current rates of smoking were the same—nearly 25%. The rates for both increased during the mid- to late 1990s, with males generally leading females, but then both rates dropped to the 1994 level again in 2005.

FIGURE 5.2

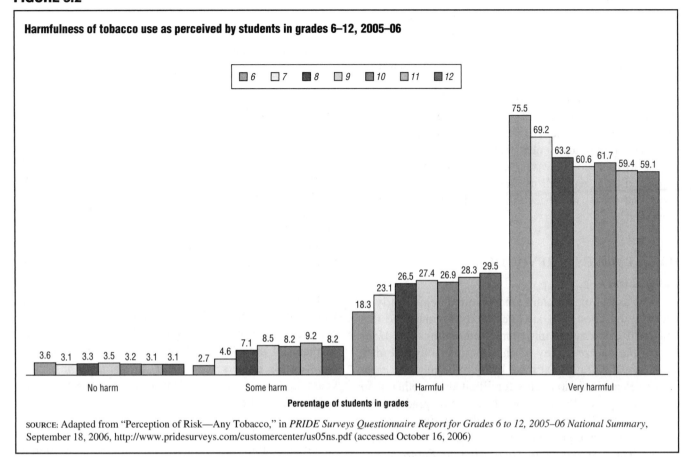

Harmfulness of tobacco use as perceived by students in grades 6–12, 2005–06

SOURCE: Adapted from "Perception of Risk—Any Tobacco," in *PRIDE Surveys Questionnaire Report for Grades 6 to 12, 2005–06 National Summary*, September 18, 2006, http://www.pridesurveys.com/customercenter/us05ns.pdf (accessed October 16, 2006)

The YRBS study shows in Table 5.6 that in 2005 white high school students (32.5%) were more likely than Hispanic high school students (24.9%) or African-American high school students (16.5%) to be current tobacco users, but whites and Hispanics were equally likely to be current cigar smokers (14.9% of whites and 14.6% of Hispanics) and African-Americans were less likely to be current cigar smokers (10.3%). In addition, whites were much more likely to currently use smokeless tobacco (10.2%) than Hispanics (5.1%) or African-Americans (1.7%).

WHERE STUDENTS LIVE. The *Monitoring the Future* survey looked at population density as a factor in student patterns of tobacco use. Eighth, tenth, and twelfth graders who lived in the largest cities in the United States (large MSAs such as Boston, New York, and Los Angeles) were the least likely to be current smokers. Those who lived in smaller cities (other MSAs) were somewhat more likely to be current smokers, and those who lived in rural areas (non-MSAs) were the most likely to be current smokers. In "Prevalence and Trends in Smoking: A National Rural Study" (*National Rural Health Association*, April 2006), Mark P. Doescher et al. determine:

> The higher prevalence of smoking in rural areas compared to urban areas . . . can be explained, in part, by lower levels of income and education attainment among

rural residents and by the greater likelihood of rural residents being white or American Indian; both groups have high rates of smoking. Additionally, persons with lower levels of income and education who reside in rural counties smoke at slightly higher rates than their urban counterparts.

PARENTAL EDUCATION. The *Monitoring the Future* survey shows an inverse relationship between current cigarette use in eighth graders and parental education: the less parental education, the more likely eighth graders were to be current smokers. This relationship is the same for tenth and eleventh graders except for the lowest parental educational level. In addition, students in all three grades who had no college plans or had plans to complete less than four years of college were much more likely to be current smokers and to have used smokeless tobacco than those with plans to complete four years of college.

Perception of Harmfulness of Tobacco Use

Figure 5.2 shows results from the *PRIDE Surveys Questionnaire Report for Grades 6 to 12, 2005–06 National Survey*. The report reveals that 75.5% of sixth graders perceived the use of tobacco as very harmful. Perception of tobacco being very harmful decreased with increasing grade level to about grade nine. About

60% of ninth, tenth, eleventh, and twelfth graders perceived tobacco use as being very harmful. Thus, a higher percentage of students in grades six through twelve perceived tobacco use as harmful than the percentage who perceived alcohol use as harmful. (See Figure 5.1.) Even though perception of risk of tobacco use stayed relatively steady in grades nine through twelve, the use of tobacco increased in these grades as the grade level increased (as shown in Table 5.6). The report also notes that, as with alcohol, easy access to tobacco increases the probability that adolescents and teenagers will use tobacco. The survey results show that access to tobacco increased as the grade level increased.

ILLICIT DRUGS AND YOUTH

Age of First Use

The use of alcohol and tobacco often begins early in life; the initiation data are presented previously in this chapter. Regarding the initiation of other drugs, the *Monitoring the Future* survey reveals that inhalants and marijuana are the drugs next most likely to be initiated early in life. Peak initiation rates for illicit drugs other than marijuana generally do not occur until grades nine through eleven in high school, and initiation rates for cocaine and crack generally occur in grades ten through twelve. The first volume of *Monitoring the Future* states:

Of all the 12th graders who reported prior use of any drug, the proportion reporting an initial use of that drug *by the end of grade 9* is presented here. This listing is a good indicator of the order of age initiation. . . .:

- cigarettes (67%)
- inhalants (61%)
- alcohol (56%)
- marijuana (54%)
- smokeless tobacco (50%)
- been drunk (49%)
- PCP (46%)
- sedatives (barbiturates) (46%)
- LSD (46%)
- daily cigarette smoking (44%)
- heroin (40%)
- crack (37%)
- narcotics other than heroin (36%)
- tranquilizers (35%)
- amphetamines (32%)
- hallucinogens (30%)
- hallucinogens other than LSD (28%)

- cocaine (25%)
- other forms of cocaine (21%)

Trends in Annual Prevalence of Drug Use in Youth

TRENDS ACROSS FIVE POPULATIONS. Annual prevalence means that a person has tried a particular drug at least once during the year prior to being surveyed about its use. Figure 5.3 compares trends in the annual prevalence of drug use across five populations: eighth-, tenth-, and twelfth-grade students, full-time college students aged nineteen to twenty-two, and all young adults through the age of twenty-eight who are high school graduates (a group that includes the college students and is referred to in Figure 5.3 as "adults"). In the early 1980s rates of drug use decreased, and college students had a higher rate of drug use than high school seniors. By the mid-1980s the annual prevalence of drug use of these two groups was somewhat equivalent. In the late 1980s, when data for young adults were added, drug use annual prevalence rates in all three groups declined dramatically. The annual prevalence of drug use by college students and twelfth graders was about the same during those years, and the annual prevalence of drug use by young adults was slightly lower.

In 1991 data for eighth and tenth graders were added. The annual prevalence of drug use rose dramatically for high school students, but the increase was less dramatic for college students. The annual prevalence of drug use increase for young adults was minor. Thus, the annual prevalence of drug use for twelfth and tenth graders became higher than the annual prevalence for college students and young adults. Around 1997 the annual prevalence of drug use for twelfth graders began to slowly drop. It dropped, then rose, then dropped again for tenth graders, and it dropped dramatically for eighth graders. However, annual prevalence rates continued to slowly climb for college students and young adults. Thus, in 2005 the annual prevalence rate of drug use was highest for twelfth graders at nearly 40%, followed by college students at about 38%, young adults at about 33%, tenth graders at about 30%, and eighth graders at about 17%.

TRENDS IN INHALANT USE IN HIGH SCHOOL STUDENTS. Inhalants have an early high rate of initiation. Of all the twelfth graders who reported prior use of inhalants in the *Monitoring the Future* survey, 61% reported an initial use of this drug by the end of ninth grade. Inhalants are volatile liquids, such as cleaning fluids, glue, gasoline, paint, and turpentine, the vapors of which are inhaled. Sometimes the sprays of aerosols are inhaled, such as those of spray paints, spray deodorants, hair spray, or fabric protector spray. These products are legal and easily accessible.

FIGURE 5.3

Trends in annual prevalence of illicit drug use, by population type, 1975–2005

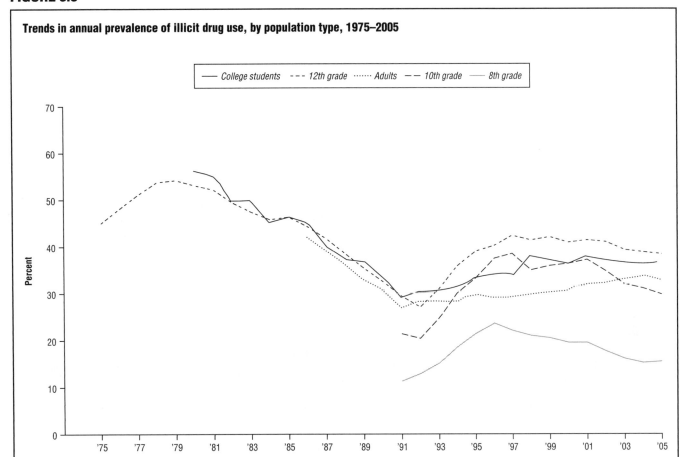

Notes: Use of "any illicit drugs" includes any use of marijuana, LSD, other hallucinogens, crack, other cocaine, or heroin, or any use which is not under a doctor's orders of other opiates, stimulants, barbiturates, methaqualone (excluded since 1990), or tranquilizers.
Beginning in 1982, the question about stimulant use (i.e., amphetamines) was revised to get respondents to exclude the inappropriate reporting of nonprescription stimulants. The prevalence rate dropped slightly as a result of this methodological change.

SOURCE: L. D. Johnston, P. M. O'Malley, J. G. Bachman, and J. E. Schulenberg, "Figure 2.1. Trends in Annual Prevalence of an Illicit Drug Use Index across Five Populations," in *Monitoring the Future National Survey Results on Drug Use, 1975–2005, Volume 2: College Students and Adults Ages 19–45,* National Institute on Drug Abuse and the University of Michigan Institute for Social Research, 2006, http://www.monitoringthefuture.org/pubs/monographs/vol2_2005.pdf (accessed October 6, 2006)

Figure 5.4 shows trends in annual prevalence of inhalant use for eighth, tenth, and twelfth graders. Since 1991, when data collection began for all three of these grade levels, eighth graders have had the highest annual prevalence of inhalant use, followed by tenth graders and then twelfth graders. Between 1991 and 1995 the annual prevalence of inhalant use rose by more than one-third among eighth and tenth graders to reach 12.8% and 9.6%, respectively, and rose by about one-fifth in twelfth graders to reach 8.4%. Annual prevalence rates for inhalant use then fell through 2002 for eighth graders to 7.7%, and through 2003 for tenth and twelfth graders to 5.4% and 4.5%, respectively. Rates rose quite steeply for eighth graders since 2002, reaching 9.6% in 2004 and steadying in 2005 at 9.5%. Rates rose less dramatically through 2005 for tenth and twelfth graders to 6% and 5.4%, respectively. *Monitoring the Future* researchers comment that "the inhalant situation may well be in the middle of an unwelcome turnaround."

TRENDS IN MARIJUANA USE IN HIGH SCHOOL STUDENTS. Besides inhalants, marijuana is one of the first drugs tried by school students. Of all the twelfth graders who reported prior use of marijuana in the *Monitoring the Future* survey, 54% reported an initial use of this drug by the end of ninth grade.

Figure 5.5 shows trends in annual prevalence rates of marijuana use for eighth, tenth, and twelfth graders. Since 1991, when data collection began for all three of these grade levels, twelfth graders have had the highest annual prevalence of marijuana use, followed by tenth graders and then eighth graders. Annual prevalence rates of marijuana use for eighth graders rose from 1991 to 1996, reaching 18.3%. These rates then dropped steadily to 11.8% in 2004 and then rose slightly to 12.2% in 2005. For tenth and twelfth graders annual prevalence rates of marijuana use rose from 1992 to 1997, reaching 34.8% and 38.5%, respectively. The rates for both held

FIGURE 5.4

Trends in annual prevalence of inhalant use among eighth, tenth, and twelfth graders, selected years 1975–2005

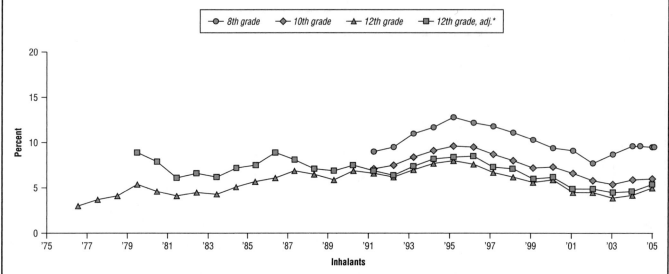

*Adjusted for underreporting of amyl and butyl nitrites.

SOURCE: Adapted from L. D. Johnston, P. M. O'Malley, J. G. Bachman, and J. E. Schulenberg, "Figure 5.4b. Various Drugs: Trends in Annual Prevalence for Eighth, Tenth, and Twelfth Graders, Inhalants," in *Monitoring the Future National Survey Results on Drug Use, 1975–2005, Volume 1: Secondary School Students*, National Institute on Drug Abuse and the University of Michigan Institute for Social Research, 2006, http://www.monitoringthefuture.org/pubs/monographs/vol1_2005.pdf (accessed October 6, 2006)

FIGURE 5.5

Trends in annual prevalence of marijuana use among eighth, tenth, and twelfth graders, 1975–2005

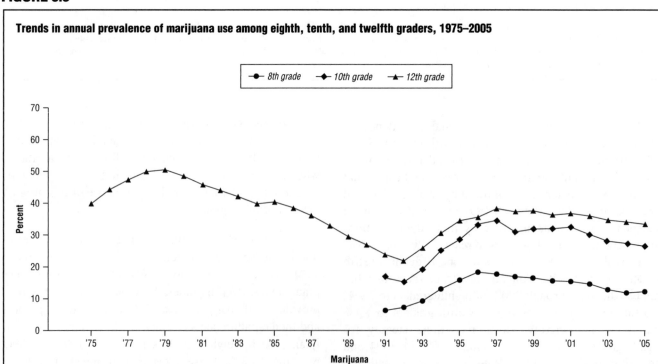

SOURCE: Adapted from L. D. Johnston, P. M. O'Malley, J. G. Bachman, and J. E. Schulenberg, "Figure 5.4a. Various Drugs: Trends in Annual Prevalence for Eighth, Tenth, and Twelfth Graders, Marijuana," in *Monitoring the Future National Survey Results on Drug Use, 1975–2005, Volume 1: Secondary School Students*, National Institute on Drug Abuse and the University of Michigan Institute for Social Research, 2006, http://www.monitoringthefuture.org/pubs/monographs/vol1_2005.pdf (accessed October 6, 2006)

FIGURE 5.6

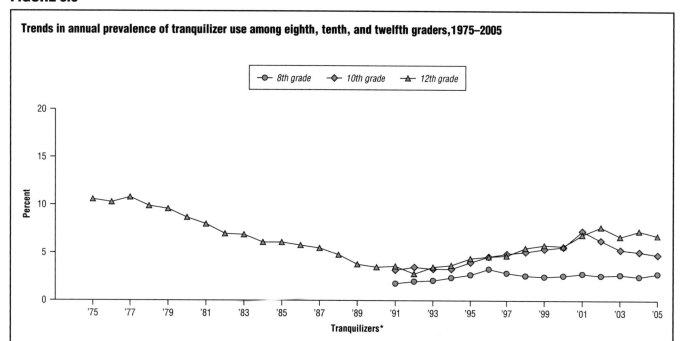

Trends in annual prevalence of tranquilizer use among eighth, tenth, and twelfth graders,1975–2005

*Beginning in 2001, a revised set of questions on tranquilizer use was introduced. From 2001 on, data points are based on the revised questions.

SOURCE: Adapted from L. D. Johnston, P. M. O'Malley, J. G. Bachman, and J. E. Schulenberg, "Figure 5.4b. Various Drugs: Trends in Annual Prevalence for Eighth, Tenth, and Twelfth Graders, Tranquilizers," in *Monitoring the Future National Survey Results on Drug Use, 1975–2005, Volume 1: Secondary School Students*, National Institute on Drug Abuse and the University of Michigan Institute for Social Research, 2006, http://www.monitoringthefuture.org/pubs/monographs/vol1_2005.pdf (accessed October 6, 2006)

relatively steady from 1998 through 2001 and then dropped to the 2005 levels of 26.6% and 33.6%, respectively.

TRENDS IN TRANQUILIZER USE IN HIGH SCHOOL STUDENTS. Of all the twelfth graders who reported prior use of tranquilizers in the *Monitoring the Future* survey, 35% reported an initial use of this drug by the end of ninth grade. Tranquilizers are drugs prescribed by physicians to relieve a patient's tension and anxiety. Drugs such as Valium, Librium, and Xanax are tranquilizers. This illicit drug and the rest to follow generally do not have high rates of early initiation as do inhalants and marijuana.

Figure 5.6 shows trends in annual prevalence rates of illicit tranquilizer use for eighth, tenth, and twelfth graders. Since 1991, when data collection began for all three of these grade levels, twelfth graders and tenth graders have had the highest prevalence of use. Eighth graders have had a lower annual prevalence rate of tranquilizer use. Annual prevalence rates for eighth graders rose slowly from 1.8% in 1991 to 3.3% in 1996. The rates then declined slightly to 2.9% in 1997 and then leveled off. The 2005 annual prevalence rate for tranquilizer use in eighth graders was 2.8%.

Annual prevalence rates of tranquilizer use for tenth and twelfth graders are hard to distinguish from one another throughout the 1990s in Figure 5.6. For tenth graders, annual prevalence rates remained fairly steady

from 1991 to 1994. These rates then rose steadily from 3.3% in 1994 to 7.3% in 2001 and then declined to 4.8% in 2005. For twelfth graders, the annual prevalence rate fell from 3.6% in 1991 to 2.8% in 1992. The rate then rose steadily from 1992, reaching 7.7% in 2002. It then declined in 2003, rose in 2004, and declined again in 2005. The 2005 annual prevalence rate of tranquilizer use in twelfth graders was 6.8% in 2005.

TRENDS IN AMPHETAMINE USE IN HIGH SCHOOL STUDENTS. Of all the twelfth graders who reported prior use of amphetamines in the *Monitoring the Future* survey, 32% reported an initial use of this drug by the end of ninth grade. Amphetamines are stimulants (uppers), drugs that produce a sense of euphoria or wakefulness. They are used to increase alertness, boost endurance and productivity, and suppress the appetite. Other stimulants include caffeine, nicotine, methamphetamine, and cocaine.

Figure 5.7 shows trends in annual prevalence rates of amphetamine use for eighth, tenth, and twelfth graders. Since 1991, when data collection began for all three of these grade levels, tenth and twelfth graders have had the highest rate of use. From 1992 through 2001 tenth-grade annual prevalence rates were higher than twelfth-grade rates. From 1991 through 2005 eighth-grade annual prevalence rates were consistently lower than those of their older classmates.

FIGURE 5.7

Trends in annual prevalence of amphetamine use among eighth, tenth, and twelfth graders, 1975–2005

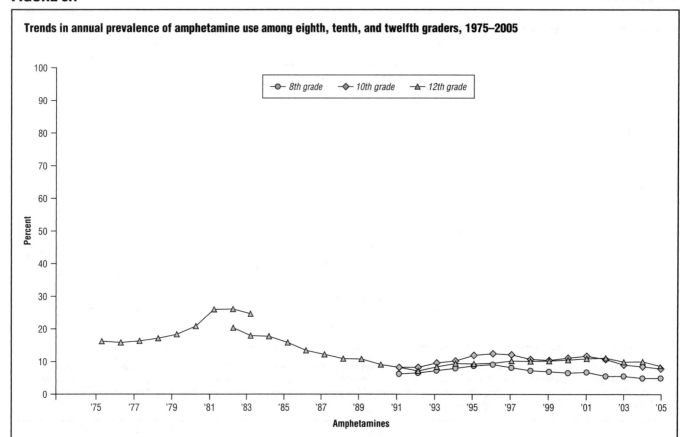

SOURCE: Adapted from L. D. Johnston, P. M. O'Malley, J. G. Bachman, and J. E. Schulenberg, "Figure 5.4a. Various Drugs: Trends in Annual Prevalence for Eighth, Tenth, and Twelfth Graders, Amphetamines," in *Monitoring the Future National Survey Results on Drug Use, 1975–2005, Volume 1: Secondary School Students*, National Institute on Drug Abuse and the University of Michigan Institute for Social Research, 2006, http://www.monitoringthefuture.org/pubs/monographs/vol1_2005.pdf (accessed October 6, 2006).

Annual prevalence rates for eighth graders rose from 6.2% in 1991 to 9.1% in 1996. The rates then declined to 6.9% in 1999 and then declined in short plateaus to 4.9% by 2005. Annual prevalence rates of amphetamine use for tenth and twelfth graders are hard to distinguish from one another throughout most years in Figure 5.7. For tenth graders, annual prevalence rates rose from 8.2% in 1991 to 11.7% in 2001, and then declined to 7.8% in 2005. For twelfth graders, the annual prevalence rate of amphetamine use generally rose throughout the 1990s and after 2000 in a slight up-and-down fashion, from 8.2% in 1991 to 11.1% in 2002. Since 2002 the annual prevalence rate of amphetamine use in twelfth graders declined to 8.6% in 2005.

TRENDS IN HALLUCINOGEN USE IN HIGH SCHOOL STUDENTS. Of all the twelfth graders who reported prior use of hallucinogens in the *Monitoring the Future* survey, 30% reported an initial use of this drug by the end of ninth grade. Hallucinogens, also known as psychedelics, distort the perception of reality. They cause excitation, which can vary from a sense of well-being to severe depression. The experience may be pleasurable or quite frightening. The effects of hallucinogens vary from use to use and cannot be predicted.

Figure 5.8 shows trends in annual prevalence rates of hallucinogen use for eighth, tenth, and twelfth graders. Since 1991, when data collection began for all three of these grade levels, twelfth graders have had the highest annual prevalence of hallucinogen use, followed by tenth graders and then eighth graders.

Annual prevalence rates of hallucinogen use for eighth graders rose from 1.9% in 1991 to 4.1% in 1996. (See Figure 5.8.) The rate then declined to 2.2% in 2004 with a "blip" of a rise in 2005 to 3.4%, which may have been because of a change that was implemented in the question for all grades the year prior. The trend patterns of annual prevalence rates of hallucinogen use for tenth and twelfth graders were similar to that of eighth graders and to each other. Annual prevalence rates for tenth and twelfth graders rose from 1991 to 1996, from 4% in 1991 to 7.8% in 1996 for tenth graders and from 5.8% in 1991 to 10.1% in 1996 for twelfth graders. The rates for both grades then declined through 2005, with some small ups and downs along the way. In 2005 the annual prevalence rates of hallucinogen use for tenth and twelfth graders were 4% and 5.5%, respectively.

FIGURE 5.8

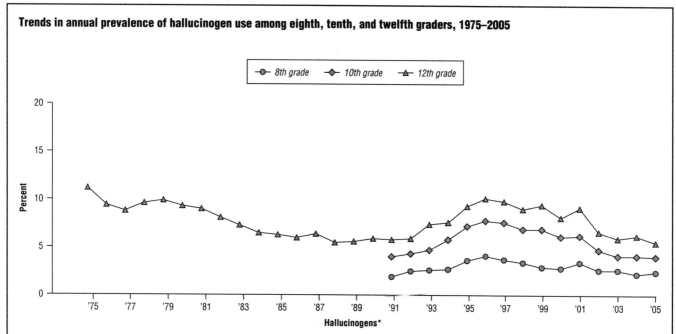

Trends in annual prevalence of hallucinogen use among eighth, tenth, and twelfth graders, 1975–2005

—●— 8th grade   —◆— 10th grade   —▲— 12th grade

Hallucinogens*

*In 2001, a revised set of questions on other hallucinogen use was introduced. Data for hallucinogens were affected by these changes. From 2001 on, data points are based on the revised questions.

SOURCE: Adapted from L. D. Johnston, P. M. O'Malley, J. G. Bachman, and J. E. Schulenberg, "Figure 5.4d. Various Drugs: Trends in Annual Prevalence for Eighth, Tenth, and Twelfth Graders, Hallucinogens," in *Monitoring the Future National Survey Results on Drug Use, 1975–2005, Volume 1: Secondary School Students*, National Institute on Drug Abuse and the University of Michigan Institute for Social Research, 2006, http://www.monitoringthefuture.org/pubs/monographs/vol1_2005.pdf (accessed October 6, 2006).

TRENDS IN MDMA/ECSTASY USE IN HIGH SCHOOL STUDENTS. MDMA (3,4-methylenedioxy-methamphetamine), or ecstasy, is a mind-altering drug with hallucinogenic properties. It is related to amphetamine and is made in illicit laboratories by making minor modifications in the chemical structure of this drug. Thus, it is called a designer drug and is one of the most popular.

Figure 5.9 shows trends in annual prevalence rates of ecstasy use for eighth, tenth, and twelfth graders. Since 1996, when data collection began for this drug, twelfth graders have had the highest annual prevalence of ecstasy use, followed by tenth graders and then eighth graders.

Annual prevalence rates of MDMA/ecstasy use for eighth graders declined initially from 2.3% in 1996 and 1997 to 1.7% in 1999. It then peaked in 2001 at 3.5% but then dropped sharply through 2004. In 2005 it held steady at the 2004 annual prevalence rate of 1.7%. The trend patterns of annual prevalence rates of MDMA/ecstasy use for tenth and twelfth graders were similar to that of eighth graders and to each other, with an initial drop, a sharp peak in 2001, and then a drop. The peak annual prevalence rate for ecstasy use for tenth graders was 6.2% and for twelfth graders was 9.2%, both in 2001. The annual prevalence rates for tenth and twelfth graders in 2005 were 2.6% and 3%, respectively. (See Figure 5.9.)

Current, Past-Year, and Lifetime Use of Illicit Drugs in Youth

Figure 4.1 in Chapter 4 shows that young people have the highest rate of current illicit drug use in the U.S. population. In 2005 the rate of current drug use starting with twelve-year-olds increased with age, peaking with eighteen- to twenty-year-olds, who had a current drug use rate of 22.3%. The rate of illicit drug use then declined with age.

Table 4.1 in Chapter 4 compares age groups twelve to seventeen, eighteen to twenty-five, and twenty-six and older regarding their past month (current), past-year, and lifetime prevalence of drug use. Those aged eighteen to twenty-five showed the highest rates of illicit drug use in all categories in both 2004 and 2005. Those aged twelve to seventeen had the next highest prevalence rate for past-year and current use.

Perception of Harmfulness of Illicit Drug Use

Figure 5.10 shows results from the *PRIDE Surveys Questionnaire Report for Grades 6 to 12, 2005–06 National Survey*. The report reveals that nearly 90% or more of students in all grades perceived the use of any illicit drug as very harmful. Only a small proportion of students (from 2.3% to 3.2%) thought that illicit drugs posed no harm to the individual. Even though perception

FIGURE 5.9

Trends in annual prevalence of ecstasy (MDMA) use among eighth, tenth, and twelfth graders,1996–2005

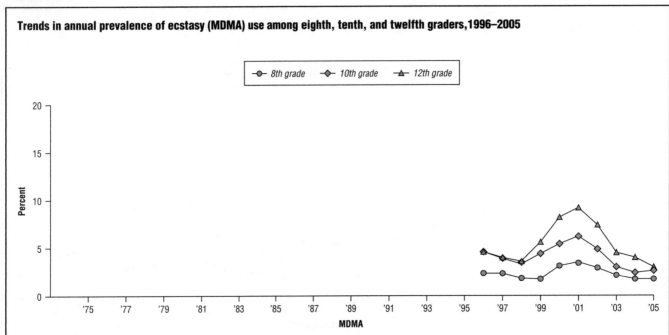

SOURCE: Adapted from L. D. Johnston, P. M. O'Malley, J. G. Bachman, and J. E. Schulenberg, "Figure 5.4h. Various Drugs: Trends in Annual Prevalence for Eighth, Tenth, and Twelfth Graders, MDMA," in *Monitoring the Future National Survey Results on Drug Use, 1975–2005, Volume 1: Secondary School Students*, National Institute on Drug Abuse and the University of Michigan Institute for Social Research, 2006, http://www.monitoringthefuture .org/pubs/monographs/vol1_2005.pdf (accessed October 6, 2006)

FIGURE 5.10

Harmfulness of illicit drug use as perceived by students in grades 6–12, 2005–06

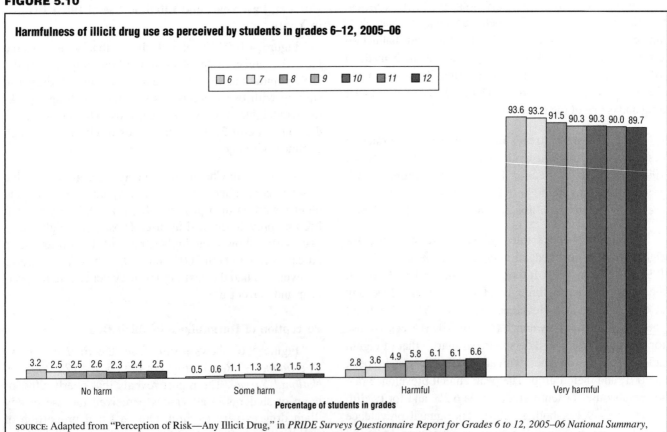

SOURCE: Adapted from "Perception of Risk—Any Illicit Drug," in *PRIDE Surveys Questionnaire Report for Grades 6 to 12, 2005–06 National Summary*, September 18, 2006, http://www.pridesurveys.com/customercenter/us05ns.pdf (accessed October 16, 2006)

of risk of illicit drug use was high, approximately one out of every five students aged twelve to seventeen had used an illicit drug at least once in the past year, and one out of every three young people aged eighteen to twenty-five had used an illicit drug at least once in the past year. (See Table 4.1 in Chapter 4.)

A Youth Phenomenon

Monitoring the Future sums up the situation of drugs and youth quite well:

> Young people are often at the leading edge of social change—and this has been particularly true of drug use. The massive upsurge in illicit drug use during the last 35 to 40 years has proven to be a youth phenomenon, and the "relapse" in the drug epidemic in the early 1990s occurred initially almost exclusively among adolescents, as this study has demonstrated. Adolescents and young adults in their 20s fall into the age groups at highest risk for illicit drug use. The original epidemic began on the nation's college campuses and then spread downward in age, but the more recent relapse phase in the epidemic first manifested itself among secondary school students and then started moving upward in age as those cohorts matured. From one year to the next, particular drugs rise or fall in popularity, and related problems occur for youth, their families, governmental agencies, and society as a whole.

CHAPTER 6
DRUG TREATMENT

DRUG ABUSE AND ADDICTION
Psychiatric Definition

Though not all experts agree on a single definition of drug addiction, the *Diagnostic and Statistical Manual of Mental Disorders-IV Text Revision* (*DSM-IV-TR*; 2000) is the most widely used reference for diagnosing and treating mental illness and substance-related disorders. In the *DSM-IV-TR*, the nation's psychiatrists draw a distinction between *substance abuse* and *substance dependence*. They stress that these terms should not be used interchangeably.

As also discussed in Chapter 1, the *DSM-IV-TR* requires that at least one of the following conditions be met within the year prior before a person can be diagnosed as a substance abuser: the person has repeatedly failed to live up to major obligations, such as on the job, at school, or in the family, because of drug use; the person has used the substance in dangerous situations, such as before driving; the person has had multiple legal problems because of drug use; or the person continued to use drugs in the face of interpersonal problems, such as arguments or fights caused by substance use.

The *DSM-IV-TR* requires that at least three of the following conditions be met in the previous year before a person can be said to be substance dependent: the patient has experienced increased tolerance; the patient experienced withdrawal; the patient had a loss of control over quantity or duration of use; the patient had a continuing wish or inability to decrease use; the patient spent inordinate amounts of time procuring or consuming drugs or recovering from substance use; the patient has given up important goals or activities because of substance use; or the patient has continued to use the substance despite knowledge that he or she has experienced damaging effects.

Essence of Drug Abuse

Alan I. Leshner, the director of the National Institute of Drug Abuse (NIDA), notes in his article "The Essence of Drug Abuse" (June 14, 2005, http://www.drugabuse .gov/Published_Articles/Essence.html), that:

> What does matter tremendously is whether or not a drug causes what we now know to be the essence of addiction: uncontrollable, compulsive drug seeking and use, even in the face of negative health and social consequences. This is the crux of how many professional organizations all define addiction, and how we all should use the term. It is really only this expression of addiction—uncontrollable, compulsive craving, seeking and use of drugs—that matters to the addict and to his or her family, and that should matter to society as a whole. These are the elements responsible for the massive health and social problems caused by drug addiction.

Disease Model of Addiction

In the last twenty years of the twentieth century, advances in neuroscience led to new understanding of how people become addicted and why they stay that way. The disease model of addiction has been proposed by psychiatric and medical researchers. Addicts, they say, respond to drugs differently than people who are not addicted. Much of the difference is associated with differences in brain functioning and can be linked to genetic factors. Approaches to treatment emphasize that addiction must be treated in the same way as other chronic diseases.

A. Thomas McLellan et al., in "Drug Dependence, a Chronic Medical Illness" (*Journal of the American Medical Association*, October 4, 2000), liken drug dependence to chronic illnesses such as diabetes, hypertension, and asthma. McLellan et al. review scientific studies of twins and children of parents who were dependent on alcohol or other drugs. They report high degrees of correlation between parental and sibling dependence, suggesting a strong genetic component in addiction and alcoholism.

FIGURE 6.1

Components of comprehensive drug abuse treatment

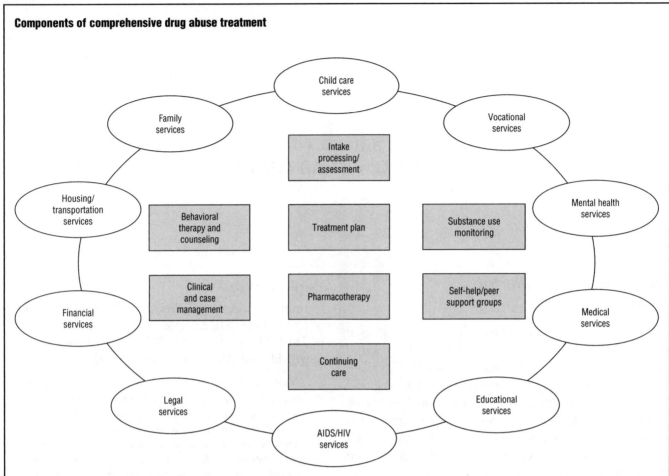

SOURCE: "Components of Comprehensive Drug Abuse Treatment," in *Principles of Drug Addiction Treatment: A Research-Based Guide*, National Institutes of Health, National Institute on Drug Abuse, October 1999, reprinted July 2000, http://www.nida.nih.gov/PDF/PODAT/PODAT.pdf (accessed October 17, 2006)

In addition, people who used drugs over long periods had different patterns of brain function, which seemed to lead them to continue to use drugs. Furthermore, in "Molecular Genetics of Addiction Vulnerability" (*NeuroRx*, July 2006), George R. Uhl posits that "classical genetic studies document strong complex genetic contributions to abuse of multiple addictive substances."

NIDA also views drug addiction (if not all substance abuse) as a disease. On its "Frequently Asked Questions" Web page (October 10, 2006, http://www.nida.nih.gov/tools/FAQ.html), the agency answers the question, "What is drug addiction?":

> Drug addiction is a complex brain disease. It is characterized by drug craving, seeking, and use that can persist even in the face of extremely negative consequences. Drug-seeking may become compulsive in large part as a result of the effects of prolonged drug use on brain functioning and, thus, on behavior. For many people, relapses are possible even after long periods of abstinence.

In *Principles of Drug Addiction Treatment: A Research-Based Guide* (October 1999, http://www.nida .nih.gov/PDF/PODAT/PODAT.pdf), NIDA points out that drug addiction is not only a brain disease but also leads to social "illness" and other diseases:

> Addiction often involves not only compulsive drug taking but also a wide range of dysfunctional behaviors that can interfere with normal functioning in the family, the workplace, and the broader community. Addiction also can place people at increased risk for a wide variety of other illnesses. These illnesses can be brought on by behaviors, such as poor living and health habits, that often accompany life as an addict, or because of [the] toxic effects of the drugs themselves.

An Integrated Approach to Treatment

The modern approach to treatment has come to reflect the complexity of the drug abuse-addiction spectrum and combines medical approaches, behavior modification, education, and social support functions intended to redress imbalances in the patient's total environment. Components of a comprehensive drug treatment approach are shown in Figure 6.1. Arrayed in the center are categories of treatment used alone or in combination and, on the periphery, social service functions that may have to be deployed to solve some of the patient's problems that led to drug use or addiction in the first place.

HOW MANY PEOPLE ARE BEING TREATED?
UFDS/N-SSATS Data

The Substance Abuse and Mental Health Services Administration (SAMHSA), an agency of the U.S. Department of Health and Human Services, has been collecting data on substance abuse facilities since 1976. The program has had various names throughout its history; it was called the Uniform Facility Data Set (UFDS) survey until 2000, when the name was changed to the National Survey of Substance Abuse Treatment Services (N-SSATS). In the course of this program's history, the data collected have changed, introducing discontinuities in reporting. Until 1998, under the UFDS, data on clients of treatment services were reported in some detail, were omitted in 1999, and reintroduced in limited format in 2000. The most recent UFDS data on the gender, racial, ethnic, and age characteristics of people in treatment were reported in 1998. Data on these breakdowns of admissions, however, have continued to be available from another SAMHSA source: the Treatment Episode Data Set, which is discussed later in this chapter.

N-SSATS numbers represent a snapshot of the treatment units on a particular day and do not indicate how many people were being treated over the course of the entire year. As of March 31, 2004, N-SSATS reported in the *National Survey of Substance Abuse Treatment Services (N-SSATS): 2004—Data on Substance Abuse Treatment Facilities* (2005, http://wwwdasis.samhsa .gov/04nssats/index.htm) that the number of people in the treatment facilities who responded to the survey stood at slightly over 1.07 million, representing a slight increase since the 1998 figure of nearly 1.04 million. (See Table 6.1.)

NSDUH Data

The SAMHSA also included questions about treatment in its 2005 National Survey on Drug Use and Health (NSDUH) to collect data from people who sought and received substance abuse treatment. Figure 6.2 shows the results of asking recipients where they received treatment for substance use in the past year at any location. People could report receiving treatment at more than one location. (This definition of treatment location is different from the specific treatment facilities reporting to the SAMHSA for N-SSATS.) The NSDUH determines that self-help groups, outpatient rehabilitation facilities, inpatient rehabilitation facilities, outpatient mental health centers, and hospital inpatient facilities are where people say they most commonly receive treatment.

The NSDUH also asked substance abusers why they did not receive the treatment they needed. SAMHSA data show that 7.6 million people needed treatment in 2005, but only a fraction of these people (the 1.07 million mentioned previously) received treatment at a specialty facility. Figure 6.3 shows that most people (44.4%) cited financial reasons for not receiving treatment. One out of five admitted that they were not yet ready to give up drugs.

Treatment Episode Data Set Data

Another source of data for the drug-treatment population comes from the SAMHSA's Treatment Episode Data Set (TEDS). This program counts admissions over the period of a year rather than the number of people in treatment on a particular date during the year. When the same person is admitted twice during the same year, he or she is counted twice, whereas in the UFDS/N-SSATS survey individuals are counted only once. As reported in *Treatment Episode Data Set (TEDS) 1994–2004: National Admissions to Substance Abuse Treatment Services* (July 2006, http://wwwdasis.samhsa.gov/teds04/tedsad 2k4web.pdf), TEDS data for 1998 showed over 1.7 million admissions (versus UFDS's nearly 1.04 million). TEDS admissions in 2004 were over 1.8 million.

CHARACTERISTICS OF THOSE ADMITTED

TEDS data from 1994 to 2004 on admissions by sex, race/ethnicity, and age are presented in Table 6.2 and Table 6.3.

Gender

As shown in Table 6.2, males represented most of those admitted for drug and/or alcohol treatment, although the percentage of men dropped slightly between 1994 and 2004 (from 71.4% to 68.5%) and that of women increased (from 28.6% to 31.5%). The number of males admitted for treatment in 2004 was nearly 1.3 million versus just over 590,000 female admissions. (See Table 6.3.) These results and data from the NSDUH reflect that a greater proportion of men abuse drugs than women in the United States. According to Table 4.1 in Chapter 4, 9.9% of males were past-month users in 2004, compared with 6.1% of females.

Race and Ethnicity

In 2004 whites were most of those admitted to substance abuse treatment facilities (60%; see Table 6.2) and were those admitted in the greatest numbers (1.1 million; see Table 6.3). They were followed by African-Americans at 22.5% (419,099). Compared with data from 1994, whites increased from 58.3% (963,257) and African-Americans decreased from 27.1% (447,945). Hispanics

TABLE 6.1

Persons admitted into substance abuse treatment, by state or region and type of care received, March 31, 2004

State or jurisdiction*	Total	Outpatient						Residential (Type of care offered)				Hospital inpatient		
		Total outpatient	Regular	Intensive	Day treatment or partial hospitalization	Detox	Methadone maintenance	Total residential	Short-term	Long-term	Detox	Total hospital inpatient	Treatment	Detox
Total	1,072,251	954,551	564,300	121,862	28,133	12,064	228,192	101,713	21,758	72,934	7,021	15,987	9,773	6,214
Alabama	12,106	10,931	1,359	4,350	280	76	4,866	1,123	381	647	95	52	32	20
Alaska	2,503	2,097	1,480	404	110	20	83	388	106	249	33	18	7	11
Arizona	23,527	21,563	13,328	2,679	469	701	4,386	1,743	438	1,163	142	221	112	109
Arkansas	3,165	2,507	1,583	436	62	124	302	555	221	288	46	103	66	37
California	140,401	121,676	71,976	16,610	3,890	2,597	26,603	17,567	2,229	14,287	1,051	1,158	733	425
Colorado	30,501	28,602	24,177	1,879	398	125	2,023	1,762	229	1,238	295	137	104	33
Connecticut	21,363	18,960	8,023	1,715	666	302	8,254	1,778	573	1,084	121	625	239	386
Delaware	3,977	3,735	2,103	228	52	23	1,329	162	10	108	44	80	68	12
District of Columbia	5,365	4,426	1,256	1,012	237	35	1,886	861	278	459	124	78	66	12
Fed. of Micronesia	—	—	—	—	—	—	—	—	—	—	—	—	—	—
Florida	45,215	38,737	25,097	2,876	1,424	262	9,078	5,487	783	4,282	422	991	595	396
Georgia	17,238	14,576	6,235	2,168	2,191	240	3,742	2,162	235	1,719	208	500	309	191
Guam	178	178	100	78	—	—	—	—	—	—	—	—	—	—
Hawaii	3,618	3,005	1,581	629	163	21	611	386	70	306	10	227	200	27
Idaho	4,017	3,768	2,907	830	17	14	—	193	70	95	28	56	28	28
Illinois	42,709	39,055	21,968	4,652	640	157	11,638	3,385	711	2,427	247	269	116	153
Indiana	25,396	24,102	15,022	5,020	393	256	3,411	998	218	715	65	296	160	136
Iowa	8,220	7,579	5,819	1,271	216	20	253	620	200	400	20	21	5	16
Kansas	9,796	8,969	6,352	1,591	157	53	816	752	318	363	71	75	54	21
Kentucky	18,261	17,001	14,157	1,409	116	14	1,305	1,021	241	686	94	239	168	71
Louisiana	12,313	10,432	5,746	1,631	215	98	2,742	1,515	427	960	128	366	213	153
Maine	7,109	6,693	4,359	434	173	121	1,606	326	52	274	—	90	40	50
Maryland	34,449	32,192	15,567	3,269	491	614	12,251	2,078	558	1,416	104	179	149	30
Massachusetts	35,998	31,866	19,958	779	582	829	9,718	3,158	477	2,342	339	974	274	700
Michigan	42,121	38,615	28,315	2,469	235	546	7,050	3,255	1,071	1,955	229	251	172	79
Minnesota	9,679	6,714	2,075	2,542	388	25	1,684	2,632	846	1,633	153	333	287	46
Mississippi	6,095	4,649	3,636	559	452	2	—	1,113	218	886	9	333	240	93
Missouri	17,566	15,593	9,541	3,520	846	36	1,650	1,653	1,083	474	96	320	235	85
Montana	2,715	2,491	2,087	377	12	15	—	165	61	45	59	59	43	16
Nebraska	4,976	4,174	3,226	720	25	17	186	744	224	473	47	58	56	2
Nevada	8,335	7,458	4,885	613	59	73	1,828	795	109	633	53	82	18	64
New Hampshire	3,517	3,211	2,604	90	6	115	396	288	103	147	38	18	6	12
New Jersey	29,687	26,609	9,259	3,599	1,259	1,815	10,677	2,482	364	2,046	72	596	433	163
New Mexico	11,517	10,802	7,518	830	165	144	2,145	622	141	367	114	93	70	23
New York	120,451	107,399	46,147	13,115	5,471	358	42,308	10,723	1,503	8,607	613	2,329	1,318	1,011
North Carolina	26,169	24,024	15,013	3,099	241	185	5,486	1,757	393	1,245	119	388	257	131
North Dakota	2,383	2,045	1,147	431	447	20	—	282	70	206	6	56	52	4
Ohio	36,133	33,417	24,225	5,654	475	218	2,845	2,262	410	1,754	98	454	288	166
Oklahoma	8,738	7,593	6,014	801	90	226	462	1,056	274	688	94	89	39	50
Oregon	18,735	17,553	11,430	3,253	102	84	2,684	1,160	218	859	83	22	9	13
Palau	42	39	29	—	10	—	—	3	—	—	—	3	—	3
Pennsylvania	38,796	33,744	18,206	4,863	825	92	9,758	4,271	1,466	2,548	257	781	640	141
Puerto Rico	10,974	6,312	1,876	204	379	98	3,755	4,222	112	3,818	292	440	345	95
Rhode Island	6,590	6,237	2,642	118	64	164	3,249	329	27	272	30	24	—	24

TABLE 6.1

Persons admitted into substance abuse treatment, by state or region and type of care received, March 31, 2004 [CONTINUED]

		Number												
		Type of care offered												
		Outpatient						Residential				Total hospital inpatient	Hospital inpatient	
State or jurisdiction*	Total	Total outpatient	Regular	Intensive	Day treatment or partial hospitalization	Detox	Methadone maintenance	Total residential	Short-term	Long-term	Detox		Treatment	Detox
South Carolina	13,641	13,019	9,570	1,070	89	44	2,246	341	96	206	39	281	152	129
South Dakota	1,991	1,495	1,026	402	51	16	—	452	139	253	60	44	44	—
Tennessee	13,139	10,949	6,738	1,414	211	32	2,554	1,823	917	819	87	367	208	159
Texas	33,820	27,278	13,363	4,013	1,117	218	8,567	5,581	1,589	3,758	234	961	586	375
Utah	9,732	8,695	5,784	987	471	105	1,348	991	68	849	74	46	29	17
Vermont	2,668	2,522	2,142	219	49	3	109	106	43	52	11	40	16	24
Virgin Islands	135	116	84	32	—	—	—	19	—	19	—	—	—	—
Virginia	22,298	20,919	15,775	1,536	575	171	2,862	1,228	348	747	133	151	66	85
Washington	34,839	32,940	22,468	6,631	166	329	3,346	1,730	750	859	121	169	119	50
West Virginia	7,103	6,677	3,226	701	176	105	2,469	371	75	277	19	55	22	33
Wisconsin	17,354	15,918	12,164	1,430	655	44	1,625	1,068	207	773	88	368	266	102
Wyoming	2,887	2,694	1,932	620	80	62	—	172	8	158	6	21	19	2

*Facilities operated by federal agencies are included in the states in which the facilities are located.

— Quantity is zero.

SOURCE: "Table 6.24a. Clients in Treatment, according to Type of Care Received, by State or Jurisdiction: March 31, 2004, Number," in *National Survey of Substance Abuse Treatment Services (N-SSATS): 2004, Data on Substance Abuse Treatment Facilities*, U.S. Department of Health and Human Services, Substance Abuse and Mental Health Services Administration, Office of Applied Studies, August 2005, http://wwdasis.samhsa.gov/04nssats/nssats_rpt_04.pdf (accessed October 17, 2006)

FIGURE 6.2

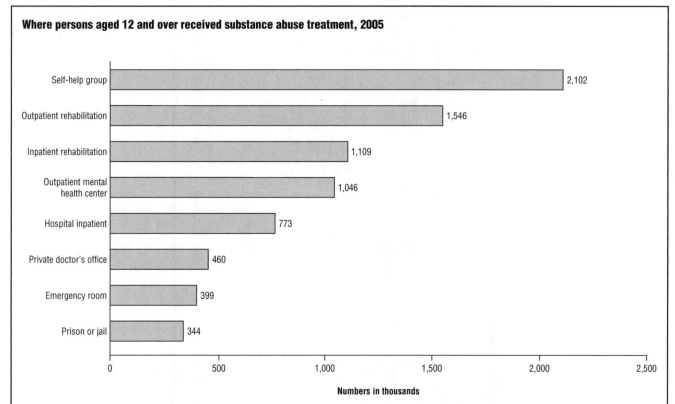

Where persons aged 12 and over received substance abuse treatment, 2005

Self-help group — 2,102
Outpatient rehabilitation — 1,546
Inpatient rehabilitation — 1,109
Outpatient mental health center — 1,046
Hospital inpatient — 773
Private doctor's office — 460
Emergency room — 399
Prison or jail — 344

Numbers in thousands

SOURCE: "Figure 7.5. Locations Where Past Year Substance Use Treatment Was Received among Persons Aged 12 or Older: 2005," in *Results from the 2005 National Survey on Drug Use and Health: National Findings*, U.S. Department of Health and Human Services, Substance Abuse and Mental Health Services Administration, Office of Applied Studies, 2006, http://www.oas.samhsa.gov/nsduh/2k5nsduh/2k5Results.pdf (accessed October 12, 2006)

increased their proportion of admissions to drug treatment facilities from 11% (181,168) in 1994 to 12.7% (235,793) in 2004. American Indians and Alaskan Natives dropped in share of those treated from 2.3% to 2.1% during this period. Asian and Pacific Islanders increased by 0.3% but remained less than 1% of the total admissions.

Age

In 1994 the age group with the largest number receiving substance abuse treatment was twenty-five- to thirty-four-year-olds (37.8% of total), followed by those aged thirty-five to forty-four years (29.1%). Ten years later, these were still the two largest groups receiving treatment, but the order was reversed: those aged thirty-five to forty-four were in the group having the highest percentage receiving substance abuse treatment and those aged twenty-five to thirty-four were in the group having the second-highest percentage. The percentage of the younger group decreased to 24.7% in 2004, whereas the percentage of the older group stayed about the same (29%), thus causing the order reversal. Those aged sixty-five and older were least represented (after those under the age of twelve), accounting for 0.8% in 1994 and 0.6% in 2004. (See Table 6.2.)

TYPES OF TREATMENT

The treatment that recovering drug addicts receive depends on the types of drugs to which they are addicted. Regardless of the substance they are addicted to, most treatment programs involve some form of rehabilitation ("rehab"). Drug rehab refers to processes that assist a drug-addicted person in discontinuing drug use and returning to a drug-free life. For many types of addiction, rehab is the only form of treatment that is needed. However, those who are addicted to opiates typically must undergo a period of detoxification ("detox") before rehab can begin. In some cases opiate addicts are given opioid substitutes to help them with their addiction.

Detox

Individuals addicted to opium-based drugs must usually undergo medical detox in an outpatient facility, a residential center, or a hospital. Medical help, including sedation, is provided to manage the painful physical and psychic symptoms of withdrawal. Counseling is always available as well; in many detox centers group therapy is available. NIDA, however, describes detoxification as a precursor to rehabilitation because that process cannot begin until the individual's body has

FIGURE 6.3

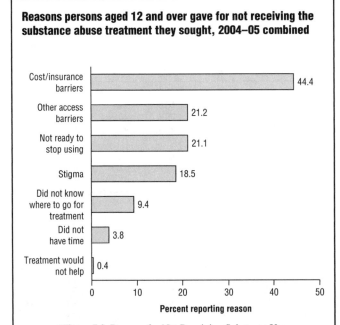

Reasons persons aged 12 and over gave for not receiving the substance abuse treatment they sought, 2004–05 combined

SOURCE: "Figure 7.8. Reasons for Not Receiving Substance Use Treatment among Persons Aged 12 or Older Who Needed and Made an Effort to Get Treatment But Did Not Receive Treatment and Felt They Needed Treatment: 2004–2005 Combined," in *Results from the 2005 National Survey on Drug Use and Health: National Findings*, U.S. Department of Health and Human Services, Substance Abuse and Mental Health Services Administration, Office of Applied Studies, 2006, http://www.oas.samhsa.gov/nsduh/2k5nsduh/2k5Results.pdf (accessed October 12, 2006)

been cleared of the drug and a certain physiological equilibrium has been established. Rehabilitation usually follows detoxification.

Rehabilitation

Rehab has many forms, but it is always designed to change the behavior of the drug abuser. Changed behavior—achieving independence of drugs or alcohol—requires understanding the circumstances that led to dependence, confidence that the individual can succeed, and changes in lifestyle so that the individual avoids occasions that produced drug-using behavior. Individual counseling, interaction with support groups, and formal education are used in combination with close supervision, incentives, and disincentives. Certain individuals require a new socialization that is achieved by living for an extended time in a structured and supportive environment in which new life skills can be acquired. Treatment may involve guiding the individual to seek help from other social agencies (as shown in the circle in Figure 6.1) to reorder his or her life.

Individuals, of course, may be mentally ill and will then receive, as part of drug rehab, mental health services in outpatient or hospital settings. Most treatment takes place in outpatient settings, with the individual reporting daily, weekly, or less frequently for periodic treatment and assessment.

OPIOID SUBSTITUTE PROGRAMS. Heroin addicts and those habituated to other opium-based substances follow usual treatment programs but may, in addition, be prescribed what are known as opioid substitutes. The best known of the opioid substitutes is methadone, which is an agonist, a chemical substance that activates brain receptors. In the case of methadone, the brain receptors it activates are the same receptors that respond to heroin. However, heroin addiction disrupts many physiological functions, whereas methadone normalizes those functions. Many studies show methadone to be effective; likewise, many thousands lead normal lives using this heroin substitute. Methadone was approved for use in 1972.

Levo-alpha-acetylmethadol (LAAM), which was approved in 1993, is another agonist used in treating drug dependency. Whereas methadone must be taken daily, LAAM can be taken three times per week. Use of LAAM and methadone is not without risk. It is possible to become dependent on them just as it is with heroin and other opioids. However, clinical experience with both methadone and LAAM indicates that these medications have a much lower potential for abuse than heroin.

Naltrexone is an antagonist, a chemical substance that reduces the effect of another chemical substance on the body. Naltrexone blocks the effect of heroin on the brain's receptors and can reduce involuntary compulsive drug craving. It can be prescribed by physicians and is effective both against alcohol dependency and in detox. As reported in "Subutex and Suboxone Approved to Treat Opiate Dependence" (*FDA Talk Paper*, October 2, 2002), buprenorphine, which was approved for use by the U.S. Food and Drug Administration in 2002, acts as an agonist at lower doses and as an antagonist at higher doses.

Distribution of Patients

The great majority of patients undergoing treatment in 2004 were receiving outpatient care, 954,551 (89%) of nearly 1.1 million patients on March 31 of that year. (See Table 6.1.) Of the remainder, 101,713 (9.5%) were in residential facilities and 15,987 (1.5%) received hospital inpatient treatment. Of those under outpatient treatment but not in detox, the majority were receiving what the SAMHSA labels regular, or nonintensive, treatment.

Of the total treatment population, 25,299 individuals (2.4% of all patients) were undergoing detox, most in outpatient settings (12,064), the rest in residential facilities (7,021) and hospitals (6,214). Among all patients under treatment, 228,192 (21.3%) were receiving methadone. (See Table 6.1.)

TABLE 6.2

Percentage of persons admitted into substance abuse treatment, by gender, ethnicity, and age at admission, 1994–2004

Sex, race/ethnicity, and age at admission	TEDS admissions*											U.S. population
	1994	1995	1996	1997	1998	1999	2000	2001	2002	2003	2004	2004
Sex												
Male	71.4	70.7	70.5	70.4	70.5	70.5	70.0	69.8	69.8	69.1	68.5	48.9
Female	28.6	29.3	29.5	29.6	29.5	29.5	30.0	30.2	30.2	30.9	31.5	51.1
Total	100.0	100.0	100.0	100.0	100.0	100.0	100.0	100.0	100.0	100.0	100.0	100.0
Race/ethnicity												
White (non-Hispanic)	58.3	59.0	59.8	59.6	59.5	59.2	58.5	59.1	58.8	58.7	60.0	70.2
Black (non-Hispanic)	27.1	26.7	25.7	25.3	24.9	24.3	24.9	24.4	24.2	24.0	22.5	12.4
Hispanic	11.0	10.7	10.4	10.9	11.3	12.0	12.0	12.0	12.6	12.7	12.7	12.0
American Indian/Alaska Native	2.3	2.3	2.5	2.4	2.4	2.4	2.3	2.2	2.1	2.0	2.1	0.8
Asian/Pacific Islander	0.6	0.6	0.6	0.7	0.7	0.8	0.8	0.8	0.9	1.0	0.9	4.3
Other	0.8	0.8	1.0	1.1	1.2	1.4	1.6	1.5	1.4	1.6	1.8	0.4
Total	100.0	100.0	100.0	100.0	100.0	100.0	100.0	100.0	100.0	100.0	100.0	100.0
Age at admission												
Under 12 years	0.2	0.2	0.2	0.2	0.2	0.2	0.2	0.1	0.1	0.2	0.2	16.4
12 to 17 years	6.6	7.4	7.9	8.2	8.1	8.0	7.8	8.2	8.3	8.4	8.3	8.8
18 to 24 years	14.0	13.8	13.4	13.8	14.4	15.0	15.8	16.6	17.1	17.4	18.1	9.9
25 to 34 years	37.8	36.1	33.9	32.2	30.3	28.4	27.0	26.0	25.1	24.7	24.7	12.8
35 to 44 years	29.1	29.9	31.0	31.6	32.2	32.6	32.6	31.9	31.1	30.3	29.0	15.0
45 to 54 years	9.1	9.5	10.3	10.8	11.5	12.4	13.2	13.8	14.7	15.3	15.8	14.3
55 to 64 years	2.5	2.4	2.5	2.5	2.6	2.7	2.8	2.7	3.0	3.1	3.2	10.0
65 years and older	0.8	0.7	0.7	0.7	0.7	0.7	0.7	0.6	0.6	0.6	0.6	12.6
Total	100.0	100.0	100.0	100.0	100.0	100.0	100.0	100.0	100.0	100.0	100.0	100.0

*Treatment episode data set.

SOURCE: "Table 2.9b. Admissions by Sex, Race/Ethnicity, and Age at Admission: TEDS 1994–2004 and U.S. Population 2004 Percent Distribution," in *Treatment Episode Data Set (TEDS) 1994–2004: National Admissions to Substance Abuse Treatment Services*, U.S. Department of Health and Human Services, Substance Abuse and Mental Health Services Administration, Office of Applied Studies, July 2006, http://wwwdasis.samhsa.gov/teds04/tedsad2k4web.pdf (accessed October 17, 2006)

STATISTICS ON ADMITTED PATIENTS

Admissions by Substance

Data on admissions by the primary substance of abuse provided by TEDS for 2004 are shown in Table 6.4. In that year alcohol alone and with a secondary drug is the primary substance for which the greatest number of people received treatment (753,464, or 40.2%, of all admissions), followed by opiates (329,138, or 17.6%, mainly heroin), marijuana (298,317, or 15.9%), cocaine (256,387, or 13.7%), and stimulants (151,404, or 8.1%, primarily methamphetamine).

The 2004 admissions for alcohol abuse (either alone or in combination with a secondary substance) of 40.2% is down from 52.8% reported by TEDS in 1994. Total alcohol-related admissions have been declining annually, largely accounting for the decreasing trend in total admissions.

The category showing the largest growth has been stimulants. In 1994 stimulants accounted for 2.7% of all admissions, whereas in 2004 they accounted for 8.1%, as indicated by the admissions numbers in Table 6.4. Within the stimulant category, admissions caused by amphetamine (particularly methamphetamine) accounted for the vast majority. Methamphetamine is addictive and

is produced in illicit makeshift laboratories around the country. Marijuana-related admissions have had the second most rapid growth, representing 15.9% of cases in 2004, up from 8.5% as reported by TEDS in 1994.

Opiate-related admissions have been growing, and cocaine-related admissions have been declining. In 1994 opiate-caused admissions were 13.8% and cocaine-caused admissions were 17.8% of the total; ten years later their percentages were reversed, with opiates accounting for 17.5% and cocaine for 13.7% of admissions, as indicated by the admissions numbers in Table 6.4. The largest decline of admissions from 1994 to 2004 has been for cases involving inhalants, declining to 0.06% of all admissions in 2004, down from 0.16% in 1994.

Demographics by Substance

A detailed examination of admissions in 2004 is provided in Table 6.4, which shows the distribution of people admitted by major drug categories, gender, race/ethnicity, and age at admission.

GENDER. As noted previously in this chapter, total male admissions (68.5%) were higher than total female admissions (31.5%) in 2004. As Table 6.4 shows, this trend held in all but two substance categories: sedatives (54.4% females versus 45.6% males) and tranquilizers

TABLE 6.3

Persons admitted into substance abuse treatment, by gender, ethnicity, and age at admission, 1994–2004

Sex, race/ethnicity, and age at admission	1994	1995	1996	1997	1998	1999	2000	2001	2002	2003	2004
Total	1,665,331	1,675,380	1,639,064	1,607,957	1,712,268	1,725,885	1,802,807	1,824,254	1,938,846	1,892,733	1,872,784
Sex											
Male	1,182,286	1,179,563	1,151,527	1,128,154	1,202,608	1,212,676	1,258,788	1,271,668	1,352,419	1,307,112	1,281,888
Female	473,884	488,715	481,191	474,350	502,961	507,136	538,888	550,169	585,538	584,984	590,043
No. of admissions	1,656,170	1,668,278	1,632,718	1,602,504	1,705,569	1,719,812	1,797,676	1,821,837	1,937,957	1,892,096	1,871,931
Race/ethnicity											
White (non-Hispanic)	963,257	981,359	973,808	948,992	1,004,115	1,008,503	1,044,157	1,069,476	1,131,619	1,103,598	1,116,708
Black (non-Hispanic)	447,945	443,964	418,514	402,619	419,784	413,754	443,894	441,260	465,187	451,247	419,099
Hispanic	181,168	178,269	169,285	173,347	191,484	203,750	213,508	217,017	242,683	238,481	235,793
American Indian/Alaska Native	38,404	37,704	40,082	38,333	40,511	40,138	40,618	40,296	41,266	37,208	38,141
Asian/Pacific Islander	9,873	9,870	10,197	10,893	11,515	13,610	14,980	14,405	16,802	17,940	16,371
Other	12,896	13,193	16,606	18,263	20,351	23,467	27,999	26,354	27,255	30,604	34,213
No. of admissions	1,653,543	1,664,359	1,628,492	1,592,447	1,687,760	1,703,222	1,785,156	1,808,808	1,924,812	1,879,078	1,860,325
Age at admission											
Under 12 years	3,211	3,616	3,469	3,704	3,390	2,987	3,050	2,484	2,486	2,931	3,677
12 to 17 years	109,122	122,909	129,858	131,194	139,129	137,596	140,996	148,848	160,856	158,397	155,585
18 to 24 years	232,063	230,645	219,406	220,714	245,508	258,208	283,375	302,548	330,298	329,178	338,295
25 to 34 years	628,260	603,148	555,300	516,346	517,297	488,394	485,287	472,698	485,505	467,386	462,148
35 to 44 years	482,401	499,650	507,067	506,624	549,754	559,649	585,376	580,546	601,594	571,839	541,498
45 to 54 years	151,320	159,111	167,899	173,335	197,211	213,538	237,555	251,555	285,247	289,284	295,039
55 to 64 years	41,052	40,390	41,377	40,736	44,096	46,299	49,505	49,704	57,087	58,701	60,432
65 years and older	12,967	11,938	11,535	11,381	11,611	11,652	12,297	11,554	11,650	11,412	11,713
No. of admissions	1,660,396	1,671,407	1,635,911	1,604,034	1,707,996	1,718,323	1,797,441	1,819,937	1,934,723	1,889,128	1,868,387

SOURCE: "Table 2.9a. Admissions by Sex, Race/Ethnicity, and Age at Admission: TEDS 1994–2004, Number," in *Treatment Episode Data Set (TEDS) 1994–2004: National Admissions to Substance Abuse Treatment Services*, U.S. Department of Health and Human Services, Substance Abuse and Mental Health Services Administration, Office of Applied Studies, July 2006, http://wwwdasis.samhsa.gov/teds04/tedsad2k4web.pdf (accessed October 17, 2006)

Alcohol, Tobacco, and Illicit Drugs

TABLE 6.4

Percentage of persons admitted into substance abuse treatment, by gender, ethnicity, and primary substance abused, 2004

Primary substance at admission

Sex and race/ethnicity	All admissions	Alcohol		Opiates		Cocaine		Mari-juana/hashish	Stimulants		Tran-quilizers	Sedatives	Hallucinogens	PCP	Inhalants	Other/none specified
		Alcohol only	With secondary drug	Heroin	Other opiates	Smoked cocaine	Other route		Metham-phetamine/amphetamine	Other stimulants						
Sex																
Total	1,875,026	416,510	336,954	265,895	63,243	184,949	71,438	298,317	150,402	1,007	8,558	4,487	2,408	3,272	1,209	66,377
Male	68.5	74.9	73.8	68.0	52.8	58.6	66.1	74.2	54.8	57.4	47.6	45.6	71.5	66.5	68.7	58.7
Female	31.5	25.1	26.2	32.0	47.2	41.4	33.9	25.8	45.2	42.6	52.4	54.4	28.5	33.5	31.3	41.3
Total	100.0	100.0	100.0	100.0	100.0	100.0	100.0	100.0	100.0	100.0	100.0	100.0	100.0	100.0	100.0	100.0
No. of admissions	1,874,173	416,336	336,808	265,842	63,212	184,895	71,403	298,139	150,343	1,006	8,556	4,485	2,403	3,272	1,207	66,266
Race/ethnicity																
White (non-Hispanic)	60.0	70.4	60.4	50.4	88.8	37.8	51.5	54.3	72.6	62.3	85.0	82.9	69.8	19.9	67.4	67.3
Black (non-Hispanic)	22.5	12.4	24.6	23.6	4.7	53.0	28.9	28.6	2.5	21.0	5.3	6.7	16.9	50.3	6.2	16.2
Hispanic origin	12.8	11.7	10.2	23.0	3.4	6.7	15.9	12.2	15.8	10.2	7.6	6.9	8.2	22.8	18.7	10.9
Mexican	5.2	6.2	3.3	5.4	1.2	2.2	5.6	5.6	12.3	4.0	1.4	3.3	2.8	11.8	13.5	1.1
Puerto Rican	3.9	1.7	3.6	12.7	1.0	2.3	5.3	3.0	0.3	2.4	3.9	1.9	2.0	6.5	1.7	1.5
Cuban	0.3	0.3	0.2	0.4	0.1	0.5	0.9	0.4	0.2	0.4	0.2	0.2	0.2	0.6	0.1	0.3
Other/not specified	3.4	3.4	3.0	4.5	1.1	1.8	4.1	3.3	3.0	3.5	2.0	1.6	3.1	3.9	3.5	8.1
Other	4.8	5.6	4.8	3.0	3.1	2.5	3.7	4.8	9.1	6.5	2.1	3.4	5.2	7.0	7.6	5.6
Alaska Native	0.1	0.1	0.1	0.2	0.1	0.1	0.1	0.1	0.1	0.1	0.1	0.2	0.1	0.4	—	*
American Indian	1.9	3.0	2.6	0.6	1.5	0.7	1.0	1.6	2.2	1.7	0.7	1.2	1.0	1.0	4.9	3.1
Asian/Pacific																
Islander	0.9	0.8	0.6	0.4	0.6	0.5	0.5	1.1	3.0	1.4	0.3	0.6	1.7	0.5	0.8	0.7
Other	1.8	1.6	1.5	1.8	1.0	1.2	2.1	2.0	3.8	3.3	1.0	1.4	2.4	5.1	1.8	1.8
Total	100.0	100.0	100.0	100.0	100.0	100.0	100.0	100.0	100.0	100.0	100.0	100.0	100.0	100.0	100.0	100.0
No. of admissions	1,862,567	414,176	335,298	264,017	62,798	184,211	70,899	296,331	149,696	1,006	8,538	4,469	2,391	3,252	1,201	64,284

*Less than 0.05 percent.
—Quantity is zero.

SOURCE: "Table 3.1a. Admissions by Primary Substance of Abuse, according to Sex and Race/Ethnicity: TEDS 2004 Column Percent Distribution," in *Treatment Episode Data Set (TEDS) 1994–2004: National Admissions to Substance Abuse Treatment Services*, U.S. Department of Health and Human Services, Substance Abuse and Mental Health Services Administration, Office of Applied Studies, July 2006, http://wwdasis.samhsa.gov/teds04/tedsad2k4web.pdf (accessed October 17, 2006)

(52.4% females versus 47.6% males). The greatest male-female differences were noted in alcohol-only admissions (74.9% males versus 25.1% females), marijuana-related admissions (74.2% males versus 25.8% females), and alcohol admissions with a secondary drug (73.8% males versus 26.2% females).

RACE AND ETHNICITY. In 2004 whites made up 60% of the substance abuse treatment admissions, African-Americans 22.5%, Hispanics 12.8%, American Indians 1.9%, and Asians and Pacific Islanders 0.9%. Whites had the highest admission rates for all drug categories except smoked cocaine and phencyclidine (PCP). African-Americans had the highest smoked-cocaine admissions (53%) and PCP-related admissions (50.3%). African-Americans were second in admission rates for all other substances of abuse except methamphetamine/amphetamine-, tranquilizer-, and sedative-related admissions. Hispanics were generally third in admission rates but were second in methamphetamine/amphetamine-, tranquilizer-, and sedative-related admissions. (See Table 6.4.) It is important to note that the Hispanics category is treated as an "ethnicity" rather than as a race and includes both white and black individuals of Hispanic origin.

It is, however, important to consider these rates of substance abuse treatment by race in the context of the overall racial composition of the United States. The 2004 TEDS data indicate that 70% of whites, 13% of Hispanics, and 12% of African-Americans made up the population. When substance abuse treatment rates are compared to these population statistics, whites were underrepresented in treatment (60% in treatment versus 70% in the population), the proportion of Hispanics in treatment was comparable to Hispanics in the population (12.8% in treatment versus 13% in the population), and African-Americans were disproportionately admitted for treatment (22.5% in treatment versus 12% in the population).

AGE AT ADMISSION. The 2004 TEDS data show that 85.4% of people admitted for alcohol-only abuse that year were between the ages of twenty and fifty-four and had an average age of thirty-nine years. Crack cocaine treatment recipients (74.9%) clustered in the thirty- to forty-nine-year-old age group and had an average age of thirty-eight years. In contrast, 46.1% of those admitted for using inhalants were aged seventeen or younger and had an average age of twenty-four years. Those being treated for marijuana abuse were another "young" group. Nearly three-quarters (73.3%) were between the ages of fifteen and twenty-nine. The marijuana treatment group had an average age of twenty-four years.

Type of Treatment

In 2004, 62.5% of those admitted to treatment were admitted into ambulatory (nonresidential) treatment facilities; of the remainder, 17.3% went into residential facilities

and 20.2% went into residential-type (twenty-four-hour) detoxification. (See Table 6.5.)

Among those going into drug-related detoxification, the largest percentages had been admitted for tranquilizer use (33%) and heroin (33.1%). Those using marijuana had the highest percentage entering ambulatory care (83.5%). The largest proportions of substance abusers assigned to residential treatment were cocaine users at 54.6%. (See Table 6.5.)

Referring Source

Table 6.6 shows the source of referral of patients to substance abuse treatment in 2004. Just over one-third of all people admitted came to get treatment at their own volition (33.7%). The largest referral source (sending 36.3% of individuals) was the criminal justice system, referring people for drug use or driving under the influence of alcohol. Much of the remaining third of all referrals came from substance abuse treatment providers and other health care agencies (10.7% and 6.9% of referrals, respectively), referring individuals for specific services. Other referrals came from schools, employers, and community agencies.

Regarding the source of referral based on the drug of abuse, Table 6.6 data show that most heroin users (57.8%) and other opiate users (49.8%) sought treatment of their own accord. Justice system sources sent most marijuana users (57%), meth users (50.4%), and PCP users (58.9%), along with many hallucinogen users (49.5%) and alcohol-only users (41.6%) to treatment.

HOW EFFECTIVE IS TREATMENT?

During the 1960s there was an opioid epidemic in the United States, and the federal government released substantial funds to substance abuse treatment programs. This funding has continued over the decades and is supplemented by state governments and private sources. Table 9.2 in Chapter 9 shows that the 2007 federal budget request for drug abuse treatment was $2.4 billion, and the request for treatment research was $605 million.

With so much money devoted to substance abuse treatment, there has been considerable research conducted on the effectiveness of the programs. The bulk of this research began in the late 1960s and extended into the 1990s.

In "New Research Documents Success of Drug Abuse Treatments" (December 15, 1997, http://www.nih.gov/news/pr/dec97/nida-15.htm), the National Institutes of Health notes that the first major study of drug-treatment effectiveness was the Drug Abuse Reporting Program (DARP), which studied more than forty-four thousand clients in more than fifty treatment centers from 1969 to 1973. Program staff then studied a smaller group of these clients

TABLE 6.5

Percentage of persons admitted into substance abuse treatment, by primary substance of abuse and type of care received, 2004

Type of service and planned use of opioid treatment	All admissions	Alcohol		Opiates		Cocaine		Marijuana/ hashish	Stimulants		Tran- quilizers	Sedatives	Hallu- cinogens	PCP	Inhalants	Other/ none specified
		Alcohol only	With secondary drug	Heroin	Other opiates	Smoked cocaine	Other route		Methamp- hetamine/ amphetamine	Other stimulants						
									Primary substance at admission							
Total	1,875,026	416,510	336,954	265,895	63,243	184,949	71,438	298,317	150,402	1,007	8,558	4,487	2,408	3,272	1,209	66,377
Type of service																
Ambulatory	62.5	59.1	58.6	51.3	56.8	52.4	63.3	83.5	65.0	68.4	49.0	59.1	71.9	70.6	68.2	81.3
Outpatient	50.2	49.2	47.6	37.4	42.1	39.0	47.9	68.3	51.7	59.0	37.0	46.9	60.1	58.9	56.2	76.9
Intensive outpatient	10.6	9.3	10.5	5.3	11.3	13.0	14.9	14.8	13.2	8.7	10.9	10.6	11.3	11.7	11.0	3.8
Detoxification	1.7	0.6	0.4	8.6	3.4	0.4	0.5	0.4	0.2	0.7	1.1	1.6	0.5	*	0.9	0.6
Detoxification (24-hour service)	20.2	29.5	22.4	33.1	25.9	19.2	10.5	2.6	9.7	13.0	33.0	20.1	7.7	5.0	13.4	10.2
Free-standing residential	16.0	24.5	16.7	22.8	20.6	17.4	9.1	2.4	9.4	11.8	19.6	15.2	6.5	4.3	12.7	7.4
Hospital inpatient	4.2	5.0	5.7	10.3	5.3	1.8	1.5	0.1	0.2	1.2	13.5	4.8	1.2	0.6	0.7	2.8
Rehabilitation/residential	17.3	11.4	19.0	15.6	17.3	28.4	26.2	13.9	25.3	18.6	18.0	20.8	20.3	24.4	18.4	8.6
Short-term (<31 days)	8.3	6.4	10.8	6.6	10.5	12.9	11.9	5.8	9.8	7.2	9.9	12.3	8.7	7.4	8.7	2.4
Long-term (31+ days)	8.0	3.9	7.2	7.6	5.4	14.7	12.7	7.6	14.9	9.5	5.9	7.2	11.0	16.4	8.7	4.5
Hospital (non-detox)	1.0	1.1	1.1	1.4	1.5	0.7	1.5	0.5	0.6	1.8	2.2	1.3	0.7	0.7	1.1	1.7
Total	100.0	100.0	100.0	100.0	100.0	100.0	100.0	100.0	100.0	100.0	100.0	100.0	100.0	100.0	100.0	100.0
No. of admissions	1,875,026	416,510	336,954	265,895	63,243	184,949	71,438	298,317	150,402	1,007	8,558	4,487	2,408	3,272	1,209	66,377

SOURCE: Adapted from "Table 3.6. Admissions by Primary Substance of Abuse, according to Type of Service and Opioid Replacement Therapy: TEDS 2004, Percent Distribution," in *Treatment Episode Data Set (TEDS) 1994–2004: National Admissions to Substance Abuse Treatment Services*, U.S. Department of Health and Human Services, Substance Abuse and Mental Health Services Administration, Office of Applied Studies, July 2006, http://wwwdasis.samhsa.gov/teds04/tedsad2k4web.pdf (accessed October 17, 2006)

TABLE 6.6

Percentage of persons admitted into substance abuse treatment, by primary substance of abuse, source of referral, and number of prior treatment episodes, 2004

Source of referral to treatment and number of prior treatment episodes	All admissions	Alcohol		Opiates		Cocaine		Marijuana/ hashish	Stimulants		Tran-quilizers	Sedatives	Hallu-cinogens	PCP	Inhalants	Other/ none specified
		Alcohol only	With secondary drug	Heroin	Other opiates	Smoked cocaine	Other route		Metham-phetamine/ amphetamine	Other stimulants						
Total	1,875,026	416,510	336,954	265,895	63,243	184,949	71,438	298,317	150,402	1,007	8,558	4,487	2,408	3,272	1,209	66,377
Source of referral to treatment																
Criminal justice/DUI[a]	36.3	41.6	35.0	14.5	16.1	26.8	34.3	57.0	50.4	38.4	19.6	27.0	49.5	58.9	28.1	19.9
Self- or individual	33.7	29.4	30.9	57.8	49.8	37.8	31.8	16.3	24.5	31.3	39.6	35.8	24.2	19.5	32.4	53.0
Substance abuse provider	10.7	9.1	13.3	16.2	14.5	15.3	12.9	5.5	5.1	8.8	17.2	12.9	8.5	7.6	8.4	2.2
Other health care provider	6.9	8.5	7.7	4.9	10.1	7.6	6.9	4.7	4.6	8.0	13.7	10.2	5.2	2.7	11.8	8.9
School (educational)	1.2	0.7	0.9	0.1	0.3	0.1	0.4	4.1	0.4	2.2	0.8	1.3	1.5	0.1	7.6	3.5
Employer/EAP[b]	0.9	1.3	1.0	0.3	1.1	0.7	1.8	1.2	0.4	0.8	0.8	1.4	0.4	0.6	0.7	0.5
Other community referral	10.4	9.4	11.3	6.3	8.1	11.6	11.9	11.2	14.6	10.5	8.2	11.4	10.7	10.6	10.9	11.9
Total	100.0	100.0	100.0	100.0	100.0	100.0	100.0	100.0	100.0	100.0	100.0	100.0	100.0	100.0	100.0	100.0
No. of admissions	1,809,407	404,574	325,665	258,776	61,241	178,777	68,268	288,179	144,552	982	8,280	4,247	2,327	3,169	1,169	59,201
No. of prior treatment episodes																
None	43.5	50.7	38.2	22.0	39.5	32.5	40.4	57.6	49.9	47.6	43.3	46.3	48.2	42.0	55.1	73.5
1	23.2	22.4	23.5	20.1	25.4	23.6	25.7	24.6	26.6	26.4	23.2	24.0	24.8	24.7	19.2	12.1
2	12.4	10.7	13.5	15.7	13.9	15.4	14.2	9.6	11.7	12.0	12.0	13.5	12.3	15.0	8.6	5.2
3	6.9	5.8	8.0	10.6	7.6	9.5	7.7	3.9	5.2	5.5	6.3	5.9	5.6	6.8	4.9	2.5
4	3.9	3.1	4.7	7.0	4.3	5.6	4.1	1.6	2.4	1.9	4.1	3.2	2.9	3.7	3.2	1.3
5 or more	10.2	7.3	12.1	24.6	9.3	13.4	7.9	2.8	4.0	6.5	11.1	7.1	6.4	7.8	9.1	5.5
Total	100.0	100.0	100.0	100.0	100.0	100.0	100.0	100.0	100.0	100.0	100.0	100.0	100.0	100.0	100.0	100.0
No. of admissions	1,531,474	333,988	262,052	210,367	53,550	164,230	58,612	262,744	131,827	890	6,569	3,879	2,000	2,929	1,059	36,778

Primary substance at admission

[a]Driving under the influence.
[b]Employee Assistance Program.

SOURCE: "Table 3.5. Admissions by Primary Substance of Abuse, according to Source of Referral to Treatment and Number of Prior Treatment Episodes: TEDS 2004, Percent Distribution," in *Treatment Episode Data Set (TEDS) 1994–2004: National Admissions to Substance Abuse Treatment Services*, U.S. Department of Health and Human Services, Substance Abuse and Mental Health Services Administration, Office of Applied Studies, July 2006, http://wwwdasis.samhsa.gov/teds04/tedsad2k4web.pdf (accessed October 17, 2006)

six and twelve years after their treatment. A second important study was the Treatment Outcome Prospective Study (TOPS), which followed eleven thousand clients admitted to forty-one treatment centers between 1979 and 1981. Both DARP and TOPS found major reductions in both drug abuse and criminal activity after treatment.

Services Research Outcomes Study

The SAMHSA's Services Research Outcomes Study (SROS) confirmed that both drug use and criminal behavior are reduced after drug treatment. Because it conducted a five-year follow-up, the SROS provided the best nationally representative data to answer the question: "Does treatment work?" This study, although now several years old and reporting on even older data, has not been repeated and is the most recent assessment available based on a national sample.

In this nationally representative sample, alcohol use decreased 14% and drug use 21%, leading to the following conclusion in the SAMHSA's SROS report (1998, http://oas.samhsa.gov/Sros/sros8006.htm): "A nationally representative survey of 1,799 persons confirms that both drug use and criminal behavior are reduced following inpatient, outpatient and residential treatment for drug abuse."

According to the SROS report (1998, http://oas.samhsa.gov/Sros/httoc.htm), decreases varied from drug to drug, with heroin use decreasing the least. It went down 13.2%, suggesting that heroin use continued for just under 87% of users. Crack use declined 16.4%, but those treated for snorting cocaine powder did better: 45.4% had abandoned the drug after treatment and continued to do so five years later—but 54.6% were still snorting cocaine. Among marijuana users 28% had given up the drug, whereas 72% continued. Results were better in all the other drug categories, but these are also the drugs of limited use by the study sample (and the population at large). The study also showed that success of treatment is higher when users are older. The exception was crack cocaine.

TYPE AND LENGTH OF TREATMENT. According to the SROS report, results by type of treatment were variable. Overall results for any illicit drug show that best results (25% decrease in drug use) were obtained by inpatient (hospital) treatment, followed by residential treatment. Outpatient methadone treatment had less favorable results (10% decrease) than outpatient drug-free treatment (19%). Outpatient methadone treatment consists of receiving methadone during visits to a treatment center; the center may also provide other services, such as counseling. Outpatient drug-free treatment consists of counseling, group therapy, and other services, but individuals receive no pharmaceutical support.

Marijuana users who were treated in inpatient facilities had better results (35% stopped using the drug) than those in residential (32%) and in methadone treatment (33%). Drug-free outpatient treatment had the lowest success rate (19%). By contrast, those using powdered cocaine benefited almost as much from drug-free outpatient treatment (42% decrease) as from inpatient treatment (47%) and did best in residential settings (55%). Crack users also did best with residential treatment (32% decrease) but had a low response to inpatient care and showed no significant decrease in use from outpatient treatment, whether with methadone or free of drugs. Heroin users responded only to methadone treatment in statistically significant numbers; 27% of those surveyed had stopped using the drug as a consequence of outpatient methadone treatment.

On average, the best results for decreasing use of all drugs, especially cocaine, were achieved with treatment that lasted six months or more; this length of treatment was also nearly the top category for marijuana use. The second length with good results (and with the best result for marijuana) was treatment lasting at least one week but less than one month. Results for crack cocaine show statistically significant results only for the "one-week-to-less-than-one-month" category. For heroin, only the "six-months-or-more" treatment duration produced significant decrease in use. Most heroin addicts require long-term methadone treatment (or treatment with a similar prescription drug) to control their habits.

CRIMINAL BEHAVIOR. The SROS report shows that treatment for substance abuse can significantly reduce crime. Criminal activities such as breaking and entering, drug sales, prostitution, driving under the influence, and theft/larceny decreased between 23% and 38% after drug treatment. However, incarceration and parole/probation violations actually increased, by 17% and 26%, respectively. Data in the study on those incarcerated or detained were less reliable than other data because of nonresponse to the survey.

More Recent Studies on Effectiveness and Cost Effectiveness of Treatment

Using data from the SROS report, Ramin Mojtabai and Joshua Graff Zivin, in "Effectiveness and Cost-Effectiveness of Four Treatment Modalities for Substance Disorders: A Propensity Score Analysis" (Health Services Research, February 2003), compare both the effectiveness and the cost-effectiveness of inpatient, residential, outpatient detox/methadone, and outpatient drug-free substance abuse treatment programs. They determine that there are only minor differences in effectiveness among these four types of programs. (Effectiveness or success is defined as abstinence and any reduction in substance use.) Mojtabai and Graff Zivin also determine that outpatient drug-free programs are the most cost-effective type of program.

FIGURE 6.4

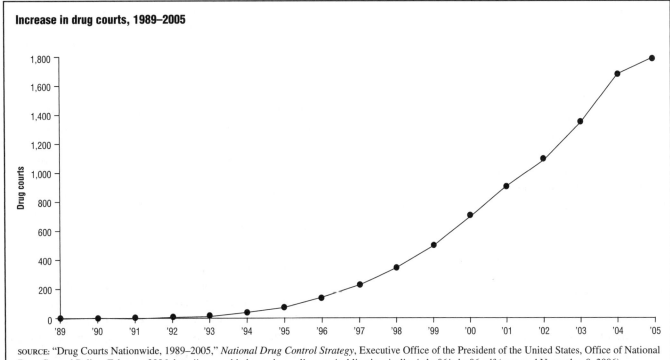

Increase in drug courts, 1989–2005

SOURCE: "Drug Courts Nationwide, 1989–2005," *National Drug Control Strategy*, Executive Office of the President of the United States, Office of National Drug Control Policy, February 2006, http://www.whitehousedrugpolicy.gov/publications/policy/ndcs06/ndcs06.pdf (accessed November 9, 2006)

More recently, Matilde P. Machado, in "Substance Abuse Treatment, What Do We Know? An Economist's Perspective" (*European Journal of Health Economics*, March 2005), compared the effectiveness and cost-effectiveness of substance abuse treatment programs by conducting a literature review and summarizing the results. Machado notes that there is no common definition of "effectiveness" but that three objectives represent most expectations about substance abuse treatment: reducing alcohol and/or drug use, improving personal and social functioning, and improving public health. Machado notes, "The evidence largely indicates that treatment is effective in each of these aspects." Drug abusers appear to agree with the research. In the 2005 NSDUH, when drug abusers were asked why they did not receive the substance abuse treatment they sought, only 0.4% answered that treatment would not help them. (See Figure 6.3.)

Nonetheless, Machado suggests that although drug treatment programs are effective, not all treatment programs are equally effective. Some may work better for patients with certain characteristics. For example, notes Machado, "stable alcoholic patients do well in short inexpensive programs while patients with more serious conditions benefit from additional services and longer treatment."

In analyzing cost-effectiveness of drug abuse treatment programs, Machado finds that most cost-effectiveness studies limited their analyses to treatment costs. She suggests that cost-effectiveness can only be determined by including all resources needed to provide treatment, such as patient costs (for example, transportation and day care) and societal costs (for example, crime and unemployment).

DRUG COURTS

Figure 6.4 shows the inception and recent increase in the use of drug courts nationwide. According to the Office of National Drug Control Policy (June 21, 2006, http://www.whitehousedrugpolicy.gov/enforce/drugcourt .html), there were 1,557 drug courts operating in the United States as of April 2006 and 394 more were in the planning stages.

Drug courts are programs that use the court's authority to offer certain drug addicted offenders to have their charges dismissed or their sentences reduced if they participate in drug court substance abuse treatment programs. Drug court programs vary across the nation, but most programs offer a range of treatment options and generally require one year of commitment from the defendant.

In *Adult Drug Courts: Evidence Indicates Recidivism Reductions and Mixed Results for Other Outcomes* (February 2005, http://www.gao.gov/new.items/d05219.pdf), the U.S. Government Accountability Office (GAO) notes that drug court programs reduce the recidivism rate (rate of reoffenses) during the time that drug abusers are enrolled in drug court treatment programs. The GAO does, however, find limited and mixed evidence of substance use relapse outcomes. Nonetheless, the GAO concludes that:

> Overall, positive findings from relatively rigorous evaluations in relation to recidivism, coupled with positive net benefit results . . . indicate that drug court programs can be an effective means to deal with some offenders. These programs appear to provide an opportunity for some individuals to take advantage of a structured program to help them reduce their criminal involvement and their substance abuse problems, as well as potentially provide a benefit to society in general.

C. West Huddleston, Karen Freeman-Wilson, and Donna L. Boone, in *Painting the Current Picture: A National Report Card on Drug Courts and Other Problem Solving Court Programs in the United States* (May 2004, http://www.ndci.org/publications/paintingcurrentpicture.pdf), assert that drug courts decrease criminal recidivism, save money, increase retention in treatment, and provide affordable treatment.

WHERE TO GO FOR HELP

> *God grant me the serenity to accept the things I cannot change, the courage to change the things I can, and the wisdom to know the difference.*

—Invocation used in most 12-Step programs

Many organizations provide assistance for addicts, their families, and friends. Most of the self-help groups are based on the 12-Step program of Alcoholics Anonymous (AA). Whereas AA is a support group for problem drinkers, Al-Anon/Alateen is for friends and families of alcoholics. Families Anonymous provides support for family members and friends concerned about a loved one's problems with drugs and/or alcohol. Other organizations include Adult Children of Alcoholics, Cocaine Anonymous, and Narcotics Anonymous. For an addict, many of these organizations can provide immediate help. For families and friends, they can provide knowledge, understanding, and support. For contact information for some of these organizations, see the Important Names and Addresses section at the back of this book.

A chief barrier to seeking help for many people habitually taking drugs is the recognition that they need help. Users often underestimate the problem and assume that they can manage without seeking professional assistance. Another barrier is the cost of drug abuse treatment, which is not always covered by a person's health insurance. Recognition of these problems has led to new programs both to help individuals recognize the need for help and to fund it.

CHAPTER 7

HOW ALCOHOL, TOBACCO, AND DRUG USE AFFECT ECONOMICS AND GOVERNMENT

The alcohol and tobacco industries play large roles in the U.S. economy. Both industries not only provide jobs and income for those involved in growing, manufacturing, and selling these products but also contribute significant tax revenues to the federal, state, and local governments. The U.S. economy also feels the effects of alcohol, tobacco, and illicit drug use in other, less beneficial, ways. All of these drugs can have significant health consequences, with associated health care costs. There are also costs in the form of loss of productivity—work that was never performed because of poor health, death, or imprisonment. The cost of enforcing drug laws, and incarcerating those convicted of breaking such laws, are significant as well.

U.S. ALCOHOL SALES AND CONSUMPTION

Retail sales of alcoholic beverages are divided into three groups: beer, wine, and distilled spirits. According to "Numbers Crunchers" (July 2006, http://www.brewer yage.com/archives/winter.spring06/IRI%203-06.pdf), of all the beverage categories in retail sales such as bottled water, carbonated beverages, and coffee, alcoholic beverages made up 38.5% of the dollars spent on beverages in 2005. Of the three alcoholic beverage categories, beer had the highest share at 20.6% of all dollars spent on all beverages, wine was second at 12%, and distilled spirits (including premixed cocktails and coolers) were last at 5.9%

Beer

The Economic Research Service (ERS; December 21, 2005, http://www.ers.usda.gov/Data/FoodConsumption/ spreadsheets/beverage.xls) notes that per capita consumption of beer fell almost steadily through the 1980s and early 1990s. Beer consumption was 24.6 gallons per person in 1981 and 21.6 gallons per person in 2003, with the 21.6 figure being relatively constant during the late 1990s and early into the twenty-first century. According

to the report "Beer State-of-the-Industry" (*Beverage Dynamics*, September–October 2005, http://www.adams bevgroup.com/bd/2005/0510_bd/0510ber.asp), in 2004 the beer industry grew by only 0.7%. The report notes, however, that beer still claims more than half the retail sales of alcoholic beverages.

There were an estimated 1,367 domestic brewers in the United States in 2005, well over four times the number in 1990, according to the Beer Institute's *Brewer's Almanac 2006* (2006, http://www.beerinstitute.org/ statistics.asp?bid=200). Microbreweries and brewpubs account for this increase. Nonetheless, the *Modern Brewery Age* (2006, http://www.breweryage.com/archives/ winter.spring06/BreweryChart%203-06.pdf) reports that Anheuser-Busch, Inc., a traditional brewery, was the top brewer in the country with a 2005 market share of 49.5%. Anheuser-Busch also controlled 55.3% of industry production in that year. Miller Brewing Company was next (20.9% of industry production), followed by Coors Brewing Company (12.4%).

Wine

Statistics gathered by the Wine Institute, in "2005 California Wine Sales Continue Growth Trend as Wine Enters Mainstream U.S. Lifestyle" (April 2006, http:// www.wineinstitute.org/industry/statistics/2006/wine_sales .php), show that 2005 wine sales in the United States grew 5.4% to 703 million gallons, for a retail sales value of $26 billion. In comparison, a total of 612 million gallons of wine were sold in the United States in 2002, for a retail sales value of $21.6 billion, up from $20.2 billion in 2001. Nonetheless, the ERS notes that per capita consumption of wine was at its peak of 2.4 gallons a year in the mid-1980s before beginning a slow decline to 1.7 gallons per capita in the early to mid-1990s. The per capita consumption rate in 2004 was 2.3 gallons per person, having risen close to the peak consumption.

The Wine Institute reports that the California wine industry accounted for a 63% share of the U.S. wine market in 2005. Red wines held a 41.7% market share in 2005, white wines a 41% share, and blush wines a 17.4% share. Chardonnay was the leading varietal wine (a wine produced from a single variety of grape) followed by Merlot.

Distilled Spirits

According to the U.S. Department of Agriculture (USDA), in *U.S. Market Profile for Distilled Spirits* (April 2005, http://www.fas.usda.gov/agx/ISMG/Distilled%20Spirits%204_19_2005.pdf), 2003 retail sales of distilled spirits (for example, whiskey, vodka, rum) were $42.7 billion, an increase of 7.1% from 2002.

How Much Do Individuals and Families Spend on Alcohol?

The U.S. Bureau of Labor Statistics reports in *Consumer Expenditures in 2004* (April 2006, http://www.bls.gov/cex/csxann04.pdf) that the average American family (or other consumer unit) spent $459 on alcoholic beverages in 2004, up from $376 in 2002 and $391 in 2003. This figure represents about 1% of the average annual expenditures for the American family. This percentage has remained relatively stable since 1993.

The amount spent on alcohol varied in 2004, depending on the characteristics of the household. On average, single parents with at least one child under age eighteen spent only $219 on alcoholic beverages in 2004, or about 0.7% of their average annual expenditures. Married couples with no children spent $567 (up from $388 in 1999), which was 0.8% of their average annual expenditures. The percentage other groups spent on alcohol varied within a range of 0.7% to 1.1%, except for the "single person and other consumer units" group. This group spent the largest proportion of its average annual expenditures on alcohol: nearly 1.3%.

U.S. TOBACCO PRODUCTION AND CONSUMPTION

Farming Trends

Thomas C. Capehart notes in "Trends in U.S. Tobacco Farming" (November 2004, http://www.ers.usda.gov/publications/tbs/nov04/tbs25702/tbs25702.pdf) that, sparked by the invention of the cigarette-making machine by James A. Bonsack in 1881, which made cigarettes cheaper and faster to manufacture, tobacco production in the United States grew from three hundred million pounds in the mid-1860s to over one billion pounds in 1909. In 1946, at the end of World War II, tobacco production was above two billion pounds. During the 1960s changes in tobacco preparation and the introduction of new machinery increased the amount of tobacco production per acre, although the number of tobacco farms dropped from about 512,000 in 1954 to 56,977 in 2002.

TABLE 7.1

Tobacco crops by area, yield, production, price, and value, 1996–2005

Year	Area harvested	Yield per acre	Production*	Marketing year average price per pound received by farmers	Value of production
	Acres	Pounds	1,000 pounds	Dollars	1,000 dollars
1996	733,060	2,072	1,518,704	1.882	2,853,739
1997	836,230	2,137	1,787,399	1.802	3,217,176
1998	717,620	2,062	1,479,891	1.828	2,700,925
1999	647,160	1,997	1,292,692	1.828	2,356,304
2000	469,420	2,244	1,053,264	1.910	2,001,811
2001	432,490	2,292	991,293	1.956	1,938,892
2002	427,310	2,039	871,122	1.936	1,686,809
2003	411,150	1,952	802,560	1.964	1,576,436
2004	408,050	2,161	881,973	1.987	1,752,335
2005	298,020	2,147	639,709	1.647	1,053,430

*Production figures are on farm-sales-weight basis.

SOURCE: "Table 2.43. Tobacco: Area, Yield, Production, Price, and Value, United States, 1996–2005," in *Agricultural Statistics 2006*, U.S. Department of Agriculture, National Agricultural Statistics Service, 2006, http://www.nass.usda.gov/Publications/Ag_Statistics/agr06/CHAP02.PDF (accessed October 17, 2006)

Table 7.1 shows that beginning in 1998 acreage devoted to tobacco and the value of production declined steadily. According to "Trends in U.S. Tobacco Farming," the number of acres used to grow tobacco fell from 1.5 million in 1954 to 717,620 in 1998 to 298,020 in 2005. The 2005 harvest produced 639.7 million pounds of tobacco, valued at about $1 billion, down from a high of $3.2 billion in 1997.

In 2005 North Carolina led in tobacco production, followed by Kentucky, Tennessee, South Carolina, Georgia, and Virginia. (See Table 7.2.) Tobacco plays a major role in the agricultural economies of the leading half-dozen tobacco-producing states.

Value and Income

According to the USDA (July 2006, http://www.ers.usda.gov/briefing/tobacco/data/table23.pdf), in 2002 tobacco crops had a value of approximately $1.7 billion in cash receipts. Preliminary USDA figures about the 2002 tobacco crop indicate it represented 0.90% of all cash receipts from crops and 1.75% of all farm commodities.

Tobacco is a labor-intensive crop to produce. Brazilian researchers estimate that it takes up to three thousand person-hours per year to grow one hectare of tobacco. (A hectare is 2.47 acres.) By comparison, vegetables take about one-tenth the labor to grow. Although tobacco pays more per hectare than any other commonly grown farm crop, more than half of tobacco growers cannot support themselves purely through tobacco farming because of high costs for labor. They must also work at other jobs to support themselves and their families.

TABLE 7.2

Area, yield, and production of tobacco, by tobacco-growing states, 2003–05

State	Area harvested			Yield per harvested acre			Production		
	2003	2004	2005[a]	2003	2004	2005[a]	2003	2004	2005[a]
	Acres	Acres	Acres	Pounds	Pounds	Pounds	1,000 Pounds	1,000 Pounds	1,000 Pounds
CT	2,180	2,360	2,430	1,321	1,574	1,674	2,880	3,714	4,067
FL	4,400	4,000	2,500	2,500	2,450	2,200	11,000	9,800	5,500
GA	27,000	23,000	16,000	2,200	2,030	1,735	59,400	46,690	27,760
IN[b]	4,200	4,200		1,950	2,050		8,190	8,610	
KY	111,650	14,950	79,700	2,016	2,044	2,099	225,042	235,003	167,260
MD[b]	1,100	1,100		1,450	1,700		1,595	1,870	
MA	1,250	1,240	1,200	1,392	1,587	1,500	1,740	1,968	1,800
MO	1,400	1,450	1,400	2,020	2,300	2,000	2,828	3,335	2,800
NC	159,700	56,100	126,000	1,878	2,246	2,213	299,995	350,560	278,900
OH	5,300	5,600	3,400	1,650	1,960	1,980	8,745	10,967	6,732
PA	3,700	4,000	5,000	2,130	2,025	2,140	7,880	8,100	10,700
SC	30,000	27,000	20,000	2,100	2,350	2,100	63,000	63,450	42,000
TN	31,140	30,260	22,950	2,108	2,161	2,251	65,632	65,381	51,670
VA	25,110	29,680	17,040	1,546	2,267	2,338	38,818	67,285	39,840
WV	1,200	1,300	400	1,300	1,300	1,700	1,560	1,690	680
WI[b]	1,820	1,810		2,338	1,956		4,255	3,541	
US	**411,150**	**408,050**	**298,020**	**1,952**	**2,161**	**2,147**	**802,560**	**881,973**	**639,709**

[a]Preliminary.
[b]Estimates discontinued in 2005.

SOURCE: "Table 2.44. Tobacco: Area, Yield, and Production, by States, 2003–2005," in *Agricultural Statistics 2006,* U.S. Department of Agriculture, National Agricultural Statistics Service, 2006, http://www.nass.usda.gov/Publications/Ag_Statistics/agr06/CHAP02.PDF (accessed October 17, 2006)

Manufacturing

In *Tobacco Situation and Outlook Yearbook* (December 2005, http://usda.mannlib.cornell.edu/reports/erssor/specialty/tbs-bb/2005/tbs2005.pdf), Thomas C. Capehart estimates that in 2005 U.S. factories produced 481.9 billion cigarettes, of which 109.2 billion were shipped to other countries. This is down from a peak output of 754.5 billion cigarettes produced by U.S. factories in 1996. Exports were high that year as well: 243.9 billion cigarettes.

Tobacco Consumption

The ERS (October 3, 2005, http://www.ers.usda.gov/Briefing/Tobacco/Background.htm) notes that cigarette smoking in the United States has been dropping almost every year since 1963, when per capita consumption reached a record high of 4,345 cigarettes. Preliminary USDA figures estimated the 2006 per capita cigarette consumption of the population aged eighteen years and older at 1,691 cigarettes. (See Table 3.1 in Chapter 3.)

Table 3.1 also shows that per capita consumption of all tobacco products generally decreased from 1996 to 2006, from 4.8 pounds in 1996 to 3.7 pounds in 2006. Per capita consumption of large cigars by males, however, increased during the period, jumping from nearly 31.9 large cigars and cigarillos (small cigars) per adult male in 1996 to 47.8 in 2006.

Consumer Spending on Tobacco

Americans spent an estimated $88.9 billion on tobacco products in 2005, more than double that of 1989 spending. (See Table 7.3.) The majority ($82 billion, or 92%) was spent on cigarettes. This was slightly less than 1% of all disposable personal income. Although the per capita consumption of cigarettes has declined, expenditures (after adjustment for inflation) have increased because of increasing cigarette prices and an increase in the population of people of smoking age.

Table 7.4 shows that the average American family (or other consumer unit) spent $288 on tobacco products and smoking supplies in 2004. In 2003 the average spent per consumer unit was $290, and in 2002 the average spent was $320. These data appear to be in contradiction with the data shown in Table 7.3, in that spending seems to be decreasing rather than increasing. However, the data in Table 7.4 are per consumer unit, and the number of consumer units increased from 2002 to 2004. In addition, the two data sets were collected differently. The data in Table 7.4 are averages of self-reported survey data, and the data in Table 7.3 are economic data (adjusted for inflation) compiled by the U.S. Department of Commerce. Thus, the data cannot be directly compared.

Exports

Capehart, in *Tobacco Situation and Outlook Yearbook*, reports that in 2005, 109.2 billion cigarettes were exported. From 1996 to 2004 cigarette exports fell by about 135 billion pieces. In 2004 most of the cigarettes exported went to Japan (71 billion), Iran (14.5 billion), and Saudi Arabia (10.7 billion). Other major importers of American cigarettes were Israel (5.1 billion), Lebanon

How Alcohol, Tobacco, and Drug Use Affect Economics and Government

TABLE 7.3

Personal spending for tobacco products, 1989–2005

Year	Total	Cigarettes	Cigars[a]	Other[b]	Disposable personal income	Percent of disposable personal income spent on tobacco products			
						All	Cigarettes	Cigars[a]	Other[b]
	Million dollars				Billion dollars	Percent			
1989	39,675	37,400	675	1,600	5,225	1.05	0.99	0.02	0.04
1990	41,920	39,500	695	1,725	5,324	1.04	0.98	0.02	0.04
1991	45,305	42,850	705	1,840	5,352	1.08	1.02	0.02	0.04
1992	48,470	45,790	715	1,965	5,536	1.08	1.02	0.02	0.04
1993	48,955	46,150	730	2,075	5,594	1.04	0.98	0.02	0.04
1994	47,297	44,544	766	1,987	5,746	0.96	0.90	0.02	0.04
1995	48,692	45,793	846	2,053	5,906	0.92	0.86	0.02	0.04
1996	50,363	47,233	1,012	2,118	6,081	0.90	0.85	0.02	0.04
1997	52,167	48,734	1,229	2,205	6,296	0.90	0.84	0.02	0.04
1998	57,273	53,236	1,607	2,430	6,664	0.96	0.88	0.03	0.04
1999	70,715	66,286	1,796	2,633	6,861	1.03	0.97	0.03	0.04
2000	77,705	72,945	1,926	2,833	7,194	1.08	1.01	0.03	0.04
2001	82,919	77,845	2,121	2,953	7,320	1.13	1.06	0.03	0.04
2002	88,220	82,873	2,270	3,077	7,830	1.13	1.06	0.03	0.04
2003[c]	86,825	81,070	2,541	3,215	8,169	1.06	0.99	0.03	0.04
2004[d]	86,315	79,958	2,935	3,422	8,664	1.00	0.92	0.03	0.04
2005[d]	88,882	82,029	3,184	3,669	9,031	0.98	0.91	0.04	0.04

[a]Includes small cigars (cigarette-size).
[b]Smoking tobacco, chewing tobacco, and snuff.
[c]Subject to revision.
[d]Estimated.
Note: Expenditures exclude sales tax.

SOURCE: Tom Capehart, "Table 21. Expenditures for Tobacco Products and Disposable Personal Income, 1989/2005," in *Tobacco Briefing Room*, U.S. Department of Agriculture, Economic Research Service, March 2006, http://www.ers.usda.gov/Briefing/Tobacco/Data/table21.pdf (accessed October 18, 2006)

(4 billion), Hong Kong (2 billion), Kuwait (1.8 billion), the United Arab Emirates (1.7 billion), and Taiwan (1.5 billion). Many of the importers in these countries then export these cigarettes to other countries.

WORLD TOBACCO MARKETS

The National Agricultural Statistics Service, in *Agricultural Statistics, 2005* (2005, http://www.usda.gov/nass/pubs/agr05/05_ch2.PDF), estimates the world production of tobacco in 2004 at 6.6 million metric tons (a metric ton equals 1,000 kilograms, or 2,204.6 pounds), down from 6.9 million in 2000. China produced over 36% (about 2.4 million metric tons). Other leading tobacco producers included Brazil (890,500 metric tons), India (665,000 metric tons), the United States (397,347 metric tons), Indonesia (158,900 metric tons), Argentina (154,300 metric tons), and Turkey (153,750 metric tons).

The Campaign for Tobacco-Free Kids reports in "Tobacco Facts" (June 2005, http://www.tobaccofreekids.org/campaign/global/docs/1.pdf) how lucrative overseas markets can be for cigarette makers. In 2003 Philip Morris had global revenue of $81.8 billion, producing 887.3 billion cigarettes, or 16.5%, of the total world cigarette production. Furthermore, more than half of all smokers in 1999 were in Asia. Concerning cigarette consumption, in 2002 China was the top consumer (2.2 trillion cigarettes) and the United States was the third-highest consumer (463 billion).

On February 27, 2005, the world's first tobacco control treaty, the World Health Organization's Framework Convention on Tobacco Control (http://www.who.int/tobacco/framework/countrylist/en/index.html), became binding international law with ratification by fifty-seven countries, including Canada. The United States signed the measure on May 10, 2004, but as of the end of 2006 had still not ratified it (become bound by it). However, 142 other countries had ratified the treaty by the end of 2006. The goal of the treaty is to improve global health by reducing tobacco consumption by setting international standards on tobacco price and tax increases, tobacco advertising and sponsorship, labeling, illicit trade, and secondhand smoke.

ALCOHOL AND TOBACCO ADVERTISING
Alcohol Advertising

The Center for Science in the Public Interest (CSPI), in "Alcoholic-Beverage Advertising Expenditures" (December 2003, http://www.cspinet.org/booze/FactSheets/AlcAdExp.pdf), the most recent fact sheet on alcohol advertising published by the CSPI, indicates that the beer industry spent approximately $1.2 billion in 2002 on advertising, up from $799.7 million in 1999. The liquor industry spent $408.1 million, up from $321.4 million in 1999. The wine industry spent $122.4 million, up from $120.5 million in 1999.

According to the CSPI fact sheet, in 2002 the beer industry focused most of its advertising dollars on television, and the wine industry on both print media (magazines,

TABLE 7.4

Average annual consumer spending and percent changes, by category, 2002–04

				Percent change	
Item	2002	2003	2004	2002–2003	2003–2004
Number of consumer units (in thousands)	112,108	115,356	116,282	—	—
Income before taxes	$49,430	$51,128	$54,453	—	—
Averages:					
Age of reference person	48.1	48.4	48.5	—	—
Number of persons in consumer unit	2.5	2.5	2.5	—	—
Number of earners	1.4	1.3	1.3	—	—
Number of vehicles	2.0	1.9	1.9	—	—
Percent homeowner	66	67	68	—	—
Average annual expenditures	$40,677	$40,817	$43,395	0.3	6.3
Food	5,375	5,340	5,781	−.7	8.3
Food at home	3,099	3,129	3,347	1.0	7.0
Cereals and bakery products	450	442	461	−1.8	4.3
Meats, poultry, fish, and eggs	798	825	880	3.4	6.7
Dairy products	328	328	371	0	13.1
Fruits and vegetables	552	535	561	−3.1	4.9
Other food at home	970	999	1,075	3.0	7.6
Food away from home	2,276	2,211	2,434	−2.9	10.1
Alcoholic beverages	376	391	459	4.0	17.4
Housing	13,283	13,432	13,918	1.1	3.6
Shelter	7,829	7,887	7,998	.7	1.4
Utilities, fuels, and public services	2,684	2,811	2,927	4.7	4.1
Household operations	706	707	753	.1	6.5
Housekeeping supplies	545	529	594	−2.9	12.3
Household furnishings and equipment	1,518	1,497	1,646	−1.4	10.0
Apparel and services	1,749	1,640	1,816	−6.2	10.7
Transportation	7,759	7,781	7,801	.3	.3
Vehicle purchases (net outlay)	3,665	3,732	3,397	1.8	−9.0
Gasoline and motor oil	1,235	1,333	1,598	7.9	19.9
Other vehicle expenses	2,471	2,331	2,365	−5.7	1.5
Public transportation	389	385	441	−1.0	14.5
Healthcare	2,350	2,416	2,574	2.8	6.5
Entertainment	2,079	2,060	2,218	−.9	7.7
Personal care products and services	526	527	581	.2	10.2
Reading	139	127	130	−8.6	2.4
Education	752	783	905	4.1	15.6
Tobacco products and smoking supplies	320	290	288	−9.4	−.7
Miscellaneous	792	606	690	−23.5	13.9
Cash contributions	1,277	1,370	1,408	7.3	2.8
Personal insurance and pensions	3,899	4,055	4,823	4.0	18.9
Life and other personal insurance	406	397	390	−2.2	−1.8
Pensions and Social Security	3,493	3,658	4,433	4.7	21.2

SOURCE: "Table A. Average Annual Expenditures of All Consumer Units and Percent Changes, Consumer Expenditure Survey, 2002–2004," in *Consumer Expenditures in 2004*, U.S. Department of Labor, U.S. Bureau of Labor Statistics, April 2006, http://www.bls.gov/cex/csxann04.pdf (accessed October 18, 2006)

newspapers, and billboards) and television. The liquor industry focused its advertising primarily on print media, but its spending on television and radio advertising rose substantially between 1999 and 2002 as a result of this industry's decision to lift its self-imposed ban on radio and television advertising.

After the liquor industry lifted its ban, the National Broadcasting Company (NBC) also ended its ban on hard liquor advertising and became the first network television station to do so. The broadcaster's 2001 decision was met with nearly universal derision, and a short time later NBC returned to its ban on hard liquor advertisements. As a response, the liquor industry developed guidelines to restrict advertising to publications or television programs with at least 70% of readers or viewers being age twenty-one or older. Stuart Elliott reports in "Thanks to Cable, Liquor Ads

Find a TV Audience" (*New York Times*, December 15, 2003) that by the end of 2003 hard liquor was being advertised on two dozen national cable networks, 140 local cable systems, and 420 local broadcast stations. In a subsequent article, "In a First, CNN Runs a Liquor Commercial" (*New York Times*, March 2, 2005), Elliott notes that CNN became the first national cable news network to air, in March 2005, ads for hard liquor with a commercial for Grey Goose vodka. Then, in August 2006 the National Highway Traffic Safety Administration (NHTSA) announced that it would use the same medium—television—to stress the threat of being arrested for driving under the influence. According to Matthew L. Wald, in "Highway Safety Agency Unveils New Campaign against Drunken Driving" (*New York Times*, August 17, 2006), the NHTSA budgeted $11 million for these television advertisements.

ALCOHOL ADVERTISING AND YOUTH. In "Effects of Alcohol Advertising Exposure on Drinking among Youth" (*Archives of Pediatric Adolescent Medicine*, January 2006), Leslie B. Snyder et al. state that their objective was "to test whether alcohol advertising expenditures and the degree of exposure to alcohol advertisements affect alcohol consumption by youth." Their results reveal that people aged fifteen to twenty-six who reported seeing more alcohol advertisements drank more, on average, than those who reported seeing fewer or no alcohol advertisements. By analyzing data on alcohol advertising expenditures on television, radio, billboards, and newspapers with the rest of the data they collected, Snyder et al. determine that young people in markets with greater alcohol advertising expenditures drank more than those in markets with less alcohol advertising expenditures. These findings suggest that attempts to reduce youth drinking must involve limiting or changing alcohol advertising to lessen its effect on youth and/or countering alcohol advertising with public health campaigns to reduce youth drinking as the NHTSA was planning in 2006.

Tobacco Advertising

According to the U.S. Federal Trade Commission (FTC), in *Cigarette Report for 2003* (2005, http://www.ftc.gov/reports/cigarette05/050809cigrpt.pdf), cigarette sales in 2003 fell 4.2% from the previous year, to 360.5 billion cigarettes. Advertising expenditures in 2003 increased 21.5% from 2002, to approximately $15.1 billion, the most ever reported to the FTC. As expenditures increased, however, per capita cigarette consumption continued to drop.

The tobacco industry is forbidden by law to advertise on radio and television. Where do the industry's advertising dollars go? The largest share (about $10.8 billion) of the approximately $15.1 billion spent in 2003 was used for price discounts, which are paid to cigarette retailers or wholesalers to discount the price of the cigarettes to the consumer. About $1.2 billion was used for retailer promotional allowances, which pays them for stocking, shelving, and displaying cigarettes.

ALCOHOL AND TOBACCO TAXATION

Taxation is an age-old method by which the government raises money. Alcoholic beverages have been taxed since colonial times, and tobacco products have been taxed since 1863. The alcohol and tobacco industries contribute a great deal of tax money to federal, state, and local governments.

Alcohol Taxes

According to the Distilled Spirits Council of the United States (2006, http://www.discus.org/issues/taxes.asp), hard liquor is the most highly taxed consumer product in the nation. The organization estimates that direct and indirect local, state, and federal taxes and fees accounted for 57% of the typical bottle price in 2006. Even though the beer and wine industries are taxed at lower levels, they still contribute a significant amount of tax revenue.

According to Table 7.5, in fiscal year (FY) 2005 the federal government collected approximately $8.9 billion in excise taxes on alcoholic beverages. (Excise taxes are monies paid on purchases of specific goods, such as alcohol and tobacco.) Federal excise taxes on distilled spirits amounted to half that total—about $4.5 billion, which included taxes on both domestic and imported distilled spirits. Distilled spirits are taxed by the proof gallon, which is a standard U.S. gallon of 231 cubic inches containing 50% ethyl alcohol by volume, or 100 proof.

Excise taxes on wine and beer make up the other half of the excise taxes collected on alcoholic beverages. The calculation of wine taxes depends on several variables, such as alcohol content and the size of the winery; in 2005 federal excise taxes on wine totaled $806.8 million. Total beer excise taxes were much higher, at $3.6 billion. (See Table 7.5.) According to the Alcohol and Tobacco Tax and Trade Bureau (TTB; 2006, http://www.ttb.gov/beer/tax.shtml), brewers who produce fewer than two million barrels (one barrel equals thirty-one gallons) get a reduced excise tax rate of $7 per barrel on the first sixty thousand barrels. Those who produce more than two million barrels pay an excise tax of $18 per barrel.

Besides the federal excise taxes, the states levy sales taxes on alcohol. In 2005 the per capita state sales tax collected on alcoholic beverages—averaged across states—was $15.99. Total state tax collections from alcohol include not only the sales tax ($4.7 billion in 2005) but also payments for alcoholic beverage licenses ($389.3 million in 2005). Taxes on alcohol amounted to about 0.7% of the nation's total state taxes collected in 2005. (See Table 7.6.)

Tobacco Taxes

The ERS (March 2006, http://www.ers.usda.gov/Briefing/Tobacco/Data/table22.pdf) reports that in 2004–05 federal, state, and local governments collected $20.3 billion in excise taxes on tobacco products. Most of this revenue came from the sale of cigarettes. According to the National Conference of State Legislatures (July 2006, http://www.ncsl.org/programs/health/Cigarette.htm), the federal excise tax on cigarettes was $0.39 per pack as of January 1, 2006.

States have raised their excise taxes on cigarettes to help defray health costs associated with tobacco, to discourage young people from starting to smoke, and to motivate smokers to stop. Table 7.7 shows state cigarette excise tax rates and rankings in 2006. New Jersey had the highest state excise tax on cigarettes at 257.5 cents per pack. Rhode Island was a close second with 246 cents excise tax per pack. South Carolina (a tobacco-growing

TABLE 7.5

Federal government tax collections on alcohol and tobacco, October 2004–September 2005

[In thousands of dollars]

Reporting period: October 2004–September 2005

Revenue source	1st quarter	2nd quarter	3rd quarter	4th quarter	Cumulative 2005	Cumulative 2004
Excise tax, total	**$4,159,910**	**$3,620,468**	**$4,375,858**	**$4,808,283**	**$16,964,519**	**$16,851,969**
Alcohol tax, total	$2,235,142	$1,879,706	$2,307,117	$2,479,399	$8,901,364	$8,725,491
Distilled spirits tax, total	$1,228,237	$911,329	$1,141,823	$1,170,010	$4,451,399	$4,295,742
Domestic	$891,760	$656,035	$867,327	$900,867	$3,315,989	$3,221,111
Imported	$336,477	$255,294	$274,496	$269,143	$1,135,410	$1,074,631
Wine tax, total	$229,302	$175,673	$192,282	$209,535	$806,792	$769,225
Domestic	$162,535	$124,745	$132,369	$147,167	$566,816	$548,839
Imported	$66,767	$50,928	$59,913	$62,368	$239,976	$220,386
Beer tax, total	$777,603	$792,704	$973,012	$1,099,854	$3,643,173	$3,660,524
Domestic	$677,761	$697,575	$846,244	$970,870	$3,192,450	$3,218,811
Imported	$99,842	$95,129	$126,768	$128,984	$450,723	$441,713
Tobacco tax, total	**$1,868,904**	**$1,687,381**	**$2,016,325**	**$2,264,654**	**$7,837,264**	**$7,910,259**
Domestic						
Regular	$1,740,955	$1,591,982	$1,911,626	$2,163,613	$7,408,176	$7,440,242
Floor stocks	−$0.250	$10	$0.000	$0.200	$9.950	$0.100
Imported	$127,949	$95,389	$104,699	$101,041	$429,078	$470,017
Unclassified alcohol and tobacco tax (domestic) Total	$43	$5	$21	$9	$78	$213
Firearms and Ammunition tax, total	$55,821	$53,376	$52,395	$64,221	$225,813	$216,006
Special (occupational) tax, total	$1,868	$1,176	$5,629	$1,516	$10,189	$102,165
Total tax collections	**$4,161,778**	**$3,621,644**	**$4,381,487**	**$4,809,799**	**$16,974,708**	**$16,954,134**

Notes:
1. This is an unofficial report. Official revenue collection figures are stated in the Alcohol and Tobacco Tax and Trade Bureau (TTB) Chief Financial Officer Annual Report.
2. All "imported" tax collection figures are obtained from U.S. Customs data.
3. Addition of current fiscal year prior quarter figures may not agree with cumulative figures for current fiscal year due to the figures being adjusted to reflect classification of unclassified alcohol and tobacco tax collections previously reported, to reflect collection adjustments for prior tax periods and to reflect rounding adjustments.
4. Source for other tax collection figures on this report is a TTB database that records tax collection data by tax return period. This data is summarized on this report by the quarter in which an incurred tax liability is satisfied.
5. Unclassified Alcohol and Tobacco Tax is tax collected, but not yet posted to a taxpayer account due to missing employer identification number (EIN), permit number, and/or other taxpayer identity information.

SOURCE: "Tax Collections TTB S 5630-FY-2005 Cumulative Summary Fiscal Year 2005 Final," in *Alcohol and Tobacco Tax and Trade Bureau Statistical Release*, U.S. Department of the Treasury, Alcohol and Tobacco Tax and Trade Bureau, April 2006, http://www.ttb.gov/statistics/final05.pdf (accessed October 18, 2006)

state) had the lowest excise tax of 7 cents per pack. The average tax in the nation in 2006 was 96.1 cents per pack.

GOVERNMENT REGULATION OF ALCOHOL AND TOBACCO

Besides taxation, the alcoholic beverage and tobacco industries are subject to federal and state laws that regulate factors such as sales, advertising, and shipping.

Alcohol Regulation

The best-known pieces of legislation regarding alcohol are the Eighteenth and Twenty-First Amendments to the U.S. Constitution. The Eighteenth Amendment prohibited the manufacture, sale, and importation of alcoholic beverages. Ratified in 1919, it took effect in 1920 and ushered in a period in U.S. history known as Prohibition. After twelve years, during which it failed to stop the manufacture and sale of alcohol, Prohibition was repealed in 1933 by the Twenty-First Amendment.

Most interpretations of the Twenty-First Amendment hold that the amendment gives individual states the power to regulate and control alcoholic beverages within their own borders. Consequently, every state has its own alcohol administration and enforcement agency. "Control states" directly control the sale and distribution of alcoholic beverages within their borders. According to the TTB (2006, http://www.ttb.gov/wine/control_board.shtml), there are eighteen control states: Alabama, Idaho, Iowa, Maine, Michigan, Mississippi, Montana, New Hampshire, North Carolina, Ohio, Oregon, Pennsylvania, Utah, Vermont, Virginia, Washington, West Virginia, and Wyoming. Some critics of this policy question whether such state monopolies violate antitrust laws. The other thirty-two states are licensure states and allow only licensed businesses to operate as wholesalers and retailers.

DIRECT SHIPMENTS—RECIPROCITY OR FELONY? A legislative controversy has developed over the direct shipment of alcoholic beverages from one state directly to consumers or retailers in another. Under the U.S. Constitution's Interstate Commerce Clause, Congress

TABLE 7.6

State government tax collections, by source of revenue, 2005

[Amounts in thousands. Per capita amounts in dollars]

Item	United States* Amount	United States* Per capita
Population, July 2005	295,860	X
Total taxes	**647,886,410**	**2,189.84**
Property taxes	11,349,052	38.36
Sales and gross receipts	311,074,039	1,051.42
General sales and gross receipts	212,246,900	717.39
Selective sales taxes	98,827,139	334.03
Alcoholic beverages	4,731,621	15.99
Amusements	5,241,621	17.72
Insurance premiums	14,842,349	50.17
Motor fuels	34,570,428	116.85
Pari-mutuels	309,789	1.05
Public utilities	11,022,793	37.26
Tobacco products	13,216,670	44.67
Other selective sales	14,891,868	50.33
Licenses	42,702,918	144.33
Alcoholic beverages	389,263	1.32
Amusements	242,023	0.82
Corporation	7,280,358	24.61
Hunting and fishing	1,263,309	4.27
Motor vehicle	18,220,765	61.59
Motor vehicle operators	2,110,390	7.13
Public utility	473,972	1.60
Occupation and business	12,068,439	40.79
Other licenses	654,399	2.21
Income taxes	258,945,643	875.23
Individual income	220,254,617	744.46
Corporation net income	38,691,026	130.77
Other taxes	23,814,758	80.49
Death and gift	5,341,720	18.05
Documentary and stock transfer	10,049,250	33.97
Severance	8,131,446	27.48
Other	292,342	0.99

*U.S. totals include the 50 state governments and do not include the District of Columbia or any local government.
Note: X=not applicable.

SOURCE: "State Government Tax Collections: 2005," U.S. Census Bureau, Governments Division, May 22, 2006, http://www.census.gov/govs/statetax/0500usstax.html (accessed October 18, 2006)

TABLE 7.7

State cigarette tax rates and rankings, 2005

Overall all states' average: 96.1 cents per pack
Major tobacco states' average: 26.5 cents per pack
Other states' average: 105.4 cents per pack

State	Tax (in cents)	Rank
New Jersey	257.5	1
Rhode Island	246	2
Washington	202.5	3
Maine	200	4
Michigan	200	4
Alaska[a]	180	6
Vermont	179	7
Montana	170	8
Hawaii[b]	160	9
Connecticut	151	10
Massachusetts	151	10
New York	150	12
Texas	141[c]	13
Pennsylvania	135	14
Ohio	125	15
Minnesota	123	16
Arizona	118	17
Oregon	118	17
Oklahoma	103	19
DC	100	20
Maryland	100	20
Illinois	98	22
New Mexico	91	23
California	87	24
Colorado	84	25
Nevada	80	26
New Hampshire	80	27
Kansas	79	28
Wisconsin	77	29
Utah	69.5	30
Nebraska	64	31
Wyoming	60	32
Arkansas	59	33
Idaho	57	34
Indiana	55.5	35
Delaware	55	36
West Virginia	55	36
South Dakota	53	38
North Dakota	44	39
Alabama	42.5	40
Georgia	37	41
Iowa	36	42
Louisiana	36	42
North Carolina	35	44
Florida	33.9	45
Kentucky	30	46
Virginia	30	46
Tennessee	20	48
Mississippi	18	49
Missouri	17	50
South Carolina	7	51
Puerto Rico	123	NA
Guam	100	NA
North Marianas	175	NA

[a]Additional 20-cent increase effective 7/1/06.
[b]Includes 20-cent increase effective 9/30/06; part of 6-stage increase through 2011.
[c]Includes $1 increase effective 1/1/07.

SOURCE: "State Cigarette Excise Tax Rates & Rankings," Campaign for Tobacco-Free Kids, September 1, 2006, http://www.tobaccofreekids.org/research/factsheets/pdf/0097.pdf (accessed October 18, 2006)

has the power to regulate trade between states. Nevertheless, the Twenty-First Amendment gives states the authority to regulate the sale and distribution of alcoholic beverages. Furthermore, it allows states to set their own laws governing the sale of alcohol within their borders.

Because the laws of the states are not uniform, several states passed reciprocity legislation, allowing specific states to exchange direct shipments, thus eliminating the state-licensed wholesalers from the exchange. Wholesalers and retailers have charged that reciprocity and direct shipment are violations of the Twenty-First Amendment. They fear being bypassed in the exchange, as do states that prohibit direct shipments of alcohol. Other stakeholders in this issue are consumers and wine producers who want the right to deal directly with each other.

ALCOHOL SALES AND THE INTERNET. In January 2001 the Twenty-First Amendment Enforcement Act became law. This legislation makes it difficult for companies to sell alcohol over the Internet or through mail-order services. It allows state attorneys general in states that ban direct alcohol sales to seek a federal injunction against companies that violate their liquor sales laws.

Within a month of the passage of this legislation, the high-tech community voiced its concern over such legislation, suggesting that if states could ban Internet wine sales they might restrict other electronic commerce as well. Senator Orrin Hatch said he crafted the bill to take other e-commerce concerns into account and insisted that the measure is narrowly tailored to deal with alcohol only.

On May 16, 2005, the U.S. Supreme Court ruled on three cases that had been consolidated under the name *Granholm v. Heald* (544 U.S. 460). At issue were state laws in Michigan and New York that prohibited out-of-state wineries from selling their products over the Internet directly to Michigan and New York residents, but allowed in-state wineries to make such sales. The Michigan and New York state governments argued that these laws were permissible under the Twenty-First Amendment. A group of wineries and business advocates argued that the state laws were unconstitutional restrictions of interstate trade. In a 5–4 decision the Court agreed that the state laws were unconstitutional, stating, "States have broad power to regulate liquor under §2 of the Twenty-first Amendment. This power, however, does not allow States to ban, or severely limit, the direct shipment of out-of-state wine while simultaneously authorizing direct shipment by in-state producers. If a State chooses to allow direct shipment of wine, it must do so on even-handed terms. Without demonstrating the need for discrimination, New York and Michigan have enacted regulations that disadvantage out-of-state wine producers. Under our Commerce Clause jurisprudence, these regulations cannot stand."

Early Tobacco Regulation and Legislation

Federal tobacco legislation has covered everything from unproved advertising claims and warning label requirements to the development of cigarettes and little cigars that are less likely to start fires. In the past the FDA prohibited the claim that Fairfax cigarettes prevented respiratory and other diseases (1953) and denied the claim that tartaric acid, which was added to Trim Reducing-Aid cigarettes, helped promote weight loss (1959).

The FTC has also been given jurisdiction over tobacco issues in several areas. As early as 1942 the FTC had issued a "cease-and-desist" order in reference to Kool cigarettes' claim that smoking Kools gave extra protection against or cured colds. In January 1964 the FTC proposed a rule to strictly regulate cigarette advertisements and to prohibit explicit or implicit health claims by cigarette companies.

The tobacco industry has managed to avoid federal regulation by being exempted from many federal health and safety laws. In the Consumer Product Safety Act the term *consumer product* does not include tobacco and

tobacco products, nor does the term *hazardous substance* in the Hazardous Substances Act. Tobacco is similarly exempted from regulation under the Toxic Substance Control Act and the Fair Packaging and Labeling Act.

Some of the legislation of the late 1980s included requiring four alternating health warnings to be printed on tobacco packaging, prohibiting smokeless tobacco advertising on television and radio, and banning smoking on domestic airline flights. In 1992 the Synar Amendment was passed. The amendment said that states must have laws that ban the sale of tobacco products to people under eighteen years of age.

In 1993 the U.S. Environmental Protection Agency released its final risk assessment on environmental tobacco smoke (ETS, or secondhand smoke) and classified it as a known human carcinogen (cancer-causing agent). In 1994 the Occupational Safety and Health Administration proposed regulations that would prohibit smoking in workplaces, except in smoking rooms that are separately ventilated. As of the end of 2006 the United States did not have federal smoking control legislation, but many states and municipalities did have legislation that banned smoking in a variety of public places and workplaces.

TOBACCO SALES AND THE INTERNET. The Internet plays a role in the distribution of tobacco as well as of alcohol. There are more than four hundred Web sites that sell tobacco products.

There are a number of problems with such Web sites. Kurt M. Ribisi, Annice E. Kim, and Rebecca S. Williams, in "Are the Sales Practices of Internet Cigarette Vendors Good Enough to Prevent Sales to Minors?" (*American Journal of Public Health*, June 2002), indicate that 18.2% of online cigarette vendors do not say that sales to minors are prohibited on their sites. More than half require that the user simply state that he or she is of legal age. According to the Campaign for Tobacco-Free Kids (October 21, 2005, http://www.tobaccofreekids.org/reports/internet/), three-quarters of Internet tobacco sellers explicitly say that they will not report cigarette sales to tax collection officials, a violation of federal law.

In July 2003 the Senate Judiciary Committee approved the Prevent All Contraband Tobacco Act (S. 1177). The Senate passed the act by unanimous consent in December 2003. Similar legislation (amended H.R. 2824) passed the House Judiciary Committee in January 2004. This legislation requires Internet tobacco vendors to register with the states in which they intend to sell their products. They are then required to comply with all state laws regarding tobacco tax collection and reporting. The bill allows states to block the delivery of cigarettes and smokeless tobacco sold by Internet vendors who fail to register with the state.

FDA REGULATION OF TOBACCO PRODUCTS. In 1994 the FDA investigated the tobacco industry to determine whether nicotine is an addictive drug that should be regulated like other addictive drugs. Weeks of testimony before Congress indicated that tobacco companies may have been aware of the addictive effects of nicotine and the likely connection between smoking and cancer as early as the mid-1950s.

In August 1995 the FDA ruled that the nicotine in tobacco products is a drug and, therefore, liable to FDA regulation. However, the tobacco, advertising, and convenience store industries filed a lawsuit against the FDA, claiming it did not have the authority to regulate tobacco as an addictive drug. After conflicting decisions in the lower courts, the Supreme Court, in *FDA v. Brown and Williamson Tobacco Corp.*, ruled 5–4 that the government lacks this authority. Although the ruling did not allow the FDA to regulate tobacco, state laws on selling cigarettes to minors were not affected.

In "FDA Regulation of Tobacco Products: Why It's Needed and What It Will Do" (March 10, 2006, http://www.tobaccofreekids.org/reports/fda/summary.shtml), the Campaign for Tobacco-Free Kids notes that in March 2005 bipartisan bills were introduced in the House and Senate to grant the FDA the authority to regulate tobacco products. The Family Smoking Prevention and Tobacco Control Act would grant the FDA the authority to control tobacco advertising and sales to children, require changes in tobacco products to make them less harmful, prohibit health claims that have no scientific backing, and require the contents and health dangers of tobacco products to be listed on the packaging. As of the end of 2006, the bills were still in committee.

ECONOMIC COSTS OF ALCOHOL, TOBACCO, AND OTHER DRUG USE

Few reports are available on the economic costs of alcohol and other drug abuse, and fewer still on the economic costs of tobacco use. The more recent prominent documents are based on the original report *The Economic Costs of Alcohol and Drug Abuse in the United States, 1992* (1998; http://www.nida.nih.gov/EconomicCosts/Index.html) by the Lewin Group for the National Institute on Drug Abuse and the National Institute on Alcohol Abuse and Alcoholism (NIAAA). The report estimated the economic cost of alcohol and drug abuse (everything from crime, treatment services, health care costs, and lost wages) to be $246 billion in 1992. Alcohol abuse and alcoholism were estimated at $148 billion, whereas drug abuse and dependence were at $98 billion. Tobacco use was not addressed.

Then in 1999 Dorothy Rice published her report "Economic Costs of Substance Abuse, 1995" (*Proceedings of the Association of American Physicians*, February

1999). In this report Rice estimated the economic costs of alcohol, other drug abuse, and smoking in 1995. She estimated the cost of alcohol and drug abuse in 1995 by updating the 1992 data from the Lewin Group report and based the smoking-attributable costs on a published study conducted by herself and her colleagues in 1993 and updated to 1995. The total economic costs of substance abuse were estimated at $428.1 billion in 1995: alcohol abuse and alcoholism at $175.9 billion, drug abuse and dependence at $114.2 billion, and smoking at $138 billion.

Economic Costs of Alcohol Abuse

After the initial Lewin Group report was prepared, the NIAAA asked the Lewin Group to develop a 1998 update for alcohol abuse alone, which resulted in *Updating Estimates of the Economic Costs of Alcohol Abuse in the United States: Estimates, Update Methods, and Data* (December 2000; http://pubs.niaaa.nih.gov/publications/economic-2000/alcoholcost.PDF). This report estimated national costs related to alcohol abuse and dependence to be approximately $185 billion in 1998, up from about $148 billion in 1992 (Lewin report) and $175.9 billion in 1995 (Rice report).

Economic Costs of Drug Abuse

Following the 1998 update, the Office of National Drug Control Policy (ONDCP) asked the Lewin Group to develop even more current data on the costs to society of illicit drug abuse alone. The report, *The Economic Costs of Drug Abuse in the United States, 1992–2002* (December 2004, http://www.whitehousedrugpolicy.gov/publications/economic_costs/economic_costs.pdf), the most current as of the end of 2006, does not include the costs of alcohol abuse or smoking-attributable costs.

Figure 7.1 shows the progression of the economic costs of drug abuse from 1992 through 2002. The 1992 figure of $98 billion from the original Lewin Group report differs from the figure of $107.5 billion shown in Figure 7.1 because the economic cost of drug abuse was reestimated for the 2002 report. The overall cost to society of drug abuse in 2002 was estimated to be $180.8 billion, rising approximately 5.3% per year from 1992 to 2002.

The ONDCP report divides the costs of drug abuse into three major cost components: productivity, health, and other. They are shown within the bars in Figure 7.1. The proportion of each cost component remained relatively stable from 1992 to 2002.

Figure 7.2 shows the proportion of each cost component in 2002. Productivity is the largest cost component at 71.2%. Productivity means *loss* from productivity. It is an indirect cost that reflects losses such as work that was never performed because of poor health, premature death, or incarceration. Productivity losses because of drug abuse were estimated to be $128.6 billion in 2002.

FIGURE 7.1

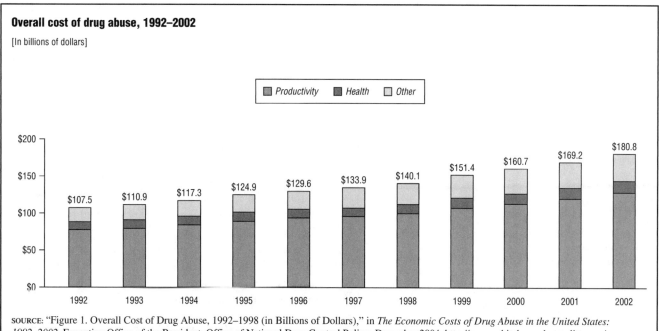

Overall cost of drug abuse, 1992–2002

[In billions of dollars]

■ *Productivity* ■ *Health* □ *Other*

SOURCE: "Figure 1. Overall Cost of Drug Abuse, 1992–1998 (in Billions of Dollars)," in *The Economic Costs of Drug Abuse in the United States: 1992–2002*, Executive Office of the President, Office of National Drug Control Policy, December 2004, http://www.whitehousedrugpolicy.gov/publications/economic_costs/economic_costs.pdf (accessed October 18, 2006)

FIGURE 7.2

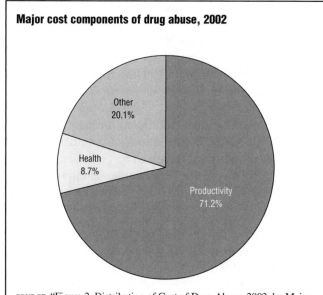

Major cost components of drug abuse, 2002

SOURCE: "Figure 2. Distribution of Cost of Drug Abuse, 2002, by Major Cost Components," in *The Economic Costs of Drug Abuse in the United States: 1992–2002*, Executive Office of the President, Office of National Drug Control Policy, December 2004, http://www.whitehousedrugpolicy.gov/publications/economic_costs/economic_costs.pdf (accessed October 18, 2006)

The second-largest cost component is "other," which includes drug-related crime costs such as the operation of prisons, state and local police protection, and victim costs. It also includes drug-related costs of the social welfare system. These costs totaled $36.4 billion in 2002.

The third-largest cost component associated with drug abuse are the health care costs. Table 7.8 compares the health care costs between 1992 and 2002 and shows the annual change. The report notes that drug abuse-related health care costs are considerable. In 2002 total health care costs were $15.8 billion, up from $10.7 billion in 1992. The largest share ($3.8 billion) was the cost of treating HIV/AIDS patients who had a history of intravenous drug use. Other significant drug-related health care costs in 2002 were hospital and ambulatory care (outpatient) costs at about $1.5 billion and federal efforts to prevent drug abuse at $1.2 billion.

Economic Costs of Tobacco Use

As mentioned previously, the 1999 Rice report estimated the economic costs of smoking at $138 billion in 1995. Another report was published a few months earlier in 1998 by the U.S. Department of the Treasury: *The Economic Costs of Smoking in the United States and the Benefits of Comprehensive Tobacco Legislation* (March 1998, http://www.treasury.gov/press/releases/reports/tobacco.pdf). The report divided the costs into direct costs (for example, adult medical spending, and lost output and workdays) and indirect costs (for example, lower productivity and health costs from secondhand smoke), concluding with a similar overall economic cost of smoking to the Rice report of about $130 billion per year.

In 2005 the Centers for Disease Control and Prevention (CDC) published "Annual Smoking-Attributable Mortality, Years of Potential Life Lost, and Productivity

TABLE 7.8

Health care costs resulting from drug abuse, 1992 and 2002

Detailed cost components	1992	2002	Annual change
Community-based specialty treatment	$3,770	$5,997	4.8%
Federally provided specialty treatment			
Department of Defense	$14	$8	−5.8%
Indian Health Services	$26	$54	7.6%
Bureau of Prisons	$17	$39	8.8%
Department of Veterans Affairs	$113	$116	0.2%
Health infrastructure and support			
Federal prevention	$616	$1,203	6.9%
State and local prevention	$89	$148	5.2%
Training	$49	$69	3.5%
Prevention research	$158	$402	9.8%
Treatment research	$195	$564	11.2%
Insurance administration	$268	$476	5.9%
Medical consequences			
Hospital and ambulatory care costs	$518	$1,454	10.9%
Special disease costs			
Drug-exposed infants	$407	$605	4.0%
Tuberculosis	$30	$19	−4.6%
HIV/AIDS	$3,489	$3,755	0.7%
Hepatitis B and C	$462	$312	−3.9%
Crime victim health care costs	$92	$110	1.8%
Health insurance administration	$340	$513	4.2%
Total	**$10,653**	**$15,844**	**4.1%**

SOURCE: "Table III.1 Health Care Costs, 1992 and 2002 (in Millions of Dollars)," in *The Economic Costs of Drug Abuse in the United States 1992–2002*, Executive Office of the President, Office of National Drug Control Policy, December 2004, http://www.whitehousedrugpolicy.gov/publications/economic_costs/economic_costs.pdf (accessed October 18, 2006)

Losses—United States, 1997–2001" (July 1, 2005, http://www.cdc.gov/mmwr/PDF/wk/mm5425.pdf), which included data on the economic costs of tobacco use. The CDC estimates the economic cost of smoking-attributable lost productivity at $92 billion annually. The CDC suggests, however, that with smoking-attributable health care expenditures added to this figure, the annual economic cost of cigarette smoking exceeds $167 billion per year.

TOBACCO COMPANIES AND RESPONSIBILITY FOR THE COSTS OF TOBACCO USE

Between 1960 and 1988 approximately three hundred lawsuits sought damages from tobacco companies for smoking-related illnesses; courts, though, consistently held that people who choose to smoke are responsible for the health consequences of that decision. This changed in 1988, when a tobacco company was ordered to pay damages for the first time. A federal jury in Newark, New Jersey, ordered Liggett Group Inc. to pay $400,000 to the family of Rose Cipollone, a longtime smoker who died of lung cancer in 1984. The case was overturned on appeal, but the Supreme Court ruled in favor of the Cipollone family in *Cipollone v. Liggett Group, Inc.* (505 U.S. 504 [1992]). In the 7–2 ruling, the Court broadened a smoker's right to sue cigarette

makers in cancer cases. The justices decided that the Federal Cigarette Labeling and Advertising Act of 1965 (PL 89-92), which required warnings on tobacco products, did not preempt damage suits. Despite the warnings on tobacco packaging, people could still sue on the grounds that tobacco companies purposely concealed information about the risks of smoking.

Tobacco Master Settlement Agreement

Following the Supreme Court's decision, the tobacco industry was faced with the possibility of never-ending lawsuits and massive damage awards. Many state governments began lawsuits against major cigarette companies, seeking to recover the costs the states had paid in caring for those with smoking-related health problems. The tobacco industry responded by negotiating with the states, offering money and changes in their business practices in exchange for an end to the lawsuits and protection from future lawsuits.

On November 23, 1998, the attorneys general from forty-six states (excluding four states that previously settled), five territories, and the District of Columbia signed an agreement with the five largest cigarette companies—Philip Morris, R. J. Reynolds, Brown and Williamson, Lorillard, and Liggett and Myers—to settle all the state lawsuits brought to recover the Medicaid costs of treating smokers. The Master Settlement Agreement (MSA) required the tobacco companies to make annual payments totaling more than $200 billion over twenty-five years, beginning in the year 2000. It also placed restrictions on how the companies could advertise, market, and promote tobacco products. Since the original signing, more than thirty additional tobacco firms have signed the MSA, and Philip Morris has contributed more than half of the payments received by the states under the agreement. Although the MSA settles all the state and local government lawsuits, the tobacco industry is still subject to class-action and individual lawsuits.

The four states that negotiated their own lawsuit settlements began receiving payments from the tobacco companies in 1998. Payments to other states began in 1999. A July 2006 fact sheet released by the Campaign for Tobacco-Free Kids details the amount of money the states have received each year since the start of the agreement. (See Table 7.9.)

HOW ARE STATES USING THE SETTLEMENT FUNDS? The MSA did not establish place any restrictions on how state governments used the funds that they received under the agreement. Anti-smoking and public health organizations have argued that the most appropriate use for MSA money is to fund smoking prevention and cessation programs. Since the November 1998 tobacco settlement, the Campaign for Tobacco-Free Kids, the American Lung Association, the American Cancer Society, and the American Heart

TABLE 7.9

Payments received from tobacco settlements, by state, 1998–2006

State	1998	1999	2000	2001	2002	2003	2004	2005	2006
Alabama	$0.0	$0.0	$131.7	$104.7	$120.0	$109.9	$101.9	$101.9	$93.4
Alaska	$0.0	$8.4	$19.6	$21.5	$24.8	$23.2	$21.5	$21.5	$19.7
Arizona	$0.0	$0.0	$120.3	$90.0	$110.4	$101.6	$92.7	$92.9	$85.2
Arkansas	$0.0	$0.0	$0.0	$124.0	$60.2	$56.3	$52.1	$52.2	$47.9
California	$0.0	$315.2	$715.9	$772.5	$956.0	$879.8	$802.4	$804.6	$737.6
Colorado	$0.0	$33.8	$78.6	$86.4	$99.6	$93.2	$86.2	$86.4	$79.2
Connecticut	$0.0	$45.8	$104.1	$112.4	$139.0	$128.0	$116.7	$117.0	$107.3
Delaware	$0.0	$9.8	$22.2	$23.9	$29.6	$27.3	$24.9	$24.9	$22.9
DC	$0.0	$15.0	$34.8	$38.2	$44.1	$41.3	$38.2	$38.3	$35.1
Florida	$562.5	$531.0	$640.9	$743.4	$765.8	$490.0	$363.9	$416.7	$440.0
Georgia	$0.0	$60.6	$140.7	$154.6	$178.4	$166.9	$154.3	$154.7	$141.8
Hawaii	$0.0	$14.9	$33.8	$36.4	$45.1	$41.5	$37.8	$37.9	$34.8
Idaho	$0.0	$9.0	$20.8	$22.9	$26.4	$24.7	$22.8	$22.9	$21.0
Illinois	$0.0	$114.9	$266.9	$293.2	$338.2	$316.6	$292.6	$293.4	$269.0
Indiana	$0.0	$50.4	$117.0	$128.5	$148.2	$138.7	$128.2	$128.6	$117.9
Iowa	$0.0	$21.5	$49.9	$54.8	$63.2	$59.2	$54.7	$54.8	$50.3
Kansas	$0.0	$20.6	$47.8	$52.5	$60.6	$56.7	$52.4	$52.5	$48.2
Kentucky	$0.0	$43.5	$98.8	$106.6	$131.9	$121.4	$110.7	$111.0	$101.8
Louisiana	$0.0	$55.7	$129.3	$142.1	$163.9	$153.4	$141.8	$142.2	$130.3
Maine	$0.0	$19.0	$44.1	$48.5	$55.9	$52.3	$48.4	$48.5	$44.5
Maryland	$0.0	$55.8	$129.6	$142.5	$164.3	$153.8	$142.1	$142.5	$130.6
Massachusetts	$0.0	$99.7	$226.5	$244.5	$302.5	$278.4	$253.9	$254.6	$233.4
Michigan	$0.0	$107.5	$244.1	$263.4	$325.9	$300.0	$273.6	$274.3	$251.5
Minnesota	$240.0	$322.8	$334.2	$352.7	$380.1	$265.4	$168.5	$175.3	$214.0*
Mississippi	$232.1	$109.8	$199.5	$231.1	$229.0	$169.6	$112.5	$116.9	$136.0*
Missouri	$0.0	$0.0	$0.0	$343.6	$167.4	$154.7	$143.0	$143.4	$131.4
Montana	$0.0	$10.5	$24.4	$26.8	$30.9	$28.9	$26.7	$26.8	$24.5
Nebraska	$0.0	$14.7	$34.1	$37.5	$43.2	$40.5	$37.4	$37.5	$34.4
Nevada	$0.0	$15.1	$35.0	$38.4	$44.3	$41.5	$38.3	$38.4	$35.2
New Hampshire	$0.0	$16.4	$38.2	$42.0	$48.4	$45.3	$41.9	$42.0	$38.5
New Jersey	$0.0	$0.0	$318.6	$244.5	$281.0	$263.0	$243.1	$243.8	$223.5
New Mexico	$0.0	$14.7	$34.2	$37.6	$43.3	$40.6	$37.5	$37.6	$34.5
New York	$0.0	$315.1	$715.8	$772.4	$955.8	$879.7	$802.3	$804.4	$737.5
North Carolina	$0.0	$57.6	$130.8	$141.2	$174.7	$160.8	$146.6	$147.0	$134.8
North Dakota	$0.0	$9.0	$21.0	$23.1	$26.6	$24.9	$23.0	$23.1	$21.2
Ohio	$0.0	$124.4	$288.9	$317.3	$366.1	$342.6	$316.7	$317.5	$291.1
Oklahoma	$0.0	$25.6	$59.4	$65.3	$75.3	$70.5	$65.1	$65.3	$59.9
Oregon	$0.0	$28.3	$64.4	$69.5	$86.0	$79.1	$72.1	$72.3	$66.3
Pennsylvania	$0.0	$0.0	$464.6	$348.1	$430.4	$396.1	$361.3	$362.2	$332.1
Rhode Island	$0.0	$17.7	$41.2	$45.3	$52.2	$48.9	$45.2	$45.3	$41.5
South Carolina	$0.0	$29.0	$67.5	$74.1	$85.5	$80.0	$73.9	$73.4	$68.0
South Dakota	$0.0	$8.6	$20.0	$22.0	$25.4	$23.7	$21.9	$22.0	$20.2
Tennessee	$0.0	$0.0	$203.4	$155.9	$177.4	$166.0	$153.4	$153.9	$141.1
Texas	$378.0	$1,018.9	$839.8	$974.2	$1,004.5	$719.0	$479.9	$498.6	$580.0*
Utah	$0.0	$11.0	$25.5	$28.0	$32.3	$30.3	$28.0	$28.0	$25.7
Vermont	$0.0	$10.2	$23.1	$24.9	$30.8	$28.3	$25.8	$25.9	$23.8
Virginia	$0.0	$50.5	$117.2	$128.8	$148.6	$139.1	$128.5	$128.9	$118.2
Washington	$0.0	$50.7	$117.7	$129.3	$149.2	$139.7	$129.1	$129.4	$118.7
West Virginia	$0.0	$21.9	$50.8	$55.8	$64.4	$60.3	$55.7	$55.9	$51.2
Wisconsin	$0.0	$51.2	$116.2	$125.4	$155.2	$142.8	$130.3	$130.6	$119.7
Wyoming	$0.0	$6.1	$13.9	$15.0	$18.6	$17.1	$15.6	$15.7	$14.4
Am. Samoa	$0.0	$0.4	$0.9	$0.9	$1.1	$1.0	$1.0	$1.0	$0.9
Guam	$0.0	$0.5	$1.2	$1.3	$1.6	$1.5	$1.4	$1.4	$1.3
No. Mariana	$0.0	$0.2	$0.5	$0.5	$0.3	$0.7	$0.5	$0.5	$0.5
Puerto Rico	$0.0	$27.7	$62.9	$67.9	$36.6	$95.8	$70.8	$70.7	$64.8
Virgin Islands	$0.0	$0.4	$1.0	$1.1	$0.6	$1.5	$1.1	$1.1	$1.0
MSA total	$0.0	$2.0 bill.	$5.9 bill.	$6.4 bill.	$7.3 bill.	$6.9 bill.	$6.3 bill.	$6.3 bill.	$5.8
Ind. state total	$1.4 bill.	$2.0 bill.	$2.0 bill.	$2.3 bill.	$2.4 bill.	$1.6 bill.	$1.1 bill.	$1.2 bill.	$14*
National total	**$1.4 bill.**	**$4.0 bill.**	**$7.9 bill.**	**$8.7 bill.**	**$9.7 bill.**	**$8.5 bill.**	**$7.4 bill.**	**$7.5 bill.**	**$7.1***

*Estimated

SOURCE: Eric Lindblom, "Actual Payments Received by the States from the Tobacco Settlements (Millions of Dollars)," Campaign for Tobacco-Free Kids, July 2006, http://www.tobaccofreekids.org/research/factsheets/pdf/0218.pdf (accessed October 18, 2006)

Association have published an annual report to monitor how states are handling the settlement funds. The FY2007 report, *A Broken Promise to Our Children: The 1998 State Tobacco Settlement Eight Years Later* (December 6, 2006, http:// www.tobaccofreekids.org/reports/settlements/2007/full report.pdf), notes that states fell short in their efforts to adequately fund tobacco prevention and cessation programs. The joint report also notes that "states that have implemented comprehensive tobacco prevention and cessation programs have achieved significant reductions in tobacco use among both adults and youth."

The report says that in FY2007 only three states—Maine, Delaware, and Colorado—were funding tobacco prevention and cessation programs at the minimum levels recommended by the CDC. Mississippi, a state that previously met the CDC recommendations, was last that year. The report suggests that this drastic change was because of the efforts of the Mississippi governor Haley Barbour to eliminate the funding. Governor Barbour, the report notes, was a former tobacco lobbyist. In FY2007 fourteen states were funding tobacco prevention and cessation programs at half the recommended minimum level, twenty-eight states and the District of Columbia were funding the programs at less than half the recommended minimum, and five states did not fund tobacco prevention programs. Together, the states allocated only 2.8% of their revenue from the settlement agreement for tobacco prevention and cessation programs in FY2007. To fund these programs at the CDC minimum level, states should have allocated 7.3% of their settlement agreement funds to this purpose.

What have states done with the tobacco settlement funds not allocated to tobacco prevention and cessation programs? The answer to this question varies among the states; they used the settlement monies to fund such things as other health- and youth-related programs, capital projects (for example, building hospitals), medical research, medical education, enforcement of tobacco control laws, and expansion of health clinics for low-income citizens. Some states also used part of the money to pay down their debt or to help balance their budgets.

CHAPTER 8
DRUG TRAFFICKING

Trafficking in drugs refers to commercial activity: the buying and selling of illegal and controlled substances without a permit to do so—a permit that, for example, a physician, pharmacist, or researcher would have. Illegal drugs are those with no currently accepted medical use in the United States, such as heroin, lysergic acid diethylamide (LSD), and marijuana. It is illegal to buy, sell, possess, and use these drugs except for research purposes. Legal drugs are those whose sale, possession, and use as intended are not forbidden by law. The use of legal psychoactive (mood- or mind-altering) drugs that have the potential for abuse, however, is restricted. These drugs, which include narcotics, depressants, and stimulants, are available only with a prescription and are called controlled substances. Drug trafficking includes all commercial activities that are integral to the buying and selling of illegal and controlled substances, including their manufacture, production, preparation, importation, exportation, supply, offering to supply, distribution, or transportation.

CRIMINAL PENALTIES FOR TRAFFICKING
Federal Penalties

The Controlled Substances Act of 1970 (PL 91-513) provides penalties for the unlawful trafficking in controlled substances, based on the schedule (rank) of the drug or substance. (See Table 1.2 in Chapter 1 for definitions of the schedules.) Generally, the more dangerous the drug and the larger the quantity involved, the stiffer the penalty. Trafficking of heroin, cocaine, LSD, and phencyclidine (PCP), all Schedule I or II drugs, includes mandatory jail time and fines. A person caught selling at least five hundred grams but less than five kilograms of cocaine powder (seventeen ounces to just under eleven pounds) will receive a minimum of five years in prison and may be fined up to $2 million for a first offense. (See Table 8.1.) The same penalty is imposed for the sale of

five to forty-nine grams of cocaine base ("crack"). Five grams are equal to the weight of six plain M&Ms candies, and forty-nine grams are a little more than a bag of M&Ms candies (47.9 grams), or about sixty M&Ms. Legislators have imposed the high penalty for selling crack in an effort to curb the use of this drug.

Following the second offense, penalties double to ten years in prison and up to $4 million in fines. When higher quantities are involved (five or more kilograms of cocaine powder, fifty grams or more of crack, etc.), penalties for the first offense are ten years and fines up to $4 million may be levied. For the second offense, twenty years and up to $8 million in fines are given, and the third offense results in mandatory life imprisonment. These examples are for an individual. Higher penalties apply if an organized group is involved or if a death or injury is associated with the arrest event.

These penalties also apply to the sale of fentanyl (a powerful painkiller medicine) or similar-acting drugs, heroin, LSD, methamphetamine, and PCP. The smallest amount, which can earn someone a minimum sentence of five years in prison and a fine of up to $2 million, involves trafficking in LSD, where a one-gram amount carries a five-year-minimum sentence in prison.

Punishments for marijuana, hashish, and hashish oil are shown in Table 8.2. Special penalties exist for marijuana trafficking because it may be traded in large quantities or grown in substantial amounts. The lower the amounts sold or the fewer the plants grown, the lower the sentence. A person cultivating one to forty-nine plants or selling less than fifty kilograms of marijuana mixture, ten kilograms or less of hashish, or one kilogram or less of hashish oil may get a maximum sentence of five years in prison and a maximum fine of $250,000. Sentences for second offenses involving large amounts of marijuana may earn the trafficker up to life imprisonment.

TABLE 8.1

Federal drug trafficking penalties, excluding marijuana

Drug/schedule	Quantity	Penalties	Quantity	Penalties
Cocaine (Schedule II)	500–4999 gms	**First offense:**	5 kgs or more	**First offense:**
Cocaine base (Schedule II)	5–49 gms mixture	Not less than 5 years, and not more than	50 gms or more mixture	Not less than 10 years, and not more than
Fentanyl (Schedule II)	40–399 gms mixture	40 years. If death or serious injury, not	400 gms or more mixture	life. If death or serious injury, not less
Fentanyl analogue (Schedule I)	10–99 gms mixture	less than 20 or more than life. Fine of not	100 gms or more mixture	than 20 or more than life. Fine of not more
Heroin (Schedule I)	100–999 gms mixture	more than $2 million if an individual,	1kg or more mixture	than $4 million if an individual, $10 million
LSD (Schedule I)	1–9 gms mixture	$5 million if not an individual		if not an individual.
		Second offense:		**Second offense:**
Methamphetamine (Schedule II)	5–49 gms pure or	Not less than 10 years, and not more than life.	10 gms or more mixture	Not less than 20 years, and not more than
	50–499 gms mixture	If death or serious injury, life imprisonment.	50 gms or more pure or	life. If death or serious injury, life
PCP (Schedule II)	10–99 gms pure or	Fine of not more than $4 million if an	500 gms or more mixture	imprisonment. Fine of not more than
	100–999 gms mixture	individual, $10 million if not an individual	100 gms or more pure or	$8 million if an individual, $20 million
			1 kg or more mixture	if not an individual.
				Two or more prior offenses:
				Life imprisonment.
Other Schedule I & II drugs	Any amount	**First offense:** Not more than 20 years. If death or serious injury, not less than 20 years, or more than life. Fine $1 million if an individual, $5 million if not an individual.		
Flunitrazepam (Schedule IV)	1 gm or more	**Second offense:** Not more than 30 years. If death or serious injury, not less than life. Fine $2 million if an individual, $10 million if not an individual.		
Other Schedule III drugs	Any amount	**First offense:** Not more than 5 years. Fine not more than $250,000 if an individual, $1 million if not an individual.		
Flunitrazepam (Schedule IV)	30 to 999 mgs	**Second offense:** Not more than 10 years. Fine not more than $500,000 if an individual, $2 million if not an individual.		
All other Schedule IV drugs	Any amount	**First offense:** Not more than 3 years. Fine not more than $250,000 if an individual, $1 million if not an individual.		
Flunitrazepam (Schedule IV)	Less than 30 mgs	**Second offense:** Not more than 6 years. Fine not more than $500,000 if an individual, $2 million if not an individual.		
All Schedule V drugs	Any amount	**First offense:** Not more than 1 year. Fine not more than $100,000 if an individual, $250,000 if not an individual.		
		Second offense: Not more than 2 years. Fine not more than $200,000 if an individual, $500,000 if not an individual.		

Note: Does not include marijuana, hashish, or hash oil.

SOURCE: Adapted from "Federal Trafficking Penalties," U.S. Department of Justice, U.S. Drug Enforcement Administration, http://www.dea.gov/agency/penalties.htm (accessed October 19, 2006)

TABLE 8.2

Federal marijuana trafficking penalties

Description	Quantity	1st offense	2nd offense
Marijuana	1,000 kg or more mixture; or 1,000 or more plants	• Not less than 10 years, not more than life • If death or serious injury, not less than 20 years, not more than life • Fine not more than $4 million individual, $10 million other than individual	• Not less than 20 years, not more than life • If death or serious injury, mandatory life • Fine not more than $8 million individual, $20 million other than individual
Marijuana	100 kg to 999 kg mixture; or 100–999 plants	• Not less than 5 years, not more than 40 years • If death or serious injury, not less than 20 years, not more than life • Fine not more than $2 million individual, $5 million other than individual	• Not less than 10 years, not more than life • If death or serious injury, mandatory life • Fine not more than $4 million individual, 10 million other than individual
Marijuana	More than 10 kgs hashish; 50–99 plants	• Not more than 20 years • If death or serious injury, not less than 20 years, not more than life	• Not more than 30 years • If death or serious injury, mandatory life
	More than 1 kg of hashish oil; 50–99 plants	• Fine $1 million individual, $5 million other than individual	• Fine $2 million individual, $10 million other than individual
Marijuana	1–49 plants; less than 50 kg mixture	• Not more than 5 years • Fine not more than $250,000, $1 million other than individual	• Not more than 10 years • Fine $500,000 individual, $2 million other than individual
Hashish	10 kg or less		
Hashish oil	1 kg or less		

Note: Marijuana is a Schedule 1 controlled substance.

SOURCE: Adapted from "Federal Trafficking Penalties—Marijuana," U.S. Department of Justice, U.S. Drug Enforcement Administration, http://www.dea.gov/agency/penalties.htm (accessed October 19, 2006)

State Laws

States have the discretionary power to make their own drug laws. Possession of marijuana may be a misdemeanor in one state but a felony in another. Prison sentences can also vary for the same charges in different states—distribution of five hundred grams of cocaine as a Class C felony may specify ten to fifty years in one state and twenty-four to forty years in another.

Changes in 1990 to the Controlled Substances Act (PL 101-647) led to more than 450 new drug laws in forty-four states and the District of Columbia. Most states follow the model of the Controlled Substances Act and enforce laws that facilitate seizure of drug trafficking profits, specify greater penalties for trafficking, and promote "user accountability" by punishing drug users.

IS THE PROFIT WORTH THE RISK?

Despite the possibility of long prison terms—up to life imprisonment—many drug dealers evidently consider the enormous potential profits of drug trafficking worth the risk. The media often report drug "busts" and indictments of people involved in multimillion- or billion-dollar operations. Paying fines of hundreds of thousands of dollars, or even millions of dollars, becomes part of doing business when the profits are so high.

SUBSTANTIAL WORLD AND U.S. TRADE

In *Economic and Social Consequences of Drug Abuse and Illicit Drug Trafficking* (1998, http://www. unodc.org/pdf/technical_series_1998-01-01_1.pdf), the United Nations estimates the total revenue of the world drug trade in 1995 at about $400 billion. The *World Drug Report, 2006, Volume 1: Analysis* (2006, http://www. unodc. org/pdf/WDR_2006/wdr2006_volume1.pdf) estimates that two hundred million people—approximately 5% of the world's population aged fifteen to sixty-four—were users of illicit drugs in 2006. About half of these two hundred million people used drugs at least once per month. About twenty-five million were addicted to drugs. Of the total population who used drugs in 2006, 162 million used cannabis and thirty-five million used amphetamine-type stimulants, cocaine, and/or opiates.

WORLD PRODUCTION OF PLANT-DERIVED (ORGANIC) DRUGS

In the *2006 International Narcotics Control Strategy Report* (March 2006, http://www.state.gov/p/inl/rls/nrcrpt/2006/), the Bureau for International Narcotics and Law Enforcement Affairs, an element of the U.S. Department of State, reports data on the amount of land cultivated to raise opium poppy, the source of heroin and other opioids; coca leaf, from which cocaine is derived; and cannabis, the hemp plant from which marijuana and hashish are derived. From estimates and observations in the report of the land cultivated, the bureau develops estimates of potential production.

According to the Department of State, the largest amount of cultivated land was dedicated to the production of opium poppy, followed by coca leaf and cannabis. (See Table 8.3.) (Note that because of reporting changes, the 2005 estimate of coca cultivation in Columbia—the

biggest producer of coca—is not included in the table, making the 2005 totals for coca cultivation misleading.) In 2004, 166,200 hectares of land were used to grow coca. (A hectare is 2.47 acres.) Opium poppy was cultivated on 256,630 hectares, a sharp increase from the previous year. The largest producer was Afghanistan. During 2004 this country experienced a severe drought; the opium poppy grows well under these conditions, whereas other crops do not. Therefore, farmers grew poppy because little else would grow. Cannabis cultivation, which excludes what is grown domestically in the United States in this tabulation, took place on 5,000 hectares in 2004. Over the seventeen-year period from 1987 to 2004, opium cultivation was higher than coca leaf cultivation in all but six years. Cannabis cultivation is a distant third, reflecting the much lower value of marijuana than of opium, cocaine, and their derivatives.

Data on production of opium gum, coca leaf, and cannabis are shown for recent years in Table 8.4. Production is measured in metric tons (a metric ton equals 1,000 kilograms, or 2,204.6 pounds). The largest tonnage of drug material is coca leaf, followed by cannabis and opium. Results for 2004 are the most recently comparable because Colombia, overwhelmingly the largest producer of coca leaf, has been left unstated in 2005. In 2004, 174,300 metric tons of coca, 17,940 metric tons of cannabis, and 5,476 metric tons of opium gum were produced. Leading producer countries were Colombia for coca, Afghanistan for opium gum, and Mexico for cannabis.

GREATEST DRUG THREAT

The National Drug Intelligence Center (NDIC), in *National Drug Threat Assessment, 2006* (January 2006, http://www.usdoj.gov/ndic/pubs11/18862/index.htm), surveyed state and local law enforcement agencies nationwide to determine what they believed to be the greatest drug threat in the United States in 2005. For the second year in a row, these agencies identified the synthetic drug methamphetamine as the drug that poses a greater threat to their area than any other drug, rather than any plant-derived drug. (See Figure 8.1.) A close runner-up was cocaine, followed far behind by marijuana, heroin, and illicitly-trafficked pharmaceuticals (prescription drugs).

The NDIC notes in its report that methamphetamine use over the last decade and a half has gradually spread from west to east across the United States. Figure 8.2 shows the progression of the methamphetamine threat from 2003 to 2005. In these three years alone, the threat can be seen moving slowly eastward across the United States.

TABLE 8.3

Illicit drug cultivation worldwide, by crop and region, 1998–2005

[In hectares]

	2005	2004	2003	2002	2001	2000	1999	1998
Opium								
Afghanistan	107,000	206,700	61,000	30,750	1,685	64,510	51,500	41,720
India								
Iran								
Pakistan		3,100		622	213	515	1,570	3,030
Total SW Asia	107,000	209,800	61,000	31,372	1,898	65,025	53,070	44,750
Burma	40,000	30,900	47,130	78,000	105,000	108,700	89,500	130,300
China								
Laos	5,600	10,000	18,900	23,200	22,000	23,150	21,800	26,100
Thailand				750	820	890	835	1,350
Vietnam				1,000	2,300	2,300	2,100	3,000
Total SE Asia	45,600	40,900	66,030	102,950	130,120	135,040	114,235	160,750
Colombia		2,100	4,400	4,900	6,500	7,500	7,500	6,100
Lebanon								
Guatemala		330						
Mexico		3,500	4,800	2,700	4,400	1,900	3,600	5,500
Total other		5,930	9,200	7,600	10,900	9,400	11,100	11,600
Total opium	152,600	256,630	136,230	141,922	142,918	209,465	178,405	217,100
Coca								
Bolivia	26,500	24,600	23,200	21,600	19,900	14,600	21,800	38,000
Colombia*		114,100	113,850	144,450	169,800	136,200	122,500	101,800
Peru	38,000	27,500	29,250	34,700	34,000	34,200	38,700	51,000
Ecuador								
Total coca	64,500	166,200	166,300	200,750	223,700	185,000	183,000	190,800
Cannabis								
Mexico				3,900	3,900	3,900	3,700	4,600
Colombia	5,000		5,000	5,000	5,000	5,000	5,000	5,000
Jamaica								
Total cannabis	5,000		5,000	8,900	8,900	8,900	8,700	9,600

*Colombian coca cultivation survey results for 2005 not available at report date.
Note: One hectare is slightly less than 2.5 acres.

SOURCE: "Worldwide Illicit Drug Cultivation: 1998–2005 (All Figures in Hectares)," in *International Narcotics Control Strategy Report, 2006*, U.S. Department of State, Bureau for International Narcotics and Law Enforcement Affairs, March 2006, http://www.state.gov/p/inl/rls/nrcrpt/2006/vol1/html/62103.htm (accessed October 19, 2006).

METHAMPHETAMINE

Methamphetamine ("meth," or "ice" in its crystalline rather than powdered form) is made in laboratories from precursor drugs rather than directly from plant material. The drug was first synthesized in 1919 and has been a factor on the drug market since the 1960s. The 2005 National Survey on Drug Use and Health (NSDUH), the results of which are published in the Substance Abuse and Mental Health Services Administration's *Results from the 2005 National Survey on Drug Use and Health: National Findings* (2006, http://www.oas.samhsa.gov/nsduh/2k5nsduh/2k5Results.pdf), reveals that 512,000 people were current users of methamphetamine in 2005. In addition, in that year 192,000 people aged twelve and older were first-time users of meth.

Methamphetamine Production

Like other synthetics, such as LSD or ecstasy, methamphetamine appeals to large and small criminal enterprises alike because it frees them from dependence on vulnerable crops such as coca or opium poppy. Even a small organization can control the whole process, from manufacture to sale on the street, of methamphetamine. The drug can be made almost anywhere and can generate large profit margins.

Clandestine meth laboratories in the United States are usually operated as temporary facilities. Drug producers make a batch, tear down the lab, and either store the lab and equipment for later use or rebuild it at another site. This constant assembling and disassembling of laboratories is necessary to avoid detection by law enforcement authorities.

Ingredients for making meth are lithium from batteries, acetone from paint thinner, lye, and ephedrine/pseudoephedrine. Anhydrous ammonia, which is used as a fertilizer, can be used to dry the drug and cut the production cycle by ten hours. The process produces ten pounds of toxic waste for every pound of meth. Making meth creates a big stench, forcing producers into remote

TABLE 8.4

Potential illicit drug production worldwide, by crop and region, 1998–2005

[In metric tons]

	2005	2004	2003	2002	2001	2000	1999	1998
Opium gum								
Afghanistan	4,475	4,950	2,865	1,278	74	3,656	2,861	2,340
India								
Iran								
Pakistan		70		5	5	11	37	66
Total SW Asia	**4,475**	**5,020**	**2,865**	**1,283**	**79**	**3,667**	**2,898**	**2,406**
Burma	380	292	484	630	865	1,085	1,090	1,750
China								
Laos	28	49	200	180	200	210	140	140
Thailand				9	6	6	6	16
Vietnam				10	15	15	11	20
Total SE Asia	**408**	**341**	**684**	**829**	**1,086**	**1,316**	**1,247**	**1,926**
Colombia		30	63	68			75	61
Lebanon								
Guatemala		12						
Mexico		73	101	58	71	21	43	60
Total other		**115**	**164**	**126**	**71**	**21**	**118**	**121**
Total opium	**4,883**	**5,476**	**3,713**	**2,238**	**1,236**	**5,004**	**4,263**	**4,453**
Coca leaf								
Bolivia*	18,800	17,500	17,210	16,600	20,200	26,800	22,800	52,900
Colombia		108,000	115,500	147,918		583,000	521,400	437,600
Peru	56,300	48,800	52,300	59,600	52,600	54,400	69,200	95,600
Ecuador								
Total coca	**75,100**	**174,300**	**185,010**	**224,118**	**72,800**	**664,200**	**613,400**	**586,100**
Cannabis								
Mexico		10,440	13,500	7,900	7,400	7,000	3,700	8,300
Colombia		4,000		4,000	4,000	4,000	4,000	4,000
Jamaica								
Belize								
Others		3,500	3,500	3,500	3,500	3,500	3,500	3,500
Total cannabis	**17,940**	**17,000**	**15,400**	**14,900**	**14,500**	**11,200**	**15,800**

*Beginning in 2001, USG surveys of Bolivian coca cover the period June to June.
Note: One metric ton is approximately 1.1 tons.

SOURCE: "Worldwide Potential Illicit Drug Production: 1998–2005 (All Figures in Metric Tons)," in *International Narcotics Control Strategy Report, 2006*, U.S. Department of State, Bureau for International Narcotics and Law Enforcement Affairs, March 2006, http://www.state.gov/p/inl/rls/nrcrpt/2006/vol1/html/62103.htm (accessed October 19, 2006)

FIGURE 8.1

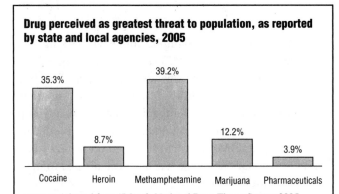

Drug perceived as greatest threat to population, as reported by state and local agencies, 2005

35.3% 8.7% 39.2% 12.2% 3.9%

Cocaine Heroin Methamphetamine Marijuana Pharmaceuticals

SOURCE: Adapted from "Map 2. National Drug Threat Survey 2005, Greatest Drug Threat as Reported by State and Local Agencies," in *National Drug Threat Assessment, 2006, Appendix A Maps*, U.S. Department of Justice, National Drug Intelligence Center, January 2006, http://www.usdoj.gov/ndic/pubs11/18862/18862p.pdf (accessed October 19, 2006)

areas to avoid arousing the suspicion of those living downwind; explosions and fires are also common.

Ephedrine, a stimulant, appetite suppressant, and decongestant, is the key ingredient for making methamphetamine. In 1989 the Chemical Diversion and Trafficking Act (PL 100-690) gave the Drug Enforcement Administration (DEA) authority to regulate bulk sales of ephedrine, but over-the-counter (without a prescription) sales were not included. As a result, manufacturers simply bought ephedrine at drugstores and then used it to manufacture meth.

The passage of the Domestic Chemical Diversion Control Act of 1993 (PL 103-200) made it illegal to sell ephedrine over the counter as well, but pseudoephedrine, a substitute, was not included in the ban. Pseudoephedrine is a decongestant and is found in more than one hundred over-the-counter drugs, including Sudafed and Actifed. Manufacturers began using pseudoephedrine to

FIGURE 8.2

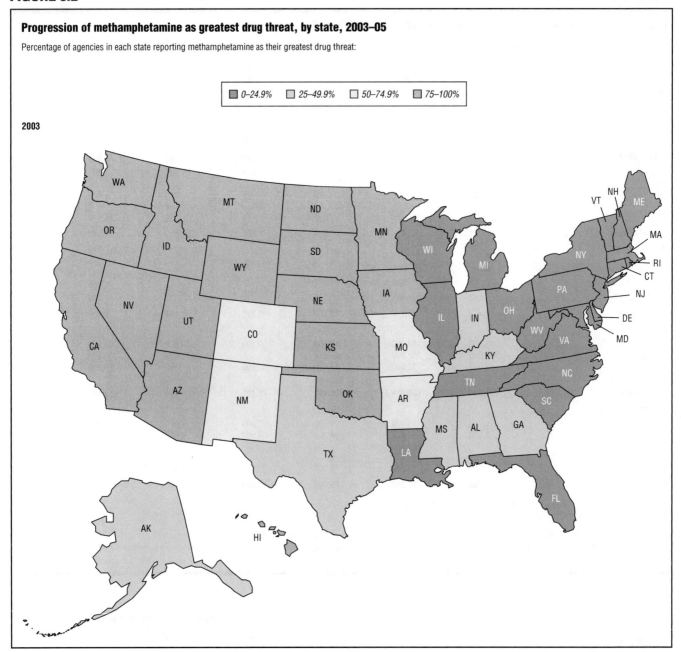

Progression of methamphetamine as greatest drug threat, by state, 2003–05

Percentage of agencies in each state reporting methamphetamine as their greatest drug threat:

☐ *0–24.9%*   ☐ *25–49.9%*   ☐ *50–74.9%*   ☐ *75–100%*

2003

make methamphetamine, often for less than they could with ephedrine. By 2005 a number of states considered and passed legislation placing restrictions on the sale and purchase of over-the-counter medication containing pseudoephedrine. Because of these restrictions on the purchase and sale of ephedrine and pseudoephedrine, the drug ephedra is often used as a substitute. Ephedra, also known as ma huang in traditional Chinese medicine, contains both ephedrine and pseudoephedrine.

The Comprehensive Methamphetamine Control Act of 1996 (PL 104-237) made it illegal to knowingly possess ephedrine and pseudoephedrine (called precursor chemicals) and doubled the possible penalty for manufacturing and/or distributing methamphetamine from ten

to twenty years. The Methamphetamine Trafficking Penalty Enhancement Act of 1998 (PL 105-277), signed into law as part of the omnibus spending agreement for 1999, further increased penalties for trafficking in meth. Authorities are targeting companies that knowingly supply chemicals essential to methamphetamine producers, domestically and internationally. The importance of controlling precursor chemicals has been established in international treaties and laws.

Importation of Methamphetamine and Its Precursors

Since the precursors ephedrine and pseudoephedrine have become difficult to get in large quantities in the United States, methamphetamine and its precursors now

FIGURE 8.2

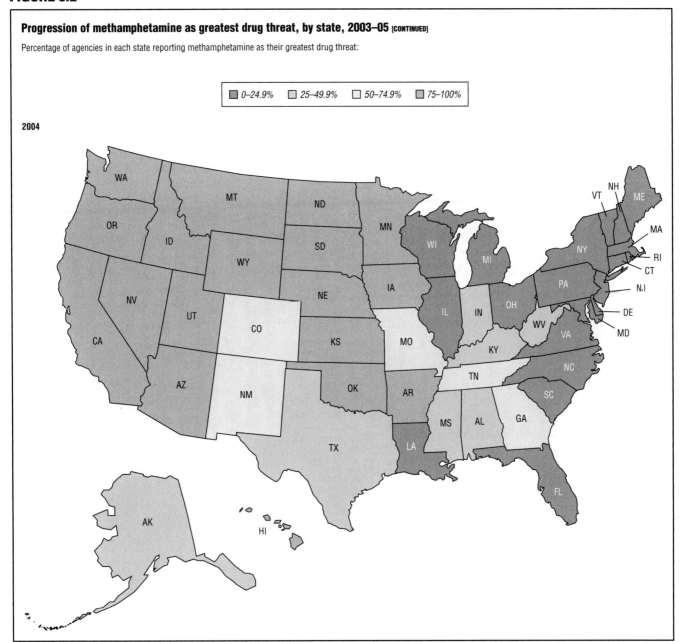

Progression of methamphetamine as greatest drug threat, by state, 2003–05 [CONTINUED]

Percentage of agencies in each state reporting methamphetamine as their greatest drug threat:

☐ 0–24.9%   ☐ 25–49.9%   ☐ 50–74.9%   ☐ 75–100%

2004

flow into the United States from other countries. According to the *National Drug Threat Assessment, 2006*, methamphetamine production in the United States is decreasing because of increased law enforcement pressure, public awareness campaigns, and regulation on the sale and use of precursor chemicals. As this downturn has occurred, the synthesis of methamphetamine in Mexico has begun, and the drug is being smuggled into the United States. Mexican sources of methamphetamine appear to be offsetting the reduction in domestic production. Nonetheless, Mexico is training law enforcement teams to investigate and destroy meth labs in their country. Canada is also working with the United States to stem trafficking of ephedrine and pseudoephedrine into and out of the country.

Figure 8.3 shows the countries that produce and export the most ephedrine: India, the Czech Republic, and Germany. Figure 8.4 shows the countries that produce and export the most pseudoephedrine: Germany, India, and China. The United States is working with these countries as well as others to control these shipments of precursor drugs in an effort to stop their diversion from legitimate uses to methamphetamine labs.

Methamphetamine Prices, Purities, and Supply

The prices and purity of illicit drugs play an important role in understanding and analyzing drug markets. The purity of a drug refers to the extent to which it is diluted, or mixed with, other substances. It is a tremendous

FIGURE 8.2

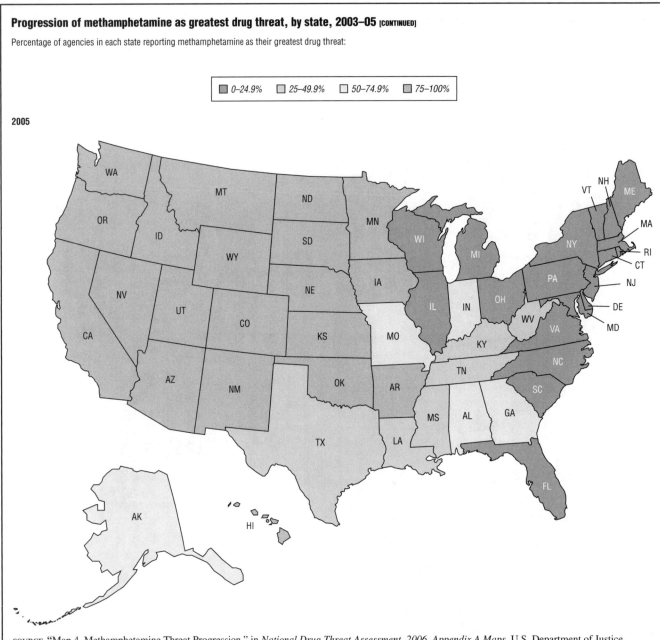

Progression of methamphetamine as greatest drug threat, by state, 2003–05 [CONTINUED]

Percentage of agencies in each state reporting methamphetamine as their greatest drug threat:

| ■ 0–24.9% | ▨ 25–49.9% | □ 50–74.9% | ▨ 75–100% |

2005

SOURCE: "Map 4. Methamphetamine Threat Progression," in *National Drug Threat Assessment, 2006, Appendix A Maps*, U.S. Department of Justice, National Drug Intelligence Center, January 2006, http://www.usdoj.gov/ndic/pubs11/18862/18862p.pdf (accessed October 19, 2006)

challenge to determine prices and purities of illicit drugs accurately, because illicit drugs are not sold in standard quantities and are generally sold at varying purities. In addition, data can only be collected from seizures and purchases by undercover agents. Thus, the data gleaned from the samples collected must be used to estimate these factors for the total drug supply for that year.

Table 8.5 shows the average price and purity of methamphetamine from 1981 to 2003. Drug prices fluctuate with supply and demand. As with other products, when supply outpaces demand, the price drops. Conversely, when the demand outpaces supply, the price

rises. In addition, the purity of drugs may drop if demand outpaces supply; it is a way for drug traffickers to stretch the drug resources they have.

In 2002 and 2003 the price per gram of methamphetamine was lower at the retail and dealer levels than in any previous year shown in Table 8.5. At the retail level, the price per gram of meth in 1981 was $401.23, more than two-and-a-half times as much as the price per gram in 2003 of $155.61. In addition, the purity of the drug was relatively high in 2002 and 2003. These figures suggest that the supply of meth since the turn of the twenty-first century has outpaced the demand. According to *Monitoring the*

FIGURE 8.3

Imports of ephedrine powder, by exporting country, 2004

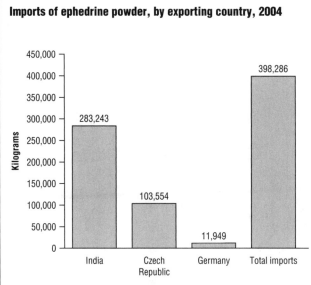

SOURCE: "2004 U.S. Imports of Ephedrine Powder," in *National Drug Control Strategy*, Executive Office of the President of the United States, Office of National Drug Control Policy, February 2006, http://www.whitehousedrugpolicy.gov/publications/policy/ndcs06/ndcs06.pdf (accessed November 9, 2006)

FIGURE 8.4

Imports of pseudoephedrine powder, by exporting country, 2004

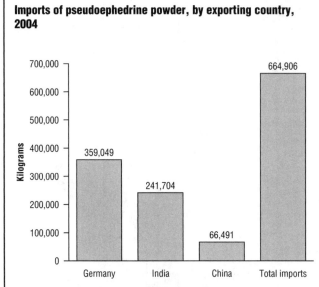

SOURCE: "2004 U.S. Imports of Pseudoephedrine Powder," in *National Drug Control Strategy*, Executive Office of the President of the United States, Office of National Drug Control Policy, February 2006, http://www.whitehousedrugpolicy.gov/publications/policy/ndcs06/ndcs06.pdf (accessed November 9, 2006)

Future National Survey Results on Drug Use, 1975–2005, Volume 2: College Students and Adults Ages, 19–45 (2006, http://www.monitoringthefuture.org/pubs/monographs/vol2_2005.pdf) by the National Institute on Drug Abuse and the University of Michigan Institute for Social Research,

TABLE 8.5

Average price and purity of methamphetamine, 1981–2003

Year	Purchases of 10 grams or less[a] Price per pure gram ($)	Purchases of 10 grams or less[a] Purity (%)	Purchases of 10–100 grams[b] Price per pure gram ($)	Purchases of 10–100 grams[b] Purity (%)	Seizures and purchases greater than 500 grams[a] Purity (%)
1981	401.23	44	153.72	51	75
1982	393.62	43	200.02	50	43
1983	396.56	40	202.75	47	14
1984	350.94	44	242.86	41	43
1985	377.34	42	190.64	50	83
1986	292.96	52	234.67	41	73
1987	269.99	51	188.26	46	78
1988	275.85	57	155.62	51	71
1989	349.46	48	162.63	51	79
1990	402.48	39	281.30	29	40
1991	449.76	36	273.82	31	32
1992	237.00	53	166.31	45	91
1993	215.37	58	132.99	53	92
1994	160.35	74	93.58	69	93
1995	254.27	56	146.02	56	88
1996	230.79	54	145.01	44	41
1997	178.26	61	110.69	50	45
1998	256.03	41	200.19	26	19
1999	210.60	43	177.22	32	22
2000	179.87	52	141.22	33	23
2001	181.72	57	113.50	42	28
2002	153.77	64	104.02	48	32
2003[c]	155.61	62	90.77	56	76

[a]Quantities purchased at the "retail" level.
[b]Quantities purchased at the "dealer" level.
[c]2003 data are preliminary, based on first two quarters of data.

SOURCE: "Table 46. Average Price and Purity of Methamphetamine in the United States, 1981–2003," in *2005 National Drug Control Strategy: Data Supplement*, Executive Office of the President of the United States, Office of National Drug Control Policy, March 2005, http://www.whitehousedrugpolicy.gov/publications/policy/ndcs06_data_supl/ds_drg_rltd_tbls.pdf (accessed October 19, 2006)

the demand for meth among nineteen- to twenty-eight-year-olds has remained relatively steady from 1999 to 2005.

Distribution of Methamphetamine

According to the DEA and the High Intensity Drug Trafficking Area (HIDTA) program, which coordinates drug control efforts among local, state, and federal law enforcement agencies, Mexican criminal groups control most of the wholesale distribution of both the powder and ice forms of methamphetamine. These groups supply midlevel distributors, which are often Mexican criminal groups as well. The DEA and the HIDTA believe that Mexican control over the distribution of meth in the United States is likely to increase as more of the drug is produced in Mexican-based labs.

Figure 8.5 shows the influence of drug trafficking organizations in the United States. The Mexican organizations are spread throughout the country. The other drug trafficking organizations shown will be mentioned throughout this chapter.

FIGURE 8.5

Areas of influence of drug trafficking organizations

Mexican organizations

Colombian organizations

Dominican organizations

Jamaican organizations

Asian organizations

Russian-Israeli organizations

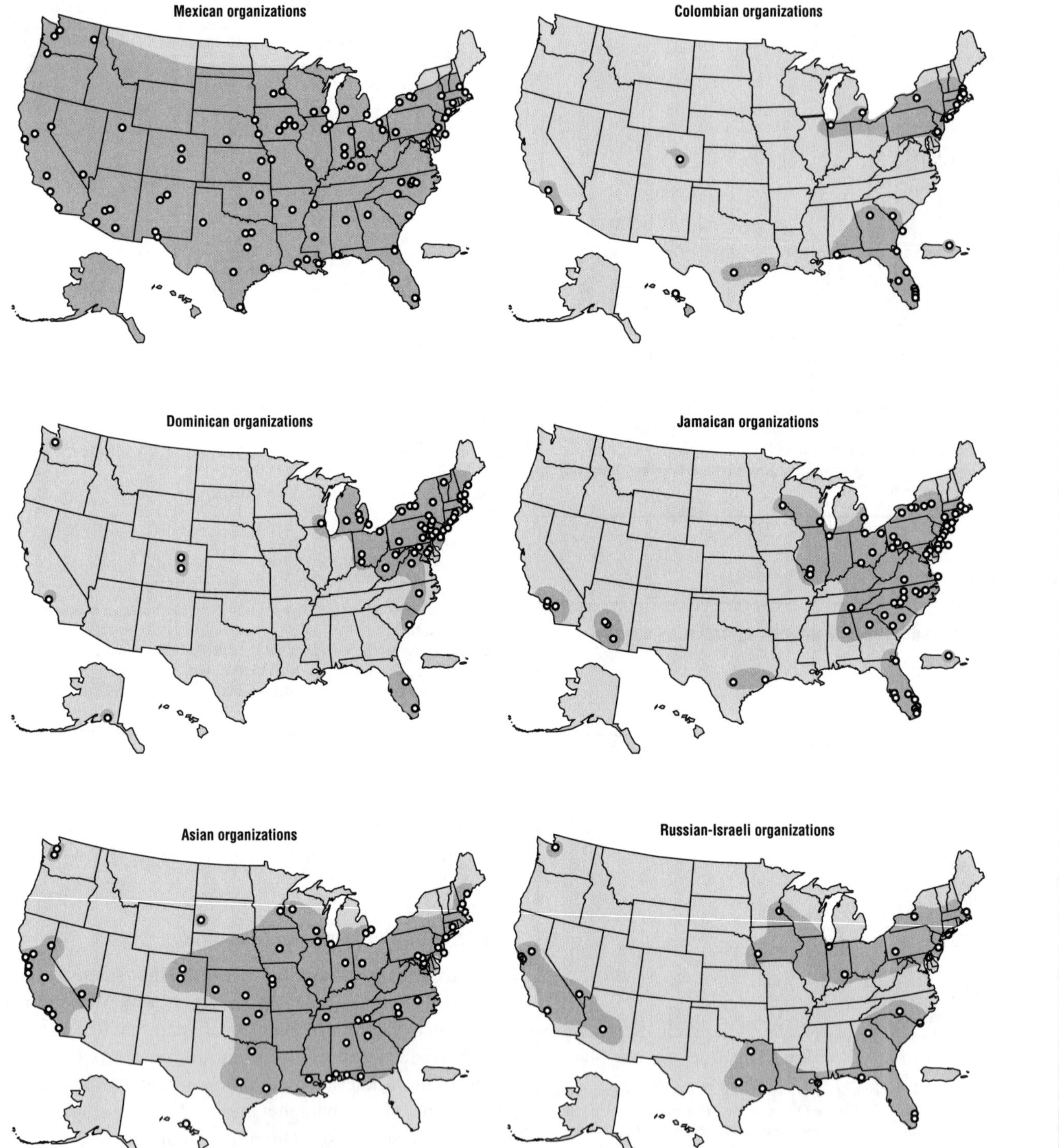

SOURCE: "Map 3. Areas of Influence of Drug Trafficking Organizations in the United States," in *National Drug Threat Assessment, 2006, Appendix A Maps*, U.S. Department of Justice, National Drug Intelligence Center, January 2006, http://www.usdoj.gov/ndic/pubs11/18862/18862p.pdf (accessed October 19, 2006)

FIGURE 8.6

Cocaine flow from South America to the United States, January–December 2004

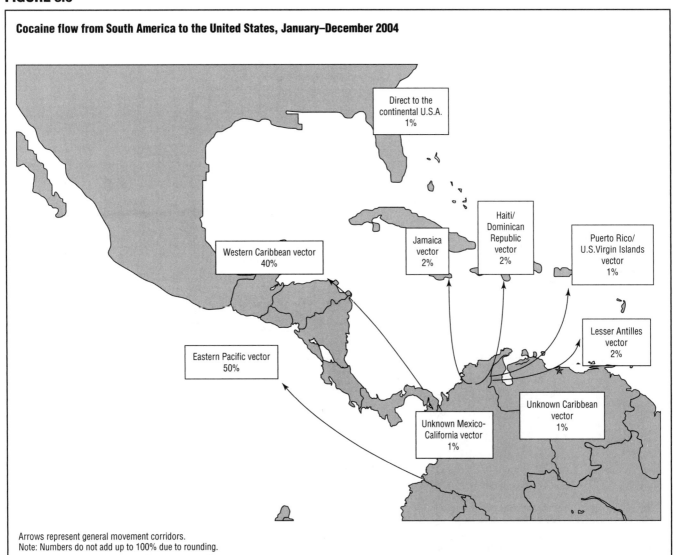

Direct to the
continental U.S.A.
1%

Haiti/
Dominican
Republic
vector
2%

Jamaica
vector
2%

Puerto Rico/
U.S. Virgin Islands
vector
1%

Western Caribbean vector
40%

Lesser Antilles
vector
2%

Eastern Pacific vector
50%

Unknown Mexico-
California vector
1%

Unknown Caribbean
vector
1%

Arrows represent general movement corridors.
Note: Numbers do not add up to 100% due to rounding.

SOURCE: "Map 5. Vectors in the Transit Zone—CCDB-Documented Cocaine Flow Departing South America, January–December 2004," in *National Drug Threat Assessment, 2006, Appendix A Maps*, U.S. Department of Justice, National Drug Intelligence Center, January 2006, http://www.usdoj.gov/ndic/pubs11/18862/18862p.pdf (accessed October 19, 2006)

COCAINE
Production and Distribution

The coca plant, from which cocaine is produced, is grown primarily in the Andean region of Colombia, Peru, and Bolivia, with Columbia being the largest producer. The first step in the production of cocaine is to mix the coca leaves with sulfuric acid in a plastic-lined hole in the ground. The leaves are then pounded to create an acidic juice. When this juice is filtered and neutralized, it forms a paste. The paste is purified into cocaine base by the addition of more chemicals and filtering. This cocaine base includes coca paste, freebase cocaine, and crack cocaine. It is transported from the jungles of Bolivia and Peru to southern Colombia, where it is processed into cocaine hydrochloride (white powder) at clandestine drug laboratories. Small, independent Bolivian and

Peruvian trafficking groups also process some cocaine. It takes three hundred to five hundred kilograms of coca leaf to make one kilogram of cocaine.

After processing, the powder is shipped to the United States and Europe. Caribbean and Central American countries serve as transit countries for the shipment of drugs into the United States. Drug traffickers shift routes according to law enforcement and interdiction pressures. In 2004, 90% of the cocaine transported from South America reached the United States through the Mexican-Central American corridor, which has both an eastern Pacific and a western Caribbean component. (See Figure 8.6.) In the eastern Pacific the drugs are smuggled primarily on fishing boats, and in the western Caribbean they are smuggled primarily on go-fast boats. Go-fast boats are small boats, usually piloted by and carrying

FIGURE 8.7

Principal drug distribution centers (PDCs)

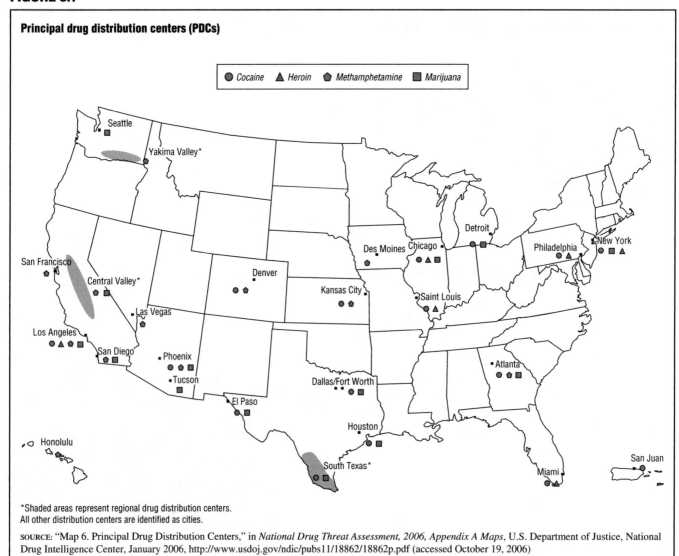

*Shaded areas represent regional drug distribution centers.
All other distribution centers are identified as cities.

SOURCE: "Map 6. Principal Drug Distribution Centers," in *National Drug Threat Assessment, 2006, Appendix A Maps*, U.S. Department of Justice, National Drug Intelligence Center, January 2006, http://www.usdoj.gov/ndic/pubs11/18862/18862p.pdf (accessed October 19, 2006)

only one person, onto which drugs have been loaded from larger supplies on a ship.

Once cocaine enters the United States, it is transported throughout the country for distribution. Although cocaine is distributed in nearly every large and midsize city in the United States, principal drug distribution centers exist. They are shown in Figure 8.7.

In 2004 Mexican drug trafficking organizations and criminal groups controlled most of the distribution of cocaine in the United States, a recent shift in power and drug control from Colombian drug trafficking organizations. The *National Drug Threat Assessment, 2006* notes that the NDIC expected this Mexican increase in control to continue, at least in the short term.

As Figure 8.5 shows, Colombian drug trafficking organizations are most active in the U.S. Northeast and Southeast. Dominican drug trafficking organizations also play a small role in the distribution of cocaine in the

United States. However, they are active generally in the northeastern and southeastern regions of the country and work with Colombian and Mexican drug trafficking organizations. Jamaican drug trafficking organizations work with Colombian drug trafficking organizations and transport multikilogram quantities of cocaine, particularly within the eastern United States.

Cocaine Prices, Purities, and Supply

Price ranges for cocaine and crack from 1981 to 2003 are shown in Table 8.6. The data show that cocaine and crack prices have dropped dramatically since 1981 at the retail and dealer levels. In 1981, for instance, cocaine at the retail level sold for $544.59 per gram. In 2003 the average retail price was $106.54 per gram. Retail crack prices were $341.61 per gram in 1986 and dropped to $189.87 per gram in 2003. The purity of crack, however, has declined over the years while the purity of cocaine has increased.

TABLE 8.6

Average price and purity of cocaine and crack, 1981–2003

| | Cocaine | | | | | Crack | | | |
| | Purchases of 2 grams or less[a] | | Purchases of 10–50 grams[b] | | Seizures and purchases greater than 750 grams[a] | Purchases of 1 gram or less[a] | | Purchases greater than 15 grams[b] | |
Year	Price per pure gram ($)	Purity (%)	Price per pure gram ($)	Purity (%)	Purity (%)	Price per pure gram ($)	Purity (%)	Price per pure gram ($)	Purity (%)
1981	544.59	40	280.55	50	88	—	—	—	—
1982	590.86	43	267.12	49	90	—	—	—	—
1983	471.88	49	215.06	61	92	—	—	—	—
1984	400.69	53	170.08	67	91	—	—	—	—
1985	389.60	51	170.56	63	89	—	—	—	—
1986	296.94	56	130.50	76	90	341.61	85	113.27	76
1987	250.55	7C	98.63	81	89	325.12	84	84.94	68
1988	223.55	73	73.79	81	89	228.01	86	71.24	78
1989	189.92	69	67.02	74	87	197.65	87	66.78	75
1990	234.94	58	84.75	63	86	254.68	81	97.59	62
1991	198.34	63	67.19	75	88	201.60	86	72.42	77
1992	153.96	68	62.19	73	88	206.69	82	66.78	76
1993	156.18	69	63.59	68	87	178.66	82	65.80	70
1994	147.43	66	55.46	73	86	174.46	81	57.84	72
1995	181.58	61	57.68	68	86	181.87	76	59.37	66
1996	150.13	73	50.67	71	86	162.37	76	54.28	66
1997	145.73	66	52.07	69	85	195.38	73	58.75	60
1998	132.09	69	47.02	70	83	161.06	75	52.41	62
1999	135.51	65	50.16	64	81	205.33	72	59.50	57
2000	161.28	61	55.26	58	78	218.55	68	63.56	52
2001	168.29	58	53.99	54	74	198.36	68	61.23	50
2002	124.54	70	47.27	60	78	172.90	70	54.80	55
2003[c]	106.54	70	44.17	62	84	189.87	74	47.47	59

[a]Quantities purchased at the "retail" level.
[b]Quantities purchased at the "dealer" level.
[c]2003 data are preliminary, based on first two quarters of data.

SOURCE: "Table 44. Average Price and Purity of Cocaine and Crack in the United States, 1981–2003," in *2005 National Drug Control Strategy: Data Supplement*, Executive Office of the President of the United States, Office of National Drug Control Policy, March 2005, http://www.whitehousedrugpolicy.gov/publications/policy/ndcs06_data_supl/ds_drg_rltd_tbls.pdf (accessed October 19, 2006)

As Figure 4.3 in Chapter 4 shows, the percent of current users of drugs in general, and cocaine in particular, remained relatively stable from 2002 to 2005. Because demand did not soften during those years, the decreasing prices suggest increased supplies and/or decreased purities. Table 8.6 shows that the purity of cocaine increased in small purchases and remained relatively stable in large purchases. Although the purity of crack dropped from 1986 to 2003, it rose from 2002 to 2003. Authorities believe this rise in purity indicates an increase in supply. However, Table 8.4 does not show increasing coca leaf production between 2002 and 2003 or increasing cultivation.

The *National Drug Threat Assessment, 2006* offers a possible answer: "Cocaine supplies appear to be stable at levels necessary to meet current domestic demand, despite record levels of seizures and declines in estimated worldwide production that have been reported over the past few years. This stability in supply could be the result of overproduction through 2002 or a time lag between coca cultivation and cocaine distribution. Time lags in reporting drug availability data also may account for apparent stability in cocaine availability in spite of decreased production and increased seizures." In addition, the NDIC notes that it is extremely difficult to estimate Andean coca cultivation. The NDIC was reviewing these estimates to determine their level of accuracy.

MARIJUANA
Production, Availability, and Distribution

Marijuana is made from the flowering tops and leaves of the cannabis plant; these are collected, trimmed, dried, and then smoked in a pipe or as a cigarette. Many users smoke "blunts," named after the inexpensive blunt cigars from which they are made. Blunt cigars are approximately five inches long and can be purchased at any store that sells tobacco products. A marijuana blunt is made from the emptied cigar casing, which is then stuffed with marijuana or a marijuana-tobacco mixture. A blunt may contain as much marijuana as six regular marijuana cigarettes. In some cases blunt users add crack cocaine or PCP to the mixture to make it more potent. These are sometimes called "turbos," "woolies," or "woolie blunts."

The Office of National Drug Control Policy (ONDCP), in *Pulse Check: Trends in Drug Abuse* (January 2004, http://www.whitehousedrugpolicy.gov/publications/drugfact/pulsechk/january04/index.html), compiled information from law enforcement and other sources across the country (ninety-seven sources in twenty-five cities). These sources reported that marijuana was readily available in the United States. Domestically grown, Mexican and Canadian grown, hydroponically grown, and the potent seedless marijuana were all available; the domestic variety was the most common.

Domestic growers cultivate cannabis in remote areas to avoid detection by law enforcement agencies. They surround their plots with camouflaging crops such as corn or soybeans. Based on eradication data collected by the DEA, California, Kentucky, Tennessee, Hawaii, and, to a somewhat lesser extent, Washington and Oregon are the primary domestic marijuana source areas. Indoor cultivation permits year-round production in a variety of settings. Growers may cultivate a dozen or so plants in a closet or operate elaborate, specially constructed (sometimes underground) greenhouses where thousands of plants grow under intense electric lighting or in sunlight. Indoor cultivators often use hydroponics, in which the plants are grown in nutrient solution rather than in soil.

Nondomestically grown marijuana arrives in the continental United States via the southwestern border with Mexico and the northern border with Canada. Mexican drug trafficking organizations control most of the wholesale distribution of marijuana throughout the United States, and marijuana has become their primary source of income. Figure 8.8 shows the estimated revenue for Mexican drug trafficking organizations. They make more money from trafficking in marijuana alone than they do from trafficking in heroin, methamphetamine, and cocaine combined.

Although Mexican criminal groups control most of the distribution of marijuana in the United States, Asian criminal groups—primarily Chinese and Vietnamese—are beginning to control distribution of the Canadian-grown drug. The distribution of Asian drug trafficking organizations can be seen in Figure 8.5.

THC Content and Price

The active ingredient in marijuana is THC (delta-9-tetrahydrocannabinol), which is most concentrated in the flowering tops (colas or buds) of the cannabis plants. The flowering tops of female plants that have not yet been pollinated and, therefore, have not yet produced seeds have the highest THC content. This plant part is called sinsemilla (literally, "without seed"). In contrast, feral hemp, commonly called ditchweed, contains a low THC content and is generally not a product drug users want.

FIGURE 8.8

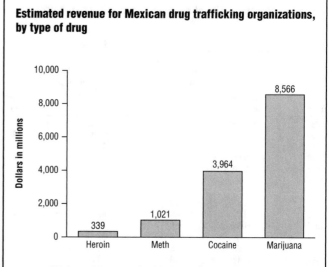

Estimated revenue for Mexican drug trafficking organizations, by type of drug

SOURCE: "Estimated Revenue for Mexican Drug Trafficking Organization," in *National Drug Control Strategy*, Executive Office of the President of the United States, Office of National Drug Control Policy, February 2006, http://www.whitehousedrugpolicy.gov/publications/policy/ndcs06/ndcs06.pdf (accessed November 9, 2006)

The DEA notes in *Illegal Drug Price/Purity Report* (April 2003) that during the 1970s and into the 1980s the THC content of commercial-grade marijuana averaged less than 2%. By 1996 potency had increased to 4.4% for marijuana and 11.3% for sinsemilla in federal seizure samples and to 2.9% for marijuana and 8.9% for sinsemilla in state and local eradication samples. In 2004 potency was even higher in federal seizure samples: 6.8% for marijuana and 14.9% for sinsemilla. Potency was lower, however, in state and local eradication samples: 2.6% for marijuana and 8.3% for sinsemilla. (See Table 8.7.)

THC levels may rise even higher. Marijuana with a THC content of more than 20% has appeared in the Netherlands and Latin America (called "skunk," "skunkweed," or "nederweed"). Raids in Alaska have also uncovered marijuana with THC content well above 20%. This marijuana is grown by indoor cultivators who focus their efforts on hybridizing, cloning, and growing high-potency marijuana.

The average price of marijuana at the retail level decreased from 1981 to 2003. (See Table 8.8.) In 1981 the retail cost of marijuana was $1,974.49 per gram; by 2003 it had dropped to $361.95. Figure 4.2 in Chapter 4 shows that 54.5% of current drug users use marijuana. Figure 4.3 in Chapter 4 shows that the demand for this drug has decreased slightly from 2003 to 2005. The *National Drug Threat Assessment, 2006* suggests that the availability of marijuana will remain high and that the demand will continue to decrease somewhat, resulting in decreasing prices. Thus, authorities expect that drug traffickers will try to expand their customer base.

TABLE 8.7

Marijuana potency, 1985–2004

	Federal seizure samples								State and local eradication samples							
	Type of cannabis								Type of cannabis							
	Ditchweed		Marijuana		Sinsemilla		All types[c]		Ditchweed		Marijuana		Sinsemilla		All types[c]	
Year	Potency[a]	Number[b]	Potency[a]	number[b]	Potency[a]	Number[b]	Potency[a]	Number[b]	Potency[a]	Number[b]	Potency[a]	Number[b]	Potency[a]	Number[b]	Potency[a]	Number[c]
1985	0.30%	9	3.44%	745	7.95%	12	3.48%	767	.50%	102	2.19%	703	7.07%	40	2.22%	845
1986	0.30%	23	2.79%	711	8.78%	14	2.80%	753	.32%	124	1.95%	661	8.16%	18	1.84%	803
1987	0.35%	17	3.16%	1,109	8.29%	17	3.20%	1,146	.34%	86	2.46%	441	7.69%	26	2.38%	553
1988	0.39%	13	3.62%	1,126	8.30%	29	3.70%	1,170	.40%	69	2.20%	513	7.33%	69	2.56%	651
1989	0.30%	7	3.68%	725	7.13%	29	3.78%	761	.29%	104	1.71%	350	6.86%	57	2.00%	511
1990	033%	15	3.78%	756	9.59%	16	3.82%	788	.33%	78	2.09%	352	10.29%	45	2.58%	475
1991	0.35%	37	3.18%	1,497	11.20%	29	3.26%	1,563	.31%	246	2.90%	651	10.10%	46	2.57%	943
1992	0.27%	21	3.09%	2,461	9.67%	33	3.16%	2,515	.31%	107	3.05%	875	7.72%	43	2.96%	1,025
1993	0.35%	11	3.67%	1,993	4.64%	5	3.65%	2,009	.37%	189	2.83%	1,039	5.82%	118	2.75%	1,346
1994	0.32%	12	3.76%	2,049	6.92%	10	3.75%	2,071	.29%	136	2.95%	980	7.55%	94	3.02%	1,210
1995	0.44%	14	3.95%	3,728	9.64%	17	3.96%	3,761	.41%	149	2.55%	701	7.26%	147	2.93%	997
1996	0.62%	3	4.40%	1,385	11.30%	22	4.50%	1,410	.37%	115	2.90%	763	8.92%	147	3.48%	1,025
1997	0.57%	3	4.92%	1,313	11.62%	19	5.00%	1,335	.48%	57	3.34%	958	11.61%	102	3.95%	1,117
1998	0.18%	6	4.71%	1,298	11.88%	37	4.89%	1,341	.40%	81	3.39%	775	12.58%	64	3.76%	920
1999	0.56%	13	4.34%	1,756	13.49%	55	4.59%	1,824	.33%	59	3.76%	691	13.31%	81	4.45%	931
2000	0.55%	4	5.10%	1,860	12.71%	63	5.34%	1,927	.34%	69	3.94%	1,066	12.71%	51	4.10%	1,186
2001	0.53%	4	5.77%	1,587	12.05%	95	6.11%	1,686	.42%	59	3.57%	806	7.87%	139	3.98%	1,004
2002	0.31%	8	5.62%	1,378	14.45%	300	7.19%	1,686	.41%	67	3.28%	408	7.31%	225	4.30%	700
2003	0.34%	8	5.62%	1,512	14.02%	342	7.14%	1,862	.39%	48	3.35%	376	7.25%	187	3.70%	611
2004[d]	0.49%	4	6.79%	721	14.87%	166	8.27%	891	.31%	20	2.57%	218	8.33%	51	3.43%	289

[a]These percentages, indicating potency, are based on simple arithmetic means calculated by dividing the sum of the delta-9 THC concentrations of each sample by the number of seizures and are not normalized by weight of seizure.
[b]Number of tested samples that yield the potency in prior column.
[c]All tested samples include a small number of Thai sticks.
[d]Preliminary data through November 8, 2004.

SOURCE: "Table 48. Potency of Tested Cannabis from Federal Seizure and State and Local Eradication Samples, by Type, 1985–2004 (Percent Delta-9 THC Concentrations and Number of Samples Tested)," in *2005 National Drug Control Strategy: Data Supplement*, Executive Office of the President of the United States, Office of National Drug Control Policy, March 2005, http://www.whitehousedrugpolicy.gov/publications/policy/ndcs06_data_supl/ds_drg_rltd_tbls.pdf (accessed October 19, 2006). Data from *Potency Monitoring Project*, Quarterly Report #87. National Center for the Development of Natural Products, Research Institute of Pharmaceutical Sciences Eradication, School of Pharmacy, University of Mississippi (January 2005).

TABLE 8.8

Average price of marijuana, 1981–2003

Year	Purchases of 1 gram or less[a]		Purchases greater than 10 grams[b]		Seizures and purchases greater than 200 grams[a]
	Price per pure gram ($)	Purity (%)	Price per pure gram ($)	Purity (%)	Purity (%)
1981	1974.49	12	1007.61	12	22
1982	1587.69	17	744.49	27	67
1983	1626.58	15	726.13	28	60
1984	1468.39	22	715.19	32	62
1985	1351.66	23	655.44	38	57
1986	1352.37	24	656.25	37	50
1987	1230.13	23	754.27	34	48
1988	1043.78	30	511.39	44	70
1989	933.97	33	485.85	52	81
1990	947.70	24	647.46	37	68
1991	895.80	31	492.31	40	69
1992	743.91	38	402.08	53	82
1993	619.73	41	325.48	58	84
1994	615.16	41	299.03	55	82
1995	544.69	45	237.73	54	86
1996	515.69	38	248.48	49	80
1997	491.04	45	208.32	51	84
1998	432.76	45	185.77	54	83
1999	426.49	42	176.05	55	82
2000	413.90	43	153.60	57	84
2001	398.28	39	134.62	55	81
2002	372.00	41	138.32	48	80
2003[c]	361.95	32	139.22	46	75

[a]Quantities purchased at the "retail" level.
[b]Quantities purchased at the "dealer" level.
[c]2003 data are preliminary based on first two quarters of data.

SOURCE: "Table 47. Average Price of Marijuana in the United States, 1981–2003," in *2005 National Drug Control Strategy: Data Supplement*, Executive Office of the President of the United States, Office of National Drug Control Policy, March 2005, http://www.whitehousedrugpolicy.gov/publications/policy/ndcs06_data_supl/ds_drg_rltd_tbls.pdf (accessed October 19, 2006)

HEROIN

Heroin users represent the smallest group using a major drug. According to the NSDUH, there were 136,000 current heroin users in the United States in 2005, and the rate of use was 0.1%. There were no significant changes in the number of current users and the rate of use between 2004 and 2005.

Heroin is a stable commodity for traffickers. In the *2001 International Narcotics Control Strategy Report* (March 2002, http://www.state.gov/p/inl/rls/nrcrpt/2001/rpt/8475.htm), the Department of State sums up the attractiveness of heroin for traffickers:

Though cocaine dominates the U.S. drug scene, heroin is lurking conspicuously in the wings. . . . [H]eroin . . . has a special property that appeals to the drug trade's long range planners: as an opiate, it allows many addicts to develop a long-term tolerance to the drug. Where constant cocaine or crack use may kill a regular user in five years, a heroin addiction can last for a decade or more, as long as the addict has access to a regular maintenance "fix." Some can even maintain a facade of normality for many years. This pernicious

property of tolerance potentially assures the heroin trade of a long-term customer base of hard-core addicts.

Heroin Production and Distribution

PRODUCTION PROCESS. The source of heroin is the opium poppy. After the leaves of the poppy fall off, only the round poppy pods remain. Heroin production begins by scoring the poppy pod with a knife. A gummy substance begins to ooze out. This opium gum is scraped off and collected. The rest of the process is explained by the Central Intelligence Agency (CIA) in "From Flowers to Heroin" (July 26, 2006, https://www.cia.gov/cia/publications/heroin/flowers_to_heroin.htm):

Once the opium gum is transported to a refinery, it is converted into morphine, an intermediate product. This conversion is achieved primarily by chemical processes and requires several basic elements and implements. Boiling water is used to dissolve opium gum; 55-gallon drums are used for boiling vessels; and burlap sacks are used to filter and strain liquids. When dried, the morphine resulting from this initial process is pressed into bricks. The conversion of morphine bricks into heroin is also primarily a chemical process. The main chemical used is acetic anhydride, along with sodium carbonate, activated charcoal, chloroform, ethyl alcohol, ether, and acetone. The two most commonly produced heroin varieties are No. 3 heroin, or smoking heroin, and No. 4 heroin, or injectable heroin.

The CIA notes that this generic process produces heroin that may be 90% pure. Variations in the process are introduced as the heroin is diluted to increase its bulk and profits. The pure heroin is mixed with various substances including caffeine, baking soda, powdered milk, and quinine.

OVERVIEW OF THE TRADE. Opium poppies are intensely cultivated in four regions of the world: Southeast Asia, Southwest Asia, Mexico, and South America. In 2004 Southwest Asia, primarily Afghanistan, accounted for approximately 92% of known opium gum production. (See Table 8.4.) Afghanistan's production was 3,656 metric tons in 2000, then dropped to 74 tons in 2001 as a consequence of steps taken by the Taliban to suppress the trade. Production went up again to 1,278 metric tons in 2002 after the Taliban fell, and more than doubled to 2,865 metric tons in 2003. In 2004 production rose to 4,950 metric tons—a 73% increase from 2003. Production was down somewhat in 2005 to 4,475 metric tons. A similar pattern is seen in the opium poppy cultivation in Afghanistan from 2000 to 2005. (See Figure 8.9.)

The DEA conducts the Heroin Signature Program (HSP). The name of the program comes from the fact that each producing region uses a unique process for deriving heroin from opium, thus the heroin has a unique "signature." Under this program heroin seized by federal authorities is analyzed to determine the purity of the

FIGURE 8.9

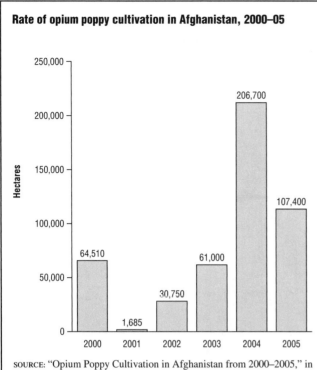

Rate of opium poppy cultivation in Afghanistan, 2000–05

SOURCE: "Opium Poppy Cultivation in Afghanistan from 2000–2005," in *National Drug Control Strategy*, Executive Office of the President of the United States, Office of National Drug Control Policy, February 2006, http://www.whitehousedrugpolicy.gov/publications/policy/ndcs06/ndcs06.pdf (accessed November 9, 2006)

heroin and its origin. In its most recent formal workup of these data, *Drug Intelligence Brief: Heroin Signature Program—2002* (March 2004), the agency determined that 80% of all heroin seized in 2002 came from South America, 10% from Southwest Asia, 9% from Mexico, and 1% from Southeast Asia. Although South America and Mexico represent about 3% of opium gum production, these countries supply most of the heroin used in the United States. The *National Drug Threat Assessment, 2006* notes that relatively little heroin produced in Afghanistan is distributed in the United States because it is sold, instead, in Asia and Europe. In addition, Colombian and Dominican criminal groups control most of the distribution of heroin in the United States, and they distribute drugs produced in Central and South America.

Mexico produces a variety of heroin called "black tar" because it looks like roofing tar. It was once considered inferior to Colombian and Asian heroin, but it has reached a level of purity high enough so that it can be snorted or smoked. Mexican heroin is targeted almost exclusively to the U.S. market. The long U.S.-Mexican land border provides many opportunities for drug smugglers to cross. Female couriers are used more frequently than males. Mexican heroin is smuggled in cars, trucks, and buses and may also be hidden on or in the body of the smuggler. Many smugglers send their drugs by overnight-package express services.

The bulk of heroin from South America comes from Colombia. Many Colombian coca traffickers have been requiring their dealers to accept a small amount of heroin along with their normal deliveries of coca. This has allowed the Colombian producers to use an existing network to introduce a pure grade of heroin into the U.S. market. Much of the growing Colombian heroin production is sent through Central America and Mexico by smugglers traveling on commercial airline flights into the United States. These smugglers hide the drugs in false-sided luggage, clothing, hollowed-out shoe soles, or inside their bodies. The Colombian-based heroin traffickers have established distribution outlets throughout the eastern half of the United States.

Purity and Price

According to the *National Drug Threat Assessment, 2006*, the purity of South American heroin decreased from 78% in 2001 to 70% in 2003. Even though the purity of Mexican heroin increased, from 30% in 2001 to 37% in 2003, it is still low. Purity is important to heroin addicts because low-purity heroin must be injected to get the most out of the drug. Many people feel uncomfortable using needles and fear contracting the human immunodeficiency virus, which can be spread by sharing a needle with an infected user. Higher purity heroin can be smoked or snorted, which makes heroin more attractive to potential users who do not want to use needles. Despite these "advantages" of higher purity heroin, an estimated three out of five heroin users continue to inject the drug no matter what its purity.

The ONDCP notes in *The Price and Purity of Illicit Drugs: 1981 through the Second Quarter of 2003* (November 2004, http://www.whitehousedrugpolicy.gov/publications/price_purity/price_purity.pdf) that heroin purity generally falls into the categories of lower purity (30% to 40%) and higher purity (60% to 75%) depending on the quantity sold. The lower purity is prevalent in purchases of less than one to ten grams. The higher purity is prevalent in purchases of ten to two hundred grams. The ONDCP suggests that higher purity levels at higher quantity levels likely means that heroin is cut when passed between quantity levels, such as between the distributor and the dealer on the street.

The ONDCP report also indicates that both wholesale and retail heroin prices have dropped dramatically since 1981. In 1981 one gram or less of heroin cost about $2,000 retail and more than ten grams cost about $1,000 wholesale. In 2003 the retail price was approximately $350 for one gram or less, and the wholesale price was approximately $150 for more than ten grams. A relative beginner in heroin use will inject between five to ten milligrams of heroin. As such, a gram delivers between one hundred and two hundred doses.

PHARMACEUTICALS

Although the abuse of prescription narcotics, depressants, stimulants, and painkillers exists in the United States, there is little trafficking in these drugs by drug trafficking organizations, according to the *National Drug Threat Assessment, 2006*. The NDIC notes that those who abuse pharmaceuticals obtain their drugs primarily through theft, forged prescriptions, doctor shopping (seeking out different doctors to prescribe more medications), and fraudulent practices of some physicians and pharmacists. However, if these means of access to prescription drugs become blocked, pharmaceutical distribution networks could arise in the future.

CHAPTER 9
ANTIDRUG EFFORTS AND THEIR CRITICISMS

The Harrison Narcotic Act of 1914 (PL 63-223), which outlawed opiates and cocaine, was the first legislation aimed at prohibiting the possession and use of mood-altering drugs. Following that act, laws were passed or amended at intervals, but the war on drugs did not begin in earnest until the early 1970s with the Comprehensive Drug Abuse Prevention and Control Act in 1970 (PL 91-513). The phrase "war on drugs" was coined in 1971 during the first Nixon administration. A national effort was launched after that to bring illicit drug use under control, and it is still very much under way.

Not everyone agrees with governmental efforts to control or prohibit the use of mood-altering substances. Prohibition came to an end because of massive public disobedience (see Chapter 2). Data from the 2005 National Survey on Drug Use and Health (NSDUH), which are published in *Results from the 2005 National Survey on Drug Use and Health: National Findings* (September 2006, http:// www.oas.samhsa.gov/nsduh/2k5nsduh/2k5Results.pdf) by the Substance Abuse and Mental Health Administration (SAMHSA), suggest a similar public response to laws that prohibit use of drugs. In 2005, 46.1% of people aged twelve or older, more than 112 million individuals, had used illicit drugs at some time in their lives. About thirty-five million had done so in the last twelve months, and nearly twenty million had used illicit drugs in the past thirty days. According to the SAMHSA, the percentage of lifetime users increased during the twenty-five preceding years; it was 31% of the age twelve-and-older population in 1979.

One criticism leveled at governmental efforts to control or prohibit the use of mood-altering substances is that they appear to be inconsistent with the public health issues they raise. Tobacco and alcohol, both legal substances, cause many more deaths per year than drugs do. In the fact sheet "Adult Cigarette Smoking in the United States: Current Estimates" (November 2006, http://www.cdc.gov/Tobacco/factsheets/AdultCigaretteSmoking_FactSheet.htm), the Cen-

ters for Disease Control and Prevention (CDC) estimates that 438,000 premature deaths occur each year as a result of smoking and exposure to secondhand smoke. Another CDC report, "Alcohol-Attributable Deaths and Years of Potential Life Lost—United States, 2001" (September 24, 2004, http:// www.cdc.gov/mmwr/preview/mmwrhtml/mm5337a2.htm), indicates that approximately 75,000 people die prematurely each year because of excessive alcohol consumption. Another 40,933 die in car crashes and other accidents that are alcohol related. In comparison, drug abuse produced 19,102 deaths in 1999, according to the *National Drug Control Strategy, 2002* (February 2002, http://www.whitehousedrugpolicy.gov/publications/pdf/Strategy2002.pdf), the most current data available. The most recent data on marijuana is in the report *Mortality Data from the Drug Abuse Warning Network 2002* (January 2004, http://oas.samhsa.gov/DAWN2k2/2k2mortality.pdf) by the SAMHSA. This report states that marijuana, which is preponderantly the drug used by most of those classified as illicit drug users, causes few fatalities and virtually none by itself. Such facts are behind efforts to legalize marijuana.

NATIONAL DRUG CONTROL STRATEGY

The Anti-Drug Abuse Act of 1988 (PL 100-690) established the creation of a drug-free America as a U.S. policy goal. As part of this initiative, Congress established the Office of National Drug Control Policy "to set priorities and objectives for national drug control, promulgate *The National Drug Control Strategy* yearly, and oversee the strategy's implementation" (February 11, 2005, http:// www.ncjrs.gov/htm/chapter1.htm). To stress the importance of the issue, the director of the ONDCP was given a cabinet-level position. John P. Walters has been the ONDCP director and the George W. Bush administration's "drug czar" since his appointment in December 2001.

The first National Drug Control Strategy (NDCS) was submitted by President George H. W. Bush in 1989. It had been prepared under the reign of the nation's first drug czar, William J. Bennett. According to the *White House Fact Sheet on the National Drug Control Strategy* (September 5, 1989, http://bushlibrary.tamu.edu/research/papers/1989/89090503.html), the NDCS's chief emphasis was on the "principle of user accountability—in law enforcement efforts focused on individual users; in decisions regarding sentencing and parole; in school, college, and university policies regarding the use of drugs by students and employees; in the workplace; and in treatment." The strategy called for directing efforts at countries where cocaine originated, improving the targeting of interdiction (preventing or stopping smuggling and intercepting drugs), increasing the capacity of treatment providers, accelerating efforts aimed at drug prevention, and focusing on the education of youth. In its details, the drug strategy laid emphasis on law enforcement activities and the expansion of the criminal justice system.

Since that time the basic building blocks of the national strategy have remained the same, but the specific emphases taken by different administrations, or by the same administration in different years, have changed. Some presidents lean more toward enforcement, others more toward fighting drug traffiickers, and yet others more toward treatment and prevention. The Clinton administration's *NDCS, 2000* (2000, http://www.ncjrs.gov/ondcppubs/publications/policy/ndcs00/strategy2000.pdf) emphasized:

1. Empowering young people to reject drugs

2. Treating drug offenders within the criminal justice system

3. Increasing treatment resources for those who need them

4. Interdicting (stopping) the flow of drugs across the nation's borders

5. Aiding other democracies to help them fight traffickers

President Bill Clinton adopted the view that the war on drugs was the wrong model because wars could be expected to end and the effort to control drugs could not. Therefore, drugs should be seen as a disease, such as cancer, requiring long-term strategies (*NDCS, 2001* 2001, http://www.ncjrs.gov/ondcppubs/publications/policy/ndcs01/strategy2001.pdf). President George W. Bush adopted the view that drug use was akin to cholera and should be fought on public health principles (*NDCS, 2003* February 2003, http://www.whitehousedrugpolicy.gov/publications/policy/ndcs03/index.html). Whatever the model, all strategies to date have had the same components: prevention and treatment (together constituting demand reduction) and law enforcement, interdiction, and international efforts (together constituting supply disruption). The emphasis given to each of these com-

TABLE 9.1

National Drug Control Strategy goals, 2005

Two-year goals:	A 10 percent reduction in current use of illegal drugs by 8th, 10th, and 12th graders.
	A 10 percent reduction in current use of illegal drugs by adults age 18 and older
Five-year goals:	A 25 percent reduction in current use of illegal drugs by 8th, 10th, and 12th graders.
	A 25 percent reduction in current use of illegal drugs by adults age 18 and older

Note: Progress toward youth goals is measured from the baseline established by the 2001 Monitoring the Future survey. Progress toward adult goals is measured from the baseline of the 2002 National Household Survey on Drug Use and Health. All strategy goals seek to reduce current use of any illicit drug. Use of alcohol and tobacco products, although illegal for youths, is not captured by "any illicit drug."

SOURCE: "National Drug Control Strategy Goals," in *National Drug Control Strategy: Update*, Executive Office of the President of the United States, Office of National Drug Control Policy, February 2005, http://www.whitehousedrugpolicy.gov/publications/policy/ndcs05/ndcs05.pdf (accessed October 20, 2006)

ponents has been reflected in federal budgets, which is discussed in the next section.

Under Bush, the ONDCP established three priorities:

• Stopping use before it starts through education and community action

• Healing drug users by helping them get treatment resources where they are needed

• Disrupting the market by attacking the economic base of the drug trade

The first two priorities are clearly aimed at demand reduction and the third at supply disruption. Each year since its first NDCS publication, the Bush administration has embraced these priorities. The *NDCS, 2006* (February 2006, http://www.whitehousedrugpolicy.gov/publications/policy/ndcs06/ndcs06.pdf) is organized by these three national priorities.

Table 9.1 presents the Bush administration's stated benchmarks for measuring the success of its strategy, and the administration has used these benchmarks from its first NDCS publication. *NDCS, 2006* asserts that the president's strategy is working and has reduced teen drug use by more than 10% from 2001 to 2003. It notes that to foster continued success, the Bush administration will use television ads and Web-based outreach to urge youth to remain "above the influence." (Drugs and youth are discussed in Chapter 5.) In addition, the administration will expand drug treatment options for drug abusers and will work to rehabilitate people with drug abuse problems who are in jails and prisons. (Drug treatment is discussed in Chapter 6.) Finally, the administration will work to disrupt drug markets by eradication (killing drug crops), stopping the flow of drugs internationally, and seizing drugs domestically.

TABLE 9.2

Distribution of federal drug control spending, by function, fiscal years 2000–07

[In millions]

Functional area	FY 2000 final	FY 2001 final	FY 2002 final	FY 2003 final	FY 2004 final	FY 2005 final	FY 2006 enacted	FY 2007 request
Demand reduction								
Drug abuse treatment	$1,990.9	$ 2,086.5	$2,236.8	$2,264.6	$2,421.1	$2,431.8	$2,365.7	$2,408.7
Drug abuse prevention	1,445.8	1,540.8	1,629.0	1,553.6	1,543.5	1,530.1	1,408.0	1,058.9
Treatment research	421.6	489.0	547.8	611.4	607.2	621.2	614.4	605.4
Prevention research	280.8	326.8	367.4	382.9	412.4	422.0	422.2	418.6
Total demand reduction	**4,139.1**	**4,443.1**	**4,781.0**	**4,812.4**	**4,984.2**	**5,005.1**	**4,810.4**	**4,491.6**
Percentage	41.7%	46.9%	44.9%	43.4%	42.0%	39.6%	38.3%	35.5%
Domestic law enforcement	**2,274.0**	**2,511.2**	**2,867.2**	**3,018.3**	**3,189.8**	**3,317.9**	**3,529.3**	**3,585.4**
Percentage	22.9%	26.5%	26.9%	27.2%	26.9%	26.2%	28.1%	28.3%
Interdiction	**1,904.4**	**1,895.3**	**1,913.7**	**2,147.5**	**2,534.1**	**2,927.9**	**2,909.4**	**3,117.4**
Percentage	19.2%	20.0%	18.0%	19.4%	21.4%	23.2%	23.1%	24.6%
International	**1,619.2**	**617.3**	**1,084.5**	**1,105.1**	**1,159.3**	**1,391.3**	**1,326.0**	**1,461.4**
Percentage	16.3%	6.5%	10.2%	10.0%	9.8%	11.0%	10.5%	11.5%
Totals	**$9,936.6**	**$9,467.0**	**$10,646.4**	**$11,083.3**	**$11,867.4**	**$12,642.3**	**$12,575.1**	**$12,655.8**

Note: Consistent with the restructured drug budget, Office of National Drug Control Policy (ONDCP) has made historical corrections to the amounts reported for fiscal years 2000 to 2006 to add the Justice Department's Prescription Drug Monitoring and Community Oriented Policing Methamphetamine Programs.

SOURCE: "Table 3. Historical Drug Control Funding by Function, FY 2000–2007 (Budget Authority in Millions)," in *National Drug Control Strategy: FY 2007 Budget Summary*, Executive Office of the President of the United States, Office of National Drug Control Policy, February 2006, http://www.whitehousedrug policy.gov/publications/policy/07budget/partii_funding_tables.pdf (accessed October 20, 2006)

THE FEDERAL DRUG BUDGET

The national drug control budget is shown in Table 9.2. The data span fiscal year (FY) 2000 to the budget request for FY2007. The federal fiscal year begins October 1 and ends September 30, so that FY2006 dollars, for example, include funding for the last quarter of calendar year 2005 and the first three quarters of 2006. The budget has grown from $9.9 billion in FY2000 to $12.7 billion in FY2007, a 27% increase over those years.

The budget is divided into two broad components: reducing the demand for drugs and disrupting their supply. Reducing the demand for drugs includes funding for priorities 1 and 2. Priority 1 funding supports research and programs that help communities work toward a drug-free environment and encourage young people to reject drug use. In Table 9.2 these funding categories are "Drug Abuse Prevention" and "Prevention Research." Priority 2 funding supports research and treatment for drug abuse and abusers. In Table 9.2 these funding categories are "Drug Abuse Treatment" and "Treatment Research." Priority 3 funding supports efforts to keep individuals and organizations from profiting from trafficking in illicit drugs, both domestically and internationally. In Table 9.2 these funding categories are "Domestic Law Enforcement," "Interdiction," and "International." The FY2000 and FY2001 budgets shown were determined during the Clinton administration, whereas the remaining budgets are during the Bush administration (including one projected budget based on the 2007 request).

As shown in Table 9.2, a high degree of budgetary fluctuation over time has been associated with international programs. Funds ranged from 6.5% of the total budget (FY2001) to 16.3% (FY2000). Significant portions of the international budget are spent on supporting international eradication efforts that, in turn, depend on the cooperation of other countries and on the U.S. drug certification program, which may temporarily deny funding to certain regimes.

Table 9.3 shows the supply and demand proportions overall from FY2005 to FY2007. Approximately 35% to 40% of drug control spending each year is allocated to reducing the demand for drugs. A much larger proportion—approximately 60% to 65%—is allocated to disrupting the drug supply. The trend in recent years has been to decrease funding for reducing the demand for drugs (prevention and treatment efforts) and to increase funding for disrupting the drug supply (law enforcement and interdiction).

Table 9.4 summarizes the drug control budget by agency. The agencies that work to reduce the demand for drugs are the Office of National Drug Control Policy (ONDCP), the Departments of Health and Human Services, Education, and Transportation (the latter indicated under "other presidential priorities"), and the U.S. Small Business Administration (also listed under "other presidential priorities"). The agencies that work to disrupt the drug supply are the Departments of Homeland Security, Justice, State, Treasury, and Defense.

Most domestic law enforcement funds are spent by the U.S. Department of Justice, or on its behalf, and underwrite the operations of the U.S. Drug Enforcement

TABLE 9.3

Federal drug control spending, by function, fiscal years 2005–07

[In millions]

	FY 2005 final	FY 2006 enacted	FY 2007 request	06–07 change dollars	%
Function:					
Treatment (w/research)	$3,053.0	$2,980.2	$3,014.1	$34.0	1.1%
Percent	24.1%	23.7%	23.8%		
Prevention (w/research)	$1,952.1	$1,830.3	$1,477.5	($352.8)	(19.3%)
Percent	15.4%	14.6%	11.7%		
Domestic law enforcement	$3,317.9	$3,529.3	$3,585.4	$56.1	1.6%
Percent	26.2%	28.1%	28.3%		
Interdiction	$2,927.9	$2,909.4	$3,117.4	$208.0	7.1%
Percent	23.2%	23.1%	24.6%		
International	$1,393.3	$1,326.0	$1,461.4	$135.4	10.2%
Percent	11.0%	10.5%	11.5%		
Total	**$12,644.3**	**$12,575.1**	**$12,655.8**	**$80.6**	**0.6%**
Supply/demand split					
Supply	$7,639.2	$7,764.7	$8,164.2	$399.5	5.1%
Percent	60.4%	61.7%	64.5%		
Demand	$5,005.1	$4,810.4	$4,491.6	($318.8)	(6.6%)
Percent	39.6%	38.3%	35.5%		
Total	**$12,644.3**	**$12,575.1**	**$12,655.8**	**$80.6**	**0.6%**

SOURCE: "Table 1. Federal Drug Control Spending by Function, FY 2005–FY 2007 (Budget Authority in Millions)," in *National Drug Control Strategy: FY 2007 Budget Summary*, Executive Office of the President of the United States, Office of National Drug Control Policy, February 2006, http://www.whitehousedrugpolicy.gov/publications/policy/07budget/partii_funding_tables.pdf (accessed October 20, 2006)

Administration (DEA), the chief domestic drug control agency. Interdiction funds are managed by the U.S. Department of Homeland Security, which now oversees all border-control functions and the U.S. Coast Guard. International funds are divided roughly equally between the Departments of State and Defense. The U.S. Department of State's Bureau of International Narcotics and Law Enforcement Affairs (INL) is the lead agency managing international programs. The U.S. Department of Defense is involved in supporting anti-insurgency programs in the Andean region and elsewhere. (Insurgencies are organized, armed rebellions against governments.)

INTERNATIONAL WAR ON DRUGS

The linkages among drugs, organized crime, and insurgencies outside the United States have long been known. A connection to terrorism is a contemporary emphasis that arose in the aftermath of the September 11, 2001 (9/11), terrorist attacks on the United States. In its *Fiscal Year 2004 Budget: Congressional Justification* (www.state.gov/documents/organization/22061.pdf), the INL made a case for the convergence between the war on drugs and the war on terror:

The September 11 attacks and their aftermath highlight the close connections and overlap among terrorists, drug traffickers, and organized crime groups. The nexus is far-reaching. In many instances, such as Colombia, the groups are the same. Drug traffickers benefit from terrorists' military skills, weapons supply, and access to clandestine organizations. Terrorists gain a source of revenue and expertise in the illicit transfer

and laundering of money for their operations. All three groups seek out weak states with feeble justice and regulatory sectors where they can corrupt and even dominate the government. September 11 demonstrated graphically the direct threat to the United States by a narcoterrorist state such as Afghanistan where such groups once operated with impunity. Although the political and security situation in Colombia is different from the Taliban period in Afghanistan—the central government is not allied with such groups but rather is engaged in a major effort to destroy them—the narcoterrorist linkage there poses perhaps the single greatest threat to the stability of Latin America and the Western Hemisphere and potentially threatens the security of the United States in the event of a victory by the insurgent groups. The bottom line is that such groups invariably jeopardize international peace and freedom, undermine the rule of law, menace local and regional stability, and threaten both the United States and our friends and allies.

Key to the international war on drugs is disruption of the drug supply. As the *NDCS, 2006* states, market disruption:

contributes to the Global War on Terrorism, severing the links between drug traffickers and terrorist organizations in countries such as Afghanistan and Colombia, among others. It renders support to allies such as the courageous administration of President Alvaro Uribe in Colombia. Market disruption initiatives remove some of the most violent criminals from society, from kingpins such as the remnants of the Cali Cartel to common thugs such as the vicious MS-13 street gang.

TABLE 9.4

Distribution of federal drug control spending, by agency, fiscal years 2005–07

[In millions]

	FY 2005 final	FY 2006 enacted	FY 2007 request
Department of Defense			
Counternarcotics central transfer account	$905.8	$936.1	$926.9
Supplemental appropriations	$242.0		
Department of Education	590.5	490.9	165.9
Department of Health and Human Services (HHS)			
National Institute on Drug Abuse	1,006.4	1,000.0	994.8
Substance Abuse and Mental Health Services Administration	2,490.5	2,442.5	2,411.1
Total HHS	3,496.9	3,442.5	3,405.9
Department of Homeland Security (DHS)			
Customs and border protection	1,429.0	1,591.0	1,796.5
Immigration and customs enforcement[a]	361.5	436.5	477.9
U.S. Coast Guard[a]	871.9	1,032.4	1,030.1
Total DHS	2,662.4	3,059.9	3,304.6
Department of Justice			
Bureau of Prisons	48.6	49.1	51.0
Drug Enforcement Administration	1,793.0	1,876.6	1,948.6
Interagency Crime and Drug Enforcement	553.5	483.2	706.1
Office of Justice programs	281.1	237.4	248.7
Total Department of Justice	2,676.2	2,646.3	2,954.3
ONDCP			
Counterdrug technology assessment center	41.7	29.7	9.6
Operations	26.8	26.6	23.3
High Intensity Drug Trafficking Area Program[b]	226.5	224.7	—
Other federal drug control programs	212.0	193.0	212.2
Total ONDCP	507.0	474.0	245.1
Department of State			
Bureau of International Narcotics and Law Enforcement Affairs	905.1	1,056.7	1,166.7
Supplemental appropriations	260.0		
Department of Treasury			
Internal Revenue Service[a]	—	55.0	55.6
Department of Veterans Affairs			
Veterans Health Administration	396.1	412.6	428.3
Other Presidential Priorities[c]	2.2	1.0	2.5
Total federal drug budget	**$12,644.3**	**$12,575.1**	**$12,655.8**

[a]In FY 2005, the Organized Crime Drug Enforcement Task Force funds for the Departments of Treasury and Homeland Security were appropriated in the Department of Justice Interagency Crime and Drug Enforcement (ICDE) accounts. Beginning in FY 2006, the Departments of Homeland Security and treasury ICDE funds are displayed as separate accounts in their respective departments.
[b]Beginning in FY 2007, the High Intensity Drug Trafficking Area Program is transferred to Justice and incorporated into the Interagency Crime and Drug Enforcement account.
[c]Includes the Small Business Administration's Drug-Free Workplace grants and the National Highway Traffic Safety Administration's Drug Impaired Driving program.

SOURCE: "Table 2. Drug Control Funding: Agency Summary, FY 2005–FY 2007 (Budget Authority in Millions)," in *National Drug Control Strategy: FY 2007 Budget Summary,* Executive Office of the President of the United States, Office of National Drug Control Policy, February 2006, http://www.whitehousedrugpolicy.gov/publications/policy/07budget/partii_funding_tables.pdf (accessed October 20, 2006)

DISRUPTING THE DRUG SUPPLY

Internationally, the federal effort is concentrated on what the INL calls the Andean ridge, the northwestern part of South America where Colombia, Ecuador, and Peru, running north to south, touch the Pacific and where land-locked Bolivia lies east of Peru. The U.S. Government Accountability Office (GAO), in *Drug Control: Aviation Program Safety Concerns in Colombia Are Being Addressed, but State's Planning and Budgeting Process Can Be Improved* (July 2004, http://www.gao.gov/new.items/d04918.pdf), estimates that 90% of all cocaine and 40% of heroin entering the United States comes from Colombia. The remaining cocaine comes from Bolivia and Peru. Besides focusing on Columbia and Mexico, the INL also concentrates on Mexico, not only because the country is a major transmission route of drugs to the United States but also because Mexico is a significant source of heroin, marijuana, and methamphetamine. The centerpiece of the effort is eradication of coca and poppy by providing airplanes and funds for spraying herbicides that kill the plants. Efforts also include assisting law enforcement and financial support provided by the U.S. Agency for International Development (USAID) for planting legal crops and improving infrastructure (roads and bridges) for delivering farm goods to market. The later measures are necessary because many of the people involved in cultivating drug-producing plants do so because it is the only source of income in the remote and undeveloped regions where they live. The USAID programs are intended to give them alternatives.

Elsewhere, the INL is concentrating on South Asia (Afghanistan and Pakistan). In all, INL programs extend to 150 countries and involve assistance in law enforcement and in the fight against money laundering (making illegally acquired cash seem as though it was legally acquired). What follows is a brief encapsulation of the INL strategy in selected high-focus areas.

Colombia

The primary effort to disrupt the drug supply in Colombia is coca eradication. The coca tree (*Erythroxylon coca*) is a densely leafed plant native to the eastern slopes of the Andes mountains and is heavily cultivated in Columbia.

Figure 9.1 shows how many hectares of Colombian coca bushes were sprayed with herbicide from 2000 to 2005. The area sprayed nearly tripled during that time span, from 47,371 hectares in 2000 to 138,000 hectares in 2005. (A hectare is 2.47 acres.)

When the source of a drug such as cocaine is diminished, two things happen: the purity of the finished product (the drug) declines and the price of it rises. There is a lag time, however, between the eradication of source plants and the detection of the decline in purity and rise in price in the United States. Thus, the *NDCS, 2006* notes that the retail price and purity data from February to September 2005 showed the results of coca eradication from years prior. During that time cocaine purity declined by 15%, whereas its price per gram increased 19%.

FIGURE 9.1

FIGURE 9.2

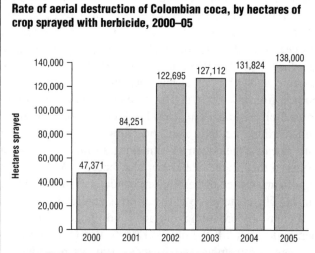

Rate of aerial destruction of Colombian coca, by hectares of crop sprayed with herbicide, 2000–05

SOURCE: "Increasing Colombian Coca Aerial Eradication: Areas in Hectares Sprayed with Herbicide," in *National Drug Control Strategy*, Executive Office of the President of the United States, Office of National Drug Control Policy, February 2006, http://www.whitehousedrugpolicy.gov/publications/policy/ndcs06/ndcs06.pdf (accessed November 9, 2006)

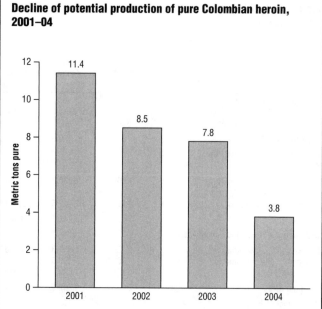

Decline of potential production of pure Colombian heroin, 2001–04

SOURCE: "Decline of Potential Production of Pure Colombian Heroin," in *National Drug Control Strategy*, Executive Office of the President of the United States, Office of National Drug Control Policy, February 2006, http://www.whitehousedrugpolicy.gov/publications/policy/ndcs06/ndcs06.pdf (accessed November 9, 2006)

Poppy eradication takes place in Colombia as well, because this country supplies 40% of the heroin entering the United States. The *NDCS, 2006* reports that there was a 68% reduction in Colombian opium poppy cultivation from 2001 to 2004. In 2004 Colombia sprayed 3,060 hectares of poppy and manually pulled up 496 hectares of the plants. These eradication measures have resulted in a 67% decline of potential production of pure Colombian heroin; potential production was 11.4 metric tons of pure heroin in 2001, and by 2004 the potential production of this drug was only 3.8 metric tons (a metric ton equals 1,000 kilograms or 2,204.6 pounds). (See Figure 9.2.)

Along with eradication, USAID has also been active in Colombia. This agency conducts what is known as the Alternative Livelihoods Program, which is aimed at providing drug farmers with alternative crops. USAID began operations in Colombia late in 2000, although this idea started in some areas more than thirty years ago.

Besides Colombia's aggressive seizure of drugs within its borders, the country is working with the United States in the resumption of the Air Bridge Denial (ABD) program. The ABD program works by forcing or shooting down aircraft that appear to be taking part in drug trafficking activities. The program was halted in 2001 when a civilian aircraft was downed in Peru and two U.S. citizens were killed. It was resumed in 2003. According to the *NDCS, 2006*, this program resulted in seven interdictions, five impounded aircraft, the destruction of two aircraft, and the seizure of 1.5 metric tons of cocaine in Colombia in 2005.

Colombia, however, illustrates some of the fundamental dilemmas of interdiction. The drug trade there is in part a symptom of a festering civil war. The Central Intelligence Agency's *World Factbook* (December 12, 2006, https://www.cia.gov/cia/publications/factbook/geos/co.html) provides this summary:

A 40-year conflict between government forces and antigovernment insurgent groups and illegal paramilitary groups—both heavily funded by the drug trade—escalated during the 1990s. The insurgents lack the military or popular support necessary to overthrow the government, and violence has been decreasing since about 2002, but insurgents continue attacks against civilians and large swaths of the countryside are under guerrilla influence. Paramilitary groups challenge the insurgents for control of territory and the drug trade. Most paramilitary members have demobilized since 2002 in an ongoing peace process, although their commitment to ceasing illicit activity is unclear. The Colombian Government has stepped up efforts to reassert government control throughout the country, and now has a presence in every one of its municipalities. However, neighboring countries worry about the violence spilling over their borders.

With an internal conflict that has lasted more than forty years, quite some time may pass before civil order is restored in Colombia and economic development has advanced enough to make drug-plant cultivation unattractive.

FIGURE 9.3

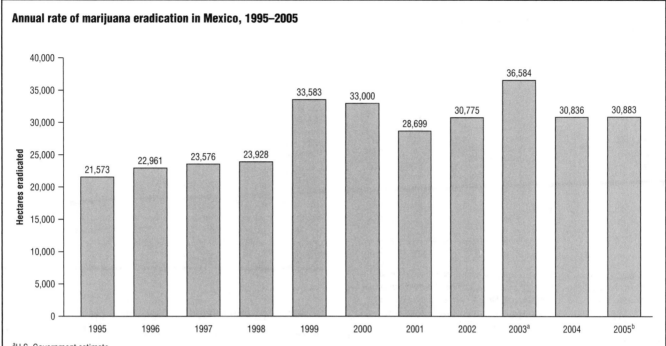

Annual rate of marijuana eradication in Mexico, 1995–2005

ᵃU.S. Government estimate.
ᵇAs reported by the government of Mexico for January through November 2005.

SOURCE: "Mexican Annual Marijuana Eradication Totals," in *National Drug Control Strategy*, Executive Office of the President of the United States, Office of National Drug Control Policy, February 2006, http://www.whitehousedrugpolicy.gov/publications/policy/ndcs06/ndcs06.pdf (accessed November 9, 2006)

Bolivia and Peru

Similar problems have hampered efforts to bring coca production under control in Bolivia, the third-largest producer of cocaine. The country is poor and has had an unsettled history (nearly two hundred coups since its independence in 1825). The country has been under democratic rule since the 1980s, but successive governments have been reluctant to support eradication programs energetically. Coca is a traditional crop and the coca leaf is chewed by the inhabitants; eradication has resulted in a popular antiestablishment movement. The INL, in the fact sheet "Counternarcotics and Law Enforcement Country Program: Bolivia" (April 5, 2005, http://www.state.gov/p/inl/rls/fs/44181.htm), notes that despite destroying eight thousand hectares of coca in 2004, coca cultivation in that year increased 6%. Eradication efforts are paralleled by replanting, and eradication is sometimes violently opposed by the population.

Peru, the second-largest producer of coca leaf and cocaine base, has organized bodies of *cocaleros* (coca growers) who enjoy sufficient popular support to hamper government action. For example, in 2002 cocaleros succeeded in briefly halting eradication efforts in several places, although by year's end some seven thousand hectares had been put out of commission. In Peru, as in Bolivia, replanting frequently follows eradication efforts. Nonetheless, the INL notes in "Country Program: Peru"

(May 8, 2002, http://www.state.gov/p/inl/rls/fs/10026.htm), the most recent report available on Peru, that Peruvian coca cultivation declined 70% from 1995 to 2001. In both Bolivia and Peru, USAID has active alternative development programs.

Mexico

Mexico is one of the principal producers of marijuana and heroin that enters the United States. Under President Vicente Fox, the Mexican government was energetic both in the eradication of the marijuana and poppy crops and in the arrest and prosecution of members of drug cartels, though efforts were hampered by severe budget constraints, corruption, and inefficiencies within law enforcement and criminal justice institutions.

In the fact sheet "Counternarcotics and Law Enforcement Country Program: Mexico" (August 10, 2005, http://www.state.gov/p/inl/rls/fs/50972.htm), the INL indicates that Mexico eradicated about 30,100 hectares of marijuana plants and 14,700 hectares of opium poppy in 2004. Figure 9.3 shows the annual marijuana eradication totals in Mexico from 1995 through 2005. Eradication of marijuana was up 43% in 2005 (30,883 hectares) from 1995 (21,573 hectares). Nevertheless, the climate and terrain of this country are such that up to three growing seasons are possible and capable of producing eleven tons of black tar heroin annually.

FIGURE 9.4

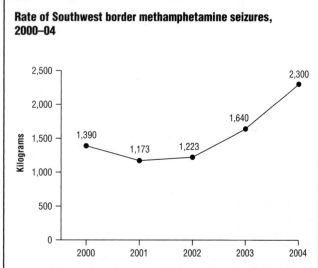

Rate of Southwest border methamphetamine seizures, 2000–04

SOURCE: "Increased Southwest Border Methamphetamine Seizures," in *National Drug Control Strategy*, Executive Office of the President of the United States, Office of National Drug Control Policy, February 2006, http://www.whitehousedrugpolicy.gov/publications/policy/ndcs06/ndcs06.pdf (accessed November 9, 2006).

TABLE 9.5

Drug-related seizure statistics in Afghanistan, fiscal year 2005

Total FY 2005 seizure statistics

Opium	42.9 metric tons
Heroin	5.5 metric tons
Morphine base	220 kg
Hashish	142.4 metric tons
Chemicals	9.4 metric tons
Clandestine conversion labs[a]	247
Heroin presses	44
Processing vats	49
Arrested/detained	32[b]

[a]Opium, morphine base, heroin.
[b]Includes one extradition to United States.

SOURCE: "Total FY 2005 Seizure Statistics," in *National Drug Control Strategy*, Executive Office of the President of the United States, Office of National Drug Control Policy, February 2006, http://www.whitehouse drugpolicy.gov/publications/policy/ndcs06/ndcs06.pdf (accessed November 9, 2006)

Mexico is also a major shipping thoroughfare for illicit drugs that are destined for the United States and Canada. Along with marijuana and heroin, one of the drugs that comes to the United States over the U.S.-Mexican border is methamphetamine, a synthetic drug that is made in illegal laboratories. This drug has become an increasing problem in the United States (see Chapter 4). U.S. law enforcement agencies have done much to combat the spread of this drug domestically, but they are also active in stopping the flow of methamphetamine and its precursors (other substances used to make methamphetamine) into the country. The INL reports in the *NDCS, 2006* that "increasing production of methamphetamine within Mexico has been indicated by increased seizures at the US southwest border." Figure 9.4 shows that methamphetamine seizures nearly doubled from 2001 to 2004.

Afghanistan

The INL indicates, in "United States Support for Afghanistan's Counternarcotics Campaign" (August 31, 2006, http://www.state.gov/r/pa/scp/2006/71700.htm), that trafficking in narcotics provided over one-third of Afghanistan's gross domestic product in 2006. This country is the world's largest supplier of opium. While under control of the fanatically religious and conservative Taliban regime, cultivated poppy acreage dropped precipitously, from 64,510 hectares in 2000 to 1,685 hectares in 2001. (See Figure 8.9 in Chapter 8.) The United States invaded Afghanistan in 2001, in a response to the terrorist attacks of September 11, 2001, and the Taliban was driven from

power. An unintended consequence of this was that poppy cultivation resumed, rising to 30,750 hectares in 2002. By 2004 poppy cultivation reached a staggering 206,700 hectares but then dropped by nearly half to 107,400 hectares in 2005. Recultivation of poppy was in part a response to the continuing drought in the region: opium poppy is hardy and can grow under adverse conditions. The Afghan drought conditions in 2004 were characterized as the worst in living memory. Thus, opium poppy was one crop that could be grown during the drought and supply income to farmers.

Afghanistan's post–9/11 government officially banned opium poppy cultivation and has pressured its regional governors to suppress the drug trade. Despite these efforts, the situation in Afghanistan was, in the immediate post–Taliban era, similar to the situation in Colombia, with a weak central government unable to assert itself in areas where autonomous warlords hold de facto power. Other countries and organizations have tried to help. For example, USAID has been active in establishing alternative development programs. The United Kingdom has conducted some eradication efforts and established a counternarcotics mobile force; Germany has provided training and equipment to establish an Afghan security force; and Italy has been involved in strengthening the country's judicial system.

The DEA developed the Foreign-Deployed Advisory Support Teams (FAST) program in Afghanistan to identify, target, investigate, and disrupt or dismantle transnational drug trafficking operations in the region. A major goal of this program is to help develop Afghanistan's antidrug abilities. Training began in 2004 and operations began in 2005. The INL reports that the drug seizure statistics for 2005, shown in Table 9.5, are evidence of the FAST program's early success.

FOSTERING INTERNATIONAL COOPERATION: THE DRUG CERTIFICATION PROCESS

The United States uses the drug certification process to promote international cooperation in controlling drug production and trafficking. Section 490 of the Foreign Assistance Act of 1961 (PL 87-195), as amended, requires the president to annually submit to Congress a list of major drug-producing and drug-transiting countries. The president must also assess each country's performance in battling narcotics trade and trafficking based on the goals and objectives of the 1988 UN Convention against Illicit Traffic in Narcotic Drugs and Psychotropic Substances. Countries that have fully cooperated with the United States or that have taken adequate steps to reach the goals and objectives of the UN convention are "certified" by the president. U.S. aid is withheld to countries that are not certified. Even though many countries resent the process, most work toward certification.

TRANSIT-ZONE AGREEMENTS

Other countries not on the list are frequently reluctant to cooperate with the United States to stop drug traffickers. The Caribbean basin, for example, is a major transit zone for drug trafficking. The Caribbean basin countries are those that border, or lie in, the Gulf of Mexico and the Caribbean Sea, such as the island nations of the West Indies, Mexico, Central American nations, and northern South American nations. Bermuda is also included, even though it is in the Atlantic Ocean. Even though most of the islands have bilateral agreements with the United States, these agreements are limited to maritime matters that permit U.S. ships to seize traffickers in the territorial waters of particular Caribbean islands. Few transit-zone countries permit U.S. planes to fly in their airspace to force suspected traffickers to land. Twelve transit-zone countries have no maritime agreements with the United States, including Ecuador and Mexico.

Bilateral agreements are not the same in each country, and some provide limited rights to U.S. law enforcement authorities. For example, a U.S.-Belize agreement allows the U.S. Coast Guard to board suspected Belizean vessels on the high seas without prior notification. The agreement with Panama requires U.S. Coast Guard vessels in Panamanian waters to be escorted by a Panamanian government ship.

DOMESTIC DRUG SEIZURES

The DEA is also at work within the United States to disrupt the drug supply. Table 9.6 shows drug seizures across the United States from 1989 to 2004. Seizures of cocaine, heroin, methamphetamine, and cannabis have varied during the time span shown but, in general, have risen. For example, seizures of cocaine have ranged from a low of 96,085 kilograms in 1990 to a high of 164,537

TABLE 9.6

Cocaine, heroin, methamphetamine, and cannabis seizures, 1989–2004

[In kilograms]

Year	Cocaine	Heroin	Metham-phetamine	Cannabis	
				Marijuana	Hashish
1989	114,903	1,311	—	393,276	23,043
1990	96,085	687	—	233,478	7,683
1991	128,247	1,448	—	224,603	79,110
1992	120,175	1,251	—	344,899	111
1993	121,215	1,502	7	409,922	11,396
1994	129,378	1,285	178	474,856	561
1995	111,031	1,543	369	627,776	14,470
1996	128,555	1,362	136	638,863	37,851
1997	101,495	1,624	1,099	698,799	756
1998	118,436	1,458	2,559	827,149	241
1999	132,063	1,151	2,779	1,075,154	797
2000	106,619	1,674	3,470	1.235,938	10,867
2001	105,748	2,496	4,051	1,214,188	161
2002	102,515	2,773	2,477	1.101,459	621
2003	117,024	2,381	3,853	1,229,615	155
2004	164,537	1,720	2,802	1,025,907	161

— Data not available.

SOURCE: "Table 49. Federal-wide Cocaine, Heroin, Methamphetamine, and Cannabis Seizures, 1989–2003 (Kilograms)," in *2005 National Drug Control Strategy: Data Supplement*, Executive Office of the President of the United States, Office of National Drug Control Policy, March 2005, http://www .whitehousedrugpolicy.gov/publications/policy/ndcs06_data_supl/ds_drg_rltd _tbls.pdf (accessed October 19, 2006)

TABLE 9.7

MDMA (ecstasy) seizures, 2000–04

Year	Reported in dosage units	Reported in kilograms	Total in dosage units[a]
2000	8,289,023	0	8,289,023
2001	10,710,509	60	10,982,509
2002	4,715,098	1,056	8,305,498
2003	1,888,475	484	3.534.075
2004[b]	594,685	172	1,179,485

[a]Conversion of seizures reported in kilograms to dosage units assumes 1 kilogram equals 3,400 impure dosage units, based DEA's *MDMA Drug Intelligence Brief* (June 1999).
[b]Provisional, based on reporting through March 2006.

SOURCE: "Table 52. Domestic Seizures of MDMA, 2000–2004," in *2005 National Drug Control Strategy: Data Supplement*, Executive Office of the President of the United States, Office of National Drug Control Policy, March 2005, http://www.whitehousedrugpolicy.gov/publications/policy/ ndcs06_data_supl/ds_drg_rltd_tbls.pdf (accessed October 19, 2006)

kilograms in 2004. Table 9.7 shows domestic seizures of MDMA, or ecstasy. These seizures varied widely from the year 2000 through 2004 as well. The year in which domestic seizures were the greatest was 2001.

Along with seizing and stopping the flow of methamphetamine at the U.S.-Mexican border, U.S. law enforcement agencies work to disrupt the supply of this drug within the United States. According to the INL in the *NDCS, 2006*, since 2005 thirty-five states have imposed new restrictions on the retail sale of the methamphetamine precursor pseudoephedrine. These restrictions

FIGURE 9.5

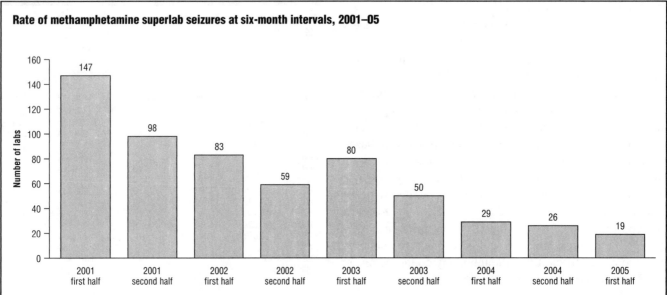

Rate of methamphetamine superlab seizures at six-month intervals, 2001–05

SOURCE: "Reduced Methamphetamine Superlab Seizures," in *National Drug Control Strategy*, Executive Office of the President of the United States, Office of National Drug Control Policy, February 2006, http://www.whitehousedrugpolicy.gov/publications/policy/ndcs06/ndcs06.pdf (accessed November 9, 2006)

have resulted in a significant national decline in methamphetamine lab seizures, because without this precursor drug the labs cannot manufacture methamphetamine. The INL also reports that the number of superlab seizures—those labs capable of producing more than ten pounds of methamphetamine per production run—has decreased as well. Figure 9.5 shows that 245 superlabs were seized in 2001, compared with 55 in 2004.

HAVE INTERDICTION AND ERADICATION HELPED?

Colombia

Colombia's rise to being a major drug producer has drawn the attention of Congress. Congress requested that the GAO conduct a number of studies of developments in Colombia. The report *Drug Control: U.S. Nonmilitary Assistance to Colombia Is Beginning to Show Intended Results, but Programs Are Not Readily Sustainable* (July 2004, http://www.gao.gov/new.items/d04726.pdf) suggests that some antidrug headway is being made in Colombia but that the program is suffering from management and budget oversight problems that call its sustainability into doubt.

The report concludes that U.S. antidrug strategy, based on a combination of interdiction, aerial eradication, and alternative development, has "resulted in a 33 percent reduction in the amount of coca cultivated in Colombia over the last two years—from 169,800 hectares in 2001 to 113,850 hectares in 2003—and a 10 percent reduction in the amount of opium poppy cultivated in 2003. However, according to DEA officials and documents, cocaine prices nationwide remained relatively stable—indicating that cocaine was still readily available."

Among the problems cited by the GAO were widespread corruption; human rights violations by the Colombian military, which have made it difficult for the United States to support Colombian military efforts; and control by insurgents (Revolutionary Armed Forces of Colombia and the National Liberation Army) of areas where coca and heroin poppy are grown.

Afghanistan

The GAO also investigated counternarcotics work in Afghanistan and reported its results in *Afghanistan Drug Control: Despite Improved Efforts, Deteriorating Security Threatens Success of U.S. Goals* (November 2006, http://www.gao.gov/new.items/d0778.pdf). The GAO finds that poppy eradication in Afghanistan had increased in 2006, but the poppy crop still grew by 50%. "However," the GAO states, "many projects have not been in place long enough to assess progress toward the overall goal of significantly reducing drug cultivation, production, and trafficking. For example, projects to provide rural credit and to field teams to discourage poppy cultivation were not in place before the 2005–2006 growing season." The GAO also notes that the security situation in Afghanistan was worsening in 2005–06. Some personnel involved in eradication were attacked, and others involved in the Alternative Livelihoods Program were killed. The GAO concludes that significant reductions in poppy cultivation and drug trafficking in Afghanistan will likely take at least a decade.

Measurement Is Difficult

The United Nations (UN), in *Global Illicit Drug Trends, 2003* (2003, http://www.unodc.org/pdf/trends2003_www _E.pdf), points out a problem with accurate reporting— namely that total production may be underestimated by governments reporting to the UN, thus potentially distorting data on the effect of interdiction programs. The UN states that in 2001 the amount of cocaine reported seized was equivalent to 44% of estimated world production. The amount of opiates (heroin and precursors) seized was 45% of supply, a much higher percentage than in previous years, but largely because of dramatically decreased production. The UN surmises that actual production of cocaine may have been well over what was reported by member states.

When estimates are too low, amounts seized can give the public a false sense of progress. In data reported by the INL for coca leaf production, Colombian production was omitted for 2001 through 2003 because measurement had changed from dry to fresh weight in Colombia. However, this omission causes a serious gap in statistical measurement in that Colombia is, by far, the largest producer of coca leaf in the world.

Another indication of the measurement problem—in tracking the success of eradication programs—is that no data have ever been produced for estimating marijuana production domestically in the United States against which U.S. eradication efforts can be measured. Furthermore, U.S. marijuana eradication is tallied by plant, whereas Mexican eradication is counted by hectare, so that U.S. and Mexican efforts cannot be compared effectively.

WHY IS THE WAR ON DRUGS SO HARD TO WIN?

The goal of the international war on drugs is a difficult one. The United States and other countries are attempting to stop the flow of a product that is in high demand, generally cheap to produce, and offers enormous profits. In reference to the United States in particular, it is undeniably the case that a significant number of Americans want drugs, are affluent, and thus create a vast market for drug traffickers.

Production costs for drugs are so low and the profit so great that even if a trafficker loses most of his or her product, he or she can earn a huge amount of money on the remainder. When one drug policy is put in place, drug traffickers change their operations to circumvent it. When one route is blocked or one method of production shut down, traffickers change to another. When one drug trafficker or grower is captured, or even if a major trafficking group is shut down, others quickly arise to take their place.

Many nations where drugs are produced, and critics of the U.S. drug policy around the world, feel that so long as demand persists, suppliers will find a way to deliver the product. Even though they may, or may not, support eradication and interdiction efforts, these critics believe that ultimately the most successful policies are those that reduce the demand for drugs.

MARIJUANA LEGALIZATION MOVEMENT

In the United States legalization of drugs almost invariably refers to the legalization of marijuana rather than, for instance, heroin and cocaine. Use of "hard drugs" such as these is relatively limited, and most Americans consider them to be highly addictive and damaging to one's physical and mental health. Marijuana's situation is different. According to the SAMHSA, in 2005 nearly three-quarters of all current drug users (74.1%) were using marijuana, and more than half of all current drug users (54.5%) used only marijuana and no other drugs. (See Figure 4.2 in Chapter 4.) Some studies suggest significant harm from marijuana use, including effects on the heart, lungs, brain, and social and learning capabilities. Others find little or no harm from moderate marijuana use. Regardless of what the research says, marijuana is generally thought of as a relatively mild drug, an opinion supported in Canada by those who introduced repeated initiatives to decriminalize marijuana possession, or in the Netherlands, where marijuana sales are tolerated in "coffee shops."

Public Opinion

Gallup polling data for selected years from 1969 to 2005 show public opinion increasingly favoring the legalization of marijuana. (See Figure 9.6.) In 1969, 84% of the public opposed legalization and 12% favored it. By 2005 those opposed had declined to 60% of the public, whereas 36% were in favor.

It is with the support of this population that a number of initiatives and referenda attempting to legalize marijuana for medical purposes or to decriminalize possession of modest quantities have appeared on state ballots. The pro-legalization constituencies express themselves through activist organizations, such as the Marijuana Policy Project, the National Organization for the Reform of Marijuana Laws, the Hemp Evolution, and state-level organizations. Some legal reform organizations, notably the American Civil Liberties Union (ACLU), advocate reform. A number of groups specialize in advocacy for the medical uses of marijuana. By contrast there are no large organizations that promote the legalization of drugs such as cocaine and heroin.

Arguments for and against Legalization

FOR LEGALIZATION. Most of those who favor legalization in some form (for medical use, decriminalization, or regulation) use two arguments in combination. The first is that an approach to drugs based on prohibition

FIGURE 9.6

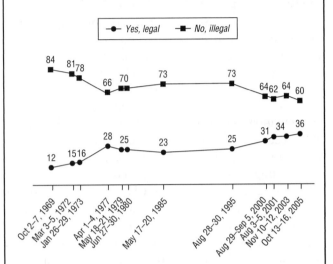

Public opinion on legalizing marijuana use, selected years 1969–2005

DO YOU THINK THE USE OF MARIJUANA SHOULD BE MADE LEGAL, OR NOT?

Numbers shown in percentages

SOURCE: Joseph Carroll, "Do you think the use of marijuana should be made legal, or not?" in *Who Supports Marijuana Legalization? Support rising; varies most by age and gender*, Gallup Poll News Service, November 1, 2005, http://www.galluppoll.com (accessed October 20, 2006). Copyright © 2005 by The Gallup Organization. Reproduced by permission of The Gallup Organization.

and criminalization does not work, produces excessive rates of incarceration, and costs a lot of money that could be more productively spent on treatment and prevention. The second is that drug use is an activity arbitrarily called a crime. It is imposed by law on some drugs and not on others, and can be seen as criminal at one time but perhaps not at another. Murder, rape, and robbery have always been considered inherently criminal acts, but drug use is just a consumption of substances; its control is arbitrary and follows fashions. Alcohol consumption was once prohibited but is now legal. Likewise, in the early 1900s opiates were sold in pharmacies and Coca-Cola contained small quantities of cocaine.

Some who advocate legalization of drugs believe that the government has no right telling people what they may and may not ingest. However, most legalization proponents recognize that many drugs can be harmful (though many dispute the degree), but they do not see this as a reason to make their use illegal. They point out that tobacco use and alcohol abuse are harmful—possibly more harmful or addictive than some drugs that are illicit—but their use is legal. The policy these legalization advocates recommend is based on educational and public health approaches like those used for tobacco and alcohol. They feel that a greater harm is imposed on society by prohibiting such substances, as evidenced by

the consequence of the Prohibition period of the early twentieth century, during which alcohol was banned and crime, racketeering, and homicide rates soared.

The general policy as advocated by most mainstream proponents of legalization is sometimes summed up in the phrase "harm reduction." The "Testimony of Executive Director Ira Glasser on National Drug Policy" (June 16, 1999, http://www.aclu.org/drugpolicy/decrim/10858leg19990616.html) outlines the following issues:

> There are two kinds of harms associated with the use of drugs. One set of harms may be caused by the drugs themselves, and varies widely, depending on the particular drug, its potency, its purity, its dosage, and the circumstances and frequency of its use. Distinctions must be made between the harms caused by heavy, compulsive use (e.g., alcoholism) and occasional, controlled use (e.g., a glass of wine each night with dinner). Distinctions must also be made between medical use (e.g., heavy dosages of morphine prescribed by doctors over a two-week period in a hospital setting or methadone prescribed daily on an outpatient basis as maintenance) and uncontrolled use (e.g., by addicts on the street using unregulated heroin and unclean needles). Distinctions must be made as well between relatively benign drugs (e.g., marijuana) and drugs with more extreme short-term effects (e.g., LSD) or more severe long-term effects (e.g., nicotine when delivered by smoking tobacco).

> The second kind of harm associated with the use of drugs is the harm caused not by the drugs themselves but by dysfunctional laws designed to control the availability of the drug. These harms include massive incarceration, much of it racially disparate, and the violation of a wide range of constitutional rights so severe that it has led one Supreme Court justice to speak of a "drug exception" to the Constitution. Dysfunctional laws have also led to reduced availability of treatment by those who desire it (e.g., methadone maintenance), as well as a number of harms created by uncontrolled and unregulated illegal markets (e.g., untaxed and exaggerated subsidies for organized criminals; street crime caused by the settling of commercial disputes with automatic weapons; unregulated dosages and impurities; unclean needles and the spread of disease, etc.)

> All laws that address the issue of drugs ought to be evaluated by assessing whether or not they reduce or enhance such harms.

Many proponents argue that legalization will result in decreased crime from trafficking, gang wars, and crimes committed to obtain drugs; lower incarceration rates and associated cost savings; and more funds available for treatment from savings and from taxes on legally distributed drugs. Legalization of drugs is also seen as making available marijuana in medical applications, such as relieving the suffering of cancer and acquired immune deficiency syndrome (AIDS) patients.

TABLE 9.8

Top ten facts on legalization of drugs cited by the U.S. Drug Enforcement Administration (DEA), 2003

Fact 1: We have made significant progress in fighting drug use and drug trafficking in America. Now is not the time to abandon our efforts.

Fact 2: A balanced approach of prevention, enforcement, and treatment is the key in the fight against drugs.

Fact 3: Illegal drugs are illegal because they are harmful.

Fact 4: Smoked marijuana is not scientifically approved medicine. Marinol, the legal version of medical marijuana, is approved by science.

Fact 5: Drug control spending is a minor portion of the U.S. budget. Compared to the social costs of drug abuse and addiction, government spending on drug control is minimal.

Fact 6: Legalization of drugs will lead to increased use and increased levels of addiction. Legalization has been tried before, and failed miserably.

Fact 7: Crime, violence, and drug use go hand-in-hand.

Fact 8: Alcohol has caused significant health, social, and crime problems in this country, and legalized drugs would only make the situation worse.

Fact 9: Europe's more liberal drug policies are not the right model for America.

Fact 10: Most nonviolent drug users get treatment, not jail time.

SOURCE: "Summary of the Top Ten Facts on Legalization," in *Speaking Out against Drug Legalization*, U.S. Department of Justice, U.S. Drug Enforcement Administration, May 2003, http://www.dea.gov/dcmand/ speakout/index.html (accessed October 20, 2006)

AGAINST LEGALIZATION. The government's case against legalization is summarized in the DEA brochure *Speaking Out against Drug Legalization* (May 2003, http:// www.dea.gov/demand/speakout/index.html). The ten arguments presented by the DEA are shown in Table 9.8.

Like legalization proponents, the DEA's position is organized around the concept of harm. Certain drugs are illegal or controlled because they cause harm. In the DEA's view, legalization of drugs—even if only marijuana—will increase the harm already suffered by the drug-using public by spreading use to ever larger numbers of people. The agency cites Alaska's experience. Marijuana was legalized there in the 1970s and the DEA states that the Alaskan teenage consumption of marijuana at more than twice the rate of teenagers elsewhere was a direct consequence of the Alaska Supreme Court ruling. In 1990 there was a voter initiative in Alaska that criminalized any possession of marijuana.

Despite the DEA's opinion, on August 29, 2003, a state appellate court affirmed the right of Alaskans to possess a small amount of marijuana in their homes; anything under four ounces is deemed "for personal use." Anything over that amount is illegal because it is assumed the person is dealing drugs.

The DEA points to National Institute on Drug Abuse studies that show that smoking a marijuana joint introduces four times as much tar into the lungs as a filtered cigarette. The agency makes the point that drugs are much more addictive than alcohol and invites the public to contemplate a situation in which commercial interests might be enabled to promote the sale of presently illicit substances.

The DEA counters the "criminalization" charge by pointing out that only 5% of drug offenders in federal prisons and 27% of drug offenders in state prisons are held for possession, the rest for trafficking. The agency points out that even these numbers are deceptive because those imprisoned for possession are usually imprisoned after repeated offenses, and many of those serving a sentence for possession were arrested for trafficking but reached plea bargains permitting them to plead guilty to the lesser offense of possession.

Would legalization reduce crime? The DEA does not believe it would. Under a regulated drug-use system, age restrictions would apply. A criminal enterprise would continue to supply those under age. If marijuana were legalized, trade in heroin and cocaine would continue. If all three of the major drugs were permitted to be sold legally, other substances, such as phencyclidine and methamphetamine, would still support a criminal trade. The DEA does not envision that a black market in drugs could be eliminated entirely, because health authorities would never permit potent drugs to be sold freely on the open market.

For all these reasons, the DEA advocates the continuation of a balanced approach to the control of drugs including prevention, enforcement, and treatment.

Contradictions and Inconsistencies

Proponents of legalization sometimes find the question of where to draw the legal line problematic. How harmful must a drug be before it should be made illegal? In an environment where public pressures are mounting against the use of tobacco, legalization of marijuana has a contradictory aspect. Funds expended now on incarcerating drug offenders may have to be expended in some future time on public health programs to treat ills caused by newly legalized drugs, though whether or how much the use of drugs such as marijuana would increase if it were legal remains entirely unknown.

Opponents of legalization have similar difficulties in addressing the issues of alcohol and tobacco. How can their legality be justified when the use of comparably harmful substances is not legal and can yield long prison sentences?

Arguments claiming that the war on drugs is succeeding because drug use is down as measured against some point in the past ignore the fact that drug use is a cyclical phenomenon with ebbs and flows. For example, in *Speaking Out* the DEA presents a chart comparing overall drug use between 1979 and 2001, showing a decline in current users from 25.4 to 15.9 million people. In that period, however, current drug use first declined to 12 million people in 1992 and then rose again to 15.9 million by 2001 while the same policies were being pursued. If the

DEA had used 1992 as its base year, it would have had to concede that its programs are not working.

MEDICAL MARIJUANA

The medicinal value of THC (delta-9-tetrahydrocannabinol), the active ingredient in marijuana, has long been known to the medical community. The drug has been shown to alleviate the nausea and vomiting caused by chemotherapy, which is used to treat many forms of cancer. Marijuana has also been found useful in alleviating pressure on the eye in glaucoma patients. Furthermore, the drug has been found effective in helping to fight the physical wasting that usually accompanies AIDS. AIDS patients lose their appetites and can slowly waste away because they do not eat. Marijuana has been found effective in restoring the appetites of some AIDS patients. Many of the newer AIDS remedies must be taken on a full stomach. This is not to say that all scientists agree that marijuana is healthy or useful. For example, other studies find that marijuana suppresses the immune system and contains a number of lung-damaging chemicals. Still, the potentially beneficial uses of marijuana as a medicine have led to a movement for it to be made legally available by prescription.

Opponents of the medical legalization of marijuana often point to Marinol as a superior alternative. Marinol is a medication that contains the active ingredient dronabinol, a laboratory-made form of THC found in marijuana. Marinol provides a standardized THC content and does not contain impurities, such as leaves, mold spores, and bacteria, which are generally found in marijuana. However, many patients do not respond to Marinol, and the determination of the right dose is variable from patient to patient. Nonresponding patients claim that smoking marijuana allows them to control the dosage they get.

Marijuana has been used illegally by an unknown number of cancer and AIDS patients on the recommendation of doctors. Nonetheless, the medical use of marijuana is not without risk. The primary negative effect is diminished control over movement. In some cases users may experience unpleasant emotional states or feelings. In addition, the usefulness of medical marijuana is limited by the harmful effects of smoking, which can increase a person's risk of cancer, lung damage, and problems (such as low birth weight) with pregnancies. However, these risks are usually not important for terminally ill patients or those with debilitating symptoms.

IMPORTANT NAMES AND ADDRESSES

AAA Foundation for
Traffic Safety
607 Fourteenth St. NW, Ste. 201
Washington, DC 20005
(202) 638-5944
FAX: (202) 638-5943
E-mail: info@aaafoundation.org
URL: http://www.aaafoundation.org/

Action on Smoking and Health
2013 H St. NW
Washington, DC 20006
(202) 659-4310
URL: http://www.ash.org/

Adult Children of Alcoholics
PO Box 3216
Torrance, CA 90510
(310) 534-1815
E-mail: info@AdultChildren.org
URL: http://www.adultchildren.org/

Al-Anon Family Group
Headquarters
1600 Corporate Landing Pkwy.
Virginia Beach, VA 23454-5617
(757) 563-1600
FAX: (757) 563-1655
E-mail: wso@al-anon.org
URL: http://www.al-anon.alateen.org/

Alcoholics Anonymous
World Services
PO Box 459
New York, NY 10163
(212) 870-3400
URL: http://www.aa.org/

Beer Institute
122 C St. NW, Ste. 350
Washington, DC 20001
(202) 737-2337
1-800-379-BREW
E-mail: info@beerinstitute.org
URL: http://www.beerinstitute.org/

Bureau for International Narcotics
and Law Enforcement Affairs
U.S. Department of State
2201 C St. NW
Washington, DC 20520
(202) 647-4000
URL: http://www.state.gov/p/inl

Centers for Disease Control and
Prevention
National Center for Chronic Disease
Prevention and Health Promotion
Office on Smoking and Health
4770 Buford Hwy. NE
Mail Stop K-50
Atlanta, GA 30341
(770) 488-5705
1-800-232-4636
E-mail: tobaccoinfo@cdc.gov
URL: http://www.cdc.gov/tobacco/

Cocaine Anonymous World Services
3740 Overland Ave., Ste. C
Los Angeles, CA 90034
(310) 559-5833
FAX: (310) 559-2554
E-mail: cawso@ca.org
URL: http://www.ca.org/

Distilled Spirits Council of the
United States, Inc.
1250 I St. NW, Ste. 400
Washington, DC 20005
(202) 628-3544
URL: http://www.discus.org/

Drug Enforcement Administration
2401 Jefferson Davis Hwy.
Alexandria, VA 22301
(202) 307-1000
URL: http://www.usdoj.gov/dea/

Drug Policy Alliance
925 Fifteenth St. NW, Second Fl.
Washington, DC 20005
(202) 216-0035

FAX: (202) 216-0803
E-mail: dc@drugpolicy.org
URL: http://www.dpf.org/

Nar-Anon Family Groups
22527 Crenshaw Blvd., #200B
Torrance, CA 90505
(310) 534-8188
1-800-477-6291
FAX: (310) 534-8688
E-mail: naranonWSO@hotmail.com
URL: http://nar-anon.org/index.html

Narcotics Anonymous World Services
PO Box 9999
Van Nuys, CA 91409
(818) 773-9999
FAX: (818) 700-0700
E-mail: fsmail@na.org
URL: http://www.na.org/

National Clearinghouse for Alcohol
and Drug Information
11300 Rockville Pike
Rockville, MD 20852
1-800-729-6686
URL: http://ncadi.samhsa.gov/

National Council on Alcoholism and Drug
Dependence
22 Cortlandt St., Ste. 801
New York, NY 10007-3128
(212) 269-7797
FAX: (212) 269-7510
E-mail: national@ncadd.org
URL: http://www.ncadd.org/

National Drug and Alcohol Treatment
Referral Routing Service
1-800-662-HELP

National Institute on Alcohol Abuse
and Alcoholism
5635 Fishers Ln., MSC 9304
Bethesda, MD 20892-9304
(301) 443-3860

FAX: (301) 480-1726
URL: http://www.niaaa.nih.gov/

National Institute on Drug Abuse
National Institutes of Health
6001 Executive Blvd., Rm. 5213
Bethesda, MD 20892-9561
(301) 443-1124
E-mail: information@nida.nih.gov
URL: http://www.nida.nih.gov/

National Organization for the Reform
of Marijuana Laws
1600 K St. NW, Ste. 501
Washington, DC 20006-2832
(202) 483-5500
FAX: (202) 483-0057

E-mail: norml@norml.org
URL: http://www.norml.org/

Office of National Drug Control Policy
Drug Policy Information Clearinghouse
PO Box 6000
Rockville, MD 20849-6000
1-800-666-3332
FAX: (301) 519-5212
URL: http://www.whitehousedrugpolicy.gov/

Office of Safe and Drug-Free Schools
U.S. Department of Education
400 Maryland Ave. SW
Washington, DC 20202
1-800-872-5327
FAX: (202) 401-0689
URL: http://www.ed.gov/about/offices/list/osdfs

U.S. Department of Health and
Human Services
Substance Abuse and Mental Health
Services Administration
One Choke Cherry Rd.
Rockville, MD 20857
(240) 276-2000
FAX: (240) 276-2010
URL: http://www.samhsa.gov/

Wine Institute
425 Market St., Ste. 1000
San Francisco, CA 94105
(415) 512-0151
FAX: (415) 442-0742
URL: http://www.wineinstitute.org/

RESOURCES

The various agencies of the U.S. Department of Health and Human Services (HHS) produce important publications on the consumption of alcohol, tobacco, and drugs in the United States and their health effects. Reports of the surgeon general and special reports to Congress are published through this office.

The Substance Abuse and Mental Health Services Administration (SAMHSA), an agency of the HHS, produces the annual National Survey on Drug Use and Health. The SAMHSA also tracks treatment services. The most recent report is the *National Survey of Substance Abuse Treatment Services (N-SSATS): 2004—Data on Substance Abuse Treatment Facilities* (2005). The SAMHSA also tracks reported episodes of drug abuse; the most recent published results are in the *Treatment Episode Data Set (TEDS) 1994–2004: National Admissions to Substance Abuse Treatment Services* (July 2006). The agency also operates the Drug Abuse Warning Network, which collects data from emergency rooms. The last report in the series from the network is *Drug Abuse Warning Network, 2004: National Estimates of Drug-Related Emergency Department Visits* (2006).

The HHS also publishes the bimonthly *Public Health Reports*, the official journal of the U.S. Public Health Service. The journal is a helpful resource on health problems, including those caused by alcohol and tobacco. The Association of Schools of Public Health has been a partner in the publication of *Public Health Reports* since 1999.

The National Institute on Alcohol Abuse and Alcoholism (NIAAA), a division of the National Institutes of Health, publishes the journal *Alcohol Research and Health*. The journal contains current scholarly research on alcohol addiction issues. The NIAAA also publishes the quarterly bulletin *Alcohol Alert*, which disseminates research findings on alcohol abuse and alcoholism.

The National Center for Health Statistics, in its annual *Health, United States*, reports on all aspects of the nation's health, including tobacco- and alcohol-related illnesses and deaths. *Morbidity and Mortality Weekly Report* is published by the Centers for Disease Control and Prevention (CDC), which also publishes numerous studies on the trends and health risks of smoking and drinking. Additionally, the American Cancer Society and the American Lung Association provide many facts on cancer and heart disease.

The U.S. Department of Agriculture (USDA) is responsible for several helpful reports concerning tobacco. Its publications *Tobacco Situation and Outlook Report* and *Tobacco: World Markets and Trade* monitor tobacco production, consumption, sales, exports, and imports. The annual *Agricultural Statistics* provides valuable information about farming, and *Food Consumption, Prices, and Expenditures* compiles data on how the nation spends its consumer dollars. Other useful information is provided by the Economic Research Service of the USDA and the U.S. Department of Labor's Bureau of Labor Statistics, which examines how people spend their income, including spending on cigarettes and alcohol.

The National Highway Traffic Safety Administration of the U.S. Department of Transportation produces the annual *Traffic Safety Facts*, which includes data on alcohol-related accidents.

The Bureau of Justice Statistics (BJS) monitors crime in the United States and focuses on criminal prosecutions, prisons, sentencing, and related subjects. Particularly helpful are *Drug Use and Dependence, State and Federal Prisoners, 2004* (October 2006) and the annual publications *Compendium of Federal Justice Statistics* and *Sourcebook of Criminal Justice Statistics*. The Federal Bureau of Investigation's annual *Crime in the United States* provides arrest statistics for the United States. The U.S.

Department of the Treasury's Alcohol and Tobacco Tax and Trade Bureau provides alcohol and tobacco tax information.

Other important annual surveys of alcohol, tobacco, and drug use in the United States are conducted by both public and private organizations. The CDC's *Youth Risk Behavior Surveillance* monitors not only alcohol, tobacco, and drug use but also other risk behaviors, such as teenage sexual activity and weapons possession. The *Monitoring the Future* survey of substance abuse among students from middle school through college is by the National Institute on Drug Abuse and the University of Michigan Institute for Social Research. The *PRIDE Questionnaire Report*, based on a survey of youth and parents, is produced by PRIDE Surveys in Bowling Green, Kentucky.

The Wine Institute (San Francisco, California), the Distilled Spirits Council of the United States Inc. (Washington, D.C.), and the Beer Institute (Washington, D.C.) are private trade organizations that track alcoholic beverage sales and consumption, as well as political and regulatory issues. Action on Smoking and Health publishes reviews concerned with the problems of smoking and the rights of nonsmokers. The Campaign for Tobacco Free Kids provides information on tobacco-related federal, state, and global initiatives; cigarette taxes; tobacco advertisements; tobacco and smoking statistics; and tobacco-related special reports.

The Gallup Organization and the Robert Wood Johnson Foundation (both Princeton, New Jersey), in the Youth Access to Alcohol Survey, provide important information about the attitudes and behaviors of the American public.

The national policy on combating drug abuse is centered in the Office of National Drug Control Policy (ONDCP). The ONDCP, which prepares a drug control policy each year for the president's signature and coordinates efforts across the federal bureaucracy, is an excellent source for statistics that are collected from many other agencies and displayed on the ONDCP's Web site at http://www.whitehousedrugpolicy.gov/. Publications consulted for this volume include *International Narcotics Control Strategy Report* (2006), *National Drug Control Strategy, 2005* (February 2005), the *National Drug Control Strategy: FY 2007 Budget Summary* (February 2006), and *National Drug Control Strategy* documents published in earlier years.

Domestic law enforcement and interdiction activities fall under the U.S. Department of Justice (DOJ). The U.S. Drug Enforcement Administration (DEA) oversees all domestic drug control activities. The DEA publishes *Drugs of Abuse*, a resource tool that educates the public about drug facts and the inherent dangers of illegal drugs.

Data on federal prisons are available from the Federal Bureau of Prisons at http://www.bop.gov/. The Federal Bureau of Investigation is a rich source for information on arrests of people for drug offenses. The data appear in annual editions of *Crime in the United States*.

The effort to control drugs beyond the nation's borders is largely under the supervision of the U.S. Department of State. The agency within the Department of State in charge of the drug control effort is the Bureau for International Narcotics and Law Enforcement Affairs. An excellent source of information is the bureau's annual *International Narcotics Control Strategy Report*.

Information Plus sincerely thanks all the organizations listed here for the valuable information they provide.

INDEX

Colombian heroin, decline of potential production of, 140 (*f*9.2)

criticisms of, 135

domestic drug seizures, 143–144

drug certification process, 143

drug supply, disruption of, 139–142

federal drug control spending, 137–138, 138*t*

federal drug control spending, distribution of, by agency, 139*t*

federal drug control spending, distribution of, by function, 137*t*

interdiction/eradication, results of, 144–145

international war on drugs, 138, 145

legalization of drugs, facts on, 147*t*

marijuana eradication in Mexico, annual rate of, 141*f*

marijuana legalization movement, 145–148, 146*f*

medical marijuana, 148

methamphetamine seizures, rate of, Southwest border, 142*f*

National Drug Control Strategy, 135–136

National Drug Control Strategy goals, 2005, 136*t*

seizures, cocaine, heroin, methamphetamine, cannabis, 143 (*t*9.6)

seizures, MDMA, 143 (*t*9.7)

seizures, rate of methamphetamine superlab seizures, 144*f*

transit-zone agreements, 143

Antismoking movement, 9, 40–41

Antisociality, 20

APA. *See* American Psychiatric Association

Aphrodisiac, 21

"Are the Sales Practices of Internet Cigarette Vendors Good Enough to Prevent Sales to Minors?" (Ribisi, Kim, and Williams), 111

Arrestee Drug Abuse Monitoring (*ADAM*) (National Institute of Justice), 59–60

Arrests

for alcohol-related offenses/DUI, 30, 30*t*

arrestee drug use, 59–61

for drug abuse violations, 59

drug arrests, 1980–2005, 60*f*

drug arrests by race, 2004, 62*t*

Asian and Pacific Islander Americans

alcohol consumption by, 18

drug treatment admissions, 92, 97

illicit drug users, 45

pain relievers and, 48

Association of Schools of Public Health, 151

ATF (Bureau of Alcohol, Tobacco, and Firearms), 1

ATF (Bureau of Alcohol, Tobacco, Firearms, and Explosives), 1

Automobile accidents. *See* Motor vehicle accidents

Avaria, Maria de Los Angeles, 25–26

Avoidant coping, 20

B

BAC. *See* Blood alcohol content

Ban, on smoking, 31

Barbiturates, 12, 52–53

Barbour, Haley, 116

Bayer Company of Germany, 11, 57

Beck, Allen J., 61, 64

Beer

advertising, 106

consumption in U.S., 15, 16*t*

history of alcohol use, 7

sales/consumption, U.S., 103

taxation, 108

Beer Institute, 103, 149, 152

"Beer State-of-the-Industry" (*Beverage Dynamics*), 103

Behavior, 93

Belize, 143

Bennett, William J., 136

Benzodiazepines, 50

Bhang, 11

Bierut, Laura J., 2

Binge drinking

current/binge/heavy alcohol use among persons aged 12 and older, by age group, 19*f*

past-month/binge/ heavy alcohol use among drinkers aged 12 and older, 17 (*t*2.2)

by pregnant women, 26

prevalence of, 16, 18

by youth, 72

Biological factors, 18–19

BJS. *See* Bureau of Justice Statistics

Black tar heroin, 57, 133

Blackouts, 18

Blood alcohol content (BAC)

alcohol and young drivers, 73, 74

intoxication levels, 22

lowering of, 28

motor vehicle accident fatalities by, 28*t*

motor vehicle crashes, drivers with BAC of 0.08 or higher killed in, 29 (*t*2.14)

motor vehicle crashes, pedestrians/ pedalcyclists with BAC of 0.08 or higher killed in, 29 (*t*2.15)

time to sober up, 23

Blood-brain barrier, 31

Blunt cigars, 129

Body

alcohol consumption, path in body, 22*f*

alcohol, long-term effects on body, 23–25

alcohol's short-term effects on, 21–23

See also Health consequences

Bolivia

cocaine production, 127

drug supply, disruption of, 139, 141

Bonsack, James A., 104

Boone, Donna L., 102

Brain

alcohol's effects on, 23

crack nicotine and, 35

drug dependence and, 4

nicotine's effects on, 31

Breast cancer, 24

Brewer's Almanac 2006 (Beer Institute), 103

British Medical Journal, 39

A Broken Promise to Our Children: The 1998 State Tobacco Settlement Eight Years Later (Campaign for Tobacco-Free Kids), 115–116

Bronchitis, 31, 36

Bronchus cancer, 38

Brown and Williamson, 114–116

Brown and Williamson Tobacco Corp., FDA v., 112

Bruess, Clint E., 25

Budget

federal drug control spending, 137–138, 138*t*

federal drug control spending, distribution of, by agency, 139*t*

federal drug control spending, distribution of, by function, 137*t*

See also Spending

Buprenorphine, 93

Bupropion, 43

Bureau for International Narcotics and Law Enforcement Affairs (INL)

contact information, 149

domestic drug seizures, 143

drug supply, disruption of, 139–142

International Narcotics Control Strategy Report, 152

management of international programs, 138

world production of plant-derived drugs, 119

Bureau of Alcohol, Tobacco, and Firearms (ATF), 1

Bureau of Alcohol, Tobacco, Firearms, and Explosives (ATF), 1

Bureau of Justice Statistics (BJS)

on arrests and race, 61

on arrests for drug abuse violations, 59

on convictions and race, 61–62

on drugs' impact on prisons, 63–64

publications of, 151

Burney, Leroy E., 9

Bush, George H. W., 13

Bush, George W.

John Walters and, 135

National Drug Control Strategy, 135–136

war on drugs and, 13–14

C

Caetano, Raul, 18
Caffeine, 2
California, 40, 103–104
Camel cigarettes, 9
Campaign for Tobacco-Free Kids
    information of, 152
    on Internet tobacco sales, 111
    on regulation of tobacco, 112
    tobacco settlement funds report,
        114–116
    on world tobacco markets, 106
Canada, 130
Cancer
    alcohol-related, 23, 25
    deaths from tobacco use, 38
    diseases/other adverse health effects
        caused by cigarette smoking, 37t
    lawsuits against tobacco companies,
        114–116
    medical marijuana and, 148
    quitting smoking and, 41
    from smoking, 9, 31, 35–36
Cancer Facts and Figures (American
    Cancer Society), 38
Cannabis
    cocaine, heroin, methamphetamine,
        cannabis seizures, 143 (*t*9.6)
    description of, 46
    hashish, hash oil from, 47–48
    history of use, 11
    illicit drug cultivation worldwide, by
        crop, region, 120t
    marijuana production, 129–130
    world production of plant-derived drugs,
        119
    See also Marijuana
Capehart, Thomas C., 104, 105, 105–106
Car accidents. *See* Motor vehicle accidents
Carbon dioxide (CO_2), 35
Carbon monoxide (CO), 35
Carcinogens, 35
Cardiovascular disease, 37t
Caribbean basin, 143
Carmona, Richard H., 26, 36
Cataracts, 36
Center for Science in the Public Interest
    (CSPI), 106–107
Centers for Disease Control and Prevention
    (CDC)
    alcohol use by high school students, 69
    contact information, 149
    deaths from tobacco use, 38
    economic costs of tobacco use, 113–114
    Fetal Alcohol Spectrum Disorders
        and, 26
    on health consequences of alcohol/
        tobacco, 135
    Master Settlement Agreement and, 116
    publications of, 151, 152

on smoking health consequences, 36, 38
    on smoking prevalence, 40
    on smoking reduction/stopping, 41
    on steroids, 59
    tobacco use trends, 31–33
    on youth and tobacco, 74–75
    Youth Risk Behavior Survey, 67, 68t
Central Intelligence Agency (CIA), 132, 140
Cerebrovascular disease (stroke), 38
Certification, drug certification process,
    137, 143
Chemical Diversion and Trafficking
    Act, 121
Children
    alcoholism's effects on, 21
    with FASD, facial characteristics of, 25,
        25f
    illicit drug use during pregnancy, 59
    secondhand smoke and, 40
    See also Youth
"Children of Addicted Parents: Important
    Facts" (National Association for
    Children of Alcoholics), 21
"Chronic Disease Notes and Reports"
    (Centers for Disease Control and
    Prevention), 31
CIA (Central Intelligence Agency), 132,
    140
Cigarette Report for 2003 (U.S. Federal
    Trade Commission), 108
"Cigarette Smoking among Adults—United
    States, 2005" (Centers for Disease
    Control and Prevention), 40
Cigarettes
    advertising, 10f, 108
    cigarette use by students in grades 9–12,
        75 (t5.7)
    consumption trends, 31–33
    diseases/other adverse health effects
        caused by, 37t–38t
    high school users of smokeless tobacco,
        smoked cigars, any tobacco product, 75
        (t5.6)
    history of, 9
    manufacturing/consumption of, 105
    past-month tobacco use of persons 12
        and older, 34 (f3.4)
    percentage of lifetime, past-year, and
        past-month cigarette users, 32 (t3.2)
    use by youth, 74, 76
    use in high school students, trends in,
        75–76
    See also Tobacco
Cigars
    cancer from, 36
    consumption trends, 33–34, 105
    high school users of, 75 (t5.6)
    history of use, 9
    past-month tobacco use of persons 12
        and older, 34 (f3.4)
    use by youth, 74, 76

Cipollone, Rose, 114
Cipollone v. Liggett Group Inc., 114
Clean Indoor Air Act, 40
Clinton, Bill, 13, 136
Club drugs, 56
CO (carbon monoxide), 35
"Co-occurring Risk Factors for Alcohol
    Dependence and Habitual Smoking"
    (Collaborative Study on the Genetics of
    Alcoholism), 35
CO_2 (carbon dioxide), 35
Coca-Cola, 11
Coca plant
    cocaine from, 53
    cocaine production, 127
    Colombian coca, rate of aerial
        destruction of, 140 (f9.1)
    Colombian production of, 145
    eradication efforts, 139, 141
    history of use, 11
    illicit drug cultivation worldwide, by
        crop and region, 120t
    interdiction/eradication, results of, 144
    world production of plant-derived
        drugs, 119
Cocaine
    crack cocaine, 13, 54
    description of, 53
    drug distribution centers, principal, 128f
    drug supply, disruption of, 139–141
    drug trafficking, 126–129
    drug trafficking penalties, 117, 118
    drug treatment admissions for, 94, 97
    drug treatment effectiveness, 100
    flow from South America to U.S., 127f
    health consequences of, 53–54
    history of use, 11–12
    past-month use of illicit drugs among
        persons aged 12 or older, 49f
    prevalence of use, 54–55
    prices, purity, supply, 128–129, 129t
    production, distribution of, 127–128
    seizures, 143, 145, 143 (*t*9.6)
    use among persons aged 18–45, by time
        of use/age group, 55f
    use during pregnancy, 59
    war on drugs and, 12
    world production of plant-derived
        drugs, 119
Cocaine Anonymous, 102, 149
Cocaine hydrochloride, 54
Collaborative Study on the Genetics of
    Alcoholism, 35
College students
    alcohol use among, 69–70, 72
    alcohol use by full-time college
        students vs. other young adults
        1–4 years beyond high school,
        70 (t5.4)
    alcohol use, trends in lifetime prevalence
        among young adults, 71t

inhalant use, trends in annual prevalence of, among eighth, tenth, twelfth graders, 80 (f5.4)

inhalants, 57

marijuana, new users over age 12, mean age at first use among those aged 12–49, 51f

marijuana use among persons aged 18–45, by time of use/age group, 50f

marijuana use, trends in annual prevalence of, among eighth, tenth, twelfth graders, 80 (f5.5)

methamphetamine, new users over age 12, mean age at first use among those aged 12–49, 53f

methamphetamine use among persons aged 18–30, by time of use/age group, 54f

most used drugs, 45–46

pain relievers, nonmedical use of, among persons aged 12 and older, 52t

past-month illicit drug use among females aged 15–44, by pregnancy status, 60t

past-month use of selected illicit drugs among persons aged 12 or older, 49f

potential illicit drug production worldwide, by crop, region, 121t

pregnancy and, 59

prisons, drugs' impact on, 63–64

psychotherapeutics, 48–53

publications on, 151–152

regulation of, 2

sentenced offenders in state prisons, percent of, by race and offense, 61t

state prison populations, impact of drugs on, 61f

tranquilizer use, trends in annual prevalence of, among eighth, tenth, twelfth graders, 81f

use of illicit drugs among persons aged 12 and older, 46t

use, trends in annual prevalence of, by population type, 79f

youth and, 78–79, 81–83, 85

See also Antidrug efforts; Drug trafficking; Drug treatment

"Implications of CYP2A6 Genetic Variation for Smoking Behaviors and Nicotine Dependence" (Malaiyandi, Sellers, and Tyndale), 35

Imports

of ephedrine powder, 125 (f8.3)

of marijuana, 130

of methamphetamine, 122–123

of pseudoephedrine powder, 125 (f8.4)

Impotence, 25

"In a First, CNN Runs a Liquor Commercial" (Elliott), 107

Incarceration

drug charges, by type/sentence lengths, 63t–64t

drug convictions and race, 61–62

drug trafficking penalties, 117–119

truth-in-sentencing, 62–63

See also Prison

Income, 104

Inhalants

definition of, 2

description of, 57

drug treatment admissions for, 94

inhalant use, trends in annual prevalence of, among eighth, tenth, twelfth graders, 80 (f5.4)

past-month use of illicit drugs among persons aged 12 or older, 49f

use by high school students, 78–79

Injuries, 23, 24 (t2.7)

INL. *See* Bureau for International Narcotics and Law Enforcement Affairs

An Inquiry into the Effects of Ardent Spirits on the Mind and Body (Rush), 8

Institute of Medicine, 16

Insurgencies, 138, 140

Interdiction

drug supply, disruption of, 139–142

federal drug budget and, 137

in National Drug Control Strategy, 136

results of, 144–145

International Classification of Diseases (ICD) (World Health Organization), 5–6, 17

International Narcotics Control Strategy Report (Bureau of International Narcotics and Law Enforcement Affairs), 152

International Opium Commission, 12

International treaties. *See* Legislation and international treaties

International war on drugs

difficulty of, 145

domestic drug seizures, 143–144

drug certification process, 143

drug supply, disruption of, 139–142

federal drug budget and, 137

illicit drug cultivation worldwide, by crop and region, 1998–2005, 120t

interdiction/eradication, results of, 144–145

international war on drugs, 138–145

potential illicit drug production worldwide, by crop, region, 1998–2005, 121t

production of plant-derived drugs, 119

terrorism and, 138

tobacco markets, 106

transit-zone agreements, 143

Internet, 110–111

Interpersonal relationships, 21

Interstate Commerce Clause, 109–110

Intoxication, 21–22

Investment in Tobacco Control State Highlights (Centers for Disease Control and Prevention), 41

J

James, Doris J., 30

Journal of the American Medical Association, 16

K

Kentucky, 104

Kim, Annice E., 111

L

LAAM (levo-alpha-acetylmethadol), 93

Labels. *See* Warning labels

Langan, Patrick A., 62–63

Laryngeal cancer, 31, 36

Lawsuits, 9–10, 114–116

Legal drugs, 1, 117

Legalization, 147t

See also Marijuana

Legislation and international treaties

Anti-Drug Abuse Act of 1988, 13, 135

Chemical Diversion and Trafficking Act, 121

Clean Indoor Air Act, 40

Comprehensive Methamphetamine Control Act of 1996, 122

Consumer Product Safety Act, 111

Controlled Substances Act of 1970, 2, 46, 117, 119

Crime Control Act of 1984, 13

Domestic Chemical Diversion Control Act of 1993, 121–122

Fair Packaging and Labeling Act, 111

Family Smoking Prevention and Tobacco Control Act, 112

Federal Cigarette Labeling and Advertising Act, 36, 114

Food, Drug, and Cosmetic Act of 1938, 12

Foreign Assistance Act of 1961, 143

Framework Convention on Tobacco Control, 106

Harrison Narcotic Act of 1914, 12, 57, 135

Hazardous Substances Act, 111

Marijuana Tax Act of 1937, 12, 46

Methamphetamine Trafficking Penalty Enhancement Act of 1998, 122

Prevent All Contraband Tobacco Act, 111

Psychotropic Substances Act of 1978, 57

Public Health Cigarette Smoking Act of 1969, 9

Pure Food and Drug Act of 1906, 11–12

Synar Amendment, 111

Toxic Substance Control Act, 111

Twenty-First Amendment Enforcement Act, 110–111

UN Convention against Illicit Traffic in Narcotics Drugs and Psychotropic Substances, 143

past-month cigarette use among females aged 15–44, by age/pregnancy status, 42f

past-month tobacco use of persons 12 and older, 34 (f3.4)

per capita consumption of tobacco products, 32 (t3.1)

percentage of lifetime, past-year, and past-month cigarette users, 32 (t3.2)

personal spending for, 106t

production/consumption, U.S., 104–106

public health and smoking, 36, 38

publications on, 151–152

regulatory issues, 2

secondhand smoke, 38–40

secondhand smoke, public opinion on harmfulness of, 41f

smoking, history of, 31

smoking status of adults, by gender, 33 (f3.1)

state cigarette tax rates and rankings, 110 (t7.7)

stopping smoking, 40–43

Surgeon General's reports on smoking/health, selected years, 39t

tax collections on alcohol and tobacco, federal government, 109t

taxation, 108–109

tobacco companies, responsibility of, 114–116

tobacco settlements, payments received from, by state, 115t

trends in use, 31–34

use by youth, 67

use, harmfulness of, as perceived by students in grades 6–12, 77f

use, history of, 9–10

world markets, 106

youth and, 74–78

"Tobacco and Smoking" (Gallup Poll), 40

Tobacco companies, 114–116

Tobacco: Deadly in Any Form or Disguise (World Health Organization), 41

"Tobacco Facts" (Campaign for Tobacco-Free Kids), 106

Tobacco industry, regulation of tobacco and, 111–112

Tobacco prevention/cessation programs, 115–116

Tobacco Situation and Outlook Report (U.S. Department of Agriculture), 151

Tobacco Situation and Outlook Yearbook (Capehart), 105

"Tobacco Smoke Is Phototoxic" (Placzek et al.), 36

Tobacco: World Markets and Trade (U.S. Department of Agriculture), 151

Tolerance, 35, 56

Toxic Substance Control Act, 111

Trade. *See* Drug trafficking

Traffic accidents, 8, 73–74

See also Motor vehicle accidents

Traffic Safety Facts, 2005 Data—Young Drivers (National Highway Traffic Safety Administration), 9, 73–74

Traffic Safety Facts (National Highway Traffic Safety Administration), 151

Trafficking. *See* Drug trafficking

Tranquilizers
as depressant, 1–2
description of, 50
drug treatment admissions, 97
tranquilizer use, trends in annual prevalence of, among eighth, tenth, twelfth graders, 81f
use by high school students, 81
use of, 50–51

Transit-zone agreements, 143

Treaties. *See* Legislation and international treaties

Treatment. *See* Drug treatment

Treatment Episode Data Set (TEDS) 1994–2004: National Admissions to Substance Abuse Treatment Services (Substance Abuse and Mental Health Services Administration)
admissions by substance, 94
drug treatment admissions by race/ethnicity, 97
drug treatment data, 89, 151

Treatment Outcome Prospective Study (TOPS), 100

"Trends in U.S. Tobacco Farming" (Capehart), 104

TTB. *See* Alcohol and Tobacco Tax and Trade Bureau

Twenty-First Amendment
Prohibition and, 8
regulation of alcohol, 109, 110, 111

Twenty-First Amendment Enforcement Act, 110–111

"2005 California Wine Sales Continue Growth Trend as Wine Enters Mainstream U.S. Lifestyle" (Wine Institute), 103

2001 International Narcotics Control Strategy Report (U.S. Department of State), 132

2006 International Narcotics Control Strategy Report (Bureau for International Narcotics and Law Enforcement Affairs), 119

Tyndale, Rachel F., 18–19, 35

U

Uhl, George R., 88

UN Convention against Illicit Traffic in Narcotics Drugs and Psychotropic Substances, 143

Uniform Facility Data Set (UFDS) survey, 89

United Nations Office on Drugs and Crime, 11

United Nations (UN)
on drug trafficking, 119
Global Illicit Drug Trends, 2003, 145
UN Convention against Illicit Traffic in Narcotics Drugs and Psychotropic Substances, 143

"United States Support for Afghanistan's Counternarcotics Campaign" (International Narcotics and Law Enforcement Affairs), 142

University of Michigan Institute for Social Research
alcohol use by high school students, 69
Monitoring the Future survey, 152
on narcotics use, 48
on youth alcohol use, 72

Updating Estimates of the Economic Costs of Alcohol Abuse in the United States: Estimates, Update Methods, and Data (National Institute on Alcohol Abuse and Alcoholism), 112

Uribe, Alvaro, 138

Urination, 21

U.S. Agency for International Development (USAID)
Afghanistan program, 142
Alternative Livelihoods Program, 140
drug supply, disruption of, 139

U.S. Bureau of Labor Statistics, 104

U.S. Coast Guard, 143

U.S. Constitution, 8, 109–111

U.S. Department of Agriculture (USDA)
on distilled spirits, 104
publications of, 151
on tobacco value, income, 104

U.S. Department of Defense, 137, 138

U.S. Department of Education, 137

U.S. Department of Health and Human Services
contact information, 150
drug control budget and, 137
publications on alcohol, tobacco, illicit drugs, 151

U.S. Department of Homeland Security, 137, 138

U.S. Department of Justice
alcohol use by arrestees, 30
on crime and illicit drugs, 64
drug control budget and, 137
responsibilities of, 152
on steroids, 59

U.S. Department of State
drug control budget and, 137, 138
on heroin trafficking, 132

U.S. Department of the Treasury, 113

U.S. Department of Transportation, 137

U.S. Drug Enforcement Administration, 13

U.S. Drug Enforcement Agency (DEA)
Afghanistan program, 142
contact information, 149
control of drugs, 1

domestic drug seizures, 143–144

drug control budget and, 137–138

drug legalization facts, 147*t*

drug schedule, 2, 3*t*–4*t*

on effects of marijuana, 47

on effects of steroids, 59

heroin seizure program, 132–133

marijuana legalization and, 147–148

on marijuana's THC content, 130

on MDMA/ecstasy use, 56

on methamphetamine distribution, 125

publications of, 152

regulation of ephedrine, 121

on stimulants, 52

U.S. Environmental Protection Agency (EPA), 39, 111

U.S. Federal Trade Commission (FTC), 108, 111

U.S. Food and Drug Administration (FDA)

drug control role, 1

on medications and alcohol, 27

opioid substitute program, 93

regulation of drugs, 12

regulation of tobacco, 111, 112

U.S. Government Accountability Office (GAO)

on drug courts, 101–102

on drug supply, 139

interdiction/eradication, results of, 144

U.S. Government Office of Technology Assessment

on marijuana, 12

on prescription of heroin, 11

war on drugs budget, 13

"U.S. Has New Plan against Smoking" (*New York Times*), 40–41

U.S. Public Health Service, 151

U.S. Sentencing Commission, 62

U.S. Small Business Administration, 137

U.S. Supreme Court, 111, 112

U.S. Surgeon General

advisory on alcohol use during pregnancy, 26 (*t*2.10)

Cipollone v. Liggett Group Inc., 114

diseases/other adverse health effects caused by cigarette smoking, 37*t*–38*t*

public health and smoking, 36

reports on smoking/health, selected years, 39*t*

on secondhand smoke, 39–40

Smoking and Health: Report of the Advisory Committee to the Surgeon General of the Public Health Service, 31

on smoking and pregnancy, 42

on smoking cessation, 41

USDA. *See* U.S. Department of Agriculture

USNoDrugs.com, 57

V

Valium, 50

Value, 104

Vicodin, 48–49

Vietnam War, 12

Virginia, 104

Vogeltanz, Nancy D., 19

Volstead Act of 1919, 8

W

Wald, Matthew L., 107

Walters, John, 13–14, 135

War on drugs

criticisms of, 135

history of, 12–14

international war on drugs, 138–145

See also Antidrug efforts

Warning labels

on alcohol, 9

on cigarettes, 36

lawsuits against tobacco companies, 114

on tobacco products, 111

"The Weed of Controversy" (Gibson), 11

White House Fact Sheet on the National Drug Control Policy, 136

WHO. *See* World Health Organization

WHO Framework Convention on Tobacco Control, 41

Wiencke, John K., 74

Wiese, Jeff, 23

Williams, Rebecca S., 111

Wilsnack, Sharon C., 19

Wilson, Woodrow, 8

Wine

advertising, 106–107

consumption in U.S., 15

history of alcohol use, 7

per capita consumption of beer, wine, distilled spirits, 16*t*

sales/consumption, U.S., 103–104

taxation, 108

Wine Institute, 150, 152

Withdrawal

drug treatment detoxification, 92–93

from heroin, 57

from nicotine, 35, 42

from stimulants, 51

Women

alcohol absorption by, 21–22

alcohol consumption by, 19–20

binge drinking by, 72

deaths from tobacco use, 38

Fetal Alcohol Spectrum Disorders, 25–26

past-month alcohol use among females aged 15–44, by pregnancy status, 27 (*t*2.11)

smoking by, 9

See also Females; Gender

World. *See* International war on drugs

World Health Organization (WHO)

alcohol abuse definition, 17

Framework Convention on Tobacco Control, 106

global reduction of tobacco use, 41

ICD definition of harmful use, 5–6

stance against smoking, 9

World War I, 9

World War II, 9

Wright, C. R. Alder, 10–11

X

Xanax, 50

Y

Young adults

alcohol use among, 69–70, 72

alcohol use by full-time college students vs. other young adults 1–4 years beyond high school, 70 (*t*5.4)

alcohol use, trends in lifetime prevalence among young adults, 71*t*

illicit drug use, annual prevalence of, 78

tobacco use among, 76

"Young Smokers Playing with Fire" (Majeski), 76

Youth

alcohol advertising and, 108

alcohol and, 67–70, 72–74

alcohol, annual prevalence of use by full-time college students vs. other young adults 1–4 years beyond high school, 70 (*t*5.4)

alcohol, past-month use of, by eighth, tenth, and twelfth graders, 70 (*t*5.3)

alcohol use, harmfulness of, as perceived by students in grades 6–12, 73*f*

alcohol use, trends in lifetime prevalence among young adults, 71*t*

amphetamine use, trends in annual prevalence of, among eighth, tenth, twelfth graders, 82*f*

cigarette use by students in grades 9–12, prevalence of, 75 (*t*5.7)

ecstasy (MDMA) use, trends in annual prevalence, among eighth, tenth, twelfth graders, 84 (*f*5.9)

hallucinogen use, trends in annual prevalence, among eighth, tenth, twelfth graders, 83*f*

harmfulness of illicit drug use as perceived by students in grades 6–12, 84 (*f*5.10)

high school students who drank alcohol, 69*t*

high school students who drank alcohol, smoked cigarettes, or tried marijuana before age 13, 68*t*

high school users of smokeless tobacco, smoked cigars, any tobacco product, 75 (*t*5.6)

illicit drug use, trends in annual prevalence of, 79*f*